Bilingual Education

Bilingual Education:
History
Politics
Theory
and
Practice

James Crawford

BILINGUAL EDUCATIONAL SERVICES, INC.
2514 SOUTH GRAND AVENUE
LOS ANGELES, CA 90007-9979
(213) 749-6213

Fourth edition, 1999

Library of Congress Cataloging-in-Publication Data

Crawford, James, 1949—
Bilingual education: history, politics, theory, and practice /
James Crawford.
p. : ill. ; cm.
Fourth, revised edition. Originally published: Trenton, N.J.:
Crane Publishing Co., 1989.
Includes index.
Bibliography: p.
I. Education, Bilingual—United States.
LC3731.C73 1989, 1991
371.97/00973 20
ISBN 0-89075-556-6

To the memory of my father

Contents

Acknowledgments

After more than a decade of writing about bilingual education, I feel indebted to an ever-expanding list of people — more, I'm afraid, than I can ever thank properly. While the judgments expressed here are my own, they reflect the contributions of countless teachers, administrators, researchers, and advocates who have patiently schooled me in the basics of the field.

At the risk of leaving out many friends, I want to mention several who have gone out of their way to help: Ellen Riojas Clark, Ginger Collier, Rosa Castro Feinberg, Michael Genzuk, Norm Gold, Kenji Hakuta, Wayne Holm, Martha Jiménez, Sandra Johnson, Steve Krashen, Dick Littlebear, Jim Lyons, Teresa McCarty, Reynaldo Macías, Dan McLaughlin, Ricardo Martínez, Geoffrey Nunberg, Carlos Ovando, Camilo Pérez-Bustillo, David Ramírez, Richard Ruíz, Shelly Spiegel-Coleman, Dick Tucker, Concepción Valadez, Arturo Vargas, Lucille and Philbert Watahomigie, Lily Wong Fillmore, and Gloria Zamora.

This book, now in its Fourth Edition, grew out of a special supplement for *Education Week* published in April 1987. My editor there, Ron Wolk, generously supported that project and granted permission to reprint portions of it here. I am also grateful to my current publisher, Jeff Penichet of Bilingual Educational Services, for his fairness and professionalism.

Finally, I owe a special debt to Mary Carol Combs, who first encouraged me to investigate the English Only movement and has continued over the years to give unsparingly of her professional expertise, editorial skills, and personal support.

James Crawford

About the Author

A graduate of Harvard College, James Crawford has worked as a journalist since the late 1970s, writing on issues ranging from job safety and health to education and language policy. As Congressional editor of *Federal Times*, he reported from Capitol Hill on matters of concern to government employees. He began writing about bilingualism at *Education Week*, initially as a staff writer and later as Washington editor. Since 1987, he has been an independent writer and lecturer. His works include *Hold Your Tongue: Bilingualism and the Politics of "English Only"* (Addison-Wesley, 1992), *Language Loyalties: A Source Book on the Official English Controversy* (University of Chicago Press, 1992), and *Best Evidence: Research Foundations of the Bilingual Education Act* (National Clearinghouse for Bilingual Education, 1997). He also served as writer-consultant to the Stanford Working Group on Federal Education Programs for Limited-English-Proficient Students.

Introduction

In the beginning was the Word. And the Word was made flesh. It was so in the beginning and it is so today. The language, the Word, carries within it the history, the culture, the traditions, the very life of a people, the flesh. Language is people. We cannot even conceive of a people without a language, or a language without a people. The two are one and the same. To know one is to know the other.

Sabine Ulibarrí

The Bilingual Education Act of 1968 marked a new outlook toward Americans whose mother tongue is not English. Previously in our history, minority languages had been accommodated at certain times, repressed at others. Most often, they had been ignored. The assumption was, and is, that non-English speakers would naturally come to see the advantages of adopting the majority language as their own. Notwithstanding episodes of intolerance — most egregiously toward Native Americans — laissez-faire has predominated, a language policy that has served to foster assimilation on a voluntary basis. Millions of immigrants have abandoned their native tongues and embraced English in what is arguably the largest, fastest, and most diverse language shift in recorded history, a phenomenon one linguist has described as "Babel in reverse."

But the neglect of minority tongues was not entirely benign. Contrary to myth, immigrant children were more likely to sink than swim in English-language classrooms. In 1908, just 13 percent of such students who were enrolled in New York City schools at age twelve went on to high school (as compared with 32 percent of white children whose parents were native-born). Some immigrants succeeded without formal schooling, thanks to strong backs, entrepreneurial talents, or political skills; they too were in the minority.

By the 1960s, while high dropout rates persisted among language-minority children, the country's economy had changed. Upward mobility was no longer an option for those without English literacy. Prospects were doubly limited for groups who faced discrimination on the basis of race as well as language: Puerto Ricans, Mexican Americans, Asian Americans, and American Indians. At the same time, the civil rights movement was beginning to energize language-minority communities. Parents who had themselves been shortchanged by English-only schools were seeking a better deal for their children. Desegregation was important, but equal opportunity demanded more than equal treatment if students could not understand the language of instruction.

Recognizing this "acute educational problem," the U.S. Congress moved to promote "new and imaginative programs" that would teach children in their native tongues while they learned English. Although bilingual education had been widespread before World War I in localities where German, French, Spanish, and other minority language speakers had amassed political clout, never before had it been endorsed as national policy. Not that Congress had a clear idea of what bilingual education meant — only a handful of such programs even existed in 1968 — but the lawmakers resolved that *something* had to be done about the schools' negligence toward children with limited English skills.

In short, the Bilingual Education Act was a leap of faith, an experiment based more on good intentions than good pedagogy. That is no longer a fair assessment. Bilingual approaches in the 1990s reflect the latest findings in linguistics and cognitive psychology. The past quarter century has brought enormous advances in curricula, methodologies, materials, and teacher training. No longer stigmatized as slow learners, language-minority children are achieving at or near grade level by the time they leave well-designed bilingual programs, even in urban schools where failure was once the norm.

The law's success is not unqualified. Title VII has sponsored many mediocre programs: crudely conceived, unsupported by administrators, or "bilingual" in name only because teachers lack fluency in the language of their students. Responding to external pressures, even well-intentioned schools have repeated mistakes of the past — for example, rushing children into regular classrooms prematurely or stigmatizing their languages and cultures. Too often, academic results have been disappointing. While poor implementation cannot invalidate bilingual education's growing roster of successes, it does make the program vulnerable to attack.

Ironically, political support was stronger in the 1960s, when the concept of bilingual education was virtually untested, than it is in the 1990s, when research has documented its benefits. Skeptics still question the wisdom of native-language instruction: Whether children are learning English or languishing in academic ghettos. Whether some students benefit, but not others. Whether school districts should have more "flexibility" to try experimental alternatives. Whether enhancing ethnic pride has taken precedence over assimilating minorities into the mainstream.

When then-Secretary of Education William Bennett began to voice these concerns in 1985, his office was swamped with fan mail. After congratulating Bennett for exposing bilingual education as a "failed" program, many correspondents went on to vent their hostility toward language minorities, Hispanics in particular, and their alleged resistance to learning English. "I think one language is enough," said a writer from Texas, who added:

> Why do we have to change our culture and life style for people who claim they want to be Americans? They want all our privileges, but still try to run our lives like they were back home. . . . Is our country going to be divided from here on? First Spanish dictates. Maybe some day, Chinese or Russian.

A Florida critic asked:

> What hope is there of assimilating these foreigners into American life if we encourage and assist them in perpetuating their own language instead of learning to speak English? We not only have our taxes frittered away with supporting [undocumented immigrants] on relief. . . . We must on top of that be taxed to educate their multitudinous offspring in their own language.

A Rhode Islander who described himself as the grandson of Norwegian and Italian immigrants wrote:

> Not only is [bilingual education] fundamentally unfair to those who learned English the best way — by experience — it is profoundly un-American and a menace to our national culture.

Clearly, there is more at stake here than questions of educational effectiveness. Bilingual education is arousing passions about issues of political power and social status that are far removed from the classroom. Rarely in American history has language been the focus of so much contention. Why did this begin happening in the 1980s?

One reason is that, with little public discussion, the Bilingual Education Act broke with the federal government's two-hundred-year-old reluctance to legislate on matters of language. It also appeared to contradict treasured assumptions about the "melting pot," or more accurately, about the Anglo-conformist ethic in American culture. The law's goals were left unclear. Was it intended to ease the transition to English or to encourage the maintenance of minority languages? For some, bilingual education was strictly a remedial effort, designed to overcome children's "language deficiency" and to assimilate them quickly into the mainstream. For others, it was an enrichment program, intended to develop students' linguistic resources and preserve their cultural heritage. Rather than settle a debate, the new policy started one.

Second, the 1965 immigration law set in motion enormous demographic changes by repealing the "national origins quota system," which had limited entry by non-English-speakers in general and by Asians in particular. By the 1980s, an increase in racial, cultural, and linguistic diversity was impossible to ignore. An estimated 7.3 million immigrants arrived during the decade, swelling the nation's foreign-born population and, not coincidentally, its language minority population by approximately 40 percent. According to the 1990 census, 31.8 million residents — one in seven Americans — now speak a language other than English at home; 14 million report some difficulty with English.[1]

The new bilingualism has proved jarring to many Americans, especially to those who came of age during a time of relative cultural homogeneity. Hearing other languages spoken freely in public has fostered the perception that English is losing ground, that newcomers no longer care to learn the national tongue. Yet the available demographic evidence suggests otherwise. Instead of slowing down, linguistic assimilation appears to be accelerating — from a three-generation pattern, common at the turn of this century, to a two-generation pattern of language loss today. That is, the children of immigrants are rapidly losing their parents' vernacular. It is a paradox that few critics of bilingual education seem to grasp: while the population of minority language speakers continues to climb, thanks primarily to immigration, today's immigrants are learning English more rapidly than ever before.

Racial and cultural changes have been equally striking. Up until the 1950s, 85 percent of immigrants to the United States had come from Europe; in the 1980s, 85 percent came from the Third World, mainly from Asia and Latin America.[2] In communities where they have concentrated, the newcomers are exerting a major and, for some of their neighbors, an unwelcome impact. A new brand of nativism has emerged in response. Early in this century, those who felt a similar threat from "alien races" raised claims of Anglo-Saxon superiority to justify the exclusion of eastern and southern Europeans. Such explicit appeals to racial loyalty are no longer acceptable in our political discourse. Language loyalties, on the other hand, remain largely devoid of associations with social injustice. While race is immutable, immigrants can and often do exchange their mother tongue for another; to insist that they learn English seems reasonable to most Americans. Yet language politics can also provide a respectable veneer for racial politics. Hence the rise of an English Only movement in the 1980s, which attacked bilingualism as a symbol of national decline and ethnic "divisiveness."

Third, bilingual education is contentious for the simple reason that it disrupts established patterns. For schools it can cause multiple headaches — the need to recruit qualified teachers, redesign curricula, reorganize class schedules — that many administrators would like to avoid. Monolingual teachers fear reassignment, loss of status, or other career setbacks. English-speaking parents worry about the neglect of their own children. Taxpayers expect the bill to be outlandish. While such fears usually prove to be exaggerated, school restructuring is rarely painless.

Nevertheless, the demographic challenge must be faced. During the decade of the 1980s, the U.S. population grew by 9.8 percent overall, while Hispanics increased by 53 percent and Asian Americans by 107 percent. Taken together, these groups will represent 15.7 percent of the U.S. population in the year 2000, 22.7 percent in 2020, and 32.8 percent in 2050, according to the Census Bureau.[3] Because language minorities are generally younger than other Americans, their impact is disproportionately felt in the schools. From 1985 through 1993, states reported an average annual increase of 9.2 percent in the enrollment of limited-English-proficient (LEP) children.[4] These students' educational needs are formidable. In study after study, a non-English-language background has been correlated with higher rates of falling behind, failing, and dropping out. Language-minority youths "are 1.5 times more likely than their English language counterparts to have discontinued school before completing twelve years," and Hispanic youths are more than twice as likely to have done so, according to a 1988 report by the Intercultural Development Research Association.

Finally, bilingual education arouses opposition because it contradicts peculiarly American notions about language. As a people we have relatively limited experience with bilingualism on the one hand, and strongly held myths about it on the other. Monolinguals in this country seldom appreciate the time and effort involved in acquiring a second language (though they may not feel up to the task themselves). Ignorance of linguistic matters is commonplace even in educated circles. So much so that Kenneth G. Wilson, professor of English and former vice president of the University of Connecticut, could write in 1987:

> Almost all the well-meaning claims for bilingual education turn out to be irrelevant because language doesn't work that way. . . . We must do everything to introduce the second language as early as possible, the ear-lier the better. Nursery school is better than kindergarten, kindergarten better than first grade, and first grade better than later grades. . . . Even twenty years ago we knew a fair number of things about the way chil-dren learn language. We knew many of these things only empirically then; today we have much more basic science in hand to explain these empirical data.

Despite his pretensions, Wilson apparently had no inkling of the advances in psycholinguistic research over the past two decades. Evidence has mounted steadily against the "critical period" hypothesis that second languages are best acquired in early childhood. Older language students, with their greater cognitive capacity and knowledge of the world, appear to have a significant edge over younger ones, according to a growing body of research.[5] Where did Wilson get his information? He cited only "personal anecdotal evidence . . . from watching my two-to-three-year-old daughter learn Norwegian."

The point here is not to single out Professor Wilson for rebuke, but to illus-trate the prevalence of opinionated discourse about language. It is a subject that is dear to all of us, bound up with individual and group identity, status, intellect, culture, nationalism, and freedom. When it comes to language, we are willing to take on the experts. Lay persons who would feel unqualified to speak on other pedagogical topics are eager to express their views about bilingual education.

Certainly, this is a matter that *should* concern all Americans. It is not just a question of how we will run our schools, but of what kind of society we aspire to be: pluralist or conformist, humane or intolerant. All the more reason that the debate should be informed. My aim in this book is to provide the factual context — the history, politics, theory, and practice of bilingual education — for those who want to understand and influence this important discussion.

Notes

1. These statistics are for U.S. residents aged 5 and above. It should be noted that the census data have several limitations that may tend to overstate or understate respondents' proficiency in English and other languages. The Census Bureau makes language estimates based on the "long form," a written questionnaire mailed to a sample population of approximately 13 percent. Obviously, this procedure is likely to overlook many U.S. residents whose English literacy is limited. Those in the survey were asked: "What language other than English does [this person] speak in the home?" but not "How well?" or "How often?" Because of this ambiguity and the lack of an oral interviewer, some respondents may have claimed to speak languages in which their skills are quite limited. On the other hand, some may not have cited languages they speak fluently, but only outside the home. To those who did respond affirmatively, the census posed a second question: "Does [this person] speak English very well, well, not well, or not at all." It did not ask about other important aspects of English proficiency: reading, writing, and understanding. In any case, such self-reports are notoriously unreliable; a variety of personal and cultural factors can incline a respondent either to brag or be self-deprecating. In a follow-up study to the 1980 census, the U.S. Department of Education concluded that respondents who said they spoke English less than "very well" were likely to have some "difficulty" with English.

2. In the 1950s the top five source countries of immigrants to the United States were (in descending order) Germany, Canada, Mexico, the United Kingdom, and Italy; in the 1980s they were Mexico, the Philippines, Vietnam, Korea, and China (including Taiwan).

3. Because Hispanics may be of any race, there may be some overlap in these figures. Projections are as follows:

(figures in thousands)

Year	Total U.S.	Hispanic Origin	%	Asian, Pacific Islander	%
1995	263,434	26,798	10.2	9,756	3.7
2000	276,241	31,166	11.3	12,125	4.4
2010	300,431	40,525	13.5	17,653	7.0
2020	325,942	51,217	15.7	22,653	7.0
2030	349,993	62,810	17.9	28,467	8.1
2050	392,031	88,071	22.5	40,508	10.3

Source: U.S. Bureau of the Census, Current Population Reports, P25-1104, *Population Projections of the United States, by Age, Sex, Race, and Hispanic Origin: 1993 to 2050* (Washington, D.C.: U.S. Government Printing Office, 1993).

4. For good reason the term LEP, "limited-English-proficient," has fallen into disfavor in recent years. Rather than recognizing children for what they have — valuable skills in languages other than English — it defines them on the basis of what they lack.

Unfortunately, in the author's view, there is currently no workable alternative. LEP has a precise meaning in federal and state education laws and court decisions. Moreover, it represents a conceptual advance over the earlier term "limited-English speaking," by encompassing proficiencies in reading, writing, and listening. The most-often-mentioned candidate to replace LEP, "English language learner" (ELL), is superficially less offensive. But it is also less precise, and it conveys a single-minded focus on learning English that tends to restrict discussion about students' pedagogical needs. Perhaps that explains why ELL is also favored by many English Only advocates.

5. Certainly, starting young is an advantage in the sense that proficiency in a second language takes several years to achieve. No researcher would dispute this rationale for early programs of English as a second language (ESL) or foreign language in elementary school (FLES). But there appears to be no pedagogical basis for hurrying LEP children into mainstream classrooms; in fact, such practices are likely to be harmful.

History

1 Bilingualism in America: A Forgotten Legacy

$\mathscr{B}$ilingual education figures nowhere in the immigrant myth: the bootstraps rise to success, the fight for social acceptance, the sink-or-swim imperative of learning English. For many Americans today, the idea of teaching children in other languages is an affront to sacred traditions. Yesterday's immigrants allegedly prospered without special programs; glad to blend into the melting pot, they struggled to master the language of their adopted homeland. By operating in English only, public schools weaned students from other tongues and opened a new world of opportunities.

Ancestral legends die hard. Undoubtedly, some early newcomers were quick to assimilate and to advance themselves. But more often, "melting" was a process of hardships that lasted several generations. The immigrants' children were typically the first to achieve fluency in English, their grandchildren the first to finish high school, and their great-grandchildren the first to grow up in the middle class. Moreover, language minorities who were also racial minorities never had the option of joining the mainstream — whether they learned English or not — before the civil rights reforms of the 1960s.

Melting pot mythology obscures the diversity of cultures that have flourished in North America since the colonial period, and the aggressive efforts to preserve them, among both immigrants and indigenous minorities. In this history bilingual education has played a central, if overlooked, role.

In 1664, when the settlement of New Netherland was ceded to the British crown, at least eighteen tongues were spoken on Manhattan Island, not counting Indian languages. Although the hegemony of English over the thirteen colonies had been decided by the late seventeenth century, the sounds of German, Dutch, French, Swedish, Irish, and Welsh were frequently heard at the time of the American Revolution, and Spanish was dominant in several soon-to-be-acquired territories. Bilingualism was common among the working classes as well as the educated, especially in the middle colonies of New York, Pennsylvania, New Jersey, and Delaware. In the mid-eighteenth century, newspaper advertisements for runaway servants, both black and white, made frequent reference to their bilingual or trilingual proficiencies.[1]

Wherever Europeans established schools in the New World, vernacular education was the rule, whether in English or another tongue. New arrivals naturally strived to preserve their heritage; language loyalties were strong. Indeed, these were among the values that had brought the Pilgrims to America. During a brief exile in Holland, religious freedom had come at a high cost: their children had begun to lose English. In Plymouth they sought a climate where not only their Puritanism but their culture could thrive.

German-speaking Americans were operating schools in their mother tongue as early as 1694 in Philadelphia.[2] Sometimes bilingual and sometimes not, German-language schooling prevailed until the early twentieth century, notwithstanding periodic attempts to replace it with English as the medium of instruction.

In the 1750s Benjamin Franklin, a politician frustrated by his inability to influence German-speaking voters, promoted one such project under the auspices of the Society for the Propagation of Christian Knowledge. All went smoothly until German parents learned that linguistic assimilation, not religious instruction, was the real purpose of these schools; whereupon they refused to enroll their children. Soon after, the Pennsylvania Germans helped to vote Franklin out of the colonial assembly.[3] As a pamphleteer Franklin expressed alarmist concerns about bilingualism that have a familiar ring today. Citing the increased use of German in public situations, he predicted that interpreters would soon be:

> necessary in the Assembly, to tell one half of our Legislators what the other half say; In short unless the stream of their importation could be turned from this to other Colonies ... [Germans] will soon so out number us, that all the advantages we have will not in My Opinion be able to preserve our language, and even our Government will become precarious.

Yet such views were rare among the nation's founders. Not only was bilingualism generally accepted as a fact of life, but the Continental Congress actively accommodated politically significant groups of non-English speakers. During the Revolutionary War it published many official documents in German and French, including the *Artikel des Bundes und der immerwährenden Eintracht zwischen den Staaten*, or Articles of Confederation.

No Official Language Policy

Anti-British sentiment aroused by the American Revolution inspired a variety of schemes to discard English in favor of German, French, Greek, or Hebrew as the national language. Notwithstanding the persistent legend that Congress came within one vote of adopting German as our official tongue, no alternative language was seriously considered.[4] As one clever patriot observed: "It would be more convenient for us to keep the language as it was and *make the English speak Greek*."

Like England, the United States has adopted neither an official language nor a government-sanctioned body to regulate speech. In 1780, John Adams's proposal to establish an American language academy "for refining, correcting, improving, and ascertaining" the English tongue was ignored by the Continental Congress. Evidence suggests that the framers of the U.S. Constitution believed that in a democracy government should leave language choices up to the people.[5] They had no interest in promoting diversity, to be sure; the concept of cultural pluralism had yet to be invented. But according to the anthropologist Shirley Brice Heath, our early leaders placed a higher premium on political liberty than on linguistic homogeneity. Hence they adopted, in effect, "a policy not to have a policy" on language.

Benjamin Rush hoped to encourage the assimilation of the Pennsylvania Germans without compromising the principles of the new nation. His solution:

bilingual higher education. A federally funded German College, he argued, would "open the eyes of the Germans to a sense of the importance and utility of the English language and become perhaps the *only possible means,* consistent with their liberty, of spreading a knowledge of the English language among them." Like other early leaders, Rush was eager to promote a common tongue, but felt the goal could better be achieved by voluntary than dictatorial means.

The work of defining and standardizing the "American language" was left to unofficial — that is, nongovernmental — arbiters. With his dictionary and speller, Noah Webster sought to differentiate what he called "Federal English" from the "corrupted" language of the mother country. "As an independent nation," he argued in 1789, "our honor requires us to have a system of our own, in language as well as government." There was also the danger that regional and class differences in speech might divide the new nation. "Our political harmony is therefore concerned in a uniformity of language." Nevertheless, the young Webster confidently predicted that the competitors of Federal English "will gradually waste away — and within a century and a half, North America will be peopled with a hundred millions of men, *all speaking the same language."*

Indeed, from 1790 to 1815, the domain of English continued to expand at the expense of rival tongues. European military conflicts and efforts to check emigration, combined with the War of 1812, made the trans-Atlantic passage difficult to impossible. Without reinforcement by new arrivals, colonial languages like French, Dutch, and German declined, especially among the young. Ethnic schools increasingly offered English, either as a class or as the medium of instruction.

In the 1830s, however, the tide turned once more, as progressively larger waves of immigrants began arriving on American shores; Germany alone provided more than 5 million during the nineteenth century. Again came an expansion of non-English-speaking enclaves, where it was only natural for children to be schooled in their native tongues. Still, no uniform language policy prevailed. Bilingual education was likely to be accepted in areas where language-minority groups had influence and to be rejected where they had none.

By mid-century, public and parochial German-English schools were operating in such cities as Baltimore, Cincinnati, Cleveland, Indianapolis, Milwaukee, and St. Louis. An Ohio law of 1839 authorized instruction in English, German, or both in areas where parents requested it. In 1847, Louisiana adopted the identical statute, except that it substituted French for German. The Territory of New Mexico, two years after its annexation in 1848, authorized Spanish-English bilingual education. Altogether more than a dozen states passed laws that provided for schooling in languages other than English, either as a subject or as a medium of instruction. Even without explicit legal authorization, local school boards provided classes in languages as diverse as Swedish, Danish, Norwegian, Italian, Polish, Dutch, and Czech.

"Ethnic politics" — not discussions of "the psychological advantages or disadvantages of bilingual training" — determined the structure of these programs, according to Joel Perlmann, an education historian. "The debates did not focus on whether kids would learn math better in German or in English, or whether they were emotionally better off learning German skills first. The central issues, the ones that were always raised, had to do with being a good American and creating a good America."

For the nineteenth century education establishment, linguistic assimilation was the ultimate goal for immigrant students. Yet coercive means were seen as counterproductive, especially for groups like the Germans, who felt strongly about maintaining their heritage. William Torrey Harris, St. Louis school superintendent in the 1870s and later U.S. Commissioner of Education, believed that the schools must "Americanize" language-minority children. At the same time, he preached cultural tolerance, arguing that "national memories and aspirations, family traditions, customs and habits, moral and religious observances cannot be suddenly removed or changed without disastrously weakening the personality."

Americanization Efforts

A resurgence of nativism in the late nineteenth century, led by the American Protective Association, marked the beginning of a gradual decline for bilingual education. Earlier opponents of immigration, such as the "Know Nothing" Party of the 1840s and 1850s, had attacked the Germans mainly for their religion or politics, rarely for their foreign speech. By the 1880s, however, language legislation was discovered to be a convenient weapon against Catholic schools. The *Chicago Tribune* editorialized against "the arrogance and presumption . . . of an Italian priest living in Rome" for encouraging immigrants to send their children to non-English schools. Ironically, at that time in the rural Midwest, a parochial-school education — whether Catholic or Lutheran — was practically synonymous with a German-language education. So, in 1889, Protestant schools became unintended victims when Wisconsin and Illinois enacted the APA's proposal to mandate English as the sole language of instruction in all schools, public and private.

Despite the religious bigotry behind the new language laws, the American

Catholic hierarchy was ambivalent in its response: disturbed by state meddling with parochial education, yet not averse to the new English requirements. Within the church, language was becoming a focus of contention, as splits developed along nationality lines. There was no hesitation among German Americans, however, who united across sectarian lines to resist this encroachment on their language rights. When was it decided that Americanization was synonymous with Anglicization? they asked. "There is no reason we should hate English, nor is there any reason why a true American should not look upon German with tender regard," argued Colonel Conrad Krez, a decorated Civil War veteran in Milwaukee. The defenders of English-only schools, such as Governor William D. Hoard of Wisconsin, tried to cast the issue as "the *duty* of the State to require, and the *right* of the children of the State to receive, instruction in the language of the country." But immigrant voters soon expelled the governor, along with virtually all his fellow-Republican officeholders, and the law was speedily repealed. An identical scenario unfolded in Illinois. Parochial schools were again free to teach as they chose, although in practice they increased their use of English.

Indeed, German-language schooling may have already begun to decline. Around this time several cities abandoned bilingual education in their public schools. St. Louis did so after German voting strength was sapped by gerrymandering and the Irish gained control of the school board. Louisville and St. Paul banished German to the status of a foreign language offered only in the upper grades. Assimilationist pressures from German parents themselves may have played an even larger role in promoting English instruction. Nevertheless, in the year 1900, according to historian Heinz Kloss, more than 600,000 American children — or about 4 percent of the elementary school population at the time, public and parochial — continued to receive instruction partly or exclusively in the German language.

By this time new strains of xenophobia had begun to multiply as Italians, Jews, and Slavs began to outnumber Irish, Germans, and Scandinavians in the immigrant stream. These "new immigrants" were more culturally diverse than their predecessors from northern Europe and more likely to settle in cities, now that the frontier was largely "closed." So their appearance, manners, living habits, and speech attracted more public notice and comment — usually negative. A poem published by the *Atlantic Monthly* in 1892 illustrates the horror these groups inspired in many of the native-born:

> Wide open and unguarded stand our gates,
> And through them presses a wild motley throng —
> Men from the Volga and the Tartar steppes,
> Featureless figures from the Hoang-Ho,
> Malayan, Scythian, Teuton, Kelt, and Slav,
> Flying the Old World's poverty and scorn;
> These bringing with them unknown gods and rites,
> Those, tiger passions, here to stretch their claws.
> In street and alley what strange tongues are these,
> Accents of menace alien to our air,
> Voices that once the Tower of Babel knew!

Responding to such sentiments, Senator Henry Cabot Lodge of Massachusetts organized the Immigration Restriction League, seeking to bar entry to any foreigner unable to pass a literacy test.[6] In 1906, Congress passed the first federal language law of any kind, an English-speaking requirement for naturalization.

Not all Americans were so unsympathetic. Muckrakers exposed squalor and exploitation in urban slums, while social reformers sought to improve immigrants' lot through protective legislation and self-help. Settlement houses worked to ease their adjustment to a new culture. Operating through organizations like the YMCA, philanthropists financed large-scale adult English instruction for the first time, while also indoctrinating immigrants in "free enterprise" values. After the Lawrence textile strike,[7] an "Americanization" campaign was taken up by industrialists hoping to counter the influence of foreign labor agitators. In 1915, the National Americanization Committee launched an "English First" project in Detroit, with the cooperation of the local Board of Commerce. Employers like Henry Ford made attendance at after-hours English classes mandatory for their foreign-born workers.

As Americanization took a coercive turn, proficiency in English was increasingly equated with political loyalty; for the first time, an ideological link was forged between speaking good English and being a "good American." The U.S. Bureau of Education became active in this propaganda effort, sponsoring conferences on "Americanization work" and publishing an *Americanization Bulletin* and other literature, all financed by private benefactors. The goal was explicitly stated: to replace immigrant languages and cultures with those of the United States. As explained by the superintendent of New York City schools in 1918,

Americanization would cultivate "an appreciation of the institutions of this country [and] absolute forgetfulness of all obligations or connections with other countries because of descent or birth." Ellwood P. Cubberly, dean of the Stanford University School of Education, added:

> Our task is to break up [immigrant] groups or settlements, to assimilate and amalgamate these people as part of our American race, and to implant in their children, as far as can be done, the Anglo-Saxon conception of righteousness, law and order, and our popular government, and to awaken in them a reverence for our democratic institutions and for those things in our national life which we as a people hold to be of abiding worth.

The Rise of Language Restrictionism

Americanization represented a break with the principle of treating other nationalities in ways "consistent with their liberty." So did the nation's new policy of imperialism, as articulated by one of its leading exponents, Senator Albert J. Beveridge of Indiana: "The rule of liberty, that all just governments derive their authority from the consent of the governed, applies only to those who are capable of self-government. . . . God has . . . been preparing the English-speaking and Teutonic peoples for a thousand years [as] master organizers of the world to establish system where chaos reigns." Cultural jingoism flowed directly out of military jingoism. Following the Spanish-American War, the U.S. government imposed English as the medium of instruction in its new colonies of Puerto Rico, Hawaii, and the Philippines.

In Puerto Rico, where the population was virtually monolingual in Spanish, the policy was an educational disaster but was justified as a political necessity. One candid official noted in 1902: "Colonization carried forward by the armies of war is vastly more costly than that carried forward by the armies of peace, whose outposts and garrisons are the public schools of the advancing nation." Another maintained that "English is the chief source, practically the only source, of democratic ideas in Porto Rico." Puerto Ricans had no say in the matter. Indeed, the island's legislature passed repeated condemnations of the English-only mandate, but to no avail. As a result, students spent much of their time parroting lessons in a language they had no occasion to use outside of school. Few found much value in such education. A 1925 study by Teachers College reported that 84 percent of Puerto Rican children were dropping out by the 3rd grade. Although the language policy was modified periodically (first to allow Spanish instruction in the early grades, later to restore initial reading in English), it remained largely intact until 1949.

Back on the mainland, former President Theodore Roosevelt applied the same philosophy to immigrants: "We have room for but one language in this country and that is the English language, for we intend to see that the crucible turns our people out as Americans, of American nationality, and not as dwellers in a polyglot boarding house." He advocated, on the one hand, expanded opportunities for immigrants to learn English, and on the other, the deportation of those who failed to do so within five years. Roosevelt framed language differences as a loyalty issue, a problem of "hyphenated Americanism"; increasingly his rhetoric targeted German Americans, as World War I approached.

After the United States entered the war in April 1917, anti-German feeling crested in an unprecedented wave of language restrictionism. Several states passed laws and emergency decrees banning German speech in the classroom, in church, in public meetings, even on the telephone. Findlay, Ohio, imposed a $25 fine for anyone who spoke the enemy's language on the street. In the Midwest at least 18,000 persons were charged under such laws by 1921. Six months after Armistice Day, Governor James M. Cox sought legislation to remove all uses of German from Ohio's elementary schools, public and private, arguing that the language posed "a distinctive menace to Americanism, and a part of a plot formed by the German government to make the school children loyal to it." The state legislature readily approved Cox's bill.

Under legal pressure or not, around this time most public school systems in the United States curtailed study of the German language. They did so with the blessings of such establishment voices as the *New York Times*, which editorialized in 1919: "Some German-American parents want German to be taught. It pleases their pride, but it does not do their children any good." German language teachers, suddenly thrown out of work, were often reassigned to instruct children in "Americanism" and "citizenship." Mobs raided schools and burned German textbooks; in Lima, Ohio, they were led by the local school superintendent. In nearby Columbus the school board sold its German books to a waste paper company for fifty cents per hundredweight.

Soon the fervor of Anglo-conformity spilled over into hostility toward all minority tongues. In the year following the war, according to legal historian Arnold Leibowitz, fifteen states legislated English as the basic language of instruction.[8] Several followed Ohio's example of forbidding any foreign-language study in the elementary grades. The most restrictive of these laws were struck down by the U.S. Supreme Court in the *Meyer v. Nebraska* case, which involved a parochial school teacher charged with the crime of reading a Bible story in German to a ten-year-old child. In reversing his conviction, the court said:

> The desire of the legislature to foster a homogeneous people with American ideals prepared readily to understand current discussions of civic matters is easy to appreciate. Unfortunate experiences during the late war and aversion toward every characteristic of truculent adversaries were certainly enough to quicken that aspiration. But the means adopted, we think, exceed the limitations upon the power of the State and conflict with rights assured . . . in time of peace and domestic tranquility. . . .
>
> The protection of the Constitution extends to all, to those who speak other languages as well as to those born with English on the tongue. Perhaps it would be highly advantageous if all had a ready understanding of our ordinary speech, but this cannot be coerced by methods which conflict with the Constitution — a desirable end cannot be promoted by prohibited means.

By the time the court handed down this ruling in 1923, the frenzy of Americanization was already starting to subside. Attempts to legislate loyalty to English were on the decline. Big city school systems were beginning to lift bans on German studies.

Yet public attitudes had changed fundamentally: learning in languages other than English now seemed less than patriotic. European immigrant groups felt stronger pressures to assimilate and less enthusiasm for preserving old-country ways. Minority tongues were devalued in the eyes of the younger generation. Meanwhile, the stream of non-English-speaking newcomers slowed to a trickle after 1924, when Congress enacted the strictest immigration quotas in the nation's history.

Bilingual instruction continued in some parochial schools, mainly in rural areas of the Midwest, but by the late 1930s, it was virtually eradicated throughout the United States. Interest in the study of foreign languages also fell off dramatically. Next to Latin, German had been the most popular foreign language in 1915, with 24 percent of American secondary school students enrolled; by 1922, less than one percent were studying German. Overall enrollments in modern language classes declined from 36 percent of secondary students in 1915 to 14 percent in 1948.[9]

Within a generation the Americanizers' goal of transforming a polyglot society into a monolingual one was largely achieved. "This linguistic equivalent of 'book burning' worked admirably well" in promoting assimilation, writes Josué González, former federal director of bilingual education. "But it worked best with the Northern European immigrants," who had a "cultural affinity" with American values and shared a "Caucasian racial history." For other language minorities, especially those with dark complexions, English-only schooling brought difficulties. While their cultures were suppressed, discrimination barred their full acceptance into American life. In addition, it was these groups — conquered peoples and racial minorities — who had suffered linguistic repression in the nineteenth century, a departure from the habitual laissez-faire toward European immigrant languages.

English as a 'Civilizing' Influence

The U.S. government recognized the language rights of the Cherokee tribe under an 1828 treaty and agreed to subsidize the first newspaper published in an Indian tongue, the *Cherokee Phoenix*. In the 1830s, however, President Andrew Jackson initiated a policy of forcible Indian removal from the eastern United States. When the Cherokees used their printing press to advocate resistance, it was confiscated and destroyed by the state of Georgia. Their ordeal became known as the Trail of Tears, as more than one-third of the tribe died en route to Oklahoma. After resettlement they established an educational system of twenty-one schools and two academies. Using Sequoyah's syllabary, or phonetic writing system, tribal members achieved a 90 percent literacy rate in the Cherokee language. According to a 1969 Senate report on Indian education, in the 1850s these schools "used bilingual materials to such an extent that Oklahoma Cherokees had a higher English literacy level than the white populations of either Texas or Arkansas." Other tribal and missionary schools also made effective use of native-language instruction.

Successful or not, such experiments in bilingual education were doomed by the federal government's hostility to Indian self-determination. In 1868, the Indian Peace Commission reported: "In the difference of language to-day lies two-thirds of our trouble. . . . Schools should be established, which children should be required to attend; their barbarous dialects should be blotted out and the English language substituted." In 1879, federal officials began separating Indian children from their families and forcing them to attend off-reservation boarding schools. Students were punished when caught speaking their tribal tongues, even if they could speak no English. Senator Ben Nighthorse Campbell of Colorado, a member of the Northern Cheyenne tribe, describes the experience: "Both my grandparents were forcibly removed from their homes and placed into boarding schools. One of the first English words Indian students learned was *soap*, because their mouths were constantly being washed out for using their native language."

This policy coincided with a broader campaign to contain Indians on reservations by repressing their cultures, for example, banning native religious ceremonies and hair braids for Indian men. The rationale was that such "civilizing" measures, including compulsory use of English, would acclimate nomadic peoples to reservation life. "To teach Indian school children in their native language is practically to exclude English, and to prevent them from acquiring it," declared J. D. C. Atkins, commissioner of Indian affairs, in 1887. "This language, which is good enough for a white man and a black man, ought to be good enough for the red man." In defense of the English-only rule, Atkins asked: "Is it cruelty to the Indian to force him to give up his scalping knife and tomahawk? Is it cruelty to force him to abandon the vicious and barbarous sun dance, where he lacerates his flesh, and dances and tortures himself even unto death?"

Senator Henry Dawes of Massachusetts used a similar line of argument to justify "allotment" of reservation lands to individual Indians: it would assimilate them into American culture by teaching them "selfishness, which is at the bottom of civilization." In practice, the Dawes Severalty Act of 1887 made them vulnerable to exploitation, foreclosure, and theft. Federal policy succeeded mainly in separating Indians from millions of acres to which they were entitled by treaty.

When whites demanded access to Oklahoma, Congress dissolved the autonomous tribal governments of the so-called Five Civilized Tribes — Cherokees, Choctaws, Creeks, Chickasaws, and Seminoles — along with their independent school systems. The Cherokees' printing press, which had been used to produce native-language teaching materials, again was confiscated. This time it was shipped to Washington, D.C., and put on display at the Smithsonian Institution. Tribal schools were taken over by the Bureau of Indian Affairs (BIA) and English-only policies were instituted. Educational attainment began a long, gradual decline. By 1969, 40 percent of Cherokee adults in eastern Oklahoma were functionally illiterate, up to 75 percent of their children were dropouts in some schools, and in one county 90 percent were receiving welfare. But virtually all of them spoke English.

In 1934, Indian Commissioner John Collier rescinded the BIA's official policy of repressing Indian vernaculars. He even tried to introduce native-language instruction in some community schools, hoping to encourage bilingualism and biliteracy. For example, on the Navajo reservation, linguists were hired to compile a Navajo dictionary and develop Navajo teaching materials. But this experiment with bilingual education was limited by a severe shortage of trained Indian teachers and by budget cuts during World War II. Despite their best efforts, Collier and his fellow reformers also failed to change the culture of BIA educators, many of whom continued to forbid children to "talk Indian" in school. In practice, punishments for native-language use continued into the 1940s and 1950s, as many Native American adults can testify from personal experience.

Strangers in Their Own Land

Spanish speakers endured similar treatment in the Southwest. As a conquered people following the Mexican-American War, they too faced repression of their language and culture to a far greater extent than European immigrants. The 1848 Treaty of Guadalupe Hidalgo promised that these new Spanish-speaking citizens of the United States "shall be maintained and protected in the free enjoyment of their liberty and property, and secured in the free exercise of their religion without restriction." While not mentioned explicitly, a guarantee of certain language rights was strongly implied.[10] Yet such rights have rarely been respected.

Although California's 1849 constitution required the publication of all laws in both Spanish and English, the practice was soon abandoned. Political power shifted abruptly as the Gold Rush attracted hordes of Anglo-American miners and land speculators. Amid the competition for wealth, language became a tool of advantage. In 1855, the legislature mandated English-only instruction in all schools, along with other measures designed to discriminate against Spanish speakers. Forced to prove title to their lands in a language and legal system foreign to them, the native *Californios* were expropriated from most of the 14 million acres they held on the eve of statehood (40 percent of their holdings went to pay the fees of English-speaking lawyers).

Californians met to rewrite their state constitution in 1878-79 during a period of unabashed nativism. One delegate proclaimed: "This State should be a State for white men. . . . We want no other race here." After stripping Chinese immigrants of virtually all their civil rights, the convention took aim at the Californios. It adopted the following provision: "All laws of the State of

California, and all official writings, and the executive, legislative, and judicial proceedings shall be conducted, preserved, and published in no other than the
English language."

Spanish speakers enjoyed a very different experience in New Mexico,
where they remained a popular majority until the early twentieth century. In the
1870s the territorial legislature still operated mainly in Spanish, with laws later
translated into English. Jury trials were held in English in only two of fourteen
counties. A mere 5 percent of New Mexico's schools used English as the language of instruction, while 69 percent taught in Spanish and 26 percent were
bilingual. With the arrival of railroads in the 1880s, the territory's demography
began to change, but not its tradition of tolerance. When New Mexico finally
became a state in 1912, its first constitution provided guarantees against language
discrimination and for the training of Spanish-language teachers.

Texas represented the opposite extreme. There Mexican American children
were commonly segregated in inferior schools, if not discouraged from attending
school altogether. English-only instruction was strictly enforced. Beginning in
1919, the Texas legislature made it a criminal offense to teach in any other language (although foreign language instruction was permissible in the upper
grades). Children were likewise punished for speaking their native language anywhere at school, even on the playground. In the Rio Grande Valley, "Spanish
detention," or being kept after school for using Spanish, persisted well into the
late 1960s, according to an investigation by the U.S. Commission on Civil Rights.
One south Texas principal, quoted in the commission's 1972 report, explained
the disciplinary policy in this way:

> Our school is predominantly Latin American — 97 percent. We try
> to discourage the use of Spanish on the playground, in the halls,
> and in the classroom. We feel that the reason so many of our pupils
> are reading two to three years below grade level is because their
> English vocabulary is so limited. We are in complete accord that it
> is excellent to be bilingual or multilingual, but we must . . . stress
> the fact that practice makes perfect — that English is a very difficult
> language to master. Our pupils speak Spanish at home, at dances,
> on the playground, at athletic events. . . . We feel the least they can
> do is try to speak English at school.

As late as 1970, a teacher was indicted in Crystal City, Texas, for using
Spanish in a high school history class. The case was subsequently dismissed,

however. Unbeknownst to the local district attorney, the legislature had repealed the English-only instruction law the previous year.

The 'Cultural Deprivation' Era

George I. Sánchez, a psychologist at the University of Texas, protested the schools' single-minded emphasis on English and became an early advocate of bilingual approaches. "Imagine the Spanish-speaking child's introduction to American education!" he wrote in 1940.

> He comes to school, not only without a word of English but without the environmental experience upon which school life is based. He cannot speak to the teacher and is unable to understand what goes on about him in the classroom. He finally submits to rote learning, parroting words and processes in self-defense. To him, school life is artificial. He submits to it during class hours, only partially digesting the information which the teacher has tried to impart. Of course he learns English and the school subjects imperfectly!

Gradually, other educators began to recognize the futility of coercive assimilation. But few were ready to accept the alternative advanced by Sánchez: that the school should build upon, rather than dismantle, the minority child's language and culture. Instead, reformers sought more effective ways to adapt the child to the school — in particular, to treat his or her "language disability."

Cultural deprivation theory, which came to dominate educational psychology in the 1950s, rejected genetic explanations for underachievement by minority students. It pointed instead to environmental factors: parents' failure to stress educational attainment, lower-class values that favored "living in the present" rather than planning for the future, and inadequate English-language skills. "To make it in America," declared sociologist W. I. Thomas, what these "culturally inferior" children needed most was to master the language and values of the dominant society. The job of the schools, he argued, was to "change their culture," that is, to overcome students' handicaps of ethnic background and enable them to assimilate.

English as a second language (ESL), a methodology developed in the 1930s to meet the needs of foreign diplomats and university students, was now prescribed for language-minority children. "Pullout classes," the most common form of ESL, removed students from regular classrooms, typically two to five times a week for a forty-five-minute period of compensatory instruction. Unlike remedial reading, ESL techniques took account of a child's lack of oral English proficiency. Still, its availability was not widespread. In a Civil Rights Commission survey, only 5.5 percent of Mexican American children in California, Arizona, New Mexico, Colorado, and Texas were enrolled in ESL classes in 1968-69 (about half that number were receiving bilingual instruction).

While ESL was an improvement over sink-or-swim language instruction, its effectiveness remained limited. "By dealing with the student simply as a non-English speaker," the commission observed in 1972, "most ESL classes fail to expose children to approaches, attitudes, and materials which take advantage of the rich Mexican American heritage." Excluding minority cultures, or providing only "fantasy" stereotypes like "caballeros and señoritas with gardenias behind their ears," was undercutting children's self-image. Instruction that strives to change students "into something else" inevitably discourages academic achievement, notes Josué González. "When children are painfully ashamed of who they are, they are not going to do very well in school, whether they be taught monolingually, bilingually, or trilingually."

From a strictly academic standpoint, ESL students were learning English too slowly to keep up in other content areas. So there was little improvement in their long-term achievement. In the 1960s the dropout rate for Puerto Rican students in New York City was estimated at 60 percent; those who remained were almost automatically assigned to vocational tracks. In 1963, the city's public schools awarded 331 academic diplomas to Puerto Ricans, representing no more than one percent of the total Puerto Rican enrollment; of these graduates, only 28 went on to college. Meanwhile, language difficulties were often ignored; students were simply labeled slow learners, or worse. Based on their performance on IQ tests administered in English, disproportionate numbers of language-minority children ended up in special education classes. As late as 1980, Hispanic children in Texas were overrepresented by 315 percent in the learning-disabled category.

Bilingual Education Reborn

The renaissance of bilingual education occurred not among Mexican Americans or Puerto Ricans, but among a relatively privileged minority: Cubans who had fled to Miami after the 1959 revolution in their homeland. The early arrivals were Hispanics of European stock, light-skinned, and largely from the professional classes. Proud of their language and culture, they brought with them education and job skills, if little ready cash. Many had taught school in Cuba, and the state of Florida helped them become recertified. Generous subsidies were available through the federal Cuban Refugee Program.

To serve this politically favored group, the Dade County Public Schools provided ESL instruction and, in 1961, initiated "Spanish for Spanish speakers" classes. Two years later the district established a full-fledged bilingual program, probably the nation's first since the 1920s. Launched at the Coral Way Elementary School, the experiment was open to both English and Spanish speakers. It was anything but a compensatory approach: the objective was fluent bilingualism for both groups. Pauline Rojas and Ralph Robinett, ESL specialists who had worked in Puerto Rico, directed the effort with the help of well-trained Cuban educators.

Beginning in September 1963, Coral Way's 350 1st, 2nd, and 3rd graders were grouped by language. Cuban children received their morning lessons in Spanish and their afternoon lessons in English; for English-speaking children, the schedule was reversed. During lunch, music, and art, as well as on the playground, the two groups were mixed. Results were immediately promising, as students appeared to progress academically and in both languages. A 1966 report by the district concluded: "The pupils in Coral Way are rapidly becoming 'culturally advantaged.' They are learning to operate effectively in two languages and two cultures."

Indeed, Coral Way was in many respects a success. In English reading, both language groups did as well as or better than their counterparts in monolingual English schools, and the Cuban children achieved equivalent levels in Spanish. The one disappointment was among Anglo students; as a group, they never reached national norms in Spanish reading achievement. "In retrospect," observes psychologist Kenji Hakuta, "the difference between the two groups was not unexpected, since the predominant language of the environment [was] English." The Cuban children had an advantage because, unlike their English-speaking peers, they received high-quality exposure to the second language outside as well as inside the classroom. In any case, Hakuta says, "the feasibility of bilingual education was established." Variants of the Coral Way approach were tried elsewhere in Dade County, and as educators saw its benefits, the "two-way" model spread to other districts (see Chapter 11).

Federal and state bilingual education laws soon followed. Government intervention changed the focus of the Coral Way experiment, however, from an enrichment model aimed at developing fluency in two languages, to a remedial effort designed to help "disadvantaged" children overcome the "handicap" of not speaking English. From its outset, federal aid to bilingual education was regarded as a "poverty program," rather than an innovative approach to language instruction. This decision would shape the development of bilingual programs, and the heated ideological battles surrounding them, over the next three decades.

Notes

1. For example: "Run away . . . from *John Orr*, near *Skuylkill, Philadelphia*, a Servant Man named *James Mitchel*. . . . He has been a Traveller, and can talk *Dutch* [probably German], *Spanish* and *Irish*"; "Run away also . . . an *Irish* Servant Man named Peter Kelley. . . . He speaks good *French*"; and "Run away from *Joseph Forman*, of New-York . . . a Negro Man named JOE. . . . [This] country born, speaks good English and Dutch." Apparently, monolingualism was unusual enough to be noteworthy: "Run away from his Master, *Theodorus Van Wyck*, of *Dutchess* County, in the Province of *New York*, a Negro Man named JAMES, aged about 22 Years . . . can talk nothing but English, and has a low Voice." These and other Colonial advertisements are cited in Allen Walker Read, "Bilingualism in the Middle Colonies, 1725-1775," *American Speech* 12 (1937): 93-99.

2. German Americans were the nation's largest ethnolinguistic minority in every decennial census from 1790 to 1950; unfortunately, useful figures on language proficiency are rarely available. In an analysis of the 1790 census, the American Council of Learned Societies estimated that persons of German background represented 8.6 percent of the population of the original thirteen states. See "Report of the Committee on Linguistic and National Stocks in the Population of the United States," in the *Annual Report of the American Historical Association for the Year 1931*, pp. 103-441. By comparison, Hispanics made up 9.0 percent of the U.S. population in the 1990 census.

3. They were especially incensed by a passage in Franklin's *Observations on the Increase of Mankind* (1755) in which he wrote: "Why should the *Palatine Boors* be suffered to swarm into our Settlements, and by herding together, establish their Language and Manners, to the Exclusion of ours? Why should Pennsylvania, founded by the *English*, become a Colony of *Aliens*, who will shortly be so numerous as to Germanize us instead of our Anglifying them?" Apparently regretting his intemperate language, Franklin excised this passage from later editions of his writings. Ironically, in 1738 he had founded one of the earliest German-language newspapers in America, *Die Philadelphische Zeitung,* though it soon failed. Toward the end of his life, Franklin became an influential supporter of German-language higher education.

4. The event that generated this confusion was a petition to the U.S. Congress by Virginia Germans who sought the printing of all federal laws in their language as well as English. In 1795, the proposal failed in the House of Representatives, 42 to 41, with Speaker Friedrich A. Muhlenberg, a Pennsylvania German, apparently casting the deciding vote. Federal documents continued to be published in German, but on an ad hoc basis. The tale that German nearly became our official language appar-

ently originated with nineteenth century adherents of *Deutschtum*, or German American cultural nationalism, and was given new life by Ripley's Believe It or Not in the 1930s. See Heinz Kloss, *American Bilingual Tradition* (Rowley, Mass.: Newbury House, 1977), pp. 26-33.

5. Seventy years earlier, the British monarchy had rejected a similar scheme by Jonathan Swift, a notorious language scold who condemned the "corruptions" of English during the Restoration era. Daniel Defoe, another enthusiast of an English language academy, wanted to make it "as criminal . . . to coin words as money." Samuel Johnson, however, in the preface to his *Dictionary*, described the idea of arresting language change by fiat as not only futile, but contrary to "the spirit of English liberty." See Albert C. Baugh and Thomas Cable, *A History of the English Language*, 3rd ed. (Englewood Cliffs, N.J.: Prentice-Hall, 1978), pp. 254-69.

6. The standard was an ability to read forty words in any language. Congress passed such legislation four times beginning in 1897, but each time it was met with presidential vetoes. The literacy test finally became law in 1917, when Congress overrode Woodrow Wilson's opposition.

7. Led by the Industrial Workers of the World, this 1912 strike in Lawrence, Massachusetts, was a watershed event in U.S. labor-management relations. Victorious despite brutal repression, the strikers demonstrated the potential of an unskilled, nonunionized, immigrant workforce composed of many nationalities. Organizers overcame ethnic divisions by conducting strike meetings in more than twenty languages.

8. This brought the total to thirty-four states. At the national level, a bill to designate English "the language of instruction in all schools, public and private," failed to pass the 66th Congress. For many, federal language legislation remained anathema.

9. According to the U.S. Center for Education Statistics, enrollment climbed to 27.7 percent in 1968, fell to 21.9 percent in 1982 (public schools, grades 9 through 12), then rebounded to 38.4 percent in 1990. Generally, these levels have paralleled trends in college entrance and graduation requirements.

10. This interpretation is consistent with statements by Nicholas Trist, the treaty's chief U.S. negotiator. In a letter to Secretary of State James Buchanan, Trist italicized what he perceived to be an "overpowering" concern of the Mexican delegation: *"a perfect devotion to their distinct nationality, and a most vehement aversion to its becoming merged in or blended with ours."* Hence it insisted on "the right of Mexicans residing there to continue there, retaining the character of Mexican citizens." Thirty years later, several delegates to a California constitutional convention cited the Treaty of Guadalupe Hidalgo in opposing an English-only mandate for state government, but they were voted down.

2 The Evolution of Federal Policy

Bilingual-bicultural education is like an impressionist painting — very attractive from a distance but unclear and confusing when one gets very close to it.

This assessment by civil rights consultant Gary Orfield, written in 1977, remains prevalent among school officials and parents today. Federal policy on bilingual education appears to be a complex array of regulations, legal precedents, funding restrictions, and assorted red tape. Critics ask: Why not let local communities decide what's best for their students? Why should federal bureaucrats dictate an instructional methodology?

In truth, the federal government requires bilingual approaches only for a portion of school districts that qualify for bilingual education grants. No teaching methodology is mandated; merely *some* use of native language in Title VII classrooms. In recent years, even this requirement has been relaxed to allow for expanded funding of "special alternative" — that is, English-only — approaches.

Much of the confusion has arisen from the "two track" approach that has characterized the federal role in bilingual education: financial aid to support programs serving limited-English-proficient (LEP) children, and civil rights efforts to ensure that these students get an equal chance to succeed. Although policies on both tracks have aimed at enhancing educational opportunities, they have not always run side by side. Funding for bilingual programs came first, before federal authorities had begun to grapple with the problem of language discrimination in the schools.

Genesis of Title VII

On January 2, 1968, when President Lyndon B. Johnson signed the Bilingual Education Act into law, the U.S. government signaled its first commitment to addressing the needs of students with limited English skills. The new Title VII of the Elementary and Secondary Education Act (ESEA) authorized resources to support educational programs, to train teachers and aides, to develop and disseminate instructional materials, and to encourage parental involvement. In spite of its name, the original Bilingual Education Act did not require schools to use a language other than English to receive funding.[1]

The law's focus was explicitly compensatory, aimed at children who were both poor and "educationally disadvantaged because of their inability to speak English." And yet, a key question of goals — whether the act was to speed the transition to English or to promote bilingualism — was left unresolved. Senator Ralph Yarborough, the measure's prime sponsor, did nothing to dispel this confusion when he told fellow lawmakers: "It is not the purpose of the bill to create pockets of different languages throughout the country . . . not to stamp out the mother tongue, and not to make their mother tongue the dominant language, but just to try to make those children fully literate in English."

Although Senator Yarborough and President Johnson were both liberal Democrats from Texas, for some years there had been bad blood between the two, and it was the White House that put up the strongest resistance to the legislation. Great Society programs and the Vietnam War had put a squeeze on the federal budget by 1967. In its precarious political position, the Johnson administration hoped to avoid further tax increases and thus sought to head off new demands on the federal treasury. Testifying before Yarborough's special subcommittee on bilingual education, Commissioner of Education Harold Howe II argued against creating a new title of the ESEA. Some additional assistance, he said, could be provided under the existing Titles I and III, which were already financing eighteen bilingual and English-as-a-second-language (ESL) programs in the Southwest.

Howe also endorsed the major criticism of Yarborough's proposal: it would have aided only Spanish-speaking children, ignoring the needs of others who might benefit from bilingual instruction.[2] Hispanic leaders quickly recognized the political pitfalls of this provision. Representative Henry B. González of Texas argued for the coverage of Louisiana Cajuns, American Indians, and other native-born language minorities. "In view of our continuing efforts to promote mutual respect and tolerance," he said, "we would be inviting grave and justly deserved criticism from many ethnic groups if we recognize the problems of only one." The critics were pacified when Representative James Scheuer of New York drafted a compromise extending the program to "children who come from environments where the dominant language is other than English," with preference given to those from low-income families.[3] Finding itself outflanked, the Johnson administration reluctantly agreed to support a new Title VII.

By the late 1960s, political winds favored increased attention for Hispanics, who had been largely passed over by antipoverty legislation. The National Education Association (NEA) had drawn attention to the plight of Mexican American children with its Tucson Survey of 1965-66. Its pamphlet *The Invisible Minority, Pero No Vencibles* painted a picture of educational neglect in that Arizona city: inadequate facilities, a lack of trained teachers, and the scandal of sink-or-swim schooling. Throughout the Southwest veteran educators like José Cárdenas of San Antonio were beginning to conclude that "just about anything was better than the existing situation." Simultaneously, a number of academic researchers and Romance language teachers were coming to the conclusion that a dual-language approach was theoretically viable. The NEA brought these forces together, along with Senator Yarborough and Texas state senator Joe Bernal, at a conference in Tucson on October 30-31, 1966. Politically speaking, this marked the birth of the "bilingual movement."

Notwithstanding differences over minor details, at the time there was remarkably little controversy about the idea of federal support for bilingual education. In endorsing Yarborough's bill, Senator George Murphy, a conservative Republican from California, noted that Governor Ronald Reagan had recently signed legislation repealing California's English-only school statute. (Five years later Reagan would approve the state's first bilingual education law.) As with any idea whose time has come politically, members of Congress scrambled to affix their names. Thirty-seven bilingual education bills were introduced in the 90th Congress (1967-68), including one sponsored by George Bush, then a freshman Congressman from Texas.

Expenditures were another matter. Under pressure from the White House, Congress approved no funding for Title VII in the first year. For 1969, it appropriated $7.5 million, just enough to finance seventy-six projects serving 27,000 children. Even this meager subsidy doubled the number of children enrolled in bilingual classrooms in the United States. By 1972, the total had risen to 112,000 of the estimated 5 million language-minority children of school age.

Beginning with New Mexico in 1969, states began to pass laws encouraging instruction in languages other than English. In 1971, Massachusetts became the first to *mandate* bilingual education in school districts with enough LEP students to make it practical. Currently, thirty states have statutes expressly permitting native-language instruction. Nine of these require it under certain circumstances,[4] and twenty-one provide some form of financial aid to bilingual programs; most set standards for certifying bilingual or ESL teachers. Although laws in seven states[5] still prohibit instruction in languages other than English, these bans are no longer enforced.

Civil Rights and Language-Minority Children

The second track of federal bilingual education policy originated in 1970, largely as a response to civil rights activism. A few months earlier La Raza Unida Party, a militant Chicano group, had taken matters into its own hands. In Crystal City, Texas, it organized school boycotts to protest the unequal treatment of Spanish-speaking students. Bilingual education was among its demands and, after the party had won a majority of seats on the local school board, among its innovations. Meanwhile, Mexican American, Puerto Rican, and Chinese parents began to file lawsuits challenging the schools' failure to address their children's language needs.

The litigation advanced a novel claim of discrimination: that *equal treatment* for children of limited English proficiency — in other words, "submersion" in mainstream classrooms — meant *unequal opportunities* to succeed. There was no question that large numbers of language-minority students were falling behind and dropping out. At issue was whether local school officials should be held accountable. The Civil Rights Act of 1964 had forbidden discrimination on the basis of national origin, but thus far in the field of education, federal authorities had confined their attention to race discrimination against Southern blacks. Nevertheless, *de facto* and *de jure* segregation of Mexican American children remained prevalent in schools throughout the Southwest.

Finally, on May 25, 1970, the U.S. government entered the fray. J. Stanley Pottinger, director of the federal Office for Civil Rights (OCR), sent a memorandum to "school districts with more than five percent national-origin-minority group children" informing them of their obligations under Title VI of the Civil Rights Act, which outlaws discrimination in federally supported programs. Where children had limited English skills, Pottinger said, "the district must take affirmative steps to rectify the language deficiency in order to open its instructional program to these students."

Although the memo did not direct school officials to establish bilingual education programs, it demanded that they offer some kind of special language instruction for children with a limited command of English. It prohibited the assignment of students to classes for the handicapped "on the basis of criteria which essentially measure or evaluate English language skills." No longer could schools shuttle children along vocational tracks toward an "educational dead-end" instead of teaching them English. Finally, administrators had to communicate with parents in a language they could understand.

While Pottinger's memo carved out new territory for OCR's enforcement of Title VI, including the threat to terminate federal education subsidies as a last resort, the immediate reaction in school districts was muted. Education historian Colman B. Stein reports that in Beeville, Texas, the superintendent's only response was to redesignate the vocational track as "career education."

If the executive branch was slow to get results, the federal courts were not. A lawsuit by Mexican American parents in New Mexico, *Serna v. Portales Municipal Schools*, led to the first court mandate for bilingual education. Based on expert testimony in this 1972 case, a federal judge ordered instruction in the children's native language and culture as part of a desegregation plan. Upholding the decision two years later, the Tenth U.S. Circuit Court of Appeals ruled that Title VI gave Hispanic students "a right to bilingual education."[*]

Other landmark cases followed. Aspira, a Puerto Rican advocacy group, sued New York City on behalf of 150,000 Hispanic students. In 1974, it won a consent decree, which remains in effect, guaranteeing bilingual instruction for the city's Spanish-dominant children. In *Ríos v. Read* (1977) a federal court found that the Patchogue-Medford, New York, school district had violated the rights of LEP students by providing a half-hearted bilingual program that relied mainly on ESL and included no bicultural component. "While the District's goal of teaching Hispanic children the English language is certainly proper," the court said, "it cannot be allowed to compromise a student's right to a meaningful education before proficiency in English is obtained."

The most sweeping order came in 1981. U.S. District Judge William Wayne Justice found that the state of Texas had not only segregated students in inferior "Mexican schools," but had "vilified the language, culture, and heritage of these children with grievous results." Accordingly, Justice mandated bilingual education in grades K through 12 throughout Texas. The following year, however, a federal appellate court reversed this ruling in the case, *U.S. v. Texas*, on factual grounds. Evidence of discriminatory practices had been insufficient to justify such a broad remedy, it said; moreover, the Texas legislature had recently enacted a strong mandate for bilingual education.

The Lau Decision

The major court decision on the rights of language-minority students, and the only such ruling by the U.S. Supreme Court, is *Lau v. Nichols*. The case originated in 1970, when a San Francisco poverty lawyer, Edward Steinman, learned that a client's child was failing in school because he could not understand the language of instruction. Steinman filed a class action suit on behalf of Kinney Lau and 1,789 other Chinese students in the same predicament.[6] These children, he alleged, were being denied "education on equal terms" (the court's standard in *Brown v. Board of Education*) because of their limited English skills. San Francisco officials responded that, unlike the 1954 *Brown* case, *Lau* involved no discrimination because there was no segregation or disparate treatment. The same instruction was offered to all students, without regard to national origin. If the Chinese children had a "language deficiency," that was unfortunate, but the district was not to blame.

Federal district and appeals courts sided with the school officials, although in a strong dissent, Judge Shirley Hufstedler of the Ninth Circuit (later U.S. Secretary of Education) dismissed the school district's premises as irrelevant:

> The state does not cause children to start school speaking only Chinese. Neither does a state cause children to have black skin rather than white nor cause a person charged with a crime to be

indigent rather than rich. State action depends upon state responses to differences otherwise created.

These Chinese children are not separated from their English-speaking classmates by state-erected walls of brick and mortar, but the language barrier, which the state helps to maintain, insulates the children from their classmates as effectively as any physical bulwarks. Indeed, these children are more isolated from equal educational opportunity than were those physically segregated Blacks in *Brown*; these children cannot communicate at all with their classmates or teachers. . . Invidious discrimination is not washed away because the able bodied and the paraplegic are given the same state command to walk.

In 1974, the Supreme Court unanimously overruled the lower courts and embraced Hufstedler's logic. "There is no equality of treatment," wrote Justice William O. Douglas, "merely by providing students with the same facilities, text-books, teachers, and curriculum; for students who do not understand English are effectively foreclosed from any meaningful education." Under Title VI of the Civil Rights Act, the Chinese-speaking children were entitled to special assistance to enable them to participate equally in the school program, the court said. Sink-or-swim was no longer acceptable. The ruling invoked no Constitutional guarantees; or in legal parlance, it "did not reach" the equal protection clause of the Fourteenth Amendment. Title VI, whose implications were spelled out by Pottinger's memorandum, was sufficient basis for requiring extra help for children with limited English skills, according to Justice Douglas.[7]

The decision stopped short of mandating bilingual education, an omission that the program's critics have since interpreted as "upholding flexibility" for school districts to use alternative methods. The plaintiffs, however, had earlier dropped their demand for bilingual instruction. So the court's failure to order that approach was in keeping with its customary reluctance to address issues not raised in a case. *Lau* said nothing for or against local option. Justice Douglas wrote in the preface to his opinion:

No specific remedy is urged upon us. Teaching English to the students of Chinese ancestry who do not speak the language is one choice. Giving instructions to this group in Chinese is another. There may be others. Petitioners ask only that the Board of

> Education be directed to apply its expertise to the problem and rec-
> tify the situation.

In the end San Francisco officials signed a consent decree agreeing to provide bilingual education for the city's Chinese, Filipino, and Hispanic children.

The *Lau* ruling attracted little public notice at the time; it received a one-sentence mention in the January 22, 1974, edition of the *New York Times*. But the Office for Civil Rights immediately grasped the magnitude of the enforcement job ahead. In 1975, OCR investigators made preliminary visits to 334 school districts with large numbers of language-minority children. "Most [districts had] utterly failed to meet their responsibilities," according to David Tatel, a director of OCR in the Carter administration. A task force led by Martin Gerry began drawing up guidelines for "educational approaches which would constitute appropriate 'affirmative steps' to be taken by a noncomplying school district 'to open up its instructional program.'"

U.S. Commissioner of Education Terrel Bell announced these so-called "Lau remedies" on August 11, 1975. The guidelines told districts how to identify and evaluate children with limited English skills, what instructional treatments would be appropriate, when children were ready for mainstream classrooms, and what professional standards teachers should meet. They also set timetables for meeting these goals. Most significant, the remedies went beyond the *Lau* decision, requiring that where children's rights had been violated, districts must provide bilingual education for elementary school students who spoke little or no English. "English as a second language is a necessary component" of bilingual instruction, the guidelines said, but "since an ESL program does not consider the affective nor cognitive development of the students . . . an ESL program [by itself] is *not* appropriate." For secondary school students, English-only compensatory instruction would usually be permissible.

Interviewed a decade later, Gerry explained this decision: "If we had given school systems a choice between bilingual instruction and ESL, they would have all gone to ESL because it was cheaper and politically popular with a lot of people — reasons that had nothing to do with the educational needs of the kids." Despite the limited research on bilingual-bicultural approaches at that time, Gerry had become "sold on" their effectiveness while serving as a court-appointed monitor of civil rights orders in Texas, he said. "These were the only programs that were working." Nevertheless, he recalled, OCR's intent was to move children into English-language classrooms as quickly as possible — not to make them proficient in two languages, as some Hispanic educators had urged.

Hastily drafted, without an opportunity for public comment, the Lau reme-dies lacked the legal status of federal regulations. In practice, however, they had the full force of the federal government behind them, as OCR embarked on a campaign of aggressive enforcement. Where investigators found civil rights infractions, they used the Lau remedies as a basis to negotiate consent agree-ments, or "Lau plans," with offenders. Threatened with a loss of federal funding if they resisted, such districts had little choice but to adopt bilingual education.

Contradictions of Title VII

By 1973-74, when the Bilingual Education Act came up for reauthorization, it had won influential allies on Capitol Hill. Title VII's budget of $45 million now sponsored 211 school projects in 26 languages, including Russian, French, Portuguese, Cantonese, Pomo, Cree, Yup'ik, and Chamorro. Still, the program was serving only about 6 percent of eligible children. Besides the problem of insufficient funding, the Senate Labor and Public Welfare Committee expressed concern about "continuing inertia on the part of the Office of Education in devel-oping a comprehensive set of goals, directions, and policies for the Title VII effort. . . . Equally disappointing [is the fact that] virtually no Title VII funds have been spent for . . . teacher training and professional development."

In response to these complaints, Senators Edward Kennedy and Walter Mondale moved to expand the program. As amended, the 1974 law dropped the poverty criterion, and for the first time it required schools receiving grants to include instruction in the children's native language and culture "to the extent necessary to allow a child to progress effectively through the educational sys-tem." The new law also expanded eligibility for participation in Title VII pro-grams to all students of "limited English-speaking ability," regardless of which language was dominant in their homes.

While "bilingual-bicultural education" was sanctioned as a route to English acquisition, the amendments again failed to resolve the tension between the goals of transition to English and maintenance of the native language. Both approaches remained eligible for funding. With their growing political clout, Hispanics provided a strong constituency for an enrichment rather than a com-pensatory model, for programs that promoted fluency in two languages rather than just one. Puerto Rico's Congressional delegate, Santiago Polanco-Abreu, had articulated this ideal during 1967 deliberations on the Bilingual Education Act:

> I wish to stress that I realize the importance of learning English by
> Puerto Ricans and other minority groups living in the States. But I
> do not feel that our educational abilities are so limited and our edu-
> cational vision so shortsighted that we must teach one language at
> the expense of another, that we must sacrifice the academic poten-
> tial of thousands of youngsters in order to promote the learning of
> English, that we must jettison and reject ways of life that are not
> our own.

He proposed:

> the establishment of programs which (a) will utilize two languages,
> English and the non-English mother tongue, in the teaching of the
> various school subjects, (b) will concentrate on teaching *both*
> English and the non-English mother tongue, and (c) will endeavor
> to preserve and enrich the culture and heritage of the non-English-
> speaking student.

Though these goals were not adopted explicitly, neither were they rejected
in the original enactment of Title VII. The Department of Health, Education, and
Welfare (HEW) appeared to endorse them in its 1971 instructions for grant applicants: "It must be remembered that the ultimate goal of bilingual education is *a
student who functions well in two languages* on any occasion" (emphasis added).
In 1974, the department's Under Secretary, Frank Carlucci, expressed a different
interpretation of Congressional intent. "The cultural pluralism of American society
is one of its greatest assets," he said, "but such pluralism is a private matter of
local choice, and not a proper responsibility of the federal government. . . . [The
goal of Title VII is] to assist children of limited- or non-English speaking ability to
gain competency in English so that they may enjoy equal educational opportunity — and *not* to require cultural pluralism."

Politically, the language maintenance issue would become bilingual education's Achilles heel. In 1972, a resurgence of ethnic pride among both whites and
racial minorities had prompted Congress to pass the Ethnic Heritage Studies Act,
which authorized federal aid to establish research centers and develop curriculum materials. The fad was short-lived, however. By the mid-1970s a backlash
began to develop against subsidies to preserve minority languages and cultures.
Critics argued against diverting federal dollars from the twin imperatives of teach-

ing English and assimilating children into the mainstream. Albert Shanker, president of the American Federation of Teachers, wrote in a 1974 editorial:

> The American taxpayer, while recognizing the existence of cultural diversity, still wants the schools to be the basis of an American melting pot. While the need for the child to feel comfortable and be able to communicate is clear, it is also clear that what these children need is intensive instruction in English so that they may as soon as possible function with other children in regular school programs.

Fuel was added to the controversy by the American Institutes for Research (AIR), which in 1977-78 released the first large-scale, comparative evaluation of bilingual education in the United States. AIR's conclusions shocked practitioners: it could find no evidence for the overall effectiveness of bilingual approaches, as compared with sink-or-swim instruction. The study's methodology, however, drew sharp criticism from other researchers in the field, who argued that bilingual education was a new approach that varied enormously in program quality, teaching methods, socioeconomic status of students, and other factors that AIR had failed to consider (see Chapter 5).

In its most explosive finding, AIR reported that federally funded bilingual programs were defying the will of Congress. When AIR had asked Title VII directors about the duration of bilingual instruction, 86 percent responded that Spanish-speaking children were retained even after they had learned enough English to join mainstream classrooms. Most programs aimed to maintain minority languages rather than to speed the transition to English, AIR concluded. Whether that goal was achieved in practice, however, was doubtful in light of another of the report's findings: 49.6 percent of "bilingual" teachers interviewed admitted they lacked proficiency in their students' mother tongue. Nevertheless, critics seized on the first statistic to argue that schools were violating the law by providing bilingual instruction beyond "the extent necessary" for English proficiency.

An especially influential critic was Noel Epstein, education editor of the *Washington Post*. In 1977, he published a monograph indicting federal policy on bilingual education, entitled *Language, Ethnicity, and the Schools*. Epstein characterized language maintenance programs as "affirmative ethnicity," linking this pedagogical approach to the legal concept of affirmative action, which was also coming under attack at that time. The implication was that both ideas were misguided attempts to compensate for past discrimination. "Cultural pluralism in the schools" was fine, Epstein said. His quarrel was not with "efforts to teach 'each about every,' to promote greater tolerance and respect across ethnic and racial groups," but with government-financed programs to foster children's allegiance to minority languages and cultures. Inculcating ethnic identity was a function best "left to families, religious groups, ethnic organizations, private schools, ethnic publications, and others."

Even President Jimmy Carter, who liked to show off his own knowledge of Spanish and who had appointed officials favorable to bilingual maintenance programs, told his Cabinet: "I want English taught, not ethnic culture." By 1978, as Congress prepared to fine-tune Title VII, the pendulum was swinging toward the transitional approach.

Perhaps the most compelling concern was that of school desegregation, which many educators saw as contradictory to any program that smacked of language maintenance. "Without any serious national debate," argued Gary Orfield in 1977,

> it seems that we have moved from a harsh assimilationist policy to a policy of linguistic and cultural separation. . . . I believe that there is a better middle position, one which would encourage integration of Hispanic children into schools which respect their cultural tradition and encourage children of diverse backgrounds to voluntarily study Spanish language and literature in classes that actually have bilingual student bodies.

Moreover, according to historian Diego Castellanos, some Hispanic leaders began to express fears that "bilingual tracks" might become an institutionalized form of *de facto* segregation. Civil rights advocate Alfredo Mathew warned that "bilingualism [could] become so insular and ingrown that it fosters a type of apartheid that will generate animosities with other groups, such as Blacks, in the competition for scarce resources, and further alienate the Hispanic from the larger society. . . . Only to the extent that bilingual programs remain open to the possibilities of involving Blacks and Whites of all nationalities will bilingualism become an important and challenging alternative."

There was no question that bilingual programs in the late 1970s tended to separate language-minority students from their English-speaking peers. And yet, segregation was nothing new in Hispanic schooling, bilingual or otherwise. In the year the Bilingual Education Act was passed, 65 percent of Spanish-background children in elementary school and 53 percent of those in high school were attending predominantly minority institutions, according to a study by Aspira. By 1976, the figures had increased to 74 percent and 65 percent, respectively. Most Title VII grants were going to highly segregated school districts.

Bilingual education was a complicating factor in several civil rights cases, as federal courts sought to reconcile the goals of racial balance and quality programs for limited-English speakers. According to José Cárdenas, speaking from long experience as a school superintendent, "desegregation efforts consistently have jeopardized special programs for minority populations," dispersed Hispanic students, and undermined parental control. In a response to Epstein, Cárdenas blamed administrators' insensitivity for this contradiction, rather than any separatist agenda among bilingual education advocates. He added that multicultural instruction was neither a subsidy for "affirmative ethnicity," nor an attempt to emphasize cultural differences, but an overdue recognition of the role of minorities in American culture.

Once again Congress grappled with these contending views in its 1978 amendments to the Bilingual Education Act. This time, however, it succeeded in clarifying the law's goals. The native language would be used "to the extent necessary to allow a child to achieve competence in the English language." Henceforth Title VII programs would be strictly transitional; no funds would be available for language maintenance. At the same time, student eligibility for assistance was expanded to all children of "limited English proficiency," that is, those who needed help with reading and writing skills in English, even if their speaking skills seemed adequate. Finally, the new law addressed the problem of national-origin desegregation by allowing up to 40 percent enrollment of English-speaking children in bilingual programs as a way to assist LEP students in learning English.

OCR: One Step Forward, Two Steps Back

Throughout the late 1970s, the federal Office for Civil Rights continued to monitor school districts' performance in serving language-minority children. Where it found violations, OCR required districts to initiate bilingual education programs and other changes under the Lau remedies. By 1980, it had negotiated 359 Lau plans to remedy past discrimination, enabling many LEP children to receive special help for the first time.

A majority of districts cooperated, albeit with some grumbling about federal heavy-handedness. The schools of Alhambra, California, for example, had no bilingual education and only minimal ESL instruction in 1977, when OCR cited the district for multiple civil rights violations. Ten years later the district had 120 bilingual classrooms, featuring instruction in Spanish, Vietnamese, Cantonese, and Mandarin (see Chapter 10). Elsewhere there was sporadic resistance to OCR's enforcement. A group of Texas school districts sought Congressional intervention after federal authorities found their services to LEP students inadequate and suspended federal aid under the Emergency School Assistance Act. OCR officials were hauled before a Congressional subcommittee and accused of making unreasonable demands that exceeded the agency's legal mandate, especially its insistence on bilingual instruction.[8]

With its controversial policy on *Lau*, OCR's lack of formal rules was becoming a handicap. To settle a 1978 lawsuit by a consortium of Alaska school districts, the federal government pledged to go through the legal process of proposing regulations, soliciting public comment, and issuing final rules on school districts' obligations under Title VI of the Civil Rights Act. Unlike the unofficial Lau remedies, the new regulations would have the force of law. OCR took its time, however, in studying the legal issues, and creation of the new U.S. Department of Education added to the delays.

On August 5, 1980, just three months before Election Day, President Carter finally acted. In what was widely interpreted as a political move to win Hispanic votes, his administration released a proposal that was even more prescriptive than the original Lau remedies. Under the formal Lau regulations, bilingual education would be mandated in schools where at least twenty-five LEP children of the same minority language group were enrolled in two consecutive elementary grades (K through 8).

Reaction was immediate and overwhelmingly negative from educators' groups; strong support came only from the National Education Association and the National Association for Bilingual Education. The Department of Education received an unprecedented 4,600 public comments, most of which opposed the proposal. Feeling the election-year heat, Congress voted to block the rules from taking effect before mid-1981. Secretary Hufstedler exacerbated the backlash when she dispatched representatives of the bilingual education office to defend the Lau proposal at hearings around the country. The effect was to strengthen the popular misconception of Title VII as a heavy-handed federal mandate.

Fairfax County, Virginia, an affluent suburban district near Washington, had been fighting since 1976 against OCR's pressure to establish a bilingual program. Local administrators argued that, with LEP students representing more than fifty language groups, intensive ESL was the only practical treatment. Based on glowing reports of students' progress and the district's financial commitment to serving them, in December 1980 federal officials relented. Still catching heavy flak for the Lau regulations, OCR wanted to show that it could be flexible. And so, in the Fairfax case, it approved the first Lau plan featuring an ESL-only approach. The *Washington Post* hailed the "Fairfax model" as a triumph for local control over "a hard-line government policy." ESL, a necessary component of bilingual education, was now popularized as a promising "alternative method." (Subsequent research, however, has failed to confirm early expectations; see Chapter 7).

If there had been any hope of salvaging the Lau regulations, it was buried under Ronald Reagan's landslide victory and his promise to "get government off our backs." Terrel Bell, the incoming Secretary of Education, withdrew the proposed rules on February 2, 1981, calling them "harsh, inflexible, burdensome, unworkable, and incredibly costly." Ironically, Bell was the same official who had issued the Lau remedies six years earlier. Now he condemned the mandate for native-language instruction as "an intrusion on state and local responsibility. . . . We will protect the rights of children who do not speak English well, but we will do so by permitting school districts to use any way that has proven to be successful."

Notwithstanding this even-handed statement of policy, the new administration's rhetoric began to tilt sharply against the bilingual alternative. In off-the-cuff remarks shortly after taking office, President Reagan made his personal views clear:

> Now, bilingual education, there is a need, but there is also a purpose that has been distorted again at the federal level. Where there are predominantly students speaking a foreign language at home, coming to school and being taught English, and they fall behind or are unable to keep up in some subjects because of the lack of knowledge of the language, I think it is proper that we have teachers equipped who can get at them in their own language and understand why it is they don't get the answer to the problem and help them in that way. *But it is absolutely wrong and against American concepts to have a bilingual education program that is now openly, admittedly dedicated to preserving their native language and never getting them adequate in English so they can go out into the job market and participate.* [Emphasis added.]

A new era had begun.

Legislative Fallout

During the first few months of the Reagan administration, attention focused anew on the effectiveness issue. Large-scale evaluation studies had thus far failed to prove the superiority of bilingual education; in the AIR study, some children fared better in sink-or-swim classrooms. As a result, alternatives like the Fairfax ESL model and "structured immersion" in English began to gain credibility. The heaviest blow was dealt by an Education Department review of the research literature by Keith Baker and Adriana de Kanter. Widely publicized in the fall of 1981, the study created a sensation by concluding that evidence for the effectiveness of bilingual education was tenuous at best.

Policymakers began to ask: Why mandate a pedagogical approach whose benefits had yet to be demonstrated? Why not adopt a policy of "local flexibility," not only in meeting civil rights obligations, but also in qualifying for Title VII funds? Why not explore English-only alternatives, especially in districts that had trouble recruiting adequate numbers of bilingual teachers?

In 1982, Bell proposed to eliminate the native-language requirement for districts receiving Title VII grants. Echoing the Reagan rhetoric on social spending, he argued that "reduced federal resources available for education [should be] focused on students who are most in need of special programs." Senator S. I. Hayakawa, the California Republican who sponsored the Reagan administration's bill, was more candid in explaining its intent:

> I believe that given the flexibility to choose their own program, local schools will emphasize English instruction. Without the expensive requirement of a full academic curriculum in foreign languages, schools will be able to teach more non-English-speaking students for the same cost [and will enable them] to join the mainstream of our society more quickly. . . . Well-intentioned transitional bilingual education programs have often inhibited [immigrants'] command of English and retarded their full citizenship.

The 1978 amendments to Title VII, Hayakawa warned, were encouraging demands for official bilingualism and thereby threatening to splinter American society into disparate cultural groups. Besides passage of a bill to limit bilingual education, he urged ratification of a constitutional amendment designating English as the official language of the United States.

Congress failed to act on either measure that year. But with Title VII up for reauthorization in 1983, its opponents were optimistic about winning major changes, perhaps even blocking an extension. They introduced several bills to restrict bilingual programs or to redirect federal aid to English-only classrooms. Sensing this adverse climate, supporters of existing law postponed the battle until the election year of 1984 — an astute decision, as it turned out. Republicans were actively courting the Hispanic vote for the first time. Suddenly the president had words of praise for "effective bilingual programs"; a White House aide described Ronald Reagan's "growing sensitivity on the issue."

In March 1984, two House Democrats, Dale Kildee of Michigan and Baltazar Corrada of Puerto Rico, introduced legislation reauthorizing Title VII. The text was drafted in large part by James J. Lyons of the National Association for Bilingual Education (NABE). To the surprise of most observers, the bill moved quickly, thanks to a deal worked out with two conservative Republican Representatives, John McCain of Arizona and Steve Bartlett of Texas. The compromise permitted a trickle of Title VII funds for "special alternative instructional programs" (SAIPs) that used no native language. Under a complicated formula, 4 percent of total appropriations up to $140 million would be reserved for SAIPs, along with half of the excess above that amount, up to a ceiling of 10 percent. The idea was to give the administration an incentive to boost Title VII funding overall by allowing an increasing share for its favored alternative methodologies.[9]

In exchange for its concession on SAIPs, NABE won several new grant programs:

- *family English literacy,* aimed at parents of children in Title VII classrooms;
- *special populations,* which would respond to the needs of preschool, gifted and talented, and special education students of limited English proficiency;
- *academic excellence,* designed to replicate exemplary instructional models; and
- *developmental bilingual education,* which reintroduced a modest authorization to support native-language maintenance.

The amendments also put a stronger emphasis on teacher training, and the academic goals of Title VII, which had been vaguely defined, were stated as "allow[ing] a child to meet grade-promotion and graduation standards." Taken together, Lyons says, these changes helped Title VII "break out of the compensatory mold." No longer would it be regarded as a single-purpose remedial program — or so he hoped.

To bilingual education advocates, the 4 percent concession to proponents of alternative methods seemed a small price to pay for the gains they had achieved. Yet, while the practical effects of the change were small, its long-term implications proved substantial. The tiny breach in the dike would grow, setting the stage for major legislative setbacks in 1987-88.

OCR's Retreat

Bell's withdrawal of the Lau regulations had thrown civil rights enforcement into disarray. OCR went back to the drawing board to develop rules that would give districts more leeway, while defining standards to ensure that LEP children's needs were addressed. Almost immediately, however, it encountered opposition from within.

Daniel Oliver, the Department of Education's new general counsel, expressed "doubts concerning the current validity of *Lau*." In line with the Reagan administration's philosophy on civil rights, Oliver argued that OCR should have to prove "discriminatory intent," rather than merely documenting "discriminatory effects," to find that a district had violated Title VI of the Civil Rights Act. Certainly, failure to provide *any* special services to LEP children would violate the law, Oliver said. On the other hand, "a school district which implements reasonably a program based upon a theory deemed sound by experts [would] demonstrate a lack of discriminatory purpose" unless federal officials could prove otherwise. Oliver's approach proved controversial within the department. A consensus was never reached on what regulations to propose, and in late 1982 the idea of issuing revised Lau regulations was abandoned. "Districts have been left free to pursue any approach based on informed educational judgment," wrote Harry Singleton, assistant secretary for civil rights. By default, Oliver's hands-off position had prevailed.

OCR operated without any publicly stated policy until December 1985, when it announced it would enforce Lau on a "case by case basis." It did not specify what a Lau violation might look like, but OCR compliance officers would presumably know one when they saw one. "There is considerable debate among educators about the most effective way to meet the educational needs of language minority students," the memorandum explained. "OCR does not presume to know which educational strategy is most appropriate in a given situation."

The Lau remedies — a detailed set of requirements for LEP student identification, assessment, exit criteria, teacher certification, staff-student ratios, and bilingual instruction — gave way to a broad statement about the obligation to provide "services . . . to meet the educational needs of LEP children." Virtually all decisions about what services would be appropriate were left up to the school district, which merely had to find an "expert" to endorse them. An expert was defined as "someone whose experience and training expressly qualifies him or her to render such judgments." The measure of success was similarly vague: to give students access to the regular educational program "within a reasonable period of time." Advertising its new flexibility, the memorandum advised "districts faced with a shortage of trained teachers, or with a multiplicity of languages" that they might not be able to staff "an intensive ESL program or a bilingual program. OCR does not require a program that places unrealistic expectations on a district" or that would require it "to divert resources from other necessary educational resources and services." Not much reading between the lines was required. Districts would have little to fear from OCR as long as they could claim to be "serving" LEP children in some fashion.

Not surprisingly, OCR's Lau enforcement fell off sharply during this period. Data compiled by the agency in 1986 at the request of Congress, showed that school districts were nine times less likely to be monitored for *Lau* compliance under the Reagan administration than under the Ford and Carter administrations. When OCR personnel did visit school districts, they found violations 58 percent of the time; nevertheless, follow-ups were rare. Nationwide in 1985, OCR's *Lau* enforcement consisted of 10 investigations of complaints against school districts, 11 reviews to ensure compliance with the law, and two monitoring visits to determine whether local officials were abiding by their Lau plans. In 1980, the comparable figures were 136 complaint investigations, 69 compliance reviews, and 195 monitoring visits.

Alicia Coro, acting director of OCR, defended her agency's reduction in enforcement activity. "It's hardly reasonable," she said, "to go back to look at 500 districts over and over and over again unless there's something that leads you back into it. . . . The Office for Civil Rights does not have the educational expertise [to make program judgments]. We're here to enforce the law. It doesn't tell us to determine which methodology is best. That's not our responsibility."

Critics, however, accused the Reagan administration of abdicating its obligation to safeguard the civil rights of language-minority students. "OCR has disappeared from the field as far as any meaningful enforcement goes," charged attorney Camilo Pérez-Bustillo. Peter Roos, his colleague in the Multicultural Education Training and Advocacy (META) project, added: "If you had a real case — anything you had a legal handle on — you wouldn't bring it to OCR [because] it would get so tied up in the bureaucracy. The regional offices don't have authority to act on their own. By the time a case gets to Washington, it's lost."

Notwithstanding its effort to tone down the strident rhetoric on bilingual education, the Bush administration did nothing to reverse the trend of declining enforcement efforts. OCR reported twelve compliance reviews in 1991, which it described as "the largest number . . . in recent years." Between 1976 and 1980, the average number was 115.

Norma Cantú, formerly a litigator for the Mexican American Legal Defense and Educational Fund, was named assistant secretary of education for civil rights in 1993. Among her first acts was to double the frequency of Lau reviews. Yet the Clinton administration has shown no interest in reopening the question of appropriate instruction for LEP students or in specifying minimum standards that districts must meet, for example, in providing adequate resources and qualified personnel for language-minority programs. In effect, OCR continues to enforce Lau "case by case."

Castañeda Standard

Parents frustrated by OCR's inaction retain the option of taking their complaints directly to federal court. A useful tool in such cases has been the Equal Educational Opportunities Act (EEOA) of 1974, as interpreted by the Fifth Circuit Court of Appeals in *Castañeda v. Pickard*. Section 1703(f) of the EEOA requires school districts to take "appropriate action to overcome language barriers that impede equal participation by its students in its instructional programs."

In its 1981 ruling, the appellate court acknowledged "serious doubts about the continuing vitality of *Lau*" raised by the *Bakke* decision (1978). In that case the Supreme Court found that government actions with "a racially disproportionate impact" are not necessarily illegal under Title VI of the Civil Rights Act or unconstitutional under the Fourteenth Amendment, unless there is a discriminatory intent. In other words, teaching all children in English, regardless of their language abilities, might now be permissible; if a history of discrimination could not be documented, "affirmative steps" to overcome limited English proficiency might no longer be required. In *Castañeda*, however, the appellate court relied on the EEOA to mandate special language assistance. It ruled that in passing this law, Congress had thrown its weight behind *Lau*, affirming that educational neglect violated the civil rights of language-minority children, whether or not they had been victims of deliberate discrimination.

The decision added that vaguely defined "good faith efforts" did not discharge school officials of their responsibilities. Since Congress had failed to define "appropriate action," the court outlined three criteria for a program serving LEP students:

- It must be based on "a sound educational theory."
- It must be "implemented effectively," with adequate resources and personnel.
- After a trial period, it must be evaluated as effective in overcoming language handicaps.

Using this analysis, in 1983 the META lawyers argued that the Denver schools were providing only a half-hearted program in transitional bilingual education. A federal court agreed. Rejecting officials' claims of "good faith," it ordered Denver to adopt sweeping changes, including criteria for evaluating staff qualifications, better training of teachers and aides, and improvements in language assessment. Other courts have applied the EEOA to state education agencies that had failed to ensure that local districts were meeting their obligations to LEP students. Illinois and Florida were among the states required to adopt minimum standards for compliance, for example, in correctly identifying and placing LEP children.

The *Castañeda* standard remains in effect, at least in the Fifth Circuit and arguably throughout the country. OCR formally adopted the test in 1991. In the courts, however, its usefulness has waned as federal judges have become more conservative. META lost its first major lawsuit in 1989, *Teresa P. v. Berkeley*, which alleged inadequate resources, staff, assessment, and placement procedures for LEP students in the Berkeley, California, schools. A major complaint was the district's failure to recruit a sufficient number of credentialed teachers to staff its bilingual classrooms. But Judge D. Lowell Jensen, a former Reagan administration official, was unconvinced. "Good teachers are good teachers, no matter what the educational challenge may be," he ruled. While applying the *Castañeda* test, he found no factual support for a civil rights violation.

Teresa P. was not decided in a political vacuum. Berkeley dipped into emergency reserves for $1.5 million to defend the lawsuit — more than three times what the district spent each year on LEP students[10] — at a time of increasing hostility toward bilingualism. Resisting the demands of Hispanic parents proved popular, even in a community renowned for its liberalism. More important, the district received practical support and encouragement from an organized lobby. Throughout the litigation "expert" witnesses were recruited, "friend of the court" briefs were filed, and press coverage was orchestrated by a group known as U.S. English.

Notes

1. In practice, all early Title VII programs made use of students' native language in one way or another, according to the first federal director of bilingual education, Albar Peña.

2   Explaining his rationale for supporting only Spanish-English bilingual education, Senator Yarborough said: "If you take the Italians, Polish, French, Germans, Norwegians, or other non-English-speaking groups, they made a definite decision to leave their old life and culture. . . . That decision to come here carried with it a willingness to give up their language, everything. That wasn't true in the Southwest. We went in and took the people over. They had our culture superimposed upon them."

3   In the final House-Senate agreement, the 1968 Bilingual Education Act gave funding priority to schools with high concentrations of students from households whose incomes were below $3,000 a year.

4. Alaska, Connecticut, Illinois, Massachusetts, Michigan, New Jersey, Rhode Island, Texas, and Wisconsin.

5. Alabama, Arkansas, Delaware, Nebraska, North Carolina, Oklahoma, and West Virginia. In 1981, Virginia adopted an "official English" law relieving school boards of any "obligation to teach the standard curriculum, except courses in foreign languages, in a language other than English," but permitting them to provide bilingual instruction on a voluntary basis.

6. Of the district's 100,000 students, 16,574 were of Chinese background, of whom 2,856 were deemed to need special help in English; 633 received one hour of remedial language instruction daily and 433 received six hours. Only one-third of the 59 remedial teachers were fluent in both Chinese and English.

7. Justices Stewart and Blackmun, joined by Chief Justice Burger, wrote concurring opinions that expressed some reservations. "I merely wish to make plain," Blackmun said, "that when, in another case, we are concerned with a very few youngsters, or with just a single child who speaks only German or Polish or Spanish or any language other than English, I would not regard today's decision . . . as conclusive upon the issue whether the statute and the [OCR] guidelines require the [federally] funded school district to provide special instruction. For me, numbers are at the heart of this case and my concurrence is to be understood accordingly."

8. Following a stern admonition from George Mahon, the Texas Democrat who chaired the House Appropriations Committee, the hearing recessed so that a compromise could be reached between OCR's Cynthia Brown and the school district officials.

9. Like many domestic programs in the Reagan years, bilingual education was a vulnerable target for budget cutters. Its funding declined from $167 million in 1980 to $133 million in 1986. While it increased to $147 million in 1988, after adjustment for inflation this still represented a reduction of more than 40 percent from the pre-Reagan level.

10. Of its $480,000 budget to fund programs for 571 LEP students in 1988, all but $35-40,000 came from the state of California.

Politics

3 English Only or English Plus?

$\mathcal{W}$hen Californians voted by a three-to-one margin to declare English their state's official language, they may not have intended to strike a blow against bilingual education. But that was the political impact of the November 1986 referendum, known as Proposition 63. At the time California had the nation's most detailed and prescriptive bilingual education law; a year later it had none.

The ballot initiative instructed public officials "to insure that the role of English as the common language of the State of California is preserved and enhanced." Nowhere did it mention bilingual education, although one provision invited lawsuits to halt state services in languages other than English. The day after the vote, Bill Honig, California's superintendent of public instruction, predicted that "programs to teach non-English speakers," bilingual or otherwise, would be unaffected by Proposition 63. "The legal basis for bilingual education," he said, "is that non-English speaking students learn English while continuing to learn other subjects as well. This goal is fully compatible with the new [state] constitutional amendment."

Nevertheless, U.S. English, the national group that spent more than $700,000 to get Proposition 63 passed, had carefully timed the campaign to coincide with the expiration of California's bilingual education statute. The ten-year-old law was popular with many parents and educators because it clarified the schools' obligations: how to evaluate and reclassify limited-English-proficient (LEP) children, when to establish bilingual classrooms, what to do about a shortage of qualified bilingual teachers. These strict requirements also bred opposition, especially among teachers who had to learn a second language or risk losing their jobs. State Assemblyman Frank Hill, a leader of the Proposition 63 campaign, argued that allowing the law to "sunset" would be "a great victory [because] districts would no longer be shackled to one instructional approach."

In the fall of 1986, virtually every school board and educators' organization in California endorsed AB 2813, a bill to extend the bilingual education law. Sponsored by Assembly Speaker Willie Brown, it breezed through the legislature. But Governor George Deukmejian vetoed the measure, citing budget constraints. Most observers blamed the climate created by the English Only initiative. Again in July 1987, despite substantial concessions by Brown to Hill and other opponents of the program, the governor turned thumbs down on a reauthorization bill. Although most districts announced plans to continue with bilingual education as before, they began the 1987-88 school year without any clear mandate to do so. Deukmejian's successor, Pete Wilson, would veto even more modest bilingual education proposals in the coming years.

On a national scale, Proposition 63 was a boon to English Only advocates in giving legislative form to a backlash against bilingualism. Between 1987 and 1998, similar proposals were considered by voters and lawmakers in thirty-nine additional states, passing in sixteen and bringing the total of "official-English" states to twenty two.[1]

Legally, there is much uncertainty about the implications of official-English measures. While opponents can point to few direct effects thus far, the political impact of this movement has been substantial. Opinion polls showing 60-to-90 percent approval rates have not gone unnoticed by legislators. At the federal level, although a constitutional English Language Amendment has languished in committee since 1981, support for bilingual education has plummeted, leaving the program vulnerable to a major overhaul in Congress (see Chapter 4).

The English Only lobby succeeded where earlier critics of bilingual education failed. By making cultural assimilation the paramount policy concern, it redefined the terms of the debate, calling into question even the transitional use of native-language instruction. In the civil rights era, policymakers asked: What pedagogical approaches, what mix of languages in the classroom, will ensure an equal chance for LEP students to succeed? Today they want to know: How can we teach children English as quickly as possible? Can that goal be achieved without resorting to native-language instruction? Bilingual education, conceived as a way to expand opportunities for LEP children and as a superior approach to teaching English, is now attacked as a barrier to students' full participation in American life. To understand how this reversal in perceptions took place, and how the English Only campaign came to be so influential, it is necessary to analyze this movement's origins and premises.

Roots of the English Only Movement

U.S. English was organized in 1983 as an offshoot of the Federation for American Immigration Reform (FAIR), a Washington, D.C.-based lobby that advocates tighter restrictions on immigration. Its founders were the late Senator S. I. Hayakawa, the first sponsor of the English Language Amendment, and Dr. John Tanton, a Michigan ophthalmologist, environmentalist, and population-control activist. Tanton served as president of Zero Population Growth before launching FAIR in the late 1970s. By highlighting the cultural impact of increasing immigration, U.S. English has served to bolster demands for stricter control of the nation's borders. The fledgling group was an immediate success. Using sophisticated direct-mail techniques, U.S. English soon outgrew its parent organization, and by 1988 it was claiming a dues-paying membership of 350,000 and an annual budget of $7 million — roughly five times the size of FAIR's.[2]

Language politics, formerly a minor theme in American history, took on a new urgency in the 1980s. U.S. English has crystallized a growing unease with bilingualism, or more precisely, with the perceived indifference toward English among recent immigrants. To many Anglo-Americans, the newcomers seem content to live in insular communities where they can work, shop, go to school, worship, watch television, and even vote in their native languages. Hispanics and Asians are transforming some cities to the extent that some English speakers feel like strangers in their own neighborhoods. Perhaps most galling to monolingual Americans, government is promoting programs like bilingual education that appear to encourage cultural Balkanization.

The U.S. English message is simple: our common language is threatened by the "mindless drift toward a bilingual society." In this nation of immigrants, the English language has been our "social glue" — not just "*a* bond, but *the* bond" that has held us together and allowed us to resolve our differences — asserts Gerda Bikales, the group's former executive director. Bilingual schooling and voting rights are beginning to weaken these ties, she charges: "They are the programs and symbols of a country which has chosen to divide itself, to adapt to and preserve division rather than to integrate and be whole."

English needs legal protection, warned the late Senator Hayakawa in U.S. English fundraising appeals. Otherwise, the country will soon find itself increasingly polarized "along language lines" and vulnerable to the kinds of social strife experienced by his native Canada. He argued that an English Language Amendment is necessary to head off a movement for official bilingualism — that is, coequal status for Spanish in the United States — and to "send a message" to immigrants that English-speaking ability is an obligation of American citizenship.

If English Only proponents get their way, that message will take a very practical form: federal, state, and local governments will be forced to curtail a range of services now provided in minority languages. On specifics U.S. English has been hard to pin down. At various times its leaders have advocated elimination of bilingual 911 operators, health services, drivers' tests, and voting rights; endorsed English Only rules in the workplace; petitioned the Federal Communications Commission to limit foreign-language broadcasting; protested Spanish-language menus at McDonald's; opposed Pacific Bell's *Páginas Amarillas en Español* and customer assistance in Chinese;[3] and complained about federal tax forms in Spanish.

During the Proposition 63 campaign, U.S. English began to distance itself from the English Only label, denying any interest in interfering with nonpublic uses of other languages or in curtailing emergency services for non-English-speakers. Still, it refused to repudiate the concept of language restrictionism, the idea that all Americans should be required to speak English in certain contexts. "There is a price to entering the social and economic and political mainstream," Bikales insists, speaking from her personal experience as a German-Jewish immigrant:

> In return for freedom and opportunity, one learns English. . . . Cultural displacement, cultural loss, is extremely painful. It doesn't come free. No one can be excused from paying it. Government should not stand idly by

and let the core culture, the shared culture formed by generations of earlier immigrants, slip away. [It] should not allow its own citizens to feel like strangers in their own land. If anyone has to feel strange, it's got to be the immigrant — until he learns the language.

This line of argument has found a receptive ear among Americans of diverse backgrounds and political persuasions, liberal and conservative, Democrat and Republican. It has captured the imagination of pundits, intellectuals, and assorted celebrities. Saul Bellow, Bruno Bettelheim, Alistair Cooke, Walter Cronkite, Eugene McCarthy, Arnold Schwarzenegger, and Gore Vidal are among those who have lent their names to the U.S. English "advisory board." Public figures from Whoopi Goldberg to Richard Nixon to Abigail Van Buren have signed the group's advertisements hailing "the value of our common language." At the same time, the English Only campaign has mobilized nativists who make no secret of their animus toward language minorities.

In 1985-86, U.S. English generated the bulk of comments supporting the Reagan administration's proposed regulations on bilingual education. Along with arguments that immigrant children should be taught English more quickly, for their own good, many of these letters expressed ethnic fears and hostilities. The latter frequently came from areas with growing language-minority populations:

> We here in Southern California are overrun with <u>all</u> sorts of aliens — Asian, Spanish, Cuban, Middle East — and it is an insurmountable task if these millions are not required to learn English. Many are <u>illerate</u> [sic] in <u>their native language</u>. [Rolling Hills, California] . . . At the rate the Latinos (and non-whites) reproduce, [we] face a demographic imbalance if we do not change several of our dangerously outdated laws. Make English the official language everywhere in the U.S.A. [Jersey City, New Jersey] . . . No other ethnic group has made the demands for bilingual education as have the Cubans. The more you give them, the more they demand. WHOSE AMERICA IS THIS? ONE FLAG. ONE LANGUAGE. [North Miami, Florida]

Such sentiments among its followers have proved an embarrassment for U.S. English, and a rallying point for its critics. Leaders of Hispanic and Asian communities, along with elected officials ranging from Tom Bradley, the Democratic mayor of Los Angeles, to William Clements, the Republican governor of Texas, have denounced the English Only movement as racially divisive.

Attorney General James Shannon of Massachusetts, a Democrat, warned that enacting an official-English measure in his state would intensify "bigotry, divisiveness, and resentment of minority groups." Senator Pete Domenici, Republican of New Mexico, called the proposed English Language Amendment to the U.S. Constitution "an insult to all Americans for whom English is not the first language. . . . It won't help anyone learn the English language. It won't improve our society. It won't lead to a more cohesive nation. In fact, it will create a more divided nation."

Charges of Racism

Is U.S. English exploiting racism to advance its agenda? Is it using the official-English campaign as a stalking-horse for a new nativist movement? In a 1986 interview, Gerda Bikales rejected these suggestions as "a very vicious series of attacks. . . . I do not believe at all that we are responsible for any of this [racial animosity]. This is a mass movement. Anybody can and does join U.S. English. We do our very best to put out responsible ideas, responsible policies. We're not hate-mongers. There's no doubt that as long as our political leadership is going to continue to bury its head in the sand, we are going to have this kind of situation that's . . . somewhat out of control."

Stung by charges of anti-Hispanic bias, in mid-1987 U.S. English hired Linda Chávez as its president. Formerly staff director of the U.S. Commission on Civil Rights and director of public liaison in the Reagan White House, Chávez was sophisticated in the ways of Washington. Immediately she began working to dispel the organization's exclusionist image and to replace it with a beneficent one. She championed official English as a way to bring newcomers into the mainstream. In frequent public appearances, she advertised the presence of immigrants on the U.S. English board of directors, including Senator Hayakawa, who had once been barred from this country under the Asian exclusion provisions of U.S. immigration law. Finally, Chávez cited her own Hispanic roots dating back three centuries in New Mexico. "Contrary to any anti-immigrant sentiment pervading the official-English movement, quite the opposite concern motivates" U.S. English, she maintained.

> Unless we become serious about protecting our heritage as a unilingual society — bound by a common language — we may lose a precious resource that has helped us forge a national character and identity from

so many diverse elements. I truly believe that the official English movement will help protect the future integration of new Americans, as it has
helped make Americans of so many generations of immigrants in the
past.

It was an effective argument, delivered by an effective spokesperson.
Chávez boosted the credibility of U.S. English, especially on Capitol Hill.
Representative Don Edwards, a liberal Democrat from California, convened the
first House subcommittee hearings on the English Language Amendment. Leaders
of language-minority communities continued to attack U.S. English as xenophobic. But such claims had limited force when a prominent Hispanic was leading
the official-English campaign and portraying it as a civil rights measure.

For Linda Chávez and U.S. English, the honeymoon ended abruptly in the
fall of 1988. First came the publication of a memorandum by John Tanton that
Chávez described as "repugnant" and "not excusable." The U.S. English chairman
predicted a Hispanic political takeover in the United States unless something was
done about Hispanic immigration and high birthrates:

> *Gobernar es poblar* translates 'to govern is to populate.' In this society,
> where the majority rules, does this hold? Will the present majority peace-
> ably hand over its political power to a group that is simply more fertile? .
> . . Can *homo contraceptivus* compete with *homo progenitiva* if borders
> aren't controlled? . . . Perhaps this is the first instance in which those with
> their pants up are going to get caught by those with their pants down. . .
> . As Whites see their power and control over their lives declining, will
> they simply go quietly into the night? Or will there be an explosion? . . .
> We are building in a deadly disunity. All great empires disintegrate; we
> want stability.

Tanton's memo, written for a private discussion group,[4] enumerated a range
of cultural threats posed by Spanish-speaking immigrants: "the tradition of the
mordida (bribe), the lack of involvement in public affairs"; Roman Catholicism,
with its potential to "pitch out the separation of church and state"; low "educabil-
ity" and high school-dropout rates; failure to use birth control; limited concern
for the environment; and, of course, language divisions.

The second damaging disclosure involved two large contributors to U.S.
English and FAIR that had financed racist propaganda about immigrants and

advocated policies of eugenic sterilization, respectively.[5] Chávez expressed dismay to learn of these connections, insisting that she had been denied access to most of the U.S. English financial records. Describing Tanton's views as "anti-Hispanic and anti-Catholic," Chávez quit her $70,000-a-year job in protest. Walter Cronkite resigned from the advisory board of U.S. English and told the group to stop using his name in its fundraising. And Tanton himself stepped down, issuing a bitter statement in which he denied any racist intent and denounced the opponents of official English for their "McCarthyite tactics of guilt by association."

Linda Chávez should not have been surprised by these revelations. On becoming president of U.S. English, she had received several racist letters from members of the organization who resigned to protest the hiring of a Hispanic. Chávez commissioned an attitude survey to determine how representative such views were among U.S. English contributors. When asked what had prompted them to support the organization, 42 percent endorsed the statement: "I wanted America to stand strong and not cave in to Hispanics who shouldn't be here."[6]

Discriminatory Potential

According to pre-election polling in the fall of 1986, few Californians were aware that Proposition 63 could jeopardize many forms of bilingual assistance provided by state and local government. In Florida, where an official-English amendment won 83 percent of the vote in 1988, the prevailing view was that the measure would promote better communication and help immigrants learn English.[7] "At first glance, the idea of an English Language Amendment seems harmless enough," write Mary Carol Combs and John Trasviña in a 1986 paper for the League of Latin American Citizens. "Why oppose a symbolic amendment to declare by law what we all know anyway, that English is already the language of our country?"

In practice, officializing English might imperil a variety of services for non-English speakers and provide a legal basis to discriminate against already disadvantaged groups. While some Americans may resent hearing languages other than English spoken in their communities, they still retain full access to government, education, and employment, Combs and Trasviña argue. "The civil and constitutional rights of monolingual English speakers are not violated by lack of an official language." Conversely, an English Only policy would "disenfranchise limited-English-proficient citizens, particularly the elderly, who rely on bilingual assistance for a fuller understanding of election issues." It might also undercut due-process rights by eliminating court interpreters.

Nevertheless, nearly a decade after its passage, Proposition 63 has yet to exert any direct legal impact on minority language services in California, notwithstanding protests and threats of litigation from English Only proponents. In large part, this reflects the resolve of state officials to treat the amendment as symbolic and advisory rather than practical and binding. Following the vote, state Attorney General John K. Van de Kamp rejected a demand by U.S. English to ban election materials published in Chinese and Spanish by San Francisco and other jurisdictions. On the other hand, Proposition 63 has fostered English Only activity in several communities — for example, campaigns to restrict business signs in other languages. In 1988, Mayor Barry Hatch of Monterey Park attempted to block the donation of 10,000 Chinese-language books to the city's public library, arguing that "English is the language of the land."[8]

Arizona's Proposition 106, passed by the voters in 1988, is thus far the most restrictive measure of its kind. It imposed a blanket English Only policy: "This state and all political subdivisions of this state shall act in English and no other language." While allowing a handful of narrow exceptions, such as bilingual instruction "to provide as rapid a transition as possible to English," the constitutional amendment outlawed numerous government functions in other tongues, from drivers' tests to tourist information to social services. It required state and local employees to speak English and only English in the performance of their duties. For example, teachers were apparently forbidden to communicate with non-English-speaking parents in their own languages. But none of these effects has been felt because Proposition 106 has never become law. In 1990, a federal court ruled that it violated the First Amendment right to free speech for Arizona's public employees. In 1998, the Arizona Supreme Court agreed. It also found that the amendment unconstitutionally restricted non-English speakers' "ability to seek and obtain information and services from government." Nevertheless, English Only advocates vowed to appeal the decision to the U.S. Supreme Court.

Questions remain about what practical changes they hope to accomplish. Geoffrey Nunberg, a linguist at the Xerox Palo Alto Research Center, argues that official-language measures may make it "harder for immigrants who have not yet mastered English to enter the social and economic mainstream," while doing nothing to help them learn the language. "The fact is that immigrants are desperate to learn English," he says, noting that when Proposition 63 passed in California, there were 40,000 adults on waiting lists for English-as-a-second-language (ESL) instruction in Los Angeles alone. To remedy the lack of space in such classes nationwide, the Congressional Hispanic Caucus sponsored the English Proficiency Act. The legislation, enacted as part of an omnibus education measure in April 1988, authorized up to $25 million a year for adult ESL, although Congress has "zero-funded" the program for most of its existence. U.S. English declined to support the bill, calling instead for the private sector, in particular Spanish-language media, to sponsor adult ESL classes. The group's position has raised doubts about its stated objective of bringing immigrants into the mainstream.

English Only: Why Now?

The framers of the U.S. Constitution rejected the idea of an official language, argues Nunberg, "because they believed citizens would agree on language standards out of their own free will. English has become the most spectacularly successful language in the world — without state interference. Language conflicts arise precisely where one group tries to impose its language on another by force of law." Before 1981 the U.S. Congress had considered only one other official-language proposal, a 1923 bill to recognize the "American language."[9]

For proponents of an English Language Amendment, a logical question arises: If the country has gotten along without an official tongue for 200 years, why does it need one now? Proponents respond that today's immigrants, unlike their predecessors, are resisting assimilation, preserving non-English-speaking enclaves, and seeking recognition for their own languages.

These charges are not without precedent. In 1911, the federal Dillingham Commission complained that the so-called "new immigrants" of the time — Italians, Jews, Greeks, and Slavs — were failing to learn English as quickly as nineteenth century newcomers from Germany and Scandinavia. These groups, in turn, had come under criticism by earlier nativists; for example, Benjamin Franklin had protested the German-English street signs in Philadelphia. It seems that Americans have always been ambivalent about immigrants: desirous of their labor, but fearful of their social impact. Hence our tendency to accept unfavorable stereotypes about the current crop and to romanticize those of previous generations.

So far U.S. English has relied on such stereotypes, rather than on empirical evidence, in arguing that "the primacy of English" is threatened in the United States today. Research by Calvin Veltman, based on the 1976 Survey of Income and Education by the National Center for Education Statistics, has yielded the opposite conclusion. Analyzing patterns of language loyalty and language shift, Veltman found that *languages other than English* are most threatened in this country. That is, without the replenishing effects of immigration, all minority tongues would gradually die out, with the possible exception of Navajo. (He might now drop that qualifier, considering the rapid erosion of Native American tongues; see Chapter 9).

Veltman's 1988 study, *The Future of the Spanish Language in the United States*, concludes that the rate of Anglicization, or shift to English dominance, is increasing among Spanish speakers. This group is fast approaching a two-generation pattern of language loss (in all parts of the United States except the Rio Grande Valley), as compared with the three-generation model typical of immigrant groups in the past. Although Hispanics are more likely than other minority groups to retain their native language, Veltman reports, "by the time they have been in the country for fifteen years, some 75 percent of all Hispanic immigrants are speaking English on a regular daily basis. . . . Seven out of ten children of Hispanic immigrant parents become English speakers for all practical purposes, and their children — the third generation — have English as their mother tongue." In a 1983 study, using the High School and Beyond database, Veltman concludes that bilingual schooling has almost no measurable impact in slowing the tendency of Spanish-speaking children to adopt English, the higher status language, as their usual tongue.[10]

Parental attitudes no doubt play a role. In a 1985 marketing survey, 98 percent of Hispanic respondents in Miami said it was "essential for their children to read and write English perfectly," as compared with 94 percent of Anglo respondents. Combs and Trasviña observe that:

> Hispanics and other ethnic minorities in the United States know probably better than anyone: English is the language of general societal, political, and economic discourse. To get ahead in these areas, one must know English. . . . Legislating an official language will not produce "better citizens" or make them feel "more American." On the contrary, the effort sends ethnic communities the message that it's un-American to be actively bilingual and that the desire to maintain ties to one's cultural and linguistic heritage is unpatriotic.

Why the sudden concern for the "functional protection of English"? asks sociolinguist Joshua Fishman. How is English endangered in a country where it is spoken by 94 percent of the population, according to the 1990 census? where "linguistic minorities overwhelmingly lose their mother tongues by the second or at most the third generation"? where "no ethnic political parties or separatist movements exist"? Fishman maintains that U.S. English and allied groups are promoting "a hidden agenda," seeking scapegoats for social ills that have little to do with language, such as terrorism abroad and economic dislocations at home. He characterizes "the English Only movement [as] a displacement of middle-class fears and anxieties from difficult, perhaps even intractable, real problems in American society, to mythical, simplistic, and stereotypic problems. . . . [It is] another 'liberation of Grenada' relative to the real causes of unrest in the world."

Official English vs. Bilingual Education

While attracting a variety of constituencies, the English Only movement has been especially appealing to the critics of bilingual education. Former Senator Steve Symms of Idaho, a perennial sponsor of the English Language Amendment, listed the repeal of Title VII among his major objectives. For Symms and others on the far Right, bilingual education has been associated with ethnic separatism and thus with political disloyalty. R. E. "Rusty" Butler, an aide to Symms, outlines the reasoning behind such fears in a 1985 monograph, "On Creating a Hispanic America: A Nation Within a Nation?":

> Bilingual education was to be a form of atonement for the nation's sins against Hispanics, and a means of easing America's "guilt." . . . The ethnic politician has a high stake in bilingual education: By it, students are molded into an ethnically conscious constituency. Pride in their heritage and language, and an allegiance to their roots rather than their country, helps to diminish a sense of Americanism. . . .
>
> A dependence on the home language and culture plays into the hands of unscrupulous politicians by isolating Hispanics. Assimilation into the mainstream culture would make political control difficult, if not impossible [by Hispanic leaders]. . . .
>
> Many scholars argue that bilingual education breeds and fosters a separatist mentality which has both economic and political implications. . . . Dutch criminal psychologist Dick Mulder has said that "there is a danger that the language situation could feed and guide terrorism in the U.S." Therefore, bilingual education and the ideal of Aztlán as a potential Hispanic homeland has [sic] national security implications.[11]

With its overtones of racial paranoia, this type of frontal assault commanded little support in Congress during the 1980s. Even among English Only proponents, the abolition of bilingual education represented an extreme position. Although English First, an explicitly conservative group, sought to terminate all funding for Title VII, the more influential U.S. English pursued a pragmatic line of attack. It proposed to expand support for "special alternative" programs that used only English and, where native-language instruction was provided, to limit its duration. "If this were a one-year program, we would have no objection," insists Gerda Bikales. But given the long-term transition to English advocated by many researchers, she says,

> you wonder what kind of opportunities that child will ever have to interface with his American peers. We just cannot afford [such] a program — even if it works, even if after five to seven years the child does know English — there are so many other losses. There is a long delay in the socialization of the child into the American mainstream. That is a major disincentive to becoming part of this society.

It was this argument, the imperative of assimilation, that U.S. English tried to impress on policymakers, with increasing success.

While the Reagan administration took no position on the English Language Amendment, nothing prevented its officials from working closely with English Only proponents. Carol Pendás Whitten, bilingual education director from 1985 to 1987, met frequently with leaders of U.S. English to discuss their views on the education of LEP children. She even commissioned one of the group's consultants, Gary Imhoff, to review the "objectivity and accuracy" of materials used in bilingual-bicultural teacher-training programs that were receiving Title VII funds. A prolific writer on behalf of U.S. English and FAIR, Imhoff had warned that native-language instruction may serve as a "crutch," making students "excruciatingly slow" to learn English.[12] After Imhoff's hiring drew protests, Whitten was forced to cancel his contract, but her ties with English Only activists continued.

As official-English efforts lagged in the states after 1988 — with proponents running out of legislatures where they could win easy victories — U.S. English focused increasingly on bilingual education. In California it lobbied for reduced state subsidies to programs serving LEP students and pressured school districts to adopt English-only approaches following the court decision in *Teresa P. v. Berkeley*. In New York it rallied public opposition to a plan to raise standards for reassigning children from bilingual to regular classrooms, taking out full-page newspaper advertisements and flying in "expert" witnesses.[13]

By the late 1980s it was spending hundreds of thousands annually on such efforts and on those of independent groups. These included Learning English Advocates Drive (LEAD), a group of teachers opposed to bilingual education in California and New York, and the Institute for Research in English Acquisition and Development (READ), which supported studies by academic enthusiasts of "structured immersion" for LEP children. READ's first director was Keith Baker, of Baker-de Kanter report fame; his successor was Rosalie Porter, a former advisor to Secretary William Bennett and author of *Forked Tongue: The Politics of Bilingual Education.*

In her book Porter criticizes the English Language Amendment as divisive, attempting to portray herself as a moderate who belongs to neither of "the extremist camps — the doctrinaire official-English supporters [or] the strident proponents of full bilingualism." When confronted with READ's financial dependence on the English Only movement, she insisted that "these grants are without strings."[14] In fact, Porter's views on bilingual education are indistinguishable from those of U.S. English, which purchased 300 copies of *Forked Tongue* and mailed them to policymakers.

Yet Porter does represent an academic viewpoint whose influence should not be overlooked: those who scorn bilingual education as a creature of ethnic politics, as a program that is ideologically motivated and thus pedagogically suspect. One need not favor English Only legislation to take this position; those who articulate it best generally do not. Their ranks include both neoconservatives like Diane Ravitch and traditional liberals like Arthur Schlesinger, Jr.

This critique has been powerful, first, because of the widespread ignorance about bilingualism (which extends to many of the critics), and second, because it forms part of a broader critique of social and cultural fragmentation in the United States, which has targeted multiculturalism as the source of our current malaise. In his bestselling book, *The Disuniting of America*, Schlesinger writes: "The national ideal had once been *e pluribus unum.* Are we now to belittle *unum* and glorify *pluribus?* Will the center hold? or will the melting pot yield to the Tower of Babel?" For those preoccupied with such grandiose questions, the pedagogical specifics are reduced to insignificance. Bilingual education becomes ensnared in the same net with Afro-centrism, cultural relativism, "political correctness," and other demons.

E. D. Hirsch adopts a similar strategy in his 1987 book, *Cultural Literacy,* which helped to popularize the notion of "cultural conservatism." Our schools' major failing, he argues, is an emphasis on skills at the expense of content. Hence their failure to transmit "cultural literacy," by which he means the content of a unitary, Anglo-American national culture. For Hirsch, bilingual education is a distraction from this central task, a concession to the wrong kind of diversity. "Linguistic pluralism . . . is much different from Jeffersonian pluralism, which has encouraged a diversity of traditions, values, and opinions." To encourage the former is to encourage social breakdown: "Multilingualism enormously increases cultural fragmentation, civil antagonism, illiteracy, and economic-technological ineffectualness."[15]

Viewed in this context, language learning would appear to be a subversive activity. Uncomfortable with this implication of his argument, Hirsch is quick to add that he has nothing against proficiency in "foreign languages." By contrast, the bilingualism of minority communities often means "literate in no language," he asserts. "In the best of worlds, Americans would be multiliterate. But surely the first step in that direction would be for all of us to become literate in our own national language and culture." In other words, while foreign-language study by English speakers is laudable, bilingual education for minorities is counterproductive.

This double standard is echoed by Linda Chávez. While no longer connected with U.S. English, she has vowed to continue promoting its ideas on "reforming bilingual education." On the one hand, Chávez praises efforts by English speakers to learn other languages and laments her own failure to acquire Spanish, the tongue of her ancestors. On the other hand, she questions the ability of most language-minority children to achieve fluent bilingualism:

> In urban schools it's an unusual child who's going to be able to learn both languages sufficiently to be able to succeed. When these children come from low-income families, with learning disabilities and lots of educational problems, my immediate concern is getting them fluent in English, the language of survival in this country. That is going to be key to getting them into the mainstream.

Ironically, such low expectations are unlikely to produce much more than "survival English." Cultural conservatism is reminiscent of cultural deprivation theory: it denigrates the children it purports to serve. A more humane — and more promising — educational approach is to build on the skills and knowledge these children already have. Research has shown that, when much is demanded, students are more apt to excel in two languages (see Chapter 8).

'English Plus' Alternative

To counter the growing influence of the English Only movement, in 1985 the League of United Latin American Citizens and the Spanish American League Against Discrimination launched a campaign known as English Plus. Osvaldo Soto, president of the latter organization, endorsed efforts to help LEP children become proficient in the nation's common language. "But English is not enough," he said. "We don't want a monolingual society. This country was founded on a diversity of language and culture, and we want to preserve that diversity."

Offering a positive alternative to language restrictionism, these advocates argued that the national interest would better be served by encouraging mastery of English, *plus* other tongues. They urged states and municipalities to declare themselves officially multilingual and multicultural. Such measures have passed in three states — New Mexico, Oregon, and Washington — and municipalities including Atlanta, Tucson, Cleveland, and Washington, D.C.

Startled by the passage of California's Proposition 63, many language educators have begun to espouse the goals of English Plus. The National Association for Bilingual Education, which had long decried the dangers of the English Only movement, was joined by professional associations such as the National Council of Teachers of English, the Modern Language Association, and the Linguistic Society of America. At its 1987 convention, the Teachers of English to Speakers of Other Languages resolved: "The considerable resources being spent to promote and implement English Only policies could be allocated more effectively for language instruction, including English as a second language, at all educational levels." In opposing the English Language Amendment, the group pledged to "support measures which protect the right of all individuals to preserve and foster their linguistic and cultural origins."

In late 1987 a coalition of ethnic, educational, and civil rights organizations founded the English Plus Information Clearinghouse (EPIC), the first national effort to combat the English Only movement. EPIC called for a reaffirmation of "cultural and democratic pluralism" and of the "need to foster multiple language skills." A policy of English Plus, it argued, would promote equal opportunities, increase cross-cultural understanding, safeguard minority language rights, and enhance the nation's position in world trade and diplomacy.

Fending off attacks on bilingual education was one of the coalition's objectives. By 1988, however, it was too late to rescue Title VII from major revisions at the hands of Congress and the Reagan administration. The policy that emerged can be summed up as *English Minus.*

Notes

1. In chronological order they are: Nebraska (constitutional amendment, 1920); Illinois (statute, 1969); Virginia (statute, 1981); Indiana, Kentucky, and Tennessee (statutes, 1984); California and Georgia (constitutional amendment, 1986); Arkansas, Mississippi, North Carolina, North Dakota, and South Carolina (statutes, 1987); Colorado, and Florida (constitutional amendments, 1988); Alabama (constitutional amendment, 1990); Montana, New Hampshire, and South Dakota (statutes, 1995), Georgia and Wyoming (statutes, 1996); Alaska and Missouri (statutes, 1998). Hawaii recognizes both English and Native Hawaiian as official languages (constitutional amendment, 1978). Arizona's Proposition 106 (1988) was ruled unconstitutional in 1998.

2. According to its federal tax returns (which the Internal Revenue Service makes available to the public in the case of nonprofit organizations), the U.S. English Foundation had a budget of $5.8 million in 1990. English First, another group founded in 1986 to lobby for official English, has claimed 200,000 contributors and annual expenditures exceeding $2 million.

3. In 1985, the Associated Press quoted Stanley Diamond, chairman of California English (and later of U.S. English) as saying that Spanish-language advertising "tends to separate our citizens and our people by language. This leads to dangerous divisiveness. . . . We certainly would feel that the corporations, the telephone company with the Spanish Yellow Pages, should change. We will do everything we can to put this advertising *in English only*" (emphasis added).

4. The group was known as "WITAN," from the Old English *witenagemot,* or "council of wise men" who advised the king. Its participants were drawn from the leadership of U.S. English, FAIR, Population-Environment Balance, and other groups in which Tanton has been active.

5. The funding sources were Cordelia Scaife May, an heiress to the Mellon fortune, and the Pioneer Fund, a little-known foundation dedicated to "racial betterment" through eugenics. During the 1980s May contributed at least $5.8 million to U.S. English, FAIR, and several affiliated organizations through the Laurel Foundation and family trust funds. In 1983, Laurel financed distribution of *The Camp of the Saints,* a futuristic novel by the French writer Jean Raspail, in which Third World immigrants destroy European civilization. Linda Chávez said she had once reviewed this "sickening book," describing it as "racist, xenophobic, and paranoid," and had been disturbed to see a U.S. English staff member reading it.

   The Pioneer Fund was created in 1937 by Harry Laughlin, former director of the Eugenics Record Office. Laughlin described the foundation's objectives as "practical population control . . . by influencing those forces which govern immigration, the sterilization of degenerates, and mate selection in favor of American racial strains and sound family stocks." The Pioneer Fund's first project was to popularize "applied genetics in present-day Germany" — that is, Adolph Hitler's program of forced sterilization for persons judged to be genetically inferior. John B. Trevor, Jr., a current officer of the Pioneer Fund, testified against the 1965 immigration law, warning that repeal of the national origins quota system would produce "a conglomeration of racial and ethnic elements" and lead to "a serious culture decline." In the 1970s the Pioneer Fund financed genetic research by William Shockley and Arthur Jensen purporting to prove that blacks have lower IQs than whites. In the 1980s it supported experiments to explore hereditary differences in learning between Chinese and American children. Tanton disclaimed any knowledge of these activities by the Pioneer Fund, although he had served as chairman of FAIR from 1982 to 1986, a period during which it received $370,000 from the eugenics foundation; by 1993, the total exceeded $1 million.

6. For 25 percent this was a "major reason," for 17 percent a "minor reason," for 53 percent "not a reason," and 5 percent had no opinion. No inquiry was made about attitudes toward Asians or other linguistic minorities. The survey also reported a "membership profile" of U.S. English that was disproportionately male (67 percent), elderly (75 percent were sixty or older), affluent (33 percent had incomes above $50,000), college educated (60 percent), conservative (67 percent), Republican (71 percent), and northern European in origin (68 percent). Among the 385 respondents who identified their ethnic heritage, there were no Mexican Americans, no Cubans, two "other Hispanics," two Asians, and three blacks. The telephone survey, conducted in April 1988 by the Gary C. Lawrence Co. of Santa Ana, Calif., was based on a random sample of 400 U.S. English members, with a margin of error of plus or minus 5 percent.

7. A 1987 poll by Hamilton, Frederick & Schneiders, commissioned by U.S. English, asked Florida supporters of official English to explain why. Only 8 percent hoped "to stop people from speaking any language but English." A larger group, 38 percent, said the amendment would "make it easier for people who come to this country and don't speak English to eventually get ahead." And 45 percent of respondents said they wanted "to make sure that people who need to communicate for health and safety reasons always can."

8. Hatch, an outspoken official-English proponent, suggested that the Chinese build their own annex for the books rather than displace English-language materials in the main library building. In Monterey Park, where Asians account for more than half the population, only 8,000 of the library's 150,000 volumes were in Chinese before the donation, half of which were checked out at any given time, according to officials.

9. Its sponsor, Representative Washington J. McCormick of Montana, wanted to strike a blow against literary Anglophiles, not against bilingualism. He argued that declaring American our official language "would supplement the political emancipation of '76 by the mental emancipation of '23. America has lost much in literature by not thinking its own thoughts and speaking them boldly in a language unadorned with gold braid. . . . Let our writers drop their top-coats, spats, and swagger-sticks, and assume

occasionally their buckskin, moccasins, and tomahawks." The proposal died in committee, but was adopted that same year by the state of Illinois.

10. Each additional year of bilingual education is associated with . . . a net decline of 0.5 percent in [the Anglicization rate] of the children of Spanish mother tongue"; *Language Shift in the United States* (Berlin: Mouton Publishers, 1983), p. 204. Veltman cautions, however, that this calculation is based on a limited sample.

11. Butler's paper was published by the Council for Inter-American Security, a lobby that favored U.S. intervention against leftist movements in Central America. Its secretary, Larry Pratt, is president of English First. After leaving Symms's staff in 1987, Butler was hired by Secretary William Bennett as a special assistant on postsecondary education.

12. In his contract with Whitten's office, Imhoff agreed to determine whether the texts "value . . . the maintenance of non-English languages and the preservation of traditional cultures more highly than the attainment of English language proficiency and the ability to acculturate to this society." Although he professed an open mind on this question, his writings suggested otherwise. "Bilingual programs have held sway for political, not educational, reasons," Imhoff alleges in *The Immigration Time Bomb*, which he coauthored with former governor Richard Lamm of Colorado. Hispanic leaders support bilingual education as a jobs program and as a way to maintain their ethnic "power base," the book continues. Assimilation must take precedence, even if that means lowered expectations for student achievement: "The measure of success cannot be that students enrolled in any special program for those with limited English-language ability have the same degree and amount of success as those with no language handicap. That is an unrealistic and unreachable goal. . . . If we can't afford school dropouts, who are a natural by-product of displacement and cultural shock, then we can't afford immigration."

13. In November 1989, the State Board of Regents nevertheless voted unanimously to raise the "exit criterion" from the 23rd to the 40th percentile.

14. Founded in 1989 with a $62,500 grant from U.S. English, READ has continued to enjoy its support. Other grants have come from the Laurel Foundation, the major benefactor behind U.S. English and the Federation for American Immigration Reform; English Language Advocates, a California group that campaigned for Proposition 63; the Smith Richardson Foundation, a funder of numerous New Right causes; and the Fordham Foundation, headed by Chester Finn, Jr., former assistant to Secretary Bennett.

15. Although Hirsch has never associated directly with advocates of language and immigration restrictions, his Cultural Literacy Foundation has received substantial support from Cordelia Scaife May.

4 The Bennett Years

*W*illiam J. Bennett had never set foot in a bilingual classroom on September 26, 1985, the day he launched a broadside against two decades of federal policy on the schooling of language-minority children. Like most Americans, the new U.S. Secretary of Education had only a vague notion of what bilingual education meant in practice. Speaking in New York City, he asserted that the program "had lost sight of the goal of [teaching] English," and instead had become "a way of enhancing students' knowledge of their native language and culture."

Of course, these were not the criteria that Bennett's department used in awarding grants under Title VII of the Elementary and Secondary Education Act. Nor did they reflect the *transitional* character of the vast majority of bilingual programs in the United States, most of which featured English as the predominant language of instruction. A California survey had recently found that the native language was used, on average, only 8 percent of the time — and sometimes it was never used — in so-called "bilingual" classrooms.

Nevertheless, Secretary Bennett's speech proved to be an astute move, yielding his most favorable press coverage since he had assumed office six months earlier. From the beginning Bennett had been in political hot water. His sarcastic proposal for "stereo divestiture" had antagonized Congressional allies of the student loan program. His advocacy of deep cuts in federal education spending had alienated Republicans as well as Democrats. Most ominously, Bennett's conservative boosters had felt betrayed when he fired Eileen Gardner and Larry Uzell, two aides with close ties to the New Right, following a flap over Gardner's insensitive statements about the handicapped.[1]

The secretary, at that time the only Reagan Cabinet member who remained a registered Democrat, worked hard to return to the good graces of "movement" conservatives. In doing so, he took up arms against one of their favorite targets. Bilingual education had come under heavy fire in a 1985 manifesto by the Heritage Foundation, a conservative think-tank. A section written by Gardner attacked the "bilingual lobby" for attempting "to promote a separate culture within the U.S." at the expense of English. Bennett's first step was to appoint or reappoint exponents of this view to the National Advisory and Coordinating Council on Bilingual Education (NACCBE).

From a low-profile consultative body, NACCBE was transformed into a headquarters for antagonists of bilingual education. Several of Bennett's appointees gave interviews and wrote editorials urging that the program be dismantled. Robert Rosier called bilingual education "the new Latin hustle" that had benefited no one except education "bureaucrats." Anthony Torres assailed it as "a job-maintenance program for people who could not have gotten a job any other way." Cipriano Castillo argued that Title VII should channel funding to "English immersion," rather than waste money on ineffective bilingual approaches. Joan Keefe asserted that "English as a second language [ESL] is vastly cheaper to provide and has an excellent track record for speed in teaching English." Howard Hurwitz criticized "a compliant Congress" for yielding to "Hispanic militants" who promoted bilingual education for self-serving ends. Rosalie Porter and Esther Eisenhower, two boosters of ESL-only approaches, were regarded as NACCBE's "moderates" because they did not favor an immediate termination of funding for bilingual approaches.

1985: Warning Shots

In the September 26 speech, Bennett announced his own position: "After seventeen years of federal involvement, and after $1.7 billion of federal funding, we have no evidence that the children whom we sought to help — that the children who deserve our help — have benefited." Calling the Bilingual Education Act "a failed path . . . a bankrupt course," he said that "too many children have failed to become fluent in English" and that the Hispanic school dropout rate remained "tragically as high now as it was twenty years ago."

Bennett criticized Title VII's requirement that programs make some use of students' native language and culture, arguing that "a sense of cultural pride cannot come at the price of proficiency in English, our common language." While bilingual education could be beneficial "in some circumstances," he conceded, research indicated that it

> was no more effective than alternative methods of special instruction using English, and in some cases . . . was demonstrably less so. Indeed, the English language skills of students in bilingual education programs seemed to be no better than the skills of those who simply remained in regular classrooms where English was spoken, without any special help. . . . We believe that local flexibility will serve the needs of these students far more effectively than intrusive federal regulation. [Emphasis in original text]

The widely reported speech reopened a national debate over bilingual education, shattering the compromise achieved a year earlier on Capitol Hill. Title VII's 4-to-10 percent share for alternative programs, created by the 1984 amendments, had represented a concession on the part of bilingual education advocates, but to many critics it now seemed parsimonious. News accounts styled Secretary Bennett as a champion of innovative approaches who dared to challenge "the powerful bilingual education lobby." The press reported the controversy largely as Bennett portrayed it: between defenders of English instruction and proponents of cultural maintenance, between local option and federal control.

While these stereotypes were neither accurate nor fair, the emotional tone of the debate did little to alter them in the public mind. "The Anglo population feels under siege. I think [Bennett] is greatly influenced by that in his ideology," declared Gene Chávez, then president of the National Association for Bilingual Education (NABE). Representative Matthew Martínez said the secretary "lives in [an] ignorant and bigoted world." Bennett should be named "Ambassador to Antarctica" as punishment for "policies which jeopardize Hispanic students' right to learn," suggested Raúl Yzaguirre, president of the National Council of La Raza. Title VII supporters from Mary Hatwood Futrell, president of the National Education Association to Augustus F. Hawkins, chairman of the House Education and Labor Committee, accused Bennett of attempting to abolish bilingual education and bring back sink-or-swim. This was not what the secretary had proposed — at least, not in so many words.

Bennett's tactics were a model of purposeful ambiguity. He decried the "failure" of bilingual education *policy*, not of bilingual education itself. At the same time, the secretary surely knew that this distinction would be lost on much of his audience, including headline writers throughout the country. The speech thus conveyed two distinct signals: a declaration of war on native-language instruction, pleasing the program's harshest critics; and a call for responsible experimentation with various methodologies, appealing to educators and others with open minds.

Supporters of bilingual education blasted Bennett's position as disingenuous. "The secretary only supports flexibility when it goes in one direction," that is, when schools abandon bilingual instruction for untested English-only alternatives, charged John Trasviña, legislative attorney for the Mexican American Legal Defense and Educational Fund.

Nevertheless, to those unfamiliar with what pedagogical flexibility had meant before the *Lau* decision, the policy seemed eminently fair, reasonable, and beneficial to language-minority children. "Secretary Bennett makes sense," the *Washington Post* editorialized, asserting that "the rigidity of federal policy is hampering this program." The *New York Times* agreed, adding that "often instruction in the foreign language goes on too long, impeding the student's mastery of English. . . . The Federal Government should not limit funds to only one pedagogical method." "Transitional help is sensible," argued the *Kansas City Times*, but "students [also] have a right to English proficiency."

Meanwhile, the Department of Education announced that hundreds of Americans were writing to voice their approval of the secretary's speech. On inspection, most of these letters turned out to have missed Bennett's literal message, if not his coded one. Many included derogatory ethnic references. A typical writer urged: "Please do not relent on your stand against bilingual education. Today's Hispanics, on the whole, lack the motivation of earlier immigrants. They seem to be complacent by nature and their learning [of English] is further delayed by the knowledge that they can fall back on their native language." Such "supporting" letters outnumbered those opposing Bennett's speech by five to one, the department reported.

As usual, the bilingual education debate moved beyond the pedagogical to the political. In a November 25, 1985, interview with the *Miami Herald*, Secretary Bennett elaborated on his earlier statements about the links between language and citizenship. All Americans "should be conversant" with the Constitution and the Declaration of Independence *in English*, he said. "They should be able to read them and understand what those words mean as they were written." (The secretary did not explain whether the same principle applied to the *Iliad* and *Anna Karenina*, or whether one could grasp the meaning of these texts in translation.)

The desirability of Bennett's goal was not at issue. No one questioned that every American child should have the English literacy skills to read these documents. Bennett's words, however, seemed to imply that non-English speakers are less than loyal Americans. Hispanics and Asians found this suggestion troubling at a time of heightened racial tensions and English Only agitation; doubly so when it came from the country's top education official. Certainly, not all critics of bilingual education were xenophobes, but the reverse seemed to hold true: anti-immigrant bias appeared to be swelling the tide of opposition to native-language instruction.

Bilingual education advocates found themselves defending the program on several flanks: clarifying its goals — including, but not limited to, English proficiency; communicating the complexities of research on second-language acquisition; refuting charges about linguistic "divisiveness"; and countering attacks on their own motives. These were formidable tasks, considering the level of public confusion not only about Title VII, but about the broader issues of second-language acquisition.

Researchers and practitioners criticized Bennett's insinuation that bilingual education barred the way to English. "The time spent teaching children in their native language is not merely a contribution to their ethnic pride, but also an investment in their eventual success as school learners and as speakers of English in addition to the native language," wrote Catherine Snow, an educational psychologist at Harvard. While true flexibility could prove beneficial, she said, if Bennett's policy "simply means that many non-English-speaking children receive no native-language instruction, the likely result is that such children may learn English a little faster, but not so well, and that they will be more likely to fail in school as a result."

Secretary Bennett's exclusive focus on English acquisition constituted a "narrow and unworkable definition of what constitutes equal educational opportunity," charged James J. Lyons, NABE's legislative counsel. Supporters of Title VII "have never discounted the importance of teaching English to language-minority students," he added. "However, no one with an ounce of sense would say that a child who has mastered English but who has not learned mathematics, history, geography, civics, and the other subjects taught in school was educated or prepared for life in this society."

José Cárdenas, director of the Intercultural Development Research Association, took issue with Bennett's claim that English-only alternatives to bilingual instruction, such as "structured immersion," looked promising. To the contrary, Cárdenas argued, there are "no data to suggest the success of the structured immersion approach. Though the replacement of bilingual programs by immersion programs has long been an [aim] of the Reagan administration, scholars have never taken this recommendation seriously due to the absence of a single study showing this method as a feasible approach to the education of limited-English-proficient [LEP] students in the United States."

1986: Preliminary Skirmishes

Bennett's "bilingual education initiative," as the Department of Education described it, had three components. First, the Office of Bilingual Education and Minority Languages Affairs (OBEMLA) proposed new regulations for awarding Title VII grants that favored programs emphasizing the transition to English "as quickly as possible." Second, the Office for Civil Rights (OCR) invited the 498 districts that had adopted Lau plans featuring bilingual education to renegotiate these agreements.[2] Finally, the Reagan administration asked Congress to remove all restrictions on Title VII funding for English-only approaches.

The regulatory proposal reminded local school officials that they had "substantial discretion to determine the extent of native language use" in federally funded bilingual programs. Ironically, this was what supporters of bilingual education had been arguing all along: that Title VII was not a case of "federal intrusiveness," as Bennett and others had charged. Still more curious, the department's rules seemed to restrict rather than encourage local discretion: "Any project funded . . . must make provision for native-language instruction of LEP participants *only* to the extent necessary to allow them to achieve competence in English and to meet local grade-promotion and graduation standards." OBEMLA explained that a "major objective" of the regulations was to "ensure that [LEP] children obtain proficiency in English *as quickly as possible* so that they can effectively participate in the regular educational program" (emphases added).

Now it was the turn of bilingual education supporters to accuse Washington of heavy-handedness. OBEMLA had overstepped its legal mandate, they charged, by attempting to rewrite Title VII's statutory definitions. The proposal's preoccupation with English acquisition, to the virtual exclusion of student progress in other subjects, seemed to narrow the law's stated goals. Responding that its intent had been misinterpreted, the department softened the disputed language when it issued final rules in the summer of 1986. No radical changes were in store for the grantmaking process, at least in the short term. Still, school districts received the clear message that quick-exit bilingual programs would be favored.

For NABE there was a message, too: the department was displeased with its adversarial stance toward Bennett's policies. An unusual breach was growing between professionals in the field of bilingual education and the federal funding and research apparatus that supported them. Department officials felt their motives had been maligned. NABE's leaders felt they had been deliberately misled.

Tensions had been building since September 1985. Shortly before Bennett's speech, Lyons and Ricardo Martínez, the chief House staffer on bilingual education, lunched with Carol Pendás Whitten, head of OBEMLA, and her deputy, Ana María Farías. According to Lyons and Martínez, they were told that the secretary planned to unveil a high-priority effort to aid LEP children that would make bilingual educators "extremely happy." OBEMLA officials provided the same preview for several Hispanic advocacy groups. A few days later the storm broke, taking bilingual education supporters by surprise. "For NABE, this was a chilling experience," Lyons recalled. "In Washington, even adversaries maintain a certain level of honesty. But this was disinformation."

After a series of miscommunications, Bennett and Whitten turned down NABE's invitations to address its April 1986 convention in Chicago. That week the secretary traveled to Arizona for his first visits to bilingual and immersion programs; Whitten remained in Washington to attend a seminar at the Heritage Foundation. For the first time in fifteen years, the Title VII office was unrepresented at NABE's annual gathering. Asked whether the department was deliberately boycotting the meeting, Farías said: "We need not subsidize NABE, and we need not explain that."

OBEMLA's symbolic act of hostilities was followed by more tangible ones in the coming weeks. In what was billed as a cost-cutting move, Whitten announced that only OBEMLA-sponsored training seminars would be authorized for Title VII grantees. If local program administrators wanted to attend professional conferences, they would have to pay their own way. While the new policy applied to training offered by other professional organizations, NABE and its state affiliates were the most affected. Attendance at many of their gatherings declined; NABE lost heavily on its 1987 conference in Denver. Whitten's new rules also attempted to limit the salaries of local Title VII administrators, another slap-in-the-face to the profession, but the unprecedented requirement was later withdrawn under threat of litigation.

LEP Estimates

Secretary Bennett ignited another brushfire in the spring of 1986 with his biennial report on "The Condition of Bilingual Education in the United States." Among several controversial points was a reduction by more than half in the government's official estimate of the LEP student population. There were now 1.2 to 1.7 million such children aged five to seventeen, Bennett's report said, and at least 94 percent of them were receiving special language assistance. This decidedly rosy picture clashed with the perception of many educators and advocates for language-minority children, who complained that the extent of need continued to outstrip available services. Six months earlier, for example, the Educational Priorities Panel, a citizen watchdog group, had reported that 44,000 of New York City's 110,000 LEP students were receiving none of the help to which they were entitled under the *Lau* decision and the Aspira consent decree.

For several years prior to 1986, the Department of Education had estimated a LEP student enrollment of 3.6 million in U.S. elementary and secondary schools. The department's previous biennial report in 1984 had suggested that this figure should be revised upward. Bear in mind that, since 1978, the population covered by Title VII included students with difficulty not only in speaking

English, but in reading and writing it as well. Then-Secretary of Education Terrel Bell concluded in 1982 that "only about a third of the [LEP] children aged 5 to 14 . . . are receiving either bilingual instruction or instruction in English as a second language. . . . Schools in general are not meeting the needs of LEP children." Furthermore, Bell projected that the number of language-minority students would increase by 40 percent over the next two decades.

Bennett's figures differed so sharply because they relied on a restrictive definition of limited English proficiency. The department was now counting children "most likely to benefit" from special services, a smaller universe than those eligible for assistance under Title VII. Its statisticians had arbitrarily lowered the LEP "cutoff" from the 43rd percentile to the 20th percentile, arguing that the former standard was too high to exclude language-minority children who were "English dominant." They insisted on other nonstatutory criteria — such as "child speaks non-English language at home," "household head speaks non-English language with children," and "child entered U.S. in last five years" — to further "reduce" the number of LEP students. "It doesn't make sense to provide bilingual services to children who are monolingual in English," argued Robert Barnes of the department's Office of Planning, Budget, and Evaluation.

Once again, Bennett was accused of flouting the law. Congress had deliberately left the definition of LEP students broad, not requiring that a child be "dominant" in another language, said Daniel Ulibarrí, former director of the National Clearinghouse for Bilingual Education. "What is relevant is whether a child is likely to [have], or is having, academic difficulties that are language-background related."

Dorothy Waggoner, a specialist in education statistics, charged that "the department has offered no evidence that children scoring at the 20th percentile, or even at the 30th or 40th percentile, are any more ready to cope with the regular school program in English than children scoring at the 19th percentile. [Its revised figures] underestimate needs and overstate the extent of services." She added that the department's LEP calculations had failed to consider the explosive growth in immigration since the 1980 census and its impact on the language-minority student population. In California, one of the few states with reliable figures, the number of LEP children had jumped from 326,000 in 1980 to 567,000 in 1986, an increase of 73 percent. Waggoner argued that an accurate national estimate, incorporating federal statistics for *legal* immigration only, would be 3.5 million to 5.3 million LEP students, representing the range of language-minority children who scored, respectively, below the 20th percentile and the 40th percentile in English.[3]

Bennett's claim that 94 percent of LEP children were getting appropriate help was derived from a sampling of school districts conducted in 1983-84 by Development Associates. The research firm estimated that 790,000 out of a nationwide total of 840,000 LEP students in grades K through 6 were being "served" in some fashion. It acknowledged, however, that "districts may tend to define and report [numbers of] LEP students in terms of services provided rather than in terms of external criteria of need." School administrators, in other words, were unlikely to report their own civil rights violations. For its part, the department was not inclined to question these figures. If the needs of virtually all LEP children were being addressed, then there would be no reason to increase the budget for bilingual education.

Legislative Proposal

Rather than seek additional funds for Title VII, in 1986 the Reagan administration asked Congress for greater leeway in spending the existing appropriation. Writing to House Speaker Tip O'Neill, Secretary Bennett criticized the 4 percent limit on support for "special alternative instructional programs" (SAIPs) using English only. He reported that OBEMLA had received more than one hundred applications for such grants, but was able to fund only a small fraction of them that year. "Without clear evidence that the transitional method is more effective," Bennett wrote, "we believe that the restriction on availability of funds for alternative programs requiring the use of the native language is unwarranted."

Bennett's legislative proposal was simple: it would undo the 1984 compromise, striking the complex formula for allocating appropriations among bilingual and English-only programs. OBEMLA would then be free to support "any type of instructional approach which a local educational agency considers appropriate for educating its limited-English-proficient children," the secretary explained.

Bilingual education advocates reacted angrily, denouncing this attempt to sabotage a bipartisan agreement less than two years old. Sara Meléndez of the American Council on Education pointed out that the secretary could expand funding flexibility under current law — up to 10 percent of Title VII appropriations — simply by increasing the program's budget; yet he refused to ask Congress for additional money.

The greatest concern was that dropping all restrictions would give Bennett a license to "defund bilingual education," said Lori Orum, a policy analyst for the National Council of La Raza. She argued that Title VII was seriously underfinanced as it was, following six years of budget cuts culminating in the Gramm-

Rudman reductions of mid-1986. While the secretary complained that OBEMLA had to reject many grant requests from alternative programs, he neglected to mention that it was turning down an even higher proportion from transitional bilingual education (TBE) programs. In 1985-86, 82 of 345 applications for new TBE grants were funded (23.8 percent), as compared with 35 of 104 applications for SAIP grants (33.7 percent). "If we were talking about new money, I would have no problem with the bill," Orum said, but Bennett appeared intent on diverting federal support to structured immersion, "a relatively untested method."

By June, when a Senate subcommittee convened hearings on the administration's bill, the early results of a federally funded study of "immersion strategies" had leaked to the press. In first-year scores analyzed by SRA Technologies, children in both "early-exit" and "late-exit" bilingual programs were significantly outperforming the immersion students in all subjects, including English reading. Generally speaking, the more exposure children had to their native language, the better they were doing. Embarrassed by the leak, Department of Education spokesmen insisted that no conclusions about immersion should be drawn from these preliminary data (see Chapter 7).

Secretary Bennett continued to justify "local flexibility" on grounds that language situations varied widely. "We should not be surprised," he told the Senate panel, "that school districts serving recent immigrants who speak seventy different languages will need different sorts of programs from school districts whose students speak only two languages."

Yet the SRA disclosures had damaged immersion's credibility. Moreover, they highlighted the slim research base on which the administration had erected its claim that there was no superior "method" for teaching LEP children. Chairman Hawkins wrote Bennett to remind him that the department had conducted more than sixty studies on bilingual education since 1979. Where were the research findings to support the secretary's position? Replying several weeks later, Bennett simply reiterated his view that the evidence was inconclusive, citing the 1981 Baker-de Kanter study and similar literature reviews.

Hawkins had no intention of moving the administration's bill in the House; it never came to a vote in the Senate, either. Early in 1987, the chairman knew, his Education and Labor Committee would begin work on legislation to reauthorize Title VII. Wanting to be ready for Bennett's arguments, Hawkins asked the General Accounting Office (GAO), a nonpartisan agency of Congress, to investigate whether the department's statements on bilingual education were supported by research.

1987: Advance and Retreat

What the GAO produced was undoubtedly the strongest endorsement of bilingual education yet to emerge from the federal government. By assembling a panel of independent experts and asking them pertinent questions about educational research, the GAO brought clarity to a confusing array of policy issues. Its conclusions firmly supported Title VII's mandate for native-language instruction and rejected any suggestion that alternative methods looked "promising." In short, the report reflected the consensus of researchers and practitioners in the field.

Of the ten members on the GAO's panel, six had been recommended by the Department of Education or cited on behalf of its views. Surprisingly, when the report appeared in March 1987, a majority of the experts took positions at odds with the department on five major points:

- "The research showed positive effects for transitional bilingual education on students' achievement of English-language competence."
- "Evidence about students' learning in subjects other than English," although less abundant than data on second-language acquisition, also "supported the requirement for using native languages."
- Research provided no reason to believe that English-only methods like structured immersion or stand-alone ESL offered promise for language-minority children in the United States.
- There was no scientific basis for claiming that high Hispanic dropout rates reflected the failure of bilingual education, because no data had been gathered on this issue.
- The research was not so inconclusive, after all; there was enough evidence to indicate both the validity of native-language instruction and the groups of children most likely to benefit from it.

Chester Finn, Jr., assistant secretary for educational research, denounced the GAO's methodology as biased and sloppy. He argued that the views of an arbitrarily chosen panel proved nothing, and questioned whether the studies they had reviewed were representative. The department's response to the GAO concluded: "Our position on bilingual education is valid and unscathed by this inept report."

Eleanor Chelimsky, director of the GAO study, defended its findings before a House subcommittee. "The bottom line," she said, "is that a majority of ten highly distinguished and recognized experts from the relevant research disciplines do not construe the research evidence in the way the [department does, believing that it] . . . understates the effectiveness of [bilingual instruction] and overstates it for all-English approaches."

Armed with the GAO's conclusions, in the spring of 1987 advocates for bilingual education believed they were in a strong position to keep Title VII intact, perhaps even to achieve some modest gains. Democrats had recently recaptured the Senate, restoring Senator Edward Kennedy, a longtime ally of the program, as chairman of the Labor and Human Resources Committee. On the House side of the Capitol, Chairman Hawkins lent his considerable prestige to the cause by sponsoring legislation to extend the Bilingual Education Act, with minor changes, until 1993. To NABE, the GAO report seemed to come at the perfect time, providing a scientific vindication of native-language instruction. At last, here was a chance for research to shape policy, for scientific consensus to triumph over political expediency. But the vagaries of the legislative process dictated otherwise. In the final outcome, the researchers' views would play no role at all.

Wavering Allies

The first hint of trouble came in the Senate. Kennedy unexpectedly scheduled a vote of the Labor and Human Resources Committee on Bennett's proposal to lift the "4 percent cap" on Title VII funding for English-only programs. The senator did so without first holding hearings on the bill, consulting experts, or even taking a vote in subcommittee. Though not unprecedented, Kennedy's move was nonetheless unusual. Congress normally hesitates to approve sweeping changes in a program without lengthy deliberations to gauge their impact. Furthermore, a committee chairman, who has enormous discretion to stall or expedite legislation, rarely bends procedural rules to benefit adversaries. Kennedy had strongly opposed Bennett's bill the previous year, when it was introduced by Senator Dan Quayle. In 1987, however, there was a new factor in the equation: "Star Schools."

Senator Kennedy had recently become an enthusiast of this scheme to address teacher shortages by beaming lessons via satellite to remote schools. The slogan "Star Schools, not Star Wars" began to appear in his speeches. The $100 million proposal was also expected to benefit business interests close to Kennedy in his home state of Massachusetts. Even as other education programs faced cuts, prospects for the Star Schools bill looked favorable, with its high-tech aura and the backing of a powerful senator. Star Schools also made an ideal legislative hostage for an opponent hoping to advance his own agenda. Enter Senator Quayle.

In late March the Indiana Republican indicated he would offer Bennett's bilingual education proposal as an amendment to Kennedy's pet project. The chairman was alarmed. Had Quayle carried out his threat, the "killer amendment" would have guaranteed a divisive floor fight over bilingual education, something the Senate's Democratic leadership wanted to avoid. Consideration of Star Schools would likely have been put off indefinitely, along with Kennedy's chance to put his stamp on an innovative piece of legislation. Then suddenly the crisis passed. Senator Kennedy agreed to hold a committee vote on bilingual education, and Quayle changed his mind about the amendment. Though never publicly acknowledged, a deal had obviously been struck. A few days later, Star Schools passed the Senate, 77 to 16, with bipartisan support.

Around this time Kennedy and other liberal Democrats on the committee began to look for common ground with the Republicans on bilingual education. Claiborne Pell, the Rhode Island Democrat who chaired the Senate education subcommittee, was already sympathetic to the "flexibility" argument. Pell entered into discussions with Quayle, and soon they arrived at a compromise. Instead of eliminating all restrictions on funding for English-only programs, as the administration wanted, they proposed to reserve 25 percent of Title VII grants for alternative methods. In addition, at the suggestion of Senator Pell, a child's enrollment in a Title VII classroom would be limited to three years.

Before holding a committee "markup" to approve the bill, Kennedy asked the General Accounting Office for advice. Was there a factual basis to Quayle's argument that bilingual education was infeasible where LEP children were geographically dispersed or divided into several language groups? Four weeks later, based on a survey of nine state education agencies, the GAO issued its tentative findings: 22 percent of LEP children "were in low concentration areas," that is, in classrooms with fewer than ten to twenty speakers of the same minority language.[4] The study noted, however, that because of its unsystematic nature, "the data should be used cautiously" in making policy decisions. The GAO made no determination of whether bilingual education was feasible in various settings.

Despite the cautionary tone of the report, Democratic senators who had previously criticized the idea of expanded funding for English-only instruction now had a rationale for accepting the compromise. A 25 percent share of Title VII funding for alternative approaches corresponded roughly to the percentage of districts where bilingual education seemed impractical. So committee Democrats jumped aboard the Quayle-Pell express. In a concession to lobbyists for NABE and the National Council of La Raza, they changed the setaside for alternative approaches from mandatory to permissible.

Thus modified, the bipartisan measure passed, 15 to 1, with limited discussion in open committee. By way of explanation, Kennedy said the bill was an attempt "to respond to the new and changing needs" of the Title VII program. The fact that the GAO's educational research panel had counseled against such radical responses went unremarked by other senators, including erstwhile supporters of bilingual education. For example, Senator Paul Simon of Illinois, who would soon announce his bid for the Democratic presidential nomination, was curiously absent during committee deliberations on the bill; later he cast a quiet vote in its favor.

Heartened by events in the Senate, in mid-April House Republican critics of bilingual education signaled their determination to fight Hawkins's proposal. The bill was now part of HR 5, a measure to reauthorize eighteen federal programs aiding elementary and secondary education. Hawkins and his staff had carefully guided the legislation through a thicket of thorny issues, including Chapter 1 compensatory education formulas, church-state relations, educational research, and impact aid. Hoping to avoid trouble over bilingual education, the chairman agreed to negotiations. As in 1984, the leading players were Steve Bartlett, a Texas Republican, and Dale Kildee, a Michigan Democrat. Also sitting in were William Goodling, Republican of Pennsylvania; Bill Richardson, Democrat of New Mexico; and Matthew Martínez, Democrat of California.

Progress was slow; the sessions dragged on for more than a week. For both sides the problem was to strike a balance between ideological and funding considerations. As New York State Commissioner of Education Gordon Ambach had argued during hearings on the bill, there was more than money at stake; there was also the "message the federal government is sending" about bilingual education.

Finally, a complex agreement was achieved. After consultations with the Department of Education, Bartlett announced that, in exchange for lifting all restrictions on funding for English-only programs, the administration would request a healthy increase in Title VII appropriations, to $167 million. TBE programs would be "held harmless" — funded at their current level — but up to 75 percent of "new money" (i.e., annual spending over $143 million) would be reserved for English-only approaches.

TBE had been shielded, at least in the short term. But Bartlett had prevailed ideologically. "By increasing flexibility, we increase our reason for new funding," he exulted after the accord was reached. Committee Democrats were less cheerful. Justifying the compromise afterward, Kildee said there would have been "bloodletting" on the House floor if Title VII had been subjected to debate. "In substance, I certainly believe that transitional bilingual education is a very effective method," he added. "But it's not understood [by most members of Congress]. The anti-bilingual smear job is growing. The attacks are real in both [party] caucuses. It's not a Democrat-Republican issue. . . . I can count votes." Hawkins added his blessing to the accord. "I think we have to do away with some emotionalism and be pragmatic," he said, to save Title VII from being "stricken altogether."

Advocates for bilingual education were bitter following a tense session in which the Education and Labor Committee ratified the deal. In a voice vote, only Richardson and Martínez, members of the Congressional Hispanic Caucus, audibly opposed the bill. "If there was a victory here, it was for political ideology," said Arturo Vargas of the National Council of La Raza. "If there was a defeat, it was for quality education for language-minority children. All the research shows that these English-only programs are the least effective, and now the committee has endorsed these least effective programs. They weren't interested in what works."

Others questioned whether the hasty retreat had been necessary, whether it was wise to make such huge concessions without a fight, and whether the agreement would ultimately yield any additional appropriations for Title VII. Privately, several observers close to the negotiations insisted that the Democrats had been outfoxed by Bartlett. This suspicion was reinforced when William Kristol, chief of staff to Secretary Bennett, denied that the department had pledged to seek a larger budget for bilingual education.[5] Hawkins did achieve his aim of smooth sailing for HR 5, which passed the House in May, 401 to 1, without any waves made over bilingual education. In December the Senate approved a comparable bill, 97 to 1, incorporating the Quayle-Pell compromise.

1988: Final Changes

When House-Senate conferees began working out their differences over these measures in early 1988, the battle over bilingual education had largely been decided: English-only methods would be eligible for a substantial boost in federal funding, at the expense of native-language instruction. The only question was whether the change would be immediate (the Senate version) or whether it would require increased appropriations (the House version).

For bilingual education advocates, all that was left was a salvage operation. NABE surprised many observers by joining the Department of Education and U.S.

English in supporting the Senate funding formula, which released up to 25 percent of program grants for English-only approaches. As Lyons explained in a letter to Hawkins, NABE could not accept the House plan to reserve three-quarters of future increases in Title VII for alternative programs:

> The political controversy over funding [formulas] has grown to a point where it overshadows virtually all other issues associated with the education of limited-English-proficient Americans. . . . NABE wants to resolve this distracting controversy so that the nation might focus on the critical problems confronting language-minority students and the schools they attend.

Since the Reagan administration supported the Senate provisions on this point, accepting them would be "more likely to produce the political peace sought through this legislative compromise," Lyons said, voicing a perennial if elusive hope among bilingual education advocates. Moreover, the Senate formula was discretionary. It would allow a future administration more sympathetic to bilingual education to spend *less than 25 percent* on English-only instruction. By contrast, the House version would reserve a growing amount for nonbilingual programs.

Secretary Bennett preferred the Senate language because he wanted to contain Title VII costs, while immediately increasing support for structured immersion and other alternative approaches. U.S. English found this logic appealing as well. It reasoned that under the Senate version, with no growth in Title VII appropriations (a safe assumption in fiscally conservative times), up to $18 million could be diverted from bilingual to English-only programs; under the House version, only half a million. In sum, the Senate bill would give the Department of Education more discretion to fund, or not to fund, alternatives to bilingual education.

Not surprisingly, the conferees adopted the Senate formula. In exchange, the House prevailed on a number of minor changes proposed by NABE: an end to OBEMLA's restrictions on travel funds, a revocation of the secretary's power to redefine terms in the law, a mandate for full disclosure of interim research findings by the Department of Education, and abolition of the pro-Bennett National Advisory and Coordinating Council on Bilingual Education.

On the other hand, the final bill retained another Senate provision that was profoundly disturbing to bilingual educators: the three-year enrollment rule. While allowing exceptions based on individual student evaluations, the new requirement implied that three years of bilingual education was enough; that more might be harmful to the child; and that programs featuring a longer transition to English were inferior or misguided. This enormous change, based on a gut-feeling by Senator Pell and passed without hearings to solicit expert advice, remained part of the legislation signed into law by President Reagan on April 28, 1988.

Postscript

Secretary Bennett's departure that summer brought a cease-fire in the rhetorical war between federal officials and bilingual educators. His replacement, Lauro Cavazos, arrived just in time to help George Bush round up Hispanic votes for his 1988 presidential campaign. The soft-spoken former president of Texas Tech University set a new tone from the outset. "I very much believe in bilingual education," Cavazos told the Texas Association for Bilingual Education a week before the election. "Move the children as quickly as possible into English. But have them retain that [native] language, whatever it might be, and have them retain that culture. A diversity of cultures has made this country."

To head the Title VII program, Cavazos chose Rita Esquivel, a former bilingual teacher who was known and respected by leaders of the profession — in contrast to her recent predecessors at OBEMLA. Arriving in the summer of 1989, she immediately began to repair relations with NABE, treating it once again as a professional resource rather than a political adversary. In school visits and public appearances, she became something of a good-will ambassador for the field. "Her coming on the scene has been extremely helpful in promoting an awareness of the LEP student population and its needs," according to NABE's James J. Lyons. "She's done a hell of a job under the circumstances."

The circumstances, however, included a boss who wanted to be known as the Education President without increasing education spending. Bush pinned his hopes on "choice," a voucher system that would enable parents to purchase their children's education wherever they liked, in public or private schools (see Chapter 12). But Congress never took the plan very seriously (nor did Bush himself, who had difficulty recalling its details). Playing the good soldier in this campaign, Secretary Cavazos insisted that "funding is truly not an issue" in school improvement.

For most educators, trying to cope with the cutbacks of the Reagan years, this position was indefensible. The secretary lost a great deal of credibility, especially among Mexican Americans, who staged a protest when he addressed the Texas legislature in 1990. Title VII spending, adjusted for inflation, had declined by more than 40 percent over the past decade, while the number of LEP students more than doubled in many states. The 1988 amendments made the financial impact even more severe. Despite their supportive statements about bilingual education, Cavazos and Esquivel presided over a diversion of resources to English-only programs that Secretary Bennett could only dream about.

While OBEMLA claimed to award grants "based on quality, not instructional approach," its funding decisions suggested the opposite. An investigation by *Education Week* in 1989 found that about the same number of new programs had been funded in each category — 75 for transitional bilingual education and 76 for special alternative instructional programs — but the latter had scored considerably lower, on average, in the competition. If merit had been the only deciding factor, twice as many TBE grants would have been awarded than SAIP grants. The double standard enabled the Bush administration to spend close to the 25 percent maximum on English-only programs authorized under the new Title VII. While this procedure was perfectly legal, that did not make it good policy. Following the lead of Congress, the administration chose, in effect, to ignore two decades of research in second-language acquisition.

Notes

1. In 1983, Gardner had written that the handicapped "falsely assume that the lottery of life has penalized them at random. This is not so. Nothing comes to an individual that he has not, at some point in his development, summoned. . . . There is no injustice in the universe. As unfair as that may seem, a person's external circumstances do fit his level of inner spiritual development. Those of the handicapped constituency who seek to have others bear their burdens and eliminate their challenges are seeking to avoid the central issues of their lives."

2. Six months later, only fourteen districts had responded, including some that sought to expand bilingual programs in response to growing populations of LEP students.

3. Waggoner has revised this estimated range, using 1990 census figures, to 5 million to 7.5 million LEP students; "Numbers of School-Agers with Spoken English Difficulty Increases by 83%," *Numbers and Needs* 3, no. 2 (March 1993), p. 2. For 1992-93, state education agencies in forty-seven states and the District of Columbia estimated a total of 2,558,487 LEP students in elementary and secondary schools, according to the U.S. Department of Education. California's more reliable language census of elementary and secondary schools reported 1,151,819 that year; extrapolating from that figure (using the state's share of the U.S. language-minority population in the 1990 census) would yield a national total of 4.2 million LEP students. Also, according to the states' reporting, 82 percent of identified LEP students nationwide were enrolled in special language programs in 1992-93.

4. According to the GAO, only nine states collect this information by school or grade-level. In a survey of seventeen states that report data by school district only, 28 percent of LEP children were in low concentration areas. This report was prepared by a different branch of the GAO from that which surveyed experts on the educational research issues.

5. In February 1988, as part of its budget request for fiscal year 1989, the Administration sought $156 million for Title VII, roughly half the increase Bartlett had promised.

Theory

5 The Effectiveness Debate

$\mathcal{D}$oes bilingual education really work? Politicians and journalists remain obsessed with this unrewarding question, which practitioners feel they answered long ago. Three decades of experience in the classroom, refinements in curriculum and methodology, and gains in student achievement have made believers out of countless parents, teachers, administrators, and school board members. While generalizations are problematic — "bilingual education" describes a variety of pedagogies — there is no question that it has helped to dismantle language barriers for a generation of students.

A growing number of bilingual programs are well designed and well implemented; others are less so. Some encourage children to maintain and develop their native-language skills, while most continue to stress a rapid transition to English. Few have worked overnight miracles. Language of instruction is hardly the only determinant of academic success for Spanish-speaking or Navajo-speaking students, any more than it is for English-speaking students. Yet thanks to bilingual education, falling behind in school is no longer a given, as it was before 1968, for any child who arrives with limited English skills. Not an insignificant accomplishment — especially when one considers the glacial pace of education reform in the United States.

Such advances, however, have failed to quell public skepticism about the concept of learning in two languages. Bilingual education still runs up against powerful myths: that young children pick up new languages quickly and effortlessly; that prolonged reliance on the native tongue reduces students' incentives to learn English; that bilingualism confuses the mind and retards school achievement. In short, bilingual education defies common sense. If we instruct children in foreign tongues, how will that teach them to speak our language?

So far education research has done little to dispel these misconceptions or to clarify the policy discussion. To the extent it has tackled the effectiveness question head-on, through program evaluation studies comparing bilingual and nonbilingual approaches, firm answers have remained elusive. For partisans, this may be the only common ground in the entire debate: a recognition that evaluation research, often poorly conceived and executed, has failed to make a strong case for the superiority of bilingual instruction. One side faults the studies; the other, the program. "Opponents of bilingual education have tended to fixate on the negative aspects of evaluations," according to researcher Rudolph Troike, "while proponents have either cavalierly ignored the findings or have argued that alternative criteria for success should be considered."

What accounts for the underdeveloped state of bilingual education research? Among several factors blamed, neglect by the federal government usually tops the list. In the first decade of Title VII, Congress appropriated $500 million for bilingual programs, but only one-half of one percent went for research. The Bilingual Education Act was originally intended to finance demonstration projects. Since native-language approaches were largely untested in 1968, summarizing experience was vital. So all Title VII grants had to include an evaluation component. Apparently, however, many of these program evaluations were of poor quality. Obviously they were of limited interest to the U.S. Office of Education, which destroyed all those submitted during the first eight years.

The AIR Study

The initial progress report on Title VII appeared in 1977-78, a national eval-uation of federally funded bilingual programs by the American Institutes for Research (AIR). The study encompassed 38 Spanish-English bilingual programs and more than 7,000 children in 150 schools. It remains the largest evaluation of Title VII ever completed. After ten years of federal funding, AIR concluded, there had been "no consistent significant impact" on the education of limited-English-proficient (LEP) children.

This was the first of several studies and "reviews of the literature" that, after combining the results of many evaluations, could find nothing conclusive to say about bilingual education. Press accounts of the AIR study stressed the lack of positive outcomes — in English reading, children actually scored higher in sink-or-swim classrooms — and critics of Title VII were quick to use the new ammu-nition. Why should government mandate native-language instruction, they asked, or give it preference in funding, when its effectiveness remained in doubt?

Bilingual education advocates responded that such poorly designed research would never yield useful findings. Rather than testing an ideal instruc-tional model, AIR had examined a patchwork of treatments labeled "bilingual" and had lumped together their overall effects without attempting to control for a multitude of variables. Some reviews of the literature have adopted the same technique: collecting evaluations, discarding those deemed unsound for method-ological reasons, and essentially "counting the votes" for or against bilingual edu-cation. "In such an analysis," wrote Tracy Gray and Beatriz Arias of the Center for Applied Linguistics, "the positive effects found with the good programs are often canceled out by the negative effects found with the bad programs."

Rudolph Troike agreed that "the AIR study can and should be faulted for its inadequacies." At the same time, he argued that "not all of the negative findings can be easily dismissed, and bilingual educators should take this report seriously as a challenge to improve the quality of programs." The point, Troike stressed in a 1978 monograph for the National Clearinghouse for Bilingual Education, is that *well-designed* bilingual programs can be effective and should be replicated. He cited a dozen evaluation studies documenting superior approaches using native-language instruction.[1]

Such success stories, however, have produced only small ripples in the effectiveness debate. In an influential article, Kenji Hakuta and Catherine Snow have argued that "evaluation studies are doing a poor job of measuring" the ben-efits of bilingual education overall. Why is this so?

The shortcomings of this type of research fall into three categories. First, large-scale evaluations and literature reviews tend to obscure the diversity of bilingual education in program design and quality; availability of resources, materials, and trained staff; the mix of English and native-language instruction; and students' class and linguistic backgrounds. When pedagogical practice varies so widely, sweeping conclusions about the effectiveness of all programs labeled "transitional bilingual education" (TBE) are scientifically dubious. Yet such conclusions are drawn nonetheless.

Second, researchers face a daunting array of technical obstacles in designing program evaluations. To gauge effectiveness, it is not enough to show that children are learning — they might well have learned more (or less) in a different program. An independent basis for comparison is needed. Students' progress can, of course, be charted against normal curves for their grade level, but such comparisons are questionable because numerous variables may distort the outcome (e.g., an exceptionally bright group of children, highly literate parents, a school principal's incompetence, drug shootouts in the neighborhood).

Ideally, an evaluation study should compare two groups of students receiving different educational treatments but otherwise identical in socioeconomic status, language background, and achievement level. Each program should be taught by teachers of comparable training and experience, with equivalent resources, preferably in the same school, over a period of several years. Needless to say, a perfect match is rarely found. While there are statistical techniques to adjust for preëxisting differences, these are imperfect, especially as variables multiply. In a pure experiment, children could be randomly assigned to each group, but in the real world there are ethical and legal obstacles to doing so. For example, since the Supreme Court's 1974 decision in *Lau v. Nichols*, "no treatment" of LEP children's language needs has been forbidden as a violation of their civil rights (see Chapter 2).

Third, evaluations are subject to political pressures, for example, in crucial decisions about study design. Clearly, bilingual education practitioners have had a professional stake in defending their field. Meanwhile, the U.S. Department of Education, the major source of research funding, has had its own ideological axes to grind, such as a desire to vindicate the alternative methods that Secretary William Bennett called "promising." Complex findings may be interpreted and packaged in various ways, depending on who controls a study's release.

Educators have begun to recognize the theoretical fallacies of gauging "program effectiveness," narrowly defined. To put a premium on bottom-line results, measured with imperfect instruments over a short period of time, makes for crude science. "Rather than emphasize research that might give insights to teachers on effective classroom practices and [on] how they might help limited-English-proficient students, [policymakers have] expended . . . much energy on research of questionable quality and validity that asks, 'Has it worked?'" concludes the Association for Supervision and Curriculum Development (ASCD). Framed by politics rather than pedagogy, this "simplistic question ignores the complexity" of bilingual programs and "serves to fuel a divisive debate," the group adds in a 1987 report.

Evaluation Research vs. Basic Research

As an alternative to evaluation research, the ASCD recommends greater reliance on the scientific study of second-language acquisition. Such *basic research,* as defined by Hakuta and Snow, "focuses on the linguistic and psychological processes in the development of bilingual children." Instead of comparing program models, basic research uses empirical data to confirm or reject theories about why LEP students succeed or fail in school; how factors like age, social status, and native-language proficiency affect the process of acquiring English; and how linguistic development interacts with cognitive development.

Rather than wait for the perfect evaluation study, Hakuta and Snow argue, policymakers should heed the results of basic research, which refute pervasive myths about bilingualism. They cite several relevant findings — or more accurately, hypotheses — supported by an accumulating body of evidence:

- Early childhood is not the optimum age to acquire a second language; older children and adults are "more efficient language learners." Thus the "sense of urgency in introducing English to non-English-speaking children and concern about postponing children's exit from bilingual programs" are misplaced.
- "Language is not a unified skill, but a complex configuration of abilities. . . Language used for conversational purposes is quite different from language used for school learning, and the former develops earlier than the latter."
- Because many skills are transferable to a second language, "time spent learning in the native language . . . is not time lost in developing English" or other subjects. To the contrary, a child with a strong foundation in the first language will perform better in English over the long term.

- "Reading should be taught in the native language, particularly for children who, on other grounds, run the risk of reading failure. Reading skills acquired in the native language will transfer readily and quickly to English, and will result in higher ultimate reading achievement in English."
- There is no cognitive cost in the development of bilingualism in children. Very possibly, bilingualism enhances children's thinking skills."

Such developments in basic research have exerted an increasing influence on the design of bilingual education programs. In the early 1980s, the California State Department of Education launched an innovative curriculum known as Case Studies in Bilingual Education, using a "theoretical framework" developed by Jim Cummins, Stephen Krashen, and others that emphasizes cognitive development in the native language (see Chapters 6 and 8).

Nevertheless, basic research on second-language acquisition had little impact on federal policy during the Reagan and Bush administrations. In 1988, when asked for an assessment of Cummins's work, bilingual research director Edward Fuentes said the Department of Education had none. Asked for his own view, Fuentes ventured: "I think he has a theory, and his theory has yet to be proved. It's one of many explanations. That's the nature of social science. People have to continue investigating."

The department's noncommittal stance was not a product of ignorance, but of political calculation. By withholding comment on basic research, it could keep debate within the bounds of evaluation research, where the outcomes of bilingual programs often remained ambiguous. It could ignore scientific explanations of second-language acquisition that made the idea of bilingual education less counterintuitive.

And yet, for defenders of Title VII, there was (and is) no avoiding the effectiveness controversy. Public skepticism must be addressed. As long as bilingual education receives federal or state support, taxpayers and their representatives will want reassurance about results — in particular, about children's progress in learning English. Even the ASCD, in releasing its 1987 report on the research issues, felt compelled to headline its press release: "Study Finds That Bilingual Education Works."

'Burdens of Proof' and Standards of Success

Critics of bilingual education have enjoyed a tactical advantage in the debate over its effectiveness. Where evidence is contradictory, the easiest position to defend, and the hardest to disprove, is that results are inconclusive. If bilingual education has "no sound basis in research . . . let us permit diversity, innovation, experimentation, and local options to flourish," proposed Chester Finn, Jr., the Reagan administration official in charge of educational research. This message had the virtues of simplicity and apparent open-mindedness. It was especially appealing to nonexperts, who had no way of sorting out the complex arguments of educational psychologists, linguists, and statisticians. Finn elaborated the administration's official agnosticism as follows:

> The logical test underlying scientific research is the question of rejection of the null hypothesis. That is to say, the burden of proof rests on those who assert that some effect or event occurs. The presumption in all scientific research is that there is no difference until proven otherwise. Thus . . . it is not incumbent on the Department of Education to prove that "transitional bilingual education" is ineffective. Rather, the burden of proof is on those who assert that such education *is* effective. When results are inconclusive, the correct scientific conclusion is to accept the null hypothesis, i.e., to conclude that those who assert effectiveness have failed to prove their claims. . . . It is the inconclusive nature of the research that supports the Department's view that this unproven method ought not be mandated by law. [Emphasis in original]

Finn's critics have pointed to several flaws in this argument. First, he asked for proof that bilingual education is universally effective in practice — with every LEP child, from every background, in every school — a standard that it has set for no other discipline. "The level of evidence demanded is extraordinary," observes Stephen Krashen, a leading theorist of second-language acquisition. "It's hard to do the perfect experiment," he adds, acknowledging that "some of the study designs have been awful. But the results are very consistent over hundreds of studies. Evidence, which varies in quality, supports [the hypothesis that] bilingual education works."

Second, the Reagan administration approached the effectiveness question from the narrow standpoint of how quickly bilingual programs teach English. This flowed from its view of Title VII as remedial education, as a way of addressing *language handicaps.* By contrast, most bilingual education researchers and practitioners judge programs on how effectively they promote all-round cognitive development. The speed of English acquisition matters less than its quality —

whether it provides a solid foundation for future academic achievement. "The only thing that counts in education is the long term," says Krashen. "We're not interested in what kids do at the end of 1st grade. We're interested in their long-term chances of success."

Third, Finn's empiricist outlook paid lip service to science, but was fundamentally antitheoretical. Rather than consider research that tests hypotheses about language and learning, he was concerned with quantitative judgments about program experience, pro or con. In a frame of inquiry determined by politics — the controversy over Title VII funding — language of instruction became the only significant variable in comparing educational treatments. Thus TBE, a grant category that could mean many things in the classroom, was conceived as a single "method." Lacking "conclusive proof" of its effectiveness in program evaluations, Finn argued, the federal government should take no stand favoring any pedagogical approach. This view both exaggerated the certainty of research findings and underestimated their value in guiding educational practice.

Krashen, by contrast, has never claimed that his theories about second-language acquisition are "proven" in any final sense. "All scientific hypotheses are fragile," he explains. "One bit of contradictory evidence can destroy them. But we owe it to the kids to use [bilingual instruction] because it's our best guess as to what works best. I can't imagine any other way."

In fact, Finn's position contained an unacknowledged — and unproven — theory of its own: the notion that *quantity of exposure* is what matters most in second-language acquisition. Christine Rossell of Boston University, a leading critic of bilingual education, has been more explicit in articulating this view. "Time on task — the amount of time spent learning a subject — is . . . a good predictor of achievement" generally, she reasons. Therefore, English-only instruction must be a superior way to teach English. This "common sense" theory, while widely supported by public opinion, is thus far unsupported by scientific evidence. Rossell, a political scientist with limited interest in pedagogical details,[2] has focused on tallying up program evaluations to confirm the conclusion that bilingual education is ineffective. But neither she nor any of her allies has ever subjected the time-on-task hypothesis to a rigorous test — that is, one in which it could be disproven.

A final fallacy in Finn's logic was the implication that evaluation research would ultimately provide clear answers about what "works." Burdened with methodological and design flaws, such studies have so far failed to prove anything conclusively. A good case in point is the Department of Education's own contribution to the effectiveness controversy.

The Baker-de Kanter Report

In August 1980, as the Carter administration prepared to issue its ill-fated Lau regulations, the White House Regulatory Analysis and Review Group asked the department to review the research literature on the effectiveness of bilingual education. The job went to the Office of Planning and Budget,[3] which had earlier directed the AIR study. It was assigned to Keith Baker and Adriana de Kanter, respectively a sociologist and a management intern. Although the Reagan administration withdrew the Lau proposal in February 1981, the project continued under the new Secretary of Education, Terrel Bell.

Baker and de Kanter defined the study in legal-political terms, asking:

1. Is there a sufficiently strong case for the effectiveness of TBE for learning English and nonlanguage subjects to justify a legal mandate for TBE?
2. Are there any effective alternatives to TBE? That is, should one particular method be exclusively required if other methods are also effective?

Equally important was what the researchers failed to ask. They made no attempt to isolate the criteria of successful and unsuccessful bilingual programs, but only to determine whether "the instructional method is uniformly effective."

After reviewing more than three hundred studies (about half of which were primary evaluations of actual programs), Baker and de Kanter judged most to be methodologically unsound. In the end they threw out all but twenty-eight because of design weaknesses — e.g., failure to adjust for preëxisting differences between experimental groups. They also disqualified research that did not feature "random assignment" of students, unless statistical measures were taken to control for extraneous variables, or that used grade-equivalent scores, which the researchers said were "almost impossible to interpret." Among the evaluations left out were all twelve cited by Troike, along with many of bilingual education's best-publicized success stories. Among those included was the AIR report, despite the controversy over its methodology.

Taken together, the studies' results were ambiguous. "No consistent evidence supports the effectiveness of transitional bilingual education," Baker and de Kanter concluded. "An occasional, inexplicable success is not reason enough to make TBE the law of the land. . . . The time spent using the home language in the classroom may be harmful because it reduces [the time for] English practice."

In a majority of the twenty-eight evaluations, they found that differences in student performance were too small to be statistically significant when transitional bilingual education was compared with "submersion," or sink-or-swim instruction. Among the studies that showed one method to be superior, the score was split about evenly between the two. (According to a later article by Baker, one in three studies showed "significant positive effects" for TBE; one in four for submersion.) They also concluded that, according to some research, TBE and submersion were less effective than either English as a second language (ESL) or "structured immersion," a monolingual approach that attempts to teach the second language through subject-matter instruction adjusted for students' level of English proficiency.

The researchers stressed the "negative effects" of bilingual programs, particularly in the AIR study, which they described as "the only American [research] designed to be nationally representative." They dismissed the central complaint raised against AIR's methodology, that the diversity and uneven quality of Title VII projects invalidates global comparisons. "Without some independent measure of the success of implementation of each project," Baker and de Kanter responded, this objection was "a meaningless tautology." In any case, they added, it might "be more cost-effective to switch to alternative instructional methods [than] to undertake large-scale efforts to redesign and properly implement TBE programs."

Summarizing the study's policy implications, Baker and de Kanter maintained that

> too little is known about the problems of educating language minorities to prescribe a specific remedy at the federal level. . . . Each school district should decide what type of special program is most appropriate for its own unique setting. . . . Although TBE has been found to work in some settings, it also has been found ineffective and even harmful in other places. Furthermore, both major alternatives to TBE — structured immersion and ESL — have been found to work in some settings.

For Baker and de Kanter, the favored alternative was immersion in English; they called for "a widespread, structured immersion demonstration program" to test such an approach. Perhaps this was because they could cite only one, unpublished study touting the benefits of immersion for language-minority children in the United States. It involved a kindergarten curriculum in McAllen, Texas, which was labeled "a modified immersion program," even though it included an hour of daily Spanish instruction.

The authors' enthusiasm for this alternative to TBE was based largely on evaluations of Canadian immersion programs, which have proved highly effective in teaching French to English-speaking children. The researchers who designed this model, however, have cautioned against extrapolating from its success to justify immersion for language-minority children in the United States. They have noted that the Canadian model is a bilingual approach. Its participants are children of the dominant language group, whose mother-tongue development is reinforced rather than threatened outside of school. For speakers of low-status minority languages, an English-only immersion program would likely be harmful, the Canadian researchers have warned.

Rejecting these objections as "untested theoretical arguments," Baker and de Kanter said that "immersion may not transfer successfully from Canada to the United States, but this is an empirical question that must be answered by direct test." Little additional evidence was available in January 1987, when the Department of Education resubmitted to Congress a proposal to allow increased funding for alternatives to bilingual education. Edward Fuentes could cite only one primary study asserting the promise of structured immersion in this country, a program evaluation in Uvalde, Texas. Moreover, initial results from the SRA immersion study, supervised by Keith Baker, showed unpromising results for structured immersion when compared with various bilingual programs. (For a detailed discussion of immersion research, see Chapter 7.)

Critiquing the Critics

Though never officially endorsed by the department, a draft of the Baker-de Kanter report surfaced in the press in September 1981. Its conclusions were widely regarded as an indictment of Title VII. For example, the *Champaign-Urbana News-Gazette*, under the headline "Bilingual Education May Be Scrapped," said the report recommended the redirection of funds to more "promising techniques" like immersion. While the authors have disavowed such interpretations, the Baker-de Kanter study has frequently been cited by the enemies of bilingual education. During the 1980s it was easily the most quoted federal pronouncement on the education of LEP children, and probably the most criticized as well.

As with the AIR study three years earlier, bilingual education supporters protested the report's methodology, describing its program labels as oversimpli-

fied and misleading. Baker and de Kanter were accused of using a double standard of methodological acceptability to exclude evaluations favorable to native-
language instruction and to include those that found it harmful. Once again, the
vote-counting approach of tallying studies on each side of the effectiveness question was assailed as a primitive research technique at best.

The most ambitious rebuttal appeared in 1985. Psychologist Ann Willig
used a sophisticated statistical procedure known as *meta-analysis* to create a
new synthesis of the Baker-de Kanter data. This technique enabled her to com-
bine *mean effect sizes* — or differences between programs that were frequently
too small to be statistically significant in individual studies — thus allowing for a
precise measurement of overall differences in student achievement between
bilingual and submersion classrooms. The meta-analysis also adjusted for 183
variables that Baker and de Kanter had not taken into account, ranging from student and teacher characteristics to instructional methods to the language of
achievement tests. Most important, Willig was able to control for design weaknesses in the evaluations under review.

The Willig study reanalyzed twenty-three of the twenty-eight evaluations
included in the Baker-de Kanter report (excluding foreign and nonprimary studies). She accepted the federal researchers' decision to disqualify a long list of
studies supporting the superiority of bilingual approaches. Nevertheless, a meta-
analysis of the Baker de-Kanter data "consistently produced small-to-moderate
differences favoring bilingual education," Willig reported. The pattern prevailed
on English tests of reading, language skills, mathematics, and total achievement,
as well as on Spanish tests of listening comprehension, reading, writing, total language, mathematics, social studies, and attitudes toward school and self.

According to Willig, these "significant positive effects" became visible only
when statistical controls were applied for methodological flaws. In other words,
the better a study's design, the better bilingual education fared. For example,
where evaluations used random assignment of subjects to experimental and comparison groups, the effect size was largest in favor of bilingual programs.

Often the weaker research designs were stacked heavily against bilingual
education. The most egregious of these were evaluations that selected as comparison groups so-called "submersion" programs — mainstream classrooms —
whose students had already "graduated" from bilingual programs because of their
improved English skills. In the AIR study, which Baker and de Kanter had rated
highly for its scientific approach, Willig determined that at least two-thirds of the
"submersion students" had previously been enrolled in bilingual classrooms. It
does not require a Ph.D. to understand why such children outperformed their

counterparts who had not yet been mainstreamed. In effect, the individual successes of Title VII were being cited as evidence of its failure.

Willig also found that the poorest studies were those that denied rather than confirmed the benefits of native-language instruction. Results were sometimes distorted because nonbilingual comparison groups were composed of children already judged to be "English dominant" rather than LEP, or that were taught by bilingual teachers who made frequent use of students' native language. In other cases children were exited from bilingual programs during the experiment and replaced by incoming LEP children who naturally depressed aggregate scores. Or there were teacher turnover and disorganization in the bilingual classroom, but not in the comparison classroom.

Critics had previously shown that such factors were biasing evaluation studies against bilingual education. Willig's contribution, using meta-analysis, was to isolate each design flaw, calculate the amount of distortion (including interactions among variables), and adjust the program comparisons. On a level playing field, she proved, bilingual education could outscore the competition: "In every instance where there did not appear to be crucial inequalities between experimental and comparison groups, children in the bilingual programs averaged higher than the comparison children."

Most of the studies reviewed by the Baker-de Kanter and Willig reports were conducted before the mid-1970s, when the federal Office for Civil Rights began to enforce the *Lau* decision. Since that time, random assignment of LEP children to sink-or-swim classrooms has been legally out of the question. The change has made evaluation research much more difficult. "True experiments" comparing pedagogical alternatives are problematic within most schools, which normally do not offer competing approaches for LEP students with identical needs. Still, some study designs are more successful than others in controlling for extraneous variables. "Until quality research in bilingual education becomes a norm rather than a scarcity," Willig concluded, educators will be handicapped in addressing the needs of language-minority children.

Willig's research was cited by several experts polled in 1986 by the U.S. General Accounting Office as evidence against Secretary Bennett's position that the case for bilingual education remains unproven (see Chapter 4). In response, the Department of Education issued its first comment on her work: "The Willig meta-analysis reviewed a non-representative and very small sample of the existing research and used an inappropriate methodology. It is by no means a comprehensive review of the literature." Asked to explain why Willig's study was any less comprehensive than the Baker-de Kanter report — after all, it relied on virtually the same body of evaluation research — Keith Baker responded that Willig had reviewed fewer studies than a 1983 version of his report. (The later edition, which encompassed thirty-nine studies, reached conclusions identical to those of the 1981 draft.)

Alan Ginsburg, Baker's superior in the Office of Planning, Budget, and Evaluation, argued further that meta-analysis was an inappropriate research tool. The issue, he said, was not whether bilingual education is effective "on average, but [whether there are] programs that might be appropriate in one community, but not in another. The averaging effect of meta-analysis is quite limiting." Averaging, of course, was what reviews of the literature like the Baker-de Kanter report and evaluations like the AIR study were all about. Willig had simply refined the process. Baker expanded on Ginsburg's reasoning in a 1987 article for the *Review of Educational Research:*

> Willig's [finding of] a net average positive effect does not necessarily justify a federal mandate for TBE, especially if many programs produce negative results and successful alternatives exist. . . . The advantage of a narrative review over meta-analysis is clear in this situation. Where the methodology of the literature being synthesized is very complex and problematical, only the narrative reviewer can fully assess the strengths and weaknesses of a study and evaluate it as a whole to determine what is and is not valid in a study. The mechanistic checklists used in meta-analysis cannot assess the gestalt of a study.

Responding to Baker in the same issue of the journal, Willig noted that the computer "coding system" at the heart of meta-analysis, "forces one to scrutinize every aspect of a study" in a way that minimizes subjective judgments. "In contrast, the narrative reviewer may omit important factors when assessing the value of a study, either because of the overload of information or . . . reviewer bias." Willig observed that Baker and de Kanter had consistently ignored flaws in evaluation studies or used partial data in ways that confirmed negative assessments of bilingual education.

Nevertheless, the larger argument about effectiveness is unlikely to be settled on the terrain of evaluation research. Tabulating the results of imperfect studies, even with the aid of statistical magic, is no way to tackle the problems of how children learn. Such questions are the province of basic research.

Notes

1. For example, among French speakers in St. John Valley, Maine; Spanish speakers in Santa Fe, New Mexico; Navajos in Rock Point, Arizona; and Chinese in San Francisco.

2. Testifying for the defense in the *Teresa P. v. Berkeley* case — a service for which she received $129,000 in fees and expenses — Rossell described her evaluation of the district's programs for LEP children. Students who received bilingual instruction in Berkeley did no better than those who received English as a second language and individual tutoring, she concluded; therefore, there was no need to expand bilingual programs. Under cross-examination, however, she admitted a minimal acquaintance with what the program labels represented in practice. It turned out that Rossell's "expert" opinion was based on (1) three minutes of classroom observation, (2) brief conversations with teachers, and (3) a partial comparison of test results for about 20 percent of Berkeley's LEP students.

3. Later renamed the Office of Planning, Budget, and Evaluation.

6 Basic Research on Language Acquisition

$\mathcal{M}$ost educated Americans can testify to the difficulty of becoming bilingual. Despite years of schooling in French, Spanish, or German, in all likelihood we cannot carry on a conversation in a language other than English. According to the American Council on the Teaching of Foreign Languages, "only 3 percent of American high school graduates, and only 5 percent of our college graduates, reach a meaningful proficiency in a second language — and many of these students come from bilingual homes." Though our foreign-language instruction may produce passable reading and writing skills, rarely does it equip us to communicate. We may earn high marks for recalling grammatical rules or parroting classroom exercises or producing flawless compositions. Yet oral exchanges with native speakers can be an ego-jarring experience.

Frustrated at having invested so much effort for so little return, we rationalize: "I started learning a language too late; the longer you wait, the harder it is." "I never had a chance to use it outside of class, and now I'm embarrassed to try." Or "I just don't have an aptitude for memorizing grammar and vocabulary."

Each of these reactions expresses a popular "theory" of second-language acquisition. As generalizations, they are inadequate to explain student failure, but they do reflect persistent problems with foreign-language teaching. Conversational facility is indeed difficult to acquire when there are limited opportunities to engage in real conversations. An emphasis on grammar drills not only bores students; it seldom trains them to *speak* the target language. Older learners tend to be especially self-conscious when forced to participate in exercises detached from any purposeful context. For years students have lodged such complaints, with little effect on the way foreign languages are taught in this country.

Historically speaking, the focus on form over function seems to be a recent development in second-language education. During the Roman Empire scholars achieved a high level of grammatical knowledge of Latin and Greek, often in connection with the rhetorical arts, but apparently such studies were never regarded as a route to language acquisition. In the bilingual schooling of Roman children, conversational dialogues were used to develop fluency in Greek. Latin, the *lingua franca* of culture and scholarship in medieval Europe, was taught for centuries with a stress on oral skills as well as reading and writing.

"Toward the end of the Renaissance," writes Barry McLaughlin, when Latin began to die out as a spoken tongue,

> emphasis began to shift from the learning of language as a practical tool to the learning of language as a means to an end — that of developing the mind. Latin and Greek were taught because it was thought that the study of grammar was good mental discipline. Since these languages were not living languages, little attention was given to oral communication. Texts were read and translated, and this — together with the study of grammar — became the essence of language training.

By the nineteenth century, the *grammar-translation approach* was being used to teach modern languages as well. Students spent their time conjugating verbs, memorizing vocabulary, learning syntactical rules and their exceptions, taking dictation, and translating written passages. Since communicative proficiency was not an important goal, oral use of the second language was minimal. In the United States such methods predominated well into the 1950s.

Acceptance of the grammatical approach has never been universal. The English philosopher John Locke wrote in 1693:

> *Latin* is no more unknown to a Child, when he comes into the World, than *English*. And yet he learns *English* without Master, Rule, or Grammar; and so might he *Latin* too, as *Tully* did, if he had some Body always to talk to him in this Language. . . . [In this way] a Child might without Pains or Chiding, get a Language, which others are wont to be whip'd for at School six or seven Years together.[1]

Perceptive educators have long recognized the potential of more natural approaches to language acquisition. Over the years a number of *direct methods* — the most famous being that of Maximilian Berlitz — have used varieties of partial or total immersion. Oral language is heavily emphasized and translation is avoided; students are encouraged to think in the second tongue. Grammar is taught inductively rather than through the application of rules. Such techniques have proved successful among diplomats, business people, and others with strong incentives to learn. More recently they have inspired innovative methods of teaching English as a second language (ESL) such as the Natural Approach, Suggestopedia, and Total Physical Response. Direct methods have been the exception, however, in high school and college foreign-language programs.

By 1957, when the shock of *Sputnik* revived Americans' interest in foreign languages, there was widespread dissatisfaction with the grammar-translation method. Clearly it was producing few if any functional bilinguals. The prevailing explanation was that, while students might become sophisticated grammarians, they were getting too little practice in oral communication. Still, there was no rush to adopt direct methods, whose approach to grammar seemed haphazard to many educators. What filled the vacuum became known as the *audiolingual method.* With backing from the Modern Language Association, it emerged as a popular alternative to the grammar-translation approach and remains in use today.[2]

Influenced by behaviorist psychology and structural linguistics, audiolingualism begins with the premise that each language is a distinct set of "speech habits." Since students already have well-developed habits in the mother tongue, the logic goes, they need systematic practice to learn new ones in the second language. Special attention must therefore be paid to differences between the two grammars; otherwise learners tend to graft new vocabulary onto first-language syntax (a pitfall of direct methods, in the audiolingualists' view). Accordingly, the audiolingual method relies on oral "pattern drills" and "memorization and mimicry" to teach grammar in a planned sequence. The idea is that, through repetition, students' use of the second language becomes automatic, allowing them to produce sentences of their own.

When it comes to communication skills, however, practice apparently does not make perfect. Evaluations have shown that audiolingual students, like their predecessors in grammar-translation classrooms, seldom reach more than a novice level of oral proficiency in the second language.

Revolutionary Theory

Audiolingualism suffered a major setback when the reigning theory of language that sponsored it was overthrown by the Chomskyan revolution in linguistics. In the behaviorist view espoused by B. F. Skinner, language learning is just another branch of learning. That is, the mind grasps grammatical forms in the same way it draws generalizations from all experience. Correct speech habits must therefore be developed in the same way as other behavioral patterns, through imitation and reinforcement, repeated at frequent intervals. (This assumption usually underlies the "time on task" arguments against bilingual education; see Chapter 5.) Implicit in Skinner's premises is the notion that, as children acquire language, they internalize a finite set of linguistic responses for all the stimuli they will encounter in life. This is an absurd claim, according to Noam Chomsky.

In any language, Chomsky demonstrates, the number of sentences is infinite; there is no limit to the grammatical combination of words. Moreover, while exposed to relatively small amounts of data, children master complex syntactic structures in their native tongue. Rather than merely repeating a limited repertoire, they learn to produce utterances that have never been heard before, by themselves or by others, which are nevertheless "correct" and comprehensible to fellow speakers of the language. Thus, in Chomsky's theory, language use is a creative, open-ended process rather than a closed system of behavioral habits. That this ability could be acquired empirically — entirely through generalizations from experience — is highly implausible.

Instead, Chomsky hypothesizes, human beings have an innate cognitive capacity for language. The mind is endowed with *linguistic universals* that enable us to formulate rules from the verbal sounds we hear. Such rules depend on the structure of language — e.g., the subject-predicate relationship — rather than on easily mimicked features such as word order. Languages differ in particulars while sharing a *universal grammar*, or set of principles that determines the grammars the mind may "construct." Conversely, according to Chomsky, these same universals "exclude other possible languages as 'unlearnable.'" Or, to use another metaphor, heredity has "prewired" the human mind to acquire certain kinds of linguistic structures. Environmental stimuli — messages received in a natural language — "throw switches" to activate the "circuits" of a possible grammar in the brain.

Beginning in the early 1960s, Chomsky's theory of generative grammar had an enormous impact. Language acquisition, no longer a subset of general learning theory, became the focus of experimental research by psychologists who were also linguists. In studying the actual speech of children, these researchers departed from Chomsky's theoretical approach, which was unconcerned with linguistic behavior in its raw state.[3] Nevertheless, the psycholinguists tended to confirm many of Chomsky's hypotheses about the "language faculty" and its relation to other cognitive functions. Studies determined, for example, that there is a *natural order* for children's mastery of grammatical structures in both first and second languages, with certain forms acquired later than others.

The Chomskyan revolution raised unsettling questions for language educators. If normal children learn their first language naturally — without behavioral guidance and reinforcement — do teachers have a significant role to play? Indeed, are languages "teachable" in any meaningful sense? Some theorists have answered no to both questions. Yet empirical evidence has shown that individuals differ widely in their ability to learn second languages after early childhood. How could this be true if the process were genetically "programmed"?

One explanation is the *critical period hypothesis*, which posits that lateralization of the language function in the left hemisphere of the brain — a process completed before puberty — impairs the capacity for natural language acquisition. But the strongest evidence for this hypothesis comes from case studies of language deprivation, unusual circumstances in which children fail to acquire a first language in their early years. Its application to second-language acquisition is dubious, according to many researchers. After all, adults can and do learn one or more additional languages, sometimes approaching native-like fluency.[4] Research indicates that older learners may be at a phonological disadvantage, unable to shed their "foreign accents" as easily as children. Some studies also suggest adults may experience a long, gradual decline in their aptitude for acquiring other aspects of language. But, as Ellen Bialystok and Kenji Hakuta argue, the literature shows no point at which language-learning potential declines drastically. Indeed, there is considerable evidence that older language students outpace younger language students, at least in the short term.

Another finding relevant to the teachability question is that schoolchildren also vary substantially in second-language acquisition. In a study of limited-English-proficient (LEP) students aged eight through ten, Lily Wong Fillmore and Barry McLaughlin found that 60 percent became "fairly proficient" in English after three years of schooling, 30 percent "were just beginning to make sense of the new language," and 10 percent "had learned virtually no English at all." While "differences in learners" played a role, these alone could not account for the dramatic disparities. At least as important, the researchers concluded, were "differences in those who provide learners with linguistic input, that is, the speakers of the target language, and . . . differences in the social settings in which the language is learned." In other words, the quality of teaching appears to be a significant variable in second-language acquisition.

The implications of Chomsky's work were not immediately self-evident in the classroom. Since generative grammar posits that language development is a process of rule formation, not habit formation, some of Chomsky's followers devised the so-called *cognitive approach*: a return to the deductive teaching of grammatical rules, combined with exercises to practice them. Yet this approach has proved no more successful than the audiolingual method in developing communicative competence. Both models have been unpopular with students, who tend to describe them as boring and repetitive. These varying methodologies seem to have produced roughly equivalent, mediocre results. Why should this be so?

What both approaches lack is an adequate theory of second-language acquisition that can account for the failures and successes of instructional programs. Why have grammar-based and audiolingual approaches failed to develop communicative skills in foreign-language classrooms, while direct methods have been more successful? Why do second-language immersion approaches benefit some students, but not others? Why do some bilingual education programs produce dramatic gains, while others do not? Why does *more* English exposure sometimes lead to *less* English acquisition by language-minority students?

Theory is essential to developing, testing, and improving an educational treatment, argues Stephen Krashen. It is not enough simply to apply the results of studies showing an advantage for one method over another. "Moving directly from research . . . to teaching is incorrect," he says. "We run the danger of choosing the wrong characteristics to utilize in class. Without theory we cannot distinguish the crucial or distinctive features from the noncrucial or nondistinctive features."

Such a theory has emerged in the past two decades. Its best-known exponents are Krashen, of the University of Southern California, and Jim Cummins, of the Ontario Institute for Studies in Education. But it incorporates the work of many researchers in Canadian immersion, bilingual education, and ESL. More than foreign-language teaching, these three fields are furnishing the data — and reaping the benefits — of a revolutionary new conception of language development.

Learning, Acquisition, and the Input Hypothesis

At its basic level, the theory draws a distinction between language acquisition and language learning. Krashen hypothesizes that fluency in a second tongue cannot be *learned*; that is, conscious mastery of grammar and vocabulary does not prepare us to use the language for communicative purposes. Rather, this proficiency must be *acquired,* or appropriated by the mind, in essentially the same way we pick up our first language. As Locke recognized three centuries ago, babies do just fine without grammar books and dictionaries. Traditionally, human beings of all ages have developed language skills "through communicative practice in real situations," Krashen says. "Even today, with the vast amount of linguistic knowledge available about the languages of the world, it is likely that most ability to communicate in another language is acquired" outside the classroom.

How does acquisition occur? "In one fundamental way," according to Krashen. "We acquire language when we understand it. What is spectacular about this idea is that it happens incidentally, involuntarily, subconsciously, and effortlessly." The key factor is *comprehensible input:* messages in the second language that make sense — ideally, just beyond the competence of the listener, who must strain a bit to understand. Not only vocabulary, but grammatical rules are internalized in this way, as we receive communications in which they are "embedded."

What counts is the quality of second-language exposure, not the quantity. As tourists thrown among strangers speaking a strange tongue, we absorb little of what we hear. On the other hand, when our foreign hosts take the trouble to make themselves intelligible through gestures, context, or simplified speech, we can pick up survival levels of their language. Taking a beginning language course before our trip would facilitate interaction with native speakers, enabling us to acquire much more.

The *input hypothesis* draws on Chomsky's theory of the language faculty, our genetically evolved *language acquisition device* that functions more or less identically in all members of the human species. When this "mental organ" receives intelligible messages in a second language, Krashen explains, the brain has "no choice but to acquire that language, just as the visual system has no choice but to see, and the pancreas has no choice but to operate as pancreases do." We acquire grammatical structures in their natural order, provided that we get sufficient amounts of high-quality input. As our language organ processes this "essential environmental ingredient," Krashen says, it generalizes rules from verbal stimuli, not empirically, but "according to innate principles" of universal grammar.

"The obvious implication," he concludes, "is that language teaching should be based on giving people messages they understand." A non-English-speaking child gets little or no comprehensible input in a sink-or-swim classroom. By contrast, if the child is first provided background knowledge, such as a lesson taught in the native language, English instruction becomes more intelligible. "The first rationale for bilingual education," he postulates, "is that information, knowledge that you get through your first language, makes English input much more comprehensible. It can take something that is utterly opaque and make it transparent."

Krashen likes to illustrate this point with an exercise in decoding a nonsense word, *rouche*. It goes as follows:

> Favorable conditions are necessary to do this activity. That is, you have to have enough *rouche*. If there is too much *rouche*, the object might break. But if conditions are too calm, you will have problems because the *rouche* makes the object go up. If there are obstacles, a serious problem can result because you cannot control the *rouche*. Usually, the *rouche* is most favorable during the spring.

Confronted with this problem by researcher Shirley J. Adams, only 13 percent of experimental subjects could define *rouche*. After background information was provided, 78 percent guessed correctly. The context that made the difference was: "This passage is about flying a kite." (For the benefit of the remaining 22 percent, if they are still wondering, *rouche* means "wind.")

English instruction in subjects other than language can provide a rich source of comprehensible input for LEP children. In such high-context situations, students readily acquire new words and syntax in the second language, Krashen says, especially if they already know something about the subject being discussed: "For ESL students, a well-taught geography lesson, if it's comprehensible, is a language lesson. In fact, it's better than an ESL class, [where] we're always wondering what to talk about." A methodology known as *sheltered English* — sometimes called "sheltered subject matter instruction" — which tailors lessons to LEP students' proficiency in English, is increasingly being incorporated into bilingual education programs, with excellent results.

On the other hand, the input hypothesis explains the pitfalls of an early, and still practiced, methodology in bilingual education known as *concurrent translation*. Using this approach, a teacher gives a lesson in two languages at once, translating each idea on the spot. Naturally, children tend to "tune out" the second language. Having no reason to pay attention, they receive no comprehensible input in English. (For the same reason, Krashen notes, few Americans have learned the Celsius scale: our thermometers alternately display temperatures in the familiar Fahrenheit scale.) Meanwhile, the teacher using concurrent translation has little incentive to make the lesson understandable in the second language, that is, to help the students "negotiate meaning." The ineffectiveness of this method has been confirmed empirically by researchers including Dorothy Legaretta-Marcaida and Lily Wong Fillmore. Various ways of alternating language use — morning-afternoon, different days, "preview-review" lessons — have proved more beneficial. Without instantaneous translations, children become more attentive and motivated to figure out what the teacher is saying in English.

Krashen's theory also underscores the futility of approaches to ESL and foreign-language teaching that stress form over function, whether through memorizing rules (grammar-translation and cognitive methods) or through mindless exercises to illustrate "the structure of the week" (the audiolingual method). Because such techniques have nothing to do with real communication, students have trouble focusing on content; comprehensible input is limited.

"Learning about" a language, knowing how to apply its syntax and usage, can serve a *monitor*, or editing, function. By applying grammatical rules, we can produce more "correct" speech or writing. But conscious knowledge alone is inadequate in communicative situations. First, grammar books are woefully incomplete, when compared with the complex set of rules internalized by native speakers of a language. Linguists "have described only a fraction" of the structure of any natural language (including English), Krashen says, and the percentage taught in class is even smaller. Second, most people are unable or unwilling to learn all these rules. For the tiny minority who can successfully "focus on form" while communicating, the process of recall is still too slow to sustain a normal conversation.

Another misplaced emphasis is teachers' impatience for oral production in a second language before students are ready. "Speaking per se does not cause language acquisition," Krashen argues, but follows from it as "a result of obtaining comprehensible input." This corollary of the input hypothesis explains why LEP children typically go through a "silent period" for as long as six months after entering school and then suddenly start speaking in English. "When they begin to speak, they are not beginning their acquisition," he says. "They are showing off their competence."

That this process occurs naturally does not mean it is easy. Psychological and attitudinal factors can, and usually do, interrupt the smooth functioning of the language acquisition device. Krashen groups such negative influences under the term *affective filter*. These include anxiety, lack of self-confidence, and inadequate motivation to speak the second language, any of which can retard acquisition by keeping comprehensible input from "getting through." Adults seem especially hindered by such barriers.

In this respect young children appear to have an advantage over their elders. Before puberty they tend to be less self-conscious about performance in a new tongue and more comfortable in their interactions with native speakers, an important source of comprehensible input. On the other hand, low self-esteem — which is common among poor, minority children who speak a low-status language — often coincides with anxiety or hostility toward learning in general and toward English in particular. Such attitudes "raise the affective filter," or reduce the amount of input that is comprehensible, thus slowing the acquisition of English.

Instructional techniques have a strong impact on the affective domain, either reinforcing or reducing the obstacles to language acquisition. Teachers who encourage students' attempts to communicate real messages tend to lower the affective filter. By contrast, calling attention to students' errors is likely to heighten their self-consciousness. Failing to respect a child's silent period and attempting to force speech production, rather than allowing English to "emerge" on its own, can be counterproductive. According to Tracy Terrell, creator of the Natural Approach to ESL, this mistake "will at best delay language acquisition . . .

and at worst may create blocks to [it], blocks which later could prove to be quite difficult to remove."

It is here, in the affective realm, that native-language instruction can supply an antidote to common problems in second-language teaching. A bilingual-bicultural curriculum, merely by recognizing the value of a minority language and culture, can enhance a LEP child's self-esteem and provide a more comfortable environment for English acquisition. And this is only the beginning of bilingual education's benefits, Krashen says, benefits that he, as a longtime ESL professional, only came to recognize in recent years.

While research is steadily demonstrating that native-language instruction facilitates English acquisition, the conclusion remains controversial. For many educators as well as lay persons, the notion of "go East to get West" — or study Spanish to learn English — appears to defy common sense. Krashen's own conversion, he recalls, came around 1980, during a discussion of Jim Cummins's work on native-language literacy.

Interaction of First and Second Languages

In exploring how first-language skills influence both second-language acquisition and academic achievement, Cummins has shattered a number of misconceptions about bilingualism. He began in the mid-1970s with a critique of oversimplified notions on both sides of the bilingual education debate. First, Cummins says, there was the "intuitively appealing argument . . . that deficiencies in English should be remediated by intensive instruction in English." In other words, teaching LEP students in their mother tongue seemed to be a costly diversion from English acquisition. Second, there was the popular rationale for bilingual instruction — indeed, the argument had shaped the first decade of federal policy — that children cannot learn in a language they have yet to master. Cummins believed that neither hypothesis could stand up to theoretical examination and that both were contradicted in practice by successful programs.

The "insufficient exposure" idea, still a mainstay of opposition to bilingual education, was summed up by the late Representative John Ashbrook of Ohio. Title VII, he charged, was

> actually preventing children from learning English. Some day somebody is going to have to teach those young people to speak English or else they are going to become public charges. . . . When children come out of the Spanish-language schools or Choctaw-lan-

guage schools which call themselves bilingual, how is our educational system going to make them literate in what will still be a completely alien tongue?

Despite the persistence of such assumptions, Cummins says, they are strongly contradicted by research: "The results of virtually every bilingual program evaluated during the past 50 years show either no relationship or a negative relationship between amount of school exposure to the majority language and academic achievement in that language."

Moreover, there is no reason to believe that first and second languages develop independently in the brain or that knowledge and skills acquired in one are not transferable to the other. A theory of *separate underlying proficiency* — which is implied by fears that native-language instruction comes at the expense of English acquisition — has "not one shred of evidence" to support it, Cummins says. Taken to its logical extreme, this cognitive model would "leave the bilingual in the curious predicament" of being unable to "communicate with himself." When switching languages, such persons would be hard-pressed to translate what they had heard or said.

In opposition to this notion, Cummins advances a hypothesis of *common underlying proficiency*: that skills in different languages inhabit the same part of the brain, reinforcing each other at the base while differing at the surface. In this "dual iceberg" model of the bilingual mind, features that are most cognitively demanding and most detached from contextual aids, such as literacy, "are interdependent across languages." On the other hand, the "surface aspects" of language differ substantially between, say, English and Swahili. Cummins's *interdependence hypothesis* predicts that a child who has mastered the basics of reading and thinking in the first language will perform well on entering a second-language environment. Common underlying proficiency will facilitate a ready transfer of academic skills. Conversely, a child who fails to reach a "threshold level" of development in the mother tongue — e.g., a LEP student who makes a premature transition to English — is likely to be academically retarded in both languages.

Successful bilingual programs provide empirical support for Cummins's theory. Studies in Sweden, Canada, and the United States have shown that language-minority children who immigrate at the ages of eight to eleven, having already learned to read, tend to do better in English than students who arrive earlier, having received little or no instruction in their native tongue. The full range of proficiencies we call literacy appears to transfer readily, even when there are radical differences between writing systems. Research has also shown that skills in content areas like mathematics and social studies, once learned in the first language, are retained when instruction shifts to the second language.

For the input hypothesis, the implications are significant. A LEP child who has kept up in math through Spanish instruction will benefit doubly when studying the subject in a sheltered English classroom. "He will not only get more math; he'll get more English" than a counterpart who is behind in math, Krashen says. "The goal of bilingual programs is English literacy. The route is through the first language. . . . You learn to read by reading, by making sense out of print. Vocabulary grows, grammar grows, spelling ability grows, good writing style grows. It's easier to make sense out of print in a language you understand." Once acquired, those skills and background knowledge provide more context for comprehensible input in English.

Two Types of Language Proficiency

Cummins also takes issue with a prevailing rationale for bilingual education, the common-sense idea that children are inevitably handicapped when there is a mismatch between the languages of home and school. The U.S. Commission on Civil Rights articulated this view in 1975: "Lack of English proficiency is the major reason for language-minority students' academic failure. Bilingual education is intended to ensure that students do not fall behind in subject matter content while they are learning English." However well-intentioned, Cummins says, this generalization has been refuted by the success of immersion programs for English-speaking children in Canada and the United States. From the outset these students learn exclusively through the second language, with English instruction phased in later.

At a theoretical level, Cummins adds, the *language mismatch hypothesis* reflects "an inadequate understanding of what is meant by 'English proficiency.'" This shortcoming is manifested in the policy of *transitional* bilingual education in the United States. Instruction in a child's first language is "much more than an interim carrier of subject matter content," he argues. "Rather, it is the means through which the communicative proficiency which underlies both [native-language] and English literacy is developed." In transitional programs, long favored by federal policymakers, the emphasis is on hurrying children into mainstream classrooms and making them English-dominant. Such an approach, Cummins warns, "is likely to result in the creation of academic deficits in language-minority students."

A premature transition is encouraged, he says, by educators' failure to distinguish between two types of language proficiency. LEP children first develop *basic interpersonal communications skills* (BICS) in English, generally within six months to two years of entering school. This primarily social language, sometimes dubbed "playground English," is heavily dependent on clues — visual gestures, conversational responses, and physical interactions — that are largely absent in the classroom. So BICS alone leaves children ill-equipped for school success, although on the surface they may appear fluent in English. As evidence Cummins cites the high incidence of failure among children who pass through quick-exit bilingual programs. *Partial* or *limited bilingualism* is often the fate of such students, he says. While they may develop adequate conversational skills in both languages, they lack higher-level thinking tools in either.

Cummins hypothesizes that children must attain *cognitive-academic language proficiency* (CALP) if they are to succeed in the "context-reduced, cognitively demanding" activities of reading, writing, mathematics, science, and other school subjects. CALP typically takes five to seven years to develop, according to studies by Cummins and others, and is best nurtured by building on the linguistic foundation that language-minority children bring to school.

Late-Exit Bilingual Model

The theoretical framework developed by Cummins and Krashen prescribes a pedagogy quite different from the quick-exit model of transitional bilingual education. Rather than replacing children's vernacular, it calls for developing their native-language skills — not only in reading, but in other conceptually demanding subjects — while students are receiving communication-based ESL and sheltered English classes. Opportunities for continued study in the first language should be provided throughout elementary school. In dividends of student achievement, the payoff takes time. Yet because of the interdependence of the two languages, Cummins argues, the late exit should entail "no cost to English."

Rudolph Troike, as director of the National Clearinghouse for Bilingual Education in the late 1970s, surveyed evaluation research to isolate characteristics of effective programs. Using this more empirical approach, he constructed a model similar to that espoused by Cummins and Krashen. As Troike explains:

> The more fully that content knowledge and skills are developed in the native language, the faster and more effectively they can be transferred into the second language. This observation indicates

that the best bilingual program might be one in which no English at all is used for the first two years, while students were developing a solid base of knowledge and skills through and in their native language.

Among the exemplary bilingual programs, he adds, "one of the most evident characteristics was that *they all continued through the 6th grade.*" In several cases where language-minority children reached national norms on standardized tests, including English reading, the "effects of bilingual instruction did not begin to become evident until the 5th or 6th grade."

Language of instruction, however, may not be the most significant variable in the success of these late-exit programs. Cummins argues that "sociocultural determinants of minority students' school failure are more fundamental than linguistic factors." Bilingual instruction is merely part of the "educational intervention" that is necessary. To be effective, he says, schooling must "counteract the power relations that exist within the broader society." That is, it must remove the racial and linguistic stigmas of being a minority child. "Power and status relations between minority and majority groups exert a major influence on school performance," he explains. The lower the status of a "dominated group," the lower the academic achievement.

Cummins cites research on the school failure of Finnish immigrants in Sweden, where historically they have faced discrimination, as compared with their success in Australia, where being a Finn carries no social stigma. Children of the Burakumin minority "perform poorly in Japan, but as well as other Japanese students in the United States." Troike gives the example of Maori children in New Zealand, who enter school speaking English, but are soon outperformed by Samoans, a nonstigmatized minority group that arrives with limited English skills.

The schools tend to perpetuate messages about minority children's social position. In reaction, these students frequently exhibit what Cummins calls *bicultural ambivalence*, or shame of the first culture and hostility toward the second. Bilingual teachers report, for example, that some Mexican American children refuse to speak their native language, even though their English skills are poorly developed.

By contrast, "empowering minority students" has academic as well as social benefits, Cummins argues. One way is to encourage them "to take pride in their cultural background," including their native tongue. In the United States this goal is often thwarted by a policy of pressuring students to discard their first language in favor of English. The success of late-exit bilingual programs, Cummins suggests, may owe more to their affirmation of the LEP child's cultural identity than to their linguistic effects. Conversely, he asks, "Is the failure of many minority students in English-only immersion programs a function of cognitive/academic difficulties, or of students' ambivalence about the value of their cultural identity?" Either way, he says, bilingual education is the more appropriate treatment.

Other Frameworks

While the theories of Cummins and Krashen have strongly influenced practitioners in bilingual education, they are not universally accepted by other researchers. Disagreements persist, for example, about the transferability of literacy skills from one language to another — especially when writing systems differ substantially (see Chapters 9 and 10). The idea that a "threshold" of native-language development must be reached to support CALP in a second language has been questioned as difficult to quantify. Perhaps most controversial is Krashen's input hypothesis, which has been criticized as a premature attempt to synthesize existing knowledge into an all-encompassing theory of second-language acquisition.

Krashen's leading critic, Barry McLaughlin, argues that there is no objective way to distinguish the subconscious process of language acquisition from the conscious process of language learning. Nor should these concepts be assigned discrete roles, in his view. "Focusing on form," he says, can serve as more than a "monitor" function for editing a speaker's production; it can also aid in the comprehension of second-language input. McLaughlin characterizes as untestable the hypothesis that acquisition occurs through "comprehensible input" alone. For one thing, he believes that this key concept has never been adequately defined. For another, he disputes the validity of empirical studies supporting any "natural order" of acquiring grammatical structures. As for the problem of how a student makes sense of language beyond his or her level of comprehension, McLaughlin regards contextual clues as a weak explanation. He disputes Krashen's insistence that speech production plays no role in language acquisition, arguing that "comprehensible output" helps learners formulate -and test their own hypotheses about the target language. And he finds the notion of an "affective filter" inadequate to account for individual differences in language learning.

"Krashen's theory . . . is counterproductive," McLaughlin concludes in a 1987 book. "If the field of second-language acquisition is to advance, it cannot, at an early stage of its development be guided by a theory that provides all the answers. . . . More limited and more specific theories are needed at this stage, not a general, all-inclusive theory." While faulting Krashen for a "tendency to make broad and sweeping claims," McLaughlin acknowledges his contributions to second-language pedagogy. He expresses the hope and expectation that the "inadequacies [of the input hypothesis] will doubtless stimulate others to improve on the theory or develop better ones."

So far, however, this has not occurred. Neither Krashen nor any other prominent researcher has responded to these criticisms in detail. Rather than a lively debate, a remarkable silence has reigned. Instead of responding directly to the issues McLaughlin has identified, others have elaborated their own, albeit less ambitious, frameworks.

Lily Wong Fillmore has advanced a model that considers the interactions between second-language learners, the speakers of the target language who serve as sources of input, and "the social setting in which the learning takes place." These components are involved in three complex "processes," which she terms:

> *cognitive* — what goes on in the heads of learners when they inter-act with the data on which they base their language learning; . . .
> *linguistic* — how linguistic knowledge figures in second language learning [including] knowledge . . . possessed by persons who pro-vide input for the learners and the knowledge of a first language possessed by the learners; . . . [and] *social* — the steps by which learners and speakers jointly create social contexts or situations in which communication in the target language is possible.

Wong Fillmore postulates that cognitive strategies differ significantly between first- and second-language acquisition. Unlike young children, second-language learners tend to be old enough to have well developed capacities for "memory, pattern recognition, induction, categorization, generalization, infer-ence, and the like." Naturally they draw upon such skills to analyze "relation-ships between forms, functions, and meanings" in the target language. While spe-cialized language-learning mechanisms still operate (i.e., Chomsky's language acquisition device), these are less prominent than in the case of first-language learning, she argues.

According to this theory, linguistic processes also differ since, unlike young children, second-language learners have first-language knowledge. Awareness of "linguistic categories such as lexical item, clause, and phrase" helps them make "educated guesses" about comparable features of the second language. Meanwhile, speakers of the target language consciously simplify its form and content, using feedback from learners, to make input more comprehensible. Finally, social processes create an environment in which learners use their background knowledge, such as understanding of social rituals, to decipher what target-language speakers are saying. The latter must participate actively to ensure that real communication takes place in a context that is meaningful to both sides.

Notwithstanding differences in explaining how language acquisition/learning takes place, Wong Fillmore's model intersects with Krashen's theory in numerous ways. The pedagogical implications are virtually identical; indeed, they represent an area of wide agreement among bilingual education researchers generally. Amid all the sound and fury, even McLaughlin endorses Krashen's "prescriptions about language teaching . . . basic assumptions about the need to move from grammar-based to communicatively oriented instruction, the role of affective factors in language learning, and the importance of acquisitional sequences in second-language development."

Cognitive Effects of Bilingualism

Preservation of languages and cultures was the overriding goal of bilingual education in the nineteenth century. Today, however, despite the growing popularity of "two-way" or "dual language" programs (see Chapter 11), few schools in the United States strive to develop lasting bilingualism. Continuing native-language instruction beyond the point at which children become proficient in English is politically suspect, even where state laws permit maintenance programs (several do not). At least in part, this resistance is due to lingering suspicions that fluency in more than one language may unduly tax the mind.

Until recent years a majority of educational psychologists regarded bilingualism as a cognitive liability for young children. As George Thompson insisted in a widely used textbook in 1952: "There can be no doubt that the child reared in a bilingual environment is handicapped in his language growth. One can debate the issue as to whether speech facility in two languages is worth the consequent retardation in the common language of the realm."

This conclusion relied largely on studies conducted in the 1920s and 1930s, when anti-immigrant biases may have influenced researchers. As an example of this problem, Kenji Hakuta cites a 1926 study by Florence Goodenough that compared language use among several ethnic groups and found an inverse correlation between median IQ and the amount of foreign speech in the home. Goodenough concluded that either the persistence of minority tongues was "one of the chief factors in producing mental retardation," or that "those nationality groups whose average intellectual ability is inferior" were slow to learn English. In this period, adds Barry McLaughlin, a number of experiments determined that "bilingual children often must think in one language and speak in another, with the result that they become mentally uncertain and confused . . . [or that] bilingualism is a mental burden for children, causing them to suffer mental fatigue."

Such studies, however, lacked controls for subjects' socioeconomic status and other factors that could affect test performance, Hakuta explains. Typically the experiments compared lower-class bilinguals with higher-class monolinguals. On the other hand, he expresses some skepticism about research that has reached the opposite conclusion: that proficiency in more than one language is a decided intellectual advantage.

A 1962 study by Elizabeth Peal and Wallace Lambert was the first of several to conclude that bilingualism enhances cognitive flexibility. Testing a group of ten-year-old French Canadian children, Peal and Lambert found that bilinguals significantly outperformed their monolingual counterparts on verbal and nonverbal intelligence tests. The study has been widely criticized, however, for selecting bilingual subjects whose English and French skills were equally developed. At a young age, the critics pointed out, such *balanced bilinguals* were likely to be gifted children. Their intellectual edge may have accounted for their bilingualism, rather than vice versa.

In his own research for the National Institute of Education, Hakuta sidestepped this methodological problem by focusing solely on children with varying degrees of bilingualism. In a three-year longitudinal study of Hispanic elementary school students in New Haven, Connecticut, he measured nonverbal intelligence (using Raven's Progressive Matrices) and *metalinguistic awareness*, or the aptitude for abstract thinking about language. The results were mixed. More balanced bilingual children clearly performed better on Raven's, but metalinguistic awareness was only weakly related to ability in both languages (it was linked more closely with Spanish proficiency). This was puzzling, Hakuta says, because "the most logical route for bilingualism to have an effect on intelligence is through language."

Over time, however, children in the study who started out with stronger Spanish skills were more likely to become balanced bilinguals. That is, as students progressed through school, there was an increasingly strong correlation between native-language proficiency and English proficiency.[5] This finding is consistent with Cummins's threshold hypothesis that a minimum level of linguistic development must be attained before cognitive skills will transfer between languages.

At the same time, Hakuta observes that bilingualism has social and economic advantages that are unquestionable, if often ignored. He echoes the frustration of many bilingual educators who complain that as a nation we are squandering linguistic resources. Spanish-speaking children, for example, are seldom given an opportunity to continue native-language study after making the transition to English, usually by the 2nd or 3rd grade. As a result, their mother-tongue skills erode or, at best, "fossilize" at that level. On reaching high school, they may enroll in Spanish I — if they are still interested.

Whether the lack of language maintenance programs also represents a wasted opportunity for cognitive development remains a question for further study. Jim Cummins, however, expresses the leaning of most researchers when he says, "Bilingualism is not bad for the brain, and it's probably good."

Notes

1. Echoing the view of classical rhetoricians, Locke acknowledged a place for grammar studies in the native tongue: "If Grammar ought to be taught at any time, it must be to one that can speak the Language already, how else can he be taught the Grammar of it. . . . Grammar being to teach Men not to speak, but to speak correctly and according to the exact Rules of the Tongue." These passages from Locke's *Some Thoughts Concerning Education* are quoted in Dennis E. Baron, *Grammar and Good Taste: Reforming the American Language* (New Haven: Yale University Press, 1982), pp. 120-21.
2. The audiolingual method was also blessed by its timing. The National Defense Education Act of 1958 opened federal coffers to foreign-language teaching for the first time, authorizing grants for the purchase of costly "language lab" equipment and facilities.
3. Chomsky drew a distinction between *performance* in using a language, which is inconsistent, and *competence*, or the intuitive grasp of a language, on which his work has focused.
4. Indeed, Eric Lenneberg, the leader of the critical period school, has argued that first-language acquisition in childhood is the key, because "the cerebral organization for language acquisition as such has taken place. . . . Since natural languages tend to resemble each other in many fundamental respects, the matrix for language skills is present"; quoted in Ellen Bialystok and Kenji Hakuta, *In Other Words: The Science and Psychology of Second-Language Acquisition* (New York: Basic Books, 1994).
5. According to Hakuta, "when [children] first entered the bilingual program, their abilities in Spanish and English were unrelated. However, by the end of three years, there

were correlations as strong as r = .70 between the languages." See Kenji Hakuta, "Cognitive Development in Bilingual Children," paper presented at a meeting of the National Clearinghouse for Bilingual Education and the Georgetown University Bilingual Education Service Center, Rosslyn, Va., July 24, 1985.

7 Alternatives to Bilingual Education

*J*im Cummins and Stephen Krashen could hardly be stronger advocates of bilingual education. And yet their work raises a series of logical questions about the potential of alternative approaches in teaching limited-English-proficient (LEP) children:

- If "comprehensible input" is the key ingredient in acquiring English, why is native-language instruction necessary? Is bilingual education, with its funding demands, teacher shortages, and political headaches, the only workable alternative?

- If communication-based approaches to English as a second language (ESL) look promising, especially when combined with sheltered English techniques for teaching other subjects, why not devote more resources to perfecting such English-only programs?

- If English-speaking children in Québec can learn French through total immersion in the early grades, with all subjects taught in the second language, why can't language-minority children learn English in the same way in the United States?

These issues have come up repeatedly since the 1981 Baker-de Kanter report. After reviewing the literature, the federal researchers concluded: "The case for the effectiveness of transitional bilingual education is so weak that exclusive reliance on this instructional method is clearly not justified." Baker and de Kanter advanced an alternative they hailed as "uniformly successful" wherever it had been evaluated: *structured immersion.*[1] As late as 1985, however, only nine "pure immersion programs" existed in the United States, according to Keith Baker, citing a survey by SRA Technologies as it embarked on a long-term evaluation of this methodology.

Thus far the bulk of research evidence about immersion has come from Canada, where the methodology has proved highly successful with language-*majority* children. Immersion "may or may not" be applicable to language-minority children in this country, according to Baker and de Kanter, but it "shows enough promise" that, at minimum, it should be tried. To evaluate this argument, it is necessary to examine what the Canadian immersion model is and is not.

Origins of French Immersion

In the early 1960s, a dozen English-speaking parents in the Montreal suburb of St. Lambert began meeting to discuss their frustrations over the linguistic and cultural segregation of their community. This was during the period of Canada's history known as the Quiet Revolution. A legacy of social inequality had resulted in the mutual estrangement of the country's two major language communities. Canada's francophone minority was starting to protest its second-class status and limited access to government services. Although the nation was bilingual, most individuals were not. Out of economic necessity, French speakers were about four times more likely to speak English than vice versa, a further source of resentment.

The anglophones of St. Lambert, who favored a more integrated and harmonious society, believed it was important for their children to learn French. Research on language attitudes had shown that bilingual Canadians — whether anglophone or francophone — had more favorable perceptions of the other ethnic group. But the public schools, segregated by both language and religion, were doing a poor job of cultivating bilingualism. According to Olga Melikoff, a leader of the St. Lambert parents,

> Children were graduating from English Protestant schools in this province with little more knowledge of French than their parents had had, despite claims that the programs had been considerably improved over the years. [After twelve years of French study,] their knowledge was not perceptibly superior to that of graduates from English provinces of Canada and was not sufficient to enable the students to communicate with their French-Canadian neighbors. . . . St. Lambert was in 1963 approximately 50 percent French, 50 percent English. It seemed inconceivable to the parents that the children of the two ethnic groups should remain "incommunicado" forever because of language differences.

Clearly, something was wrong with the prevalent audiolingual method of French instruction.

Working with Wallace Lambert and Wilder Penfield, two McGill University researchers on bilingualism, the parents pressed the local Protestant school board to try a new approach. After initial resistance, in the fall of 1965 the board agreed to an experiment in French immersion, while expressing skepticism about its prospects. Fred Genesee, a psychologist at McGill, describes the program's stated goals:

- to provide the participating children with functional competence in both written and spoken aspects of French;
- to promote and maintain normal levels of English language development;
- to ensure achievement in academic subjects commensurate with students' academic ability and grade level; [and]
- to instill in the students an understanding and appreciation of French Canadians, their language, and culture without detracting in any way from the students' identity with and appreciation for English-Canadian culture.

The initial class of twenty-six English-speaking kindergartners entered a school program conducted entirely in French. In this *early total immersion* model, children first learned to read in the second language. One period of English language arts was introduced in the 2nd grade.[2] Gradually the proportion of English was increased in other subjects until it reached about 60 percent by the end of elementary school. In grades 7 through 12, students were offered various courses in French "to maintain and further promote second-language competence," Genesee says.

Immersion students were not mixed with native French speakers, so that instruction could be conducted in a simplified version of the second language, featuring physical and contextual clues to make input comprehensible. Although the teachers were fluent bilinguals, at the outset they spoke to the children in French only. Recognizing that speech production lags comprehension in a second language — a phenomenon that results in a "silent period" of up to six months — the program's designers allowed students to use English to ask questions in class until the end of the 1st grade.

To minimize students' anxiety, instructors avoided "overcorrecting" their errors in French, even as the study of grammar was incorporated. The curriculum placed an emphasis on teaching the second language *incidentally,* without making students conscious of their performance. The expectation, Genesee explains, was that children would be motivated to learn French if instruction fostered "a desire in the student to . . . learn the language to engage in meaningful and interesting communication." In addition, out of concern that the program might breed negative attitudes toward English-Canadian language and culture, pains were taken to ensure "a respect for English."

Judged against the standard of traditional foreign-language classes, immersion was a nearly unqualified success in teaching French. By the end of elementary school, says Jim Cummins, children achieved "native-like levels in the receptive aspects of the language, in their listening skills and their reading skills." Their speaking and writing skills were less developed, probably because they had limited interactions with francophone peers, he says. Nevertheless, the immersion students became "quite fluent and quite comfortable in speaking French, for the most part." But what about their overall progress in school? Did becoming bilingual impede their cognitive growth? Were children falling behind in academic subjects taught in French? Was the program retarding their English-language abilities?

To the relief of parents and researchers alike, the experiment had none of these potential consequences. It confirmed the hypothesis that bilingualism could be attained *at no cost* to achievement in English or other subjects. Pupils can achieve functional competence in a second language, Lambert says,

> without detriment to their home language skill development; without falling behind in the all-important content areas of the curriculum, indicating that the incidental acquisition of French does not distract the students from learning new and complex ideas; without any form of mental confusion or loss of normal cognitive growth; and without a loss of identity or appreciation of their own ethnicity. Most important of all in the present context, immersion pupils also develop a deeper appreciation for French Canadians and a more balanced outlook toward them by having learned about the group and its culture.

Changes in the students' social attitudes were somewhat contradictory, however. Alongside a strong identification with the culture of France, their reactions to French Canadians were less positive, especially as ethnic tensions heightened in Québec during the late 1960s. Functional bilingualism did enable these anglophones to form friendships with French-speaking children. Yet their contacts with members of the other language community remained unrepresentative.[3]

As anglophone parents learned about the success of French immersion at St. Lambert, demand for the program spread throughout Canada. By the early 1990s, enrollment had surpassed 250,000 students. Program variations now include *delayed immersion,* beginning in the middle elementary grades, and *late immersion,* beginning early in secondary school. Where school administrators have remained resistant, Genesee says, efforts to persuade them have usually succeeded with the aid of a pesky group known as Canadian Parents for French.

Immersion for Language Minorities?

There are virtually no English immersion programs for French-speaking children in Canada. Nor should there be, according to the unanimous view of Canadian-immersion researchers, who insist that this approach is appropriate only for language-majority children. Baker and de Kanter's proposal to substitute immersion for bilingual education in the United States is especially dangerous, the researchers warn. Richard Tucker, coauthor of the major study of the St. Lambert experiment, explains: "Although the general assertion that many children can acquire a second language and content material coincidentally is, in all probability correct, it does not imply that the most effective way to educate every child, regardless of demographic, sociopolitical, or other circumstances, is by total [immersion] in a second language." That is, social and linguistic variables are crucial in determining whether an educational treatment will be helpful or harmful to students.

The St. Lambert curriculum has proved effective because it provides sustained amounts of comprehensible second-language input in a low-anxiety environment. But this is only part of the story. As practiced in Canada, immersion is a *bilingual* program, which aims to develop students' cognitive-academic language proficiency in English as well as French. A measure of its success is that, when tested in English, children do well in subjects they have learned in French — an indication that skills and knowledge are transferring across languages.

Early schooling in the second language does not appear to impede first-language development for these students. For minority children, however, initial neglect of the native tongue often retards proficiency in either language. Why the contrast in outcomes? According to Wallace Lambert, immersion means fundamentally different things to each group. For native speakers of the dominant language, the educational treatment is *additive bilingualism,* as exemplified by Canadian immersion. For language-minority children it amounts to *subtractive bilingualism*, the philosophy behind structured immersion in the United States. This distinction reflects the programs' varying goals, as well as sociolinguistic variables beyond educators' control.

Among English-speaking children in Canada, French immersion poses no threat to native-language development, Lambert says, because English is the high status tongue throughout the country and even in the province of Québec. If immersion programs ignored English altogether, barring major social upheavals, anglophone students would probably remain secure in their ethnic identity. Certainly they would have no shortage of opportunities to perfect their English skills. In the St. Lambert model, immersion offers pupils an opportunity to add a language to their repertoire, *without giving up their mother tongue*. Bilingualism becomes an educational "extra" that will pay social, academic, and economic dividends in the future. Lambert adds that there are likely to be cognitive benefits as well.

For French-speaking children, the social and cultural dominance of English makes the first language "vulnerable to neglect and replacement," he argues. Therefore, an English immersion program "would result in a slow subtraction of the students' French and its replacement by English." Subtractive bilingualism,

Lambert explains,

> can be devastating for children [who] are induced through social
> pressure in the school, community, and even in the home to put
> aside their home language and replace [it] as quickly and thorough-
> ly as possible with English. . . . The trouble is that for most lan-
> guage-minority children, the home language has been the critical
> linguistic system associated with the development of basic concepts
> from infancy on. It would be an enormous mental-gymnastic feat
> for these children to replace and reprogram these concepts in
> English . . . and at the same time, try to keep up with English-
> speaking peers in subject matters that introduce new ideas which
> build on basic concepts. . . . [They] are placed in a psycholinguistic
> limbo where neither the home language nor English is useful as a
> tool of thought and expression.

It should come as no surprise, then, that subtractive approaches, including early-
exit bilingual education, produce a disproportionate number of children who fall
behind in class, question their ethnic identity, and drop out of school.

In choosing among educational treatments for promoting bilingualism,
Lambert and Tucker have formulated the following guideline: "Priority in early
years of schooling should be given to the language . . . least likely to be developed otherwise — in other words, the language most likely to be neglected."
This principle, they say, should signal a strong warning against structured immersion.

Unlike the *bilingual enrichment* approach of St. Lambert, the Baker-de
Kanter model is a *monolingual remedial* method, calculated to replace the languages of minority children. Rather than encouraging proficiency in two languages, structured immersion emphasizes linguistic and cultural assimilation. As
such, it is a "trivialized version" of Canadian immersion, argues researcher
Eduardo Hernández-Chávez. Regarded narrowly, "as a methodology for language
development, the two types of programs differ only in detail," he says. "On the
other hand, they differ sharply in terms of their principles and their structure."

Canadian immersion not only promotes fluent bilingualism, but also uses
second-language acquisition to strengthen skills in the first language. Explaining
the latter point, Lambert and Tucker quote the Russian psychologist L. S.
Vygotsky on the reciprocal benefits of bilingualism:

The child can transfer to a new language the system of meanings

he already possesses on his own. The reverse is also true — a foreign language facilitates mastering the higher forms of the native
language. The child learns to see his language as one particular system among many, to view its phenomena under more general categories, and this leads to awareness of his linguistic operations.
Goethe said with truth that "he who knows no foreign language
does not truly know his own."

By contrast, structured immersion treats children's native-language ability as a
handicap to be overcome. It interrupts students' linguistic development before
they reach "a minimum threshold of cognitive-academic skills," making it unlikely that they will ever attain full proficiency in English, says Hernández-Chávez.
"Academic achievement, related language proficiencies, and cognitive abilities all
suffer."

U.S. Evidence on Structured Immersion

Keith Baker rejects these "theoretical" objections to immersion for language-minority children in the United States, insisting that the method must be
judged in practice. In effect, Baker advances his own hypothesis (so far unsupported by program data) about why structured immersion *should* work. "Practice
makes perfect," he argues. "English is best learned by using it as much as possible throughout the school day."

Testing this assertion has been problematic, since there are only a handful
of English-only immersion programs in existence. Although California's bilingual
education law gave school districts the chance to test such "planned variations,"
few ever petitioned to do so, according to state officials. Under a Texas statute,
eight districts tried English-only approaches with LEP children, but the pilot projects ended in 1987 after most of them failed, reports Ramón Magallanes of the
Texas Education Agency. In Houston, for example, the immersion students who
scored highest on achievement tests were among the 60 percent who were
repeating a grade.

With immersion being hailed as a panacea on the nation's editorial pages,
some fear it could function more as a placebo, a sugar pill to conceal the neglect
of LEP children. In 1986, Philadelphia introduced a curriculum known as ESOL
Plus Immersion to cope with its rising enrollment of immigrants and refugees.
The rationale, expressed by one district administrator, was that students would
learn English faster if they could "interact with native speakers." In practice,

"immersion" meant simply that LEP students would spend more time in main-stream classrooms, where they understood little of what went on, and less time receiving ESL or native-language instruction. Community activists, teachers, and parents attacked the program as a return to sink-or-swim.

The ambiguity of program labels also complicates research to evaluate alternatives to bilingual education. Inevitably, when models are compared, disputes arise over terminology. So-called immersion programs that have been favorably evaluated, such as the McAllen, Texas, kindergarten experiment cited by Baker and de Kanter, often turn out to share similarities with bilingual education; that is, they employ native-language instruction in various guises.

In the summer of 1987, news of a moderately successful "bilingual immersion" program in El Paso, Texas, became a public relations coup for the enemies of bilingual education when a journalist mischaracterized it as an English-only approach. Repeated in other press accounts, the error was featured prominently in the 1988 report of the National Advisory and Coordinating Council on Bilingual Education.[4] In fact, according to the El Paso school district, this was a "true bilingual education program" that included sixty to ninety minutes of Spanish instruction each day. On some standardized tests the bilingual immersion students performed better, on others worse, than their counterparts in classrooms featuring greater amounts of native-language instruction. In most cases, the district's evaluation found, there were no significant differences between the two groups.

Nevertheless, immersion enthusiasts continued to point to El Paso as proof of their method's superiority. In 1993, Rosalie Porter, director of the Institute for Research in English Acquisition and Development, released yet another evaluation of the district's programs under the headline "Immersion Boosts Student Achievement, Study Finds." According to the study by Russell Gersten, John Woodward, and Susan Schneider, 4th, 5th, and 6th grade students in the "bilingual immersion" program outscored their peers in transitional bilingual education (TBE) on the Iowa Test of Basic Skills in language, reading, mathematics, and vocabulary. By the 7th grade, however, the differences between the two programs were "negligible." In other words, children receiving more native-language instruction eventually "caught up" with those receiving somewhat less native-language instruction.

Obviously, such findings could be interpreted in numerous ways, and the study provided few details about how the native language was used; variables other than language of instruction may also have contributed to the slight differences between the two programs. But Porter had no hesitation in concluding:

"The data definitely dispel the notion that transitional bilingual education is a superior approach to English immersion. While both methods seem equally effective for teaching language minority children, they take different periods of time to achieve the same academic results." Because it "boosted" English achievement-test scores faster, El Paso's bilingual immersion program proved more "cost effective . . . in a time of tightening school budgets," Porter argued.

Such politicized approaches do little to resolve the pedagogical issues. Indeed, they obscure a central question: What distinguishes structured immersion from transitional bilingual education, especially in cases where TBE features limited instruction in the native language?[5]

Keith Baker has offered contradictory answers, alternately saying that

> immersion programs use the native language only . . . to clarify a point that was not understood when it was taught in English;

and that

> most immersion programs also teach language arts [in the native language] for 30 to 60 minutes a day.

Baker's critics maintain that his vagueness on this point muddles the discussion of pedagogical alternatives. Ann Willig accuses Baker of confusing the concepts *program* and *methodology*. "Immersion is a specific and successful methodology," she says, "that can be used in any type of program, including a bilingual program." For example, sheltered English, a form of immersion, is one component of the highly regarded Case Studies bilingual curriculum (see Chapter 8).

Such debates over program labels are hardly trivial. According to the hypotheses of Cummins and Krashen, how the native language is employed can be crucial to the success of an educational treatment. The questions involve quality, not quantity: Does the program use the mother tongue to provide translations or to cultivate cognitive-academic language proficiency? Is contextual information taught in the native language so as to facilitate the acquisition of English? Do teachers employ strategies that encourage the transfer of academic skills from one language to the other?

When asked for evidence that monolingual-English immersion is effective, Reagan administration officials often cited a program in Uvalde, Texas. Evaluator Russell Gersten described this compensatory model as follows:

> All academic instruction . . . is conducted in English; no prior
> knowledge of English is assumed. Teachers and paraprofessionals
> translate problematic words into questions phrased in the child's
> native language. The carefully controlled vocabulary in the direct
> instruction programs allows teachers to "preteach" any new words
> that come up in the math, reading, or language lessons. Ninety-
> eight percent of the students in the program are Hispanic; 60 to 80
> percent are classified as limited-English-proficient upon entry. The
> majority of the 15 teachers and all 15 paraprofessionals are bilin-
> gual. . . . There is a high rate of parent and community involve-
> ment in the program, which has been in existence for 16 years.

Gersten's 1984 study reported that students scored near national norms in language arts and mathematics, and at the 34th percentile in reading after four years
of English-only instruction. Because no comparable group of students was
receiving bilingual instruction in Uvalde, Gersten contrasted these results with
the scores of bilingual program students in the 1978 Title VII evaluation by the
American Institutes for Research.[6]

Again, however, critics have questioned whether a clear line of demarcation
can be drawn between this immersion approach and quick-exit bilingual models
that make similar use of the native language. They also note that, lacking a comparison group, the Gersten study falls short of the Baker-de Kanter standards for
"acceptable" evaluation research.

Longitudinal Immersion Study

SRA Technologies, which was commissioned to conduct a $4.1 million
study of alternative methodologies for the U.S. Department of Education, worked
hard to overcome such problems in research design.[7] The objective was to compare the effectiveness "early-exit" bilingual education — a.k.a. TBE — the category that has received most Title VII funding over the years, with two other con-
tenders, "immersion strategies" in English and "late-exit" or developmental bilingual education. David Ramírez, the study's principal investigator, went to great
lengths to ensure that comparison groups were carefully matched. Rather than
add together apples and oranges, then take an average — the crude procedure
of the Baker-de Kanter report — he paid close attention to consistency in program labeling and selected only the best examples of each approach, so as to
minimize the effects of poor implementation.

Initial classroom monitoring determined that the immersion programs were conducted in English more than 90 percent of the time, with the native language used "on an informal basis" for purposes of clarification. The early-exit programs, which mainstreamed children after two to three years, used English 65 to 75 percent of the time. And the late-exit programs, which extended bilingual instruction through the 6th grade, used increasing amounts of English — from 10 percent in kindergarten to 60 percent by the 4th grade. This four-year longitudinal study involved more than 2,000 Spanish-speaking students enrolled in nine school districts in California, Florida, New Jersey, New York, and Texas. Student achievement was monitored beginning with the 1984-85 school year and ending in 1987-88.

Interim findings from this research became a closely guarded secret after its first-year data were leaked to the press in 1986. The sneak preview revealed that students in bilingual classrooms were outperforming their peers in immersion classrooms — in reading, language, and mathematics — and that the children who scored highest *when tested in English* were enrolled in late-exit programs that featured the most Spanish instruction. These findings were "unexpected," according to a memorandum by Ramírez. Certainly they came as a shock to "time-on-task" theorists, who asserted that the more English children heard in school, the faster they would acquire English.

Embarrassed by the disclosure, the study's project officer insisted that no conclusions should be drawn from a single year's scores. "It's like trying to call the winner of the Kentucky Derby based on the horse that reaches the first pole," argued Keith Baker. With his own horse trailing badly, however, Baker was inclined to modify his theory about the value of "using English as much as possible throughout the school day." Extended exposure to the second language, he hypothesized in April 1986, "may fatigue the learner so that learning becomes very difficult." (Soon thereafter, he resumed his optimistic statements about the promise of structured immersion.[8]) Meanwhile, the Department of Education clamped a tight lid on the immersion study and refused to release further test data, despite requests to do so from Capitol Hill.

On both sides expectations for the study remained high, and so did the political stakes. If the early findings held up, they would relieve some of the pressure to divert Title VII funding to English-only programs. If not, opponents of bilingual education would have a formidable new weapon to brandish in policy battles.

When finally released in February 1991, however, the Ramírez report pro-

vided less clarity than many had anticipated. For the most part, only minor differences in achievement were detected between students in immersion and early-
exit bilingual classrooms. While children clearly excelled in the late-exit classrooms, for technical reasons their performance was not directly compared with
that of their peers. The Department of Education, in releasing the study, declared
"the three most common bilingual education methods" [sic] to be "effective in
teaching LEP students." Therefore, "school administrators can choose the method
best suited to their students, confident that, if well implemented, it will reap positive results."

This simplistic message was duly disseminated by the press. While
reporters had the option of purchasing a copy of the full report (for approximately $130), none did so, according to a department spokeswoman. News sto-
ries, relying on the department's press release and an "executive summary," thus
ignored or muddied several of the study's more significant findings. These may
be summarized as follows:

- In immersion and early-exit programs — which taught children almost
  exclusively in English (with Spanish used only for clarification) or mostly
  in English (two-thirds to three-quarters of the time) — academic growth
  roughly paralleled that of English-proficient children in regular classrooms.
  But in both immersion and early-exit classrooms, student achievement lev-
  eled off well below national norms.
- In late-exit programs — which featured the most native-language instruction (90 percent in kindergarten, declining to 40 percent in grades 4
  through 6) — progress in student achievement accelerated over time,
  approaching national norms by the 6th grade.
- These outcomes were further confirmed by variations among the late-exit
  programs themselves. In one district that lapsed into an early-exit model
  during the study, scores fell off dramatically. In another where Spanish
  was used most extensively, children's progress was most dramatic.
- Regardless of treatment, students generally took five years or longer to
  acquire academic proficiency in English. Only one-fourth of the children
  in immersion programs and one-fifth of those in early-exit programs had
  been mainstreamed after four years.
- In late-exit programs, parents were more likely to help with homework
  and take an interest in their children's schooling, apparently because of
  their greater familiarity with the language.

- Across the board, parents favored approaches that would give children a chance to develop competency in their native language as well as in English; only the late-exit programs offered this choice.
- In all three programs, teacher-centered methodologies provided a passive learning environment that gave students limited encouragement to think critically or to speak out in class.

Sensitive to the controversies surrounding bilingual education, David Ramírez chose to take a cautious statistical approach in analyzing his data. This meant paying close attention to comparability among students, teachers, communities, and a host of other variables. Because none of the districts that offered late-exit programs also provided immersion or early-exit programs, he explains, it was impossible to make comparisons among all three while controlling for "school-level effects." Only immersion and early-exit approaches could be matched directly against each other.

Ramírez did draw indirect comparisons, however, by analyzing growth curves in student achievement. The study found that the progress of immersion and early-exit students slowed down by the 3rd grade; their achievement paralleled but remained well below national norms. By contrast, late-exit students demonstrated a steeper learning curve; while they had yet to overtake their English-speaking peers by the 6th grade, they showed promise of doing so. Ramírez believes the implications are significant:

> If your instructional objective is to help kids stay where they are — around the 25th percentile — then give them immersion or early exit and they'll keep their place in society. If your concern is to help kids catch up to the norming population, use more primary language. In the late-exit programs, they're growing faster in content areas and in English, too. It's really clear that you will not slow down a child's acquisition of English by providing large amounts of native-language instruction.

While the study concludes that structured immersion can be a viable alternative for LEP children, Ramírez adds a number of qualifiers. Immersion teachers need special training in oral language development and literacy; they need to master "sheltered English" techniques; and they need to be sufficiently bilingual to provide clarification in the students' native language. "The danger," he explains, "is in lifting the cap [on funding for alternative programs] without any clear specifications. When most districts talk about immersion, they mean taking regular teachers and placing them in a bilingual classroom, looking for a way to exit kids as quickly as possible." In such cases students receive little more than sink-or-swim, with some ESL on the side. "We know that doesn't work," Ramírez says. In a few situations — for example, where bilingual teachers are unavailable or where students speak numerous languages — a quality immersion approach "may be all we can do," he concedes. "But is it really what we want? It doesn't cost you any more to provide a late-exit program than an immersion program. It's just a philosophical or political question. Do you want to help kids catch up? Or do you want to keep them down on the farm?"

Nevertheless, the Ramírez report failed to transcend some perennial pitfalls of evaluation research, according to an expert panel of the National Research Council (NRC).[9] After a detailed review, the panel declined to endorse most of the study's findings because of perceived weaknesses in its design and execution. Statistical techniques used to compensate for preëxisting differences were inadequate, the NRC concluded. It questioned whether comparability had been achieved between programs in different school districts and even in different schools within the same district. Thus it rejected the growth-curve analysis in which late-exit programs appeared to be superior.

The NRC did, however, accept as "compelling" one finding of the Ramírez report: when comparisons were made between kindergarten and 1st grade classrooms in the same school, early-exit bilingual students scored significantly higher in English reading than the immersion students. More generally, the panel found no evidence that native-language instruction impedes the acquisition of English. To the contrary, it noted the "convergence" of evidence in the Ramírez report and other research that "suggest[s], under certain conditions, the importance of primary-language instruction in second-language achievement in language arts and mathematics."

Submersion, Plus ESL

Where native-language development is absent, its benefits are sometimes most obvious. English-as-a-second-language programs alone, even if well designed and implemented, have failed to provide the short-cut to English acquisition that some enthusiasts had predicted, according to a study of this approach in Fairfax County, Virginia.

Critics of bilingual education often describe ESL as an "alternative method" for teaching children with limited English skills. This is somewhat misleading, considering that ESL is an integral component of virtually every bilingual program in the United States. Since 1976, the major professional organization in the field, Teachers of English to Speakers of Other Languages, has firmly endorsed bilingual education and recognized its contribution to second-language acquisition. As a practical matter, however, because of bilingual-teacher shortages, many LEP students are still assigned to ESL-only programs — or, more accurately, to submersion in regular classrooms combined with varying amounts of ESL. Usually this means "pullout" language instruction for a brief period each day, sometimes in conjunction with sheltered English classes in other subjects.

Stand-alone ESL is the only feasible approach in school districts where LEP students come from diverse backgrounds, argues Esther Eisenhower, architect of the Fairfax County program. "Given scattered and multilingual populations like ours," she says, "the children can achieve just as well [in an] English-only treatment — if it is provided properly. We would be hard-put to find the number of teachers [needed] to deliver the Fairfax County curriculum" in seventy-five languages. In 1980, citing the district's large investment and achievement test scores that suggested ESL students were making progress, Eisenhower and her superiors convinced the federal Office for Civil Rights to approve a Lau plan for the district that included no bilingual education (see Chapter 2).

Fairfax thus became a test case for the ESL "alternative," whose effectiveness was unknown. As Rudolph Troike observed around that time, "There is extraordinarily little evidence for English-only programs showing much promise. There is an enormous methodological base in ESL, oriented toward whether one method works better or not," but almost no research assessing the effectiveness of ESL *as a substitute* for bilingual instruction. The Fairfax model represented an improvement over sink-or-swim, most educators agreed, but how significant an improvement remained a matter of debate. Were children likely to catch up with their peers after learning English, or to suffer long-term harm from the neglect of their native language? Were some LEP students more at risk than others?

Some answers are offered by a 1988 study, the first of its kind in the United States, which compared the rates at which children of different ages achieve cognitive-academic proficiency in a second language. This is basic research focusing on a narrow range of issues, not a full-fledged program evaluation. Yet it provides a rare glimpse at the outcomes of an ESL-only treatment. All subjects in the study were currently or formerly enrolled in Fairfax County's ESL program. Though diverse in ethnic makeup — Hispanics, Koreans, Vietnamese, Chinese, and Cambodians, among others — the 2,014 participants were generally "advantaged children," based on socioeconomic status in their home countries and their parents' strong middle-class aspirations. The researchers, Virginia Collier and Wayne Thomas of George Mason University, analyzed achievement test scores from the district's massive data base, covering student performance in the 4th, 6th, 8th, and 11th grades over a six-year period beginning in 1981.

The results came as a shock to Fairfax administrators: the ESL-only students took four to nine years to reach grade level in English, according to Collier and Thomas. The age-group differences were even more striking. Children who arrived at ages five to seven scored poorly in all subjects, as compared with their counterparts who entered the ESL program at ages eight to eleven — usually after learning to read in their native language before immigrating. By the 6th grade, these later arrivals were outperforming earlier arrivals who had been in the United States at least two or three years longer. "The only known variable that differentiated" the two groups, the researchers said, was the limited mother-tongue schooling of the five-to-seven-year-olds. More English instruction did not correlate with more English acquisition.

A third group in the study, those who arrived at ages twelve to fifteen, did the worst, a phenomenon the researchers attributed to the quicker pace and higher cognitive demands of the upper grades. In mathematics achievement, newly arrived 8th graders scored consistently above the 50th percentile, reflecting the transfer of skills learned back home (particularly in Asia, where math curricula tend to be more demanding than in this country). Over the next three to four years — the time it took these students to acquire English — they slipped steadily behind. By the time their scores began to rise again, high school was nearly over. Collier and Thomas concluded that native-language instruction would benefit this oldest group of students by helping them keep up in other content areas, and also the youngest group by providing a foundation for cognitive language skills.

Among basic researchers on second-language acquisition, these results are regarded as highly significant. They confirm Cummins's "threshold hypothesis" that literacy and other skills transfer to a second tongue only after a minimum level of cognitive-academic language proficiency (CALP) has been achieved in the first. They are also consistent with his prediction that CALP takes five to seven years to develop in a second language. Contrary to time-on-task assumptions, English-only approaches do nothing to speed up the process. Indeed, they may slow it down precisely because they fail to utilize and cultivate the skills children have acquired in their native language.

Esther Eisenhower, who has long insisted that bilingual education is inappropriate for Fairfax County, conceded that the study's findings, especially the sharp differences in performance by age group, "threw me for a loop." At the same time, she argued that the superior results for the eight-to-eleven-year-old group had vindicated her ESL-only approach. "You cannot tell me that bilingual education is the only way to serve all populations all of the time," she said, noting the difficulty of recruiting teachers competent in Asian languages. What about the Spanish-speaking children who could be helped in bilingual classrooms? Eisenhower responded: "I cannot, in all fairness, say that the 20 percent of Hispanics we have here are entitled to a treatment that the Asians are not."

Echoing other enthusiasts of English-only methodologies, Eisenhower warned that bilingual education may keep children from entering the mainstream: "While you're teaching about Mayan culture, you're neglecting to teach the child how to navigate American society. [Educators] are delinquent in their duties if they don't teach these skills from the first day."[10] This "common sense" view, reinforced by Anglocentric prejudices and linguistic myths, prevails despite mounting evidence to the contrary. It is contradicted not only by basic research in second-language acquisition, but increasingly by program experience.

Notes

1. Baker and de Kanter popularized this term for English-only immersion to distinguish it from *submersion*. Unlike sink or swim, the researchers said, this approach provides a "structured" second-language environment for LEP students.
2. Later variations of the program have sometimes postponed use of the native language until grade 3.
3. The immersion students had some contact with French-speaking Protestant children, largely of lower socioeconomic status, who attended separate classes at the St. Lambert school. Stigmatized as academically slow and prone to disciplinary problems, however, the francophone children were not well accepted when integrated into some of the immersion classes. See Wallace E. Lambert and G. Richard Tucker, *Bilingual Education of Children: The St. Lambert Experiment* (Rowley, Mass.: Newbury House, 1972), pp. 160-63.
4. Robert Rosier, a partisan of U.S. English who edited this report, declined to correct several factual mistakes about the El Paso program after they were pointed out to him by Rosita Apodaca, chairwoman of the advisory council. Apodaca and five other members filed a minority report in protest.
5. For example, in 1985, when school officials in Elizabeth, New Jersey, initiated an

immersion program (as part of the Ramírez study for SRA Technologies), they told parents it would use about the same amount of native language as the district's TBE program had done in the past.

6. In AIR's national sample, collected in the mid-1970s, comparable "low income Hispanic students in bilingual programs [scored in reading] at or below the 20th percentile," according to Gersten.

7. This contract was later reassigned to Aguirre International, an educational research firm based in San Mateo, California.

8. After reviewing the study's final report, Baker changed his mind once again. In an August 1991 interview, he opined: "Bilingual education works, but not the way Cummins says it does. It works in the first three years, but after that point it flips — children do better in all-English programs." Though he had yet to work out any theoretical explanation, he said, these results could be due to "mental fatigue" among LEP children in English-only classrooms.

9. The council, a branch of the National Academy of Sciences, was asked to review the Ramírez report by the U.S. Department of Education. Along with authorities on statistics and research design, the fourteen-member panel included two experts on language-minority education, Kenji Hakuta of Stanford University and Luis Moll of the University of Arizona.

10. Since Eisenhower's retirement in 1990, the Fairfax County Schools have quietly initiated some limited experiments with bilingual approaches.

Practice

8 Theory into Practice: The Case Studies Project

$\mathcal{B}$ilingual education existed on a tiny scale in the United States before Title VII. In 1969, the first year of federal funding, there were a few hundred experienced teachers nationwide, virtually no native-language materials, and only limited models for curriculum and methodology. After a fifty-year hiatus, bilingual education was starting again virtually from scratch. "Imagine trying to construct an impressive, majestic brick cathedral without bricks or mortar, with inexperienced workers and very limited resources for training them," writes María Medina Swanson, an early president of the National Association for Bilingual Education. "Yet that is how most bilingual programs got off the ground."

It was another decade, following the U.S. Supreme Court's *Lau v. Nichols* decision (1974) and the federal government's aggressive civil rights enforcement, before most school districts got around to trying the idea. Inevitably, with a limited research base on which to build, there was much trial and error in the design of bilingual programs, and overnight successes were rare. It was a disorderly, uneven process. Still, there was no other way for practitioners to amass experience or researchers to test hypotheses.

Bilingual educators were outraged in 1978 by Title VII's mediocre report card from the American Institutes for Research (AIR). With its crude methodology, the study lumped the good with the bad, the failures with success stories. It obscured the growing number of schools in which formerly limited-English-proficient (LEP) children were beginning to score near national norms for the first time (see Chapter 5).

Yet AIR's critics had to admit that serious shortcomings continued to plague many bilingual programs. Some were bilingual in name only, making limited use of LEP students' native language because qualified teachers were in short supply. Other schools favored instruction in English because it was the language of achievement tests, or because officials felt external pressures to "mainstream" children quickly. Many programs continued to employ discredited methodologies, such as concurrent translation and grammar-based approaches to English as a second language (ESL). Bilingual classrooms, perceived as compensatory, were frequently ghettoized within a school or neglected by administrators, while minority languages were treated with disrespect.

LEP children tended to perform poorly in such programs, which shared little in common with proven approaches to bilingual education, as identified by both basic research and evaluation research. Increasingly, evidence was confirming the importance of native-language development, communication-based ESL, and bicultural efforts to enhance students' self-esteem. But these findings were slow to reach the classroom teacher. Even where there was enthusiasm for bilingual approaches, educational theory was having a limited effect on educational practice. It was in this context that the Case Studies project began.

Theory First

Recognizing that the implications of research are rarely self-evident, in 1980 the California Department of Education set out to develop a "theoretically sound" model for bilingual education and to test it in selected school districts. Known as Case Studies in Bilingual Education, the project was designed "to bridge the gap between educational research and program practices." The emphasis was on school improvement rather than on further effectiveness research. (No attempt was made, for example, to include comparison groups.) At the same time, state officials hoped that Case Studies would yield program experience that could be generalized to help other schools in serving language-minority students.

It was understood that such an ambitious project would take time. "We weren't just going to do a workshop on basic principles and then walk into the classroom and see instruction change overnight," recalls Norm Gold, then a consultant in the California Bilingual Education Office. Schools' needs had to be assessed. A curriculum had to be developed. Teachers had to be trained and, in many cases, won over to a new approach. A range of logistical hurdles had to be cleared.

Before undertaking any of these practical tasks, the first step was to summarize the state of the art in second-language acquisition. The California officials solicited articles from researchers in cognitive psychology, linguistics, and literacy. Contributors included two of the leading theorists, Jim Cummins and Stephen Krashen, as well as researchers on effective teaching for language-minority children: Dorothy Legaretta-Marcaida, an expert on native-language methodologies; Tracy Terrell, an ESL program designer; and Eleanor Thonis, a reading specialist. The result, *Schooling and Language-Minority Students: A Theoretical Framework,* was published in December 1981, a 218-page book that elaborated a coherent theory of second-language acquisition and its practical applications in the classroom. The Bilingual Education Office further synthesized the research into five "basic principles for the education of language-minority students" (see p. 161).

Meanwhile, the state consultants sought out schools where the theory's validity could be tested. Using a computer search, they identified 134 schools that met their criteria: K through 6 programs, large concentrations of LEP children whose native language was Spanish, and "a core group of qualified bilingual teachers." Of the thirty schools that expressed interest, five were selected for the project in late 1981. While the sites were geographically and demographically diverse, from a small town on the Mexican border to an urban barrio, the students had much in common: poverty, limited English skills, and chronic underachievement. All five schools seemed to be trying hard to make bilingual education work, but with LEP enrollments that had increased by 46 percent over the previous four years, their students' test scores were among the lowest in California. The 3rd graders at one site were at the 2nd percentile in English reading, in another at the 6th percentile.

Basic Principles of the Case Studies Project

The following theoretical principles, along with their practical implications in the classroom, form the pedagogical basis of the Case Studies project. They are adapted from *Basic Principles for the Education of Language-Minority Students: An Overview,* a 1983 publication of the California State Department of Education.

1. For bilingual students, the development of proficiencies in both the native language and English has a positive effect on academic achievement.
2. Language proficiency is the ability to use language for both basic communicative tasks and academic purposes.
3. For limited-English-proficient students, reaching the "threshold" of native-language skills necessary to complete academic tasks forms the basis for similar proficiency in English. Implications:
   - Students are provided substantial amounts of instruction in and through the native language.
   - Initial reading classes and other cognitively demanding subjects are taught in the native language.
   - Sufficient texts and supplementary materials are available in the native language.
   - A sufficient number of well-trained teachers with high levels of native-language proficiency are available to provide instruction.
   - Teachers avoid mixing English and the native language during instruction.
   - Teachers accept regional and nonstandard varieties of the native language.
4. Acquisition of basic communicative competency in a second language is a function of comprehensible second-language instruction and a supportive environment. Implications:
   - Comprehensible second-language input is provided through both English-as-a-second-language (ESL) classes and sheltered English instruction in academic content areas.
   - When content areas are used to provide comprehensible English input, subjects are selected in which the cognitive demands are low to moderate.
   - ESL instruction is communication-based rather than grammar-based and is characterized by the following: (a) content is based on the students' communicative needs; (b) instruction makes extensive use of contextual clues; (c) the teacher uses only English, but modifies speech to students' level and confirms their comprehension; (d) students are permitted to respond in their native language when necessary; (e) the focus is on language function or content, rather than grammatical form; (f) grammatical accuracy is promoted not by correcting errors overtly, but by providing more comprehensible input; and (g) students are encouraged to respond spontaneously and creatively.
   - Opportunities for comprehensible English input are provided for LEP students when grouped by language proficiency and when interacting with fluent English-speaking peers.
5. The perceived status of students affects the interaction between teachers and students and among students themselves. In turn, student outcomes are affected. Implications:
   - Teachers use positive interactions in an equitable manner with both language-majority and language-minority students.
   - Language-majority and language-minority students are enrolled in content area classes in which cooperative learning strategies are used.
   - Whenever possible, language-majority students are enrolled in classes designed to develop second-language proficiency in the minority language(s) represented in the school.
   - Administrators, teachers, and students use the minority language(s) represented in the school for noninstructional purposes.

By 1986-87, after five years of the Case Studies treatment, median scores for the 3,500 children in these schools were well above district norms in English reading, writing, and mathematics. News of this dramatic progress, especially at the Eastman Avenue School in East Los Angeles, the Rockwood School in Calexico, and the Furgeson School in Hawaiian Gardens, has prompted numerous other districts to adopt the Case Studies model. Tens of thousands of California students are now enrolled in variations of the basic curriculum, says Gold, and its influence is spreading to a much wider circle of educators.

Therefore, it came as a surprise to many admirers of the Case Studies approach when the U.S. Department of Education decided in 1986 to terminate the project's Title VII grant two years ahead of schedule.[1] California's education department, facing budgetary problems of its own, declined to fill the gap. While the curriculum remains in place at several schools with local funding, federally financed evaluations and support services have been terminated. Apparently, what made Case Studies successful also made it controversial.

Thinking in the First Language

At the core of the Case Studies approach is intensive native-language development. Its goals are more ambitious than those of many bilingual programs, which strive primarily to keep students from falling behind in content areas while they learn English. The Case Studies curriculum not only teaches LEP children to read in their mother tongue. It also cultivates thinking skills in the first language, a process that generally takes four to five years, before children complete the transition to mainstream classrooms.

From kindergarten to about the 4th grade, Case Studies students receive instruction in ESL, while other subjects are taught in the native language, through sheltered English techniques, or in mainstream classrooms. Yet there is no hurry to complete students' transition to all-English instruction. Indeed, Case Studies teachers are trained to resist societal pressures to do so — another break with traditional practices in bilingual education.

The Case Studies curriculum was developed on the theory that academic success demands higher-level linguistic and cognitive skills that, once developed, will transfer readily from the native language to English. On the other hand, the program designers believed, if children leave bilingual programs as soon as they acquire "surface levels" of English, they will be ill-equipped to keep up in class. Thus cognitive-academic language proficiency (CALP) became a central goal of the curriculum, even though it takes considerably longer to cultivate than basic interpersonal communications skills (BICS), or "playground English."

In practice, this emphasis has paid off, according to the educators who participated in Case Studies. "People are in such a hurry to get kids into English, thinking they're doing the right thing," says Bonnie Rubio, principal of the Eastman Avenue School during the project's first four years. Before Case Studies, she explains, "we were cutting off [native-language instruction] before they developed the thinking process, even the reading comprehension skills, at about 1st grade." Lacking a solid base in their native language, many students were being shortchanged. Rubio says it was common to see 6th graders "still on bunny books" because they had trouble learning to read in English. Initially, she recalls, Eastman's bilingual teachers resisted the late-exit approach of Case Studies, but as scores began to rise, "we had converts like you wouldn't believe."

"Most of our 3rd and 4th graders now [make the] transition [into regular classrooms] just about at grade level," says Roqué Berlanga, principal of Furgeson Elementary in suburban Los Angeles. "Whereas before, when we were moving them across earlier, we found there would be a year to a year and a half deficiency. And that would increase as they [rose] through the grades, being frustrated and probably failing."

Before the Case Studies curriculum was launched, a quick-exit philosophy was one of several instructional failings at the five project schools. In their initial visits the state consultants noted that, while teachers were generally supportive of bilingual education, few were familiar with effective methodologies in initial literacy or ESL. "Beyond instruction in reading, Spanish was infrequently used as a medium of instruction with any degree of regularity," according to a the project's 1986 report. Bilingual teachers were basically on their own in deciding how and when to use Spanish or English. Because there were generally too few Spanish-proficient teachers, untrained aides were conducting lessons in some classrooms. As for Spanish-language materials, the schools had basal readers, but few texts in other subjects or books for supplementary reading.

The assessment also determined that concurrent translation was the prevalent method of bilingual instruction. Teachers simply repeated each point of a lesson in both languages, an approach that has been criticized by researchers because it allows students to ignore the English component of the lesson. Even though teachers averaged 4.5 years of experience at the five schools, most were uncertain about when to initiate English reading for LEP pupils. Meanwhile, ESL instruction stressed memorization of grammar and vocabulary rather than attempts to use the second language for communication. Generally students received little or no comprehensible input in English.

Curriculum Design

Dennis Parker, one of the Case Studies consultants, observes that an educational program is like a symphony: without a conductor or score, it can only produce noise, no matter how talented the musicians are. At the outset, Parker says, the project schools "had bilingual teachers who came from the community, they were good ethnic role models, they believed in bilingual education, they were very experienced, [but] the kids were still scoring at the 2nd percentile."

Clearly, if Case Studies was to test a new instructional model, teachers and administrators would have to apply its methods and curriculum with consistency. Toward that end, the state consultants stressed three fundamental points: intensive staff development, careful monitoring of classroom practices, and a long-term outlook. Teachers had to be instructed in the *Theoretical Framework* and trained to apply it. Their understanding and practice of the new approach, as well as student progress, needed to be evaluated constantly. Administrators had to be patient but firm, recognizing that it would take time for the treatment's effects to be felt, while ensuring that the curriculum was faithfully observed.

Coordination was also essential because of the complexity of the Case Studies model. With slight variations among schools, it has developed as follows: Students are grouped not by grade, but by language proficiency in both English and Spanish. A child's progress through the program's "phases" reflects his or her performance on the Student Oral Language Observation Matrix (SOLOM), a test of conversational English. All children study essentially the same material; only the language of instruction differs. For Spanish-speaking children the medium gradually moves toward English (see Chart 8-1).

Phase I, generally lasting two years for LEP students who start in kindergarten, begins with Spanish-language instruction in subjects that are intellectually challenging and "context reduced": language arts, science, health, social studies, and mathematics. Comprehensible doses of English are provided through ESL and through mainstream classes in art, music, and physical education, subjects that make limited cognitive demands and offer a rich context for understanding what is said in the second language.

In Phase II, typically grades 2 and 3, Spanish continues as the medium of instruction in language arts and social studies. At the same time, children begin to receive sheltered English classes in math and science, with instruction tailored to their level of English proficiency. In such classrooms, according to the Case Studies program design, "teachers change their speech register by slowing down; limiting their vocabulary and sentence length; repeating, emphasizing, and

CHART 8–1.
The Case-Studies Curriculum Model

Phase	Spanish	Sheltered English	Mainstream English
I. Non-English-Proficient (K-grade 1)* (SOLOM 5-11)	Language Arts Mathematics Science/Health Social Studies	ESL	Art Music Physical Education
II. Limited-English-Proficient (grades 2-3)* (SOLOM 12-18)	Language Arts Social Studies	ESL Mathematics Science/Health	Art Music Physical Education
III. Limited-English-Proficient (grades 3-4)* (SOLOM 19-25)	Language Arts	Traditional Language Arts Social Studies	Art Music Physical Education Mathematics Science/Health
IV. Fully-English-Proficient (grades 4-6)* (SOLOM 25+)	Language Arts (extended Spanish activities)		Art Music Physical Education Mathematics Science/Health Social Studies Language Arts

* Typical grade level for each phase.

explaining key concepts; and using examples, props, visual clues, and body language to convey and reinforce meaning carried by the language of instruction." ESL continues in Phase II, and for art, music, and physical education, LEP children are again mixed with fluent English speakers.

In Phase III, generally grades 3 and 4, students receive some instruction in English language arts, and social studies becomes a sheltered English subject. All other lessons, including math and science, are taught in mainstream classrooms.

By Phase IV children are no longer LEP. The transition to English instruction is complete, except that classes in language arts and sometimes social studies continue in Spanish (a language maintenance feature of the Case Studies model that was never eligible for federal funding). Generally speaking, children who enter the program in kindergarten make the transition to Phase IV sometime in the 4th grade.

Adapting the Model

Although the curriculum looked good on paper, as the schools prepared to adopt it in the 1982-83 school year, they encountered a variety of administrative obstacles. The project schools differed in size, in their concentrations of LEP children, and in the availability and enthusiasm of trained staff. Eastman, with more than 1,700 students in grades K through 6 and twelve 1st grade classrooms, had more flexibility in grouping students than Furgeson did, a suburban school with an enrollment of less than 600. At the same time, Eastman had fewer certified bilingual teachers; only twenty-one were available to staff forty-eight bilingual classrooms. Rockwood was located in a small town just across the border from Mexicali — some of its students slipped across from Mexico each day — and about 95 percent of children arrived speaking only Spanish. While their problems differed in particulars, administrators at each site grappled with the realities of low-income communities, from family violence to absenteeism.

Staff resistance had to be overcome at all five Case Studies schools. Although about two-thirds of teachers expressed support for the concept of bilingual education, many resented being told that the methods they had used for years were inadequate, even counterproductive, for their students.

Moreover, the state consultants were theorists, not practitioners, Rubio explains, and their ideas were sometimes cumbersome. Original plans for sheltered English and mainstream classrooms "would have meant that we'd be juggling children all day long for them to be getting the proper instruction in the right mode," she says. The solution, arrived at after consultation with Eastman's teachers, was *language grouping*. Classrooms would be divided on the basis of English proficiency, an arrangement that necessitated a waiver of California law, which at the time required that English speakers comprise at least one-third of all bilingual classrooms. The new plan led to civil rights concerns among some teachers, Rubio says, but "it didn't make any difference in East L.A. We were 99.9 percent Hispanic. There was no one else to integrate with." In any case LEP students were always mixed with fluent English speakers for art, music, and physical education.

Organizationally, language grouping proved to be both cost-effective and educationally effective, says Lilia Stapleton, bilingual coordinator for the ABC Unified School District, where Furgeson is located. "Now the teacher doesn't have to teach in two languages," she explains. "It's cut down on planning time and allows our students to be more on task than before because there's no waiting time [during translations]." And because they no longer spend time with flu-

CHART 8–2.
Two Models of Bilingual Education

	Traditional Bilingual Program	Case Studies Model
Grouping	1/3 English speakers, 2/3 LEP; broad range of English skills; divided by grade level and reading level for all classes	grouped by levels of language proficiency, grade level and reading level for core subjects; mixed 1/3-2/3 for art, music, and physical education
Methodology	concurrent translation; grammar-based ESL	language separated during all subjects (no translation); communication-based ESL
Content Areas	taught in native language and/or mainstream English	increasingly taught in sheltered English, geared to student proficiency
Curriculum	focus is on basics, especially English language arts	instruction is balanced between language and other subject areas
Exit	transition before students develop high-level cognitive skills in the native language	transition after students are exposed to higher-level cognitive skills in the native language
Staffing	requires large number of bilingual teachers; more dependence on aides; little staff development or coordination among bilingual and English teachers	needs fewer bilingual teachers because of language grouping; less dependence on aides; much emphasis on training in teaching strategies; team teaching and cooperative planning
Accountability	responsibility for teaching the LEP child rests primarily on the bilingual staff; no involvement by principal	responsibilities for educating the LEP child rests on all school staff; requires heavy administrative commitment

SOURCE: Adapted from "Eastman Curriculum Design Project," Los Angeles Unified School District, 1986

ent English-speaking children, bilingual teachers are used more efficiently. At Eastman the number of bilingual classrooms was reduced by nearly 40 percent and fewer instructional aides were needed.

Case Studies gave teachers no choice. They had to change their methods and they had to work closely with their colleagues. Teaming was mandatory, not a popular idea at the outset, Rubio recalls: "It meant there was more accountability and the need to stay on a tight schedule. [Previously] some teachers did reading for two hours, spelling during math time, health if they thought of it. Some did science and some didn't do science because they didn't like it." Now teachers had to cooperate and keep on schedule, rather than going at their own pace or favoring one subject at the expense of another. In the Case Studies program, a team typically made up of two bilingual teachers and one monolingual English teacher consulted on the needs of each student, divided children up for various classes, and followed their progress. This collegial approach, along with growing indications of student progress, had a salutary effect on staff morale, according to administrators.

In the beginning, recalls Simón López, principal of the Rockwood School in Calexico, his staff was polarized into "different camps," with bilingual teachers on one side and monolingual English teachers on the other. "Everybody was doing their own thing" in the classroom, he says, with teachers usually absorbed by their own problems. As they began sharing responsibility for instruction, attitudes changed; the staff began to "focus on the child." A major benefit of Case Studies, López says, has been in "giving us a real mission, a vision of what it is we're trying to do." Stapleton adds: "It's really brought the staffs together. And by exposing the monolingual teachers to ESL techniques, [teaming has helped them to] understand what the children are going through in the process of acquiring English. And they have a little bit more empathy for these kids."

Introducing the Case Studies curriculum meant revolutionizing the entire school program, a process that is never painless. Rubio explains: "It changes [principals'] whole lives: 'We want you to redo your school totally; reschedule all your schedules; change the way you assign children in classrooms; affect all the training for your school staff, the teachers, the aides; change the way you relate to parents.'" At the same time, she argues, aggressive leadership by the principal is essential to the success of the Case Studies model. In an early stage at Eastman, Rubio bluntly told resisters on her staff either to teach the curriculum — whether they agreed with it or not — or to transfer out. It takes the flak of change until you can get to the benefits of change," she says. "If you're willing to take the flak, believe me, it'll be worth it in the end."

Tight organization is also necessary to ensure that a "balanced curriculum" is taught, one that focuses not just on language, but on all-round cognitive development, as well. John Myers, who initiated a similar instructional model as principal of Bell Gardens Elementary School near Los Angeles, argues that the mark of a poor-quality bilingual program is inordinate concentration on language teaching at the expense of academic content areas:

> Because the kids can't read English, they give them more reading in
> English, along with language arts, spelling, and some math. But the
> thinking areas of science and social studies and health — these sub-
> jects where you're picking up the major ideas you're going to deal
> with in life — aren't being taught. And so the minority children are
> set over to one side, most of them being poor and already having a
> disadvantage, and they're not getting an equal opportunity.

By contrast, in the Case Studies model, no student is treated as a remedial
case simply because he or she lacks English proficiency. Language of instruction
is incidental to the curriculum, except that LEP children pick up English as they
progress from one phase to another. Rubio explains the results:

> One of the things that's exciting is, you can walk into a classroom
> and the 2nd graders are doing science experiments and — talking,
> talking — they're doing committee work. These are the same kids
> that in another [program] would be just sitting there wondering
> what was going on, or in a corner with a translator. To me, that
> made it all worthwhile. There's nothing wrong with them. Because
> they can't speak the English language doesn't mean they can't
> learn. And for them to be doing the same type of things the other
> kids are doing — you can imagine how that affects their self-image.
> We found that it eliminated a lot of the stigma, when they saw the
> teacher was using their [native] language.

Student Outcomes

Case Studies set the following goals: (1) after three years 100 percent of
students would achieve basic oral communicative skills in English, as measured
by the SOLOM; (2) after seven years at least 50 percent would score at or above
national norms on the Comprehensive Test of Basic Skills (CTBS) in reading, language arts, and mathematics. These were high expectations at schools where the
median reading scores for 6th graders in 1981 ranged from the 1st to the 12th
percentile.

By the end of the third year, 1985-86, when funding for the Case Studies
project was terminated, only one of the goals had been reached, on average, at

all five schools: at least 60 percent of students in grades 2 through 6 who entered the program in kindergarten were scoring at or above California norms in math. In 1984-85, the most recent year for which overall figures are available,[2] 52 percent of 2nd graders had achieved oral English proficiency; 72 percent of 3rd graders; and 91 percent of 4th graders. (The goal of 100 percent after three years may be unrealistic, say the Case Studies designers, suspecting that the oral SOLOM test may include "aspects of academic language proficiency that take longer to attain.") In English reading 39 percent of 3rd graders had reached state norms, as had 30 percent of 6th graders.

Despite the project's failure to reach all of its original goals, evaluators were heartened by a steady upward trend in every category of achievement. They documented strong correlations between Spanish reading proficiency and scores in English reading two years later, lending support to Cummins's interdependence hypothesis that literacy skills are transferable from the native language to English. Significantly, Gold reports, the "schools where the curriculum was fully implemented" achieved the best results. Administrative problems at two of the Case Studies sites, the Mission Education Center in San Francisco and the Huron Elementary School in the Coalinga-Huron Joint Unified School District, kept the model from being thoroughly tested there, he says. Students progressed more rapidly and consistently at the other three schools.

In 1981-82, the year before Case Studies began, Rockwood Elementary was Calexico's lowest-achieving school; by 1983-84 it was the district's highest, based on California Assessment Program (CAP) results.[3] Under Case Studies there was a steady, upward pattern of achievement; at other schools in the district, scores continued to fluctuate widely from year to year. In 1981-82, Rockwood's 3rd graders were at the 6th percentile in reading on the CTBS. By 1984-85, as 6th graders, this cohort had reached the 38th percentile. In language arts they progressed from the 7th to the 44th percentile over the same period; in math from the 19th to the 64th. For other groups of Rockwood students, the pattern has been the same. In 1985-86, 6th graders scored at the 32nd percentile in reading, the 46th in language, and the 59th in mathematics.

The Eastman Avenue School posted similar progress.[4] Between 1982-83 and 1985-86, the school's CAP scores climbed from well below average for Los Angeles to generally above average in reading, writing, and mathematics. On the CTBS in 1986, Eastman's 4th graders averaged up to 15 percentiles higher in reading and 25 percentiles higher in math than their counterparts in East Los Angeles (on national norms they scored at the 45th and 66th percentiles, respectively).

Like all achievement test results, Eastman's vary somewhat from year to year, but since Case Studies was introduced, the overall curve has been one of substantial improvement. In 1987 CAP scores, the school's 3rd graders made their most impressive gains to date; in reading (257) they surpassed the Los Angeles citywide median by 16 points; in language (274) by 27 points; and in math (285) by 41 points. Notwithstanding a slight dip in 1987, Eastman's 6th graders also showed substantial improvements since 1980 (see Chart 8-3).

Flexibility or Leadership?

For the California education department, Case Studies marked a departure from its normal "top down" approach, says Fred Tempes, who directed the project until 1986. "We [used to] say, 'Here's what's best for all kids, no matter what the concentrations or what languages they speak, because the state law tells us so. And here's what thou shalt do to make it happen.'" The state's bilingual education statute, before it was allowed to expire in 1987, was "very beneficial," he adds, "but the law by itself [was not] sufficient." Quality programs for LEP children cannot be legislated, Tempes maintains. Instead, school districts need to see successful models that they can adapt for their own students.

Secretary of Education William Bennett and others who question the effectiveness of bilingual education have criticized the idea of a government-prescribed "method," arguing that school districts need the flexibility to experiment with different approaches. Dennis Parker responds that "local option" is a recipe for educational neglect or chaos; furthermore, it is not what school administrators are seeking. He quotes the plea of one district official: "We don't need flexibility. We need leadership. We don't know what to do with these kids. We need some guidance." Parker concludes: "Don't tell people, 'Do whatever you think is right, and we'll reward you if you come up with some good programs,' but rather, 'Here are some things we think you should try.'" Developing and popularizing effective approaches are essential, Tempes adds:

> We worked with [the Eastman] school for five years. People may say that's a poor use of resources. You've got these state consultants who spend 50 percent of their time with one elementary school when you've got 7,000 elementary schools [in California]. What happened was, they were doing an excellent job and — we didn't even promote this — people started calling and asking, "Can

CHART 8–3.
Eastman School Outcomes
(California Assessment Program, 1980-87)

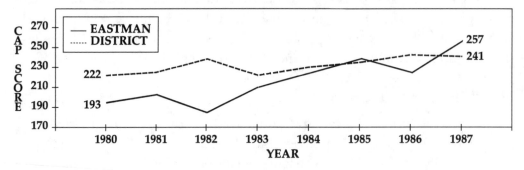

3rd grade reading scores.

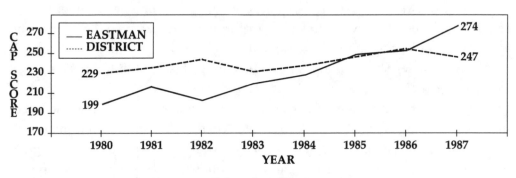

3rd grade writing scores.

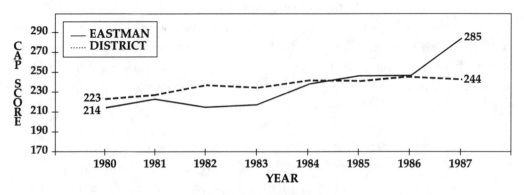

3rd grade mathematics scores.

CHART 8–3.
Eastman School Outcomes (cont.)
(California Assessment Program, 1980-87)

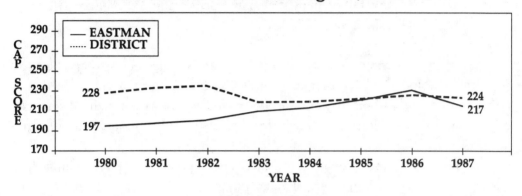

6th grade reading scores.

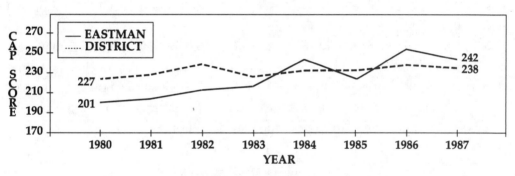

6th grade writing scores.

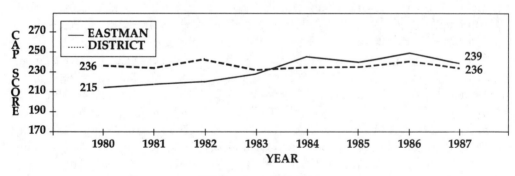

6th grade mathematics scores.

we come over and take a look?" Lots of [districts] are on the look-
out for innovation. They hear about something, and they want to
see what it is; they want to evaluate it and use it if they can. That
seems to work better than state laws mandating excellence. The
excellence really is out there.

By 1985, following enthusiastic stories in Los Angeles newspapers, Eastman
began to give tours of its program. Soon it was receiving more attention than it
could handle, and visiting days had to be limited to one per month. Meanwhile,
other California educators decided to try the Case Studies model. The Ontario-
Montclair School District adopted it for all elementary schools. Los Angeles
County began planning a replication project encompassing several medium-sized
districts, including a Portuguese bilingual program in ABC Unified. In 1986, Los
Angeles city schools appropriated $250,000 and hired Bonnie Rubio to replicate
Eastman's approach at seven schools serving 10,000 students; in 1987 the project
was expanded to twenty additional sites.

Taking a dimmer view of the Case Studies experiment, the U.S. Department
of Education not only terminated its Title VII grant, but also declined to fund
Rubio's replication project. Undaunted by federal opposition, however, the Los
Angeles school board voted in 1988 to make the "Eastman model" the corner-
stone of a $20 million expansion of bilingual education.

Notes

1. Title VII funding began in the project's second year, 1983-84, and was expected to
    continue through 1987-88. It was terminated in 1986 following a dispute with the
    federal Office of Bilingual Education and Minority Languages Affairs (OBEMLA). Case
    Studies had previously received permission to send teachers to a summer language
    institute in Mexico subsidized in part by the Secretaría de Educación Pública, the
    Mexican counterpart of the U.S. Department of Education. But in late May 1986,
    shortly before the scheduled trip, OBEMLA's deputy director, Ana María Farías,
    moved to block this use of Title VII funds. Fred Tempes of the California State
    Department of Education sought help from allies on Capitol Hill, and ultimately the
    travel funds were approved, but this was a Pyrrhic victory. According to Tempes,
    Farías told him that "although the Case studies project is eligible to apply for [a
    fourth and fifth year of] funding, we would be wasting our time by applying"
    because "of her belief that [it was] a research project rather than a program of transi-
    tional bilingual education." In October, Case Studies received formal notification that
    its grant would be discontinued because "your project has not made substantial and

measurable progress in achieving the specific educational goals contained in the approved application." Shortly thereafter, commenting generally on Title VII funding decisions, OBEMLA director Carol Pendás Whitten said that preference had been given to grant applicants that promised to mainstream children "as quickly as possible."

2. An ambitious final evaluation, which would have tracked the progress of individual students who received the full Case Studies treatment, was canceled for lack of Title VII funding.

3. These scores include the one-third of Rockwood's students who were not enrolled in the bilingual program.

4. Available test data is school-wide. About 60 percent of Eastman students receive bilingual instruction.

9 Indian Bilingual Education

$\mathcal{A}$pproximately 175 indigenous languages are still spoken in the United States — more than all the immigrant tongues combined — but fewer than one-quarter of these are still being learned by children. Without intergenerational transmission, they are considered "moribund," or destined to die out in the near future. As many as forty-five Native American languages, spoken primarily by elders in their 70s and 80s, could disappear by the year 2000. Most face the prospect of extinction in the next two or three generations. If current trends continue, only twenty will remain alive by 2050, according to Michael Krauss of the Alaska Native Language Center.

In this context the need for bilingual education among American Indians and Alaska Natives is sometimes questioned. Many who would not dispute the importance of special language programs for newly arrived Cambodians or Salvadorans assume that, since most Native American children are dominant in English when they start school, bilingual instruction is unwarranted. Why waste time teaching them native languages when they already speak English? This assumption stems from a failure to recognize what is special about these students.

First, while language shift has affected many Native American communities, it is usually a nonstandard dialect of English that has displaced the tribal tongue among younger generations. Today's parents may retain some of their native language, but tend to be dominant in a variety of "Indian English"; hence their children learn this dialect at home. While such children grow up with no knowledge (or only passive knowledge) of the indigenous language, they have little exposure to standard English before entering school. In other words, for academic purposes they are limited-English-proficient (LEP). So they encounter many of the same language barriers as LEP immigrant students, although the barriers may be less obvious — for the first decade of Title VII, programs serving English-dominant children were ineligible for funding. Recognizing this problem, in 1978 Congress expanded the definition of limited English proficiency to include "American Indian and Alaska Native students who come from environments where a language other than English has had a significant impact on their level of English language proficiency."[1]

The second thing that needs to be understood is that cultural loss has academic consequences. It diminishes Native American children's sense of identity and pride in their origins, which they need to counter society's negative messages about "Indianness." Students who lack the cultural tools to define themselves — especially if they come from "disadvantaged" or socially stigmatized backgrounds — are likely to encounter problems in school. The native language is an essential resource. For indigenous peoples in particular, language serves as the central repository of tribal history, customs, and values, little of which exist in written form. When a language dies, so does much of the culture that it expressed, along with an important symbol of group identity. Preserving and revitalizing endangered languages must therefore be recognized as an educational priority.

Bilingual programs, if correctly designed, can address both of these problems. They can help children acquire standard English while learning other subjects, and they can teach the ancestral language, keeping it alive for future generations.

Nevertheless, Indian bilingual education has faced resistance — and not just from unsympathetic whites. For many parents, the idea of using tribal languages for instruction represents a confusing reversal of government policy. When Title VII programs were first introduced on Montana reservations in the late 1960s, adults recalled with bitterness their own educational experiences. In Bureau of Indian Affairs (BIA) schools, many had been punished severely for violating "speak English only" rules. Submersed in sink-or-swim classrooms, they had come to associate Indian languages with academic difficulties. Why should a new generation of students, many of whom spoke little Crow or Cree or Cheyenne, risk similar humiliations? parents asked. Some required children to use English in the home, for their own good. Why should the schools do anything less?

Ted Risingsun, a longtime school board member in Busby, Montana, worked hard to change such attitudes. He urged fellow members of the Northern Cheyenne tribe to take pride in their language and to recognize the benefits of preserving it for future generations. Risingsun also stressed its educational value: "We found that those who learn Cheyenne well learn English well." Parents were invited into the classroom to see for themselves. By the end of the first year, he recalls, the bilingual program had "almost 100 percent support" on the reservation.

Growing up in the 1930s, Risingsun himself had been forbidden by white educators to speak Cheyenne, the only language he knew. "I'd never spoken English," he says, "but at school I was expected to use it. I didn't even know my name [in English] was Ted Risingsun. I hung my head. If there had been a bilingual teacher there, things would have been different."

Rose Chesarek, a Crow educator, tells a similar story about her sink-or-swim experience. "When you come in the school doors, everything is totally foreign. You shed everything at the door, sit at a desk, and you don't understand one word of what goes on. I don't know how I got to 4th grade, because I don't remember too much of anything until then." Her school's ban on using Crow lasted into the 1950s, part of a policy of suppressing everything about students that was Indian, Chesarek says. "All the way through school, I was told they just wanted to make me a white person, so I'd succeed. The teachers would tell me everything about me was bad. I'd go home and think about it: 'What in the hell got me to be an Indian? Why?'"

Now a bilingual teacher, Chesarek is determined to break the pattern of low self-esteem and underachievement still suffered by many Crow children. Native-language instruction, she explains, can play an important role in developing students' pride in their Indian identity, a factor that research has linked to improved achievement in school. And, based on her own teaching experience, she has no doubts about the long-term, cognitive benefits of bilingual education.

In 1973-74, when linguists were still developing the Crow alphabet, Chesarek became the first teacher of reading in that language. Her class of fifteen monolingual Crow speakers received initial literacy and mathematics instruction in Crow, along with English as a second language (ESL). Although the children did well, the reading program was abandoned after a year, and Chesarek resigned because of disorganization and controversy within the early Title VII program. Those students have now graduated from high school, she says. "All through the years, I would follow them, talk to their parents and ask how they were doing. And most parents would say, 'Oh, that one is doing so well, but my others are not. I wonder why.'"

LEP Indian Children: A Special Case

A major cause of school failure among Native Americans, and among other language minorities as well, is students' failure to develop cognitive-academic proficiency (CALP) in either English or the tribal tongue. The problem, explains William Leap, an American University anthropologist, is that the "variety of English common to their home and community [bears] many similarities (in sounds used, in sentence forms, and in style and structure of speaking) to the ancestral language of the community. It [is] their knowledge of the locally appropriate 'Indian English' code — not their knowledge of their ancestral language *per se* — which [is] creating the classroom difficulties."

Dick Littlebear, a Alaska-based consultant to Title VII programs, agrees with this diagnosis: "You find these kids floating between two nonstandard languages, a population growing up without a linguistic home. The kids haven't had the basis to develop reasoning skills." By the time such children reach the age of five or six, creating a solid linguistic foundation becomes problematic for educators. Attempts to impose standard English through the correction of errors and other remedial techniques is not the answer, Leap says. It can

> lead to serious consequences for the child . . . [whose] control over his community's Indian English variety may be his only link to ancestral language fluency. It may, for example, help explain why

> Indian students say they "understand" their grandparents when they talk, yet they cannot "speak" to their grandparents in their [tribal] language. Remediation destroys these linkages — hence student rejection of attempts to [impose] standard language structures, [especially when schools offer them] no alternative other than to acquire it or reject it.

Bilingual education offers a way out of this dilemma, Leap argues. By studying their native language, students can acquire "better control over the non-English grammar" they have internalized. In this way they become conscious of structural differences between the standard English of academic pursuits and the vernacular used on the reservation.

George Reed, a former Crow educator and linguist, complains that many of his reservation's youth grow up speaking "Crowlish," a blend of the Indian language and English. Native-language instruction can play a role in "helping Indian children sort out their identity" and in slowing the erosion of Indian tongues, he says. "My lexicon is my way of life. Culture is expressed by the language, and my language is tied up with the culture."

Although limited, research evidence suggests there are academic advantages for Indian children whose language is preserved and used in the home. This was the conclusion of a five-year longitudinal study conducted in the 1970s by Steve Chesarek, an administrator in several reservation schools, who tracked Crow students' patterns of achievement, with and without bilingual education. In those days native-language instruction at Crow Agency, Montana, was just getting started. After the departure of Chesarek's wife, Rose, it was "basically an oral program," he says. "But what we found was that if you utilize the kids' own language, you see some rapid growth in a number of areas, including English development. Kids who are fluent Crow speakers learn English very quickly, if somebody sets out to teach them English. And they do well in other academic areas, too."

While Crow students are more likely to speak their native language, as compared with students on other Montana reservations, some Crow parents still try to raise their children in English only. This decision can have negative effects on school achievement, according to Steve Chesarek: "English is their only language, but [by kindergarten] they're already limited-English speakers. They're hearing two Crow-speaking parents, or maybe a Crow and a Cheyenne, who are dealing in their short suit [when using English]. Typically, if one of the parents was a fluent English speaker, the child had no problem with English. But there weren't very many of those."

Out of tradition or necessity, Indian grandparents play a major role in child-rearing, says Minerva Allen, federal programs director for the Hays/Lodge Pole school district in northeastern Montana. "The grandparents have always raised kids; it's a cultural value. And a lot are raised by the grandparents because of [parents'] alcoholism, teen-age pregnancy, or the parents go off to look for a job." While this social pattern helps to maintain an appreciation of Indian traditions, it also tends to perpetuate limited English proficiency. Members of the older generations are more likely to be monolingual, or at least dominant, in the tribal language.

As a group, students who grow up in homes where English is spoken, but spoken poorly, are likely to start behind and stay behind, says Steve Chesarek. By contrast, proficient Crow speakers may begin school two to three years behind, but they quickly catch up, according to his research. Crow children who speak only English, he says,

> tend to become somewhat isolated. The Crow-speaking kids aren't as likely to play with them because they don't speak Crow, and the white kids aren't as likely to play with them because they're Indian. And so they form their own play group, and they reinforce the limited English that they have. If you want to draw a generalization: It doesn't matter which language you raise your child[ren] in; as long as you're fluent in it, they'll become fluent in it.[2]

Early Title VII Efforts

The federal government's first foray into Indian bilingual education came in 1969, when it financed a "pan-Indian" project involving the Crow, Rocky Boy, and Northern Cheyenne reservations. Little is known about the results of this early effort, says Cheryl Crawley, assistant superintendent of the school district that includes the towns of Hardin and Crow Agency. "But people found out that you can't have a pan-Indian bilingual program because of the enormous differences between tribes and languages."

"One of the fallacies that white people have about Indians is that they think we're generic," says Dick Littlebear, a member of the Northern Cheyenne tribe. American Indian tongues vary enormously, falling into more than fifty distinct "families" as different from each other as Romance languages and Chinese. Language situations also vary among indigenous communities. The extent to which a vernacular has been preserved, what role it plays in reservation life, whether it is written as well as spoken, how language attitudes fit into tribal politics — such questions are crucial in designing Indian bilingual education programs.

On the Rocky Boy reservation, a long tradition of Cree literacy has been nurtured and guarded by the tribal elders, says Steve Chesarek. "They already knew how to read and write Cree [when bilingual education programs began], and so they'd teach the young kids who were going to be teachers. There was no question whether it was culturally pure; it was coming from the experts. There's a whole body of Cree literature that's never been translated into English. They're very jealous of their own copyright. For kids old enough to realize this, there's a motivation to learn to read in Cree."

Attempts to put Crow into written form began in the 1960s, when the Wycliffe Bible translators began to develop an orthography, or functional writing system. The project continued into the late 1970s with the aid of academic experts, including G. H. Matthews of the Massachusetts Institute of Technology and two native Crow speakers who had studied linguistics at MIT. The first comprehensive Crow dictionary was finally completed in 1986. When Crow Agency won a new Title VII grant in 1977 and administrators began looking for teachers, there were only eleven adults known to be literate in the language. That number has increased substantially, thanks to teacher training and a Crow Studies curriculum at the reservation's Little Big Horn Community College, which is directed by Dale Old Horn, one of the MIT-trained linguists.

Initially the idea of teaching Crow literacy was foreign to parents who had never read a word in their native tongue. Many questioned whether the program's emphasis on Crow culture was time well spent, an attitude that reflected dissatisfaction with an earlier Title VII program featuring large amounts of beadwork and other traditional crafts. "In the beginning, our biggest goal was public relations," Cheryl Crawley explains, "getting parents to understand what we were trying to do. We emphasized that culture in the classroom meant doing academics embedded in a familiar cultural context that Indian children could understand." Using a newsletter and calendars with monthly messages about bilingual education, the Crow Agency program gradually won over the community. Parents stopped asking for their children to be excused from native-language instruction and stopped insisting on English at home.

Among other pedagogical problems, the Crow Agency program had to cope with a dearth of instructional materials in Crow. Beginning in 1979, Title VII financed a Bilingual Materials Development Center that published tribal legends and history, along with original stories by its staff, in both English and Crow. The center produced bilingual calendars, workbooks, Crow-language flash cards, filmstrips, and bulletin board exhibits. It also took charge of compiling the Crow dictionary.

While located on the Crow reservation, the center also published materials in other Indian languages until the U.S. Department of Education withdrew its funding in 1986. This was a significant setback for Indian bilingual education, Crawley says. "Materials development is vital. No commercial publisher is going to do it because they can't make any kind of profit," owing to the limited market for Indian language publications. Although Crow Agency was able to divert part of its Title VII grant to produce materials, the amount was far short of what was needed, according to Marlene Walking Bear, the program's director. The tribal government would like to help out, she adds, but its budget is tight, and other expenditures usually get priority on the economically depressed reservation.

Introducing Crow Literacy

While perhaps an extreme case, Crow Agency illustrates Indian students' pressing need for language assistance. Most of the bilingual school's 250 children in grades K through 6 come from homes where Crow is spoken. Although many appear fluent in conversational English, Walking Bear reports that 99 percent are assessed as LEP. "They don't have the academic language," she explains. "They can hear and follow directions, but they may not be able to produce."

On entering the program, children are taught oral concepts in Crow, and about half their time is spent in reading-readiness and ESL instruction. Basic reading skills are taught in English. The percentage of native language in other subjects is gradually reduced to about 20 percent by the 4th grade, when Crow reading is introduced. This language enrichment program continues through grade 6, along with lessons in Crow history, and its benefits appear to be more than cultural. "More and more, kids are reading close to grade level" in English, Walking Bear says. While they have yet to reach national norms, students have been raising their scores steadily since 1977.

Crawley, who developed this instructional model, says that the lack of a basal reader in Crow has made initial reading instruction impractical in the native tongue. "I think the kids find it easier to learn to read English than to read Crow," she argues, "because the Crow words are so long, because the exposure they've had to print already is in English, and they're used to [English] combinations of vowels and consonants."

As in many Indian languages, Crow words for some simple concepts can be difficult. For example, the six-syllable word for chair is *baleaalawaache,* or "something to sit on." This is one of many "compound words that came about through contact with whites," Crawley explains. "It's a description of an object rather than a simple, everyday word that has been in the language longer." Attempting to decode such words is likely to overwhelm the beginning reader, she argues. "Once kids have learned the techniques in English, and they get to 4th grade motivated to learn to read in their own language, then learning to read in Crow comes quite easy for them [and will help] to build self-esteem."

Several educators and researchers, however, take issue with this argument, noting that the Finnish, Magyar, Welsh, and Samoan languages feature word length and syntactical complexity comparable to those of Crow and other Indian tongues. "A foreign language always looks formidable to a person who's going to learn it," says Dick Littlebear. He notes that Americans who saw *Mary Poppins* now "can say 'supercalifragilisticexpialidocious,' and that's longer than any of the Cheyenne words." Rose Chesarek reports that her students in the early 1970s learned Crow literacy with ease and were soon reading "a book a week," because Crow's sounds and its phonetic alphabet are similar to those of English, with only a few exceptions.

Needed: Indian Teachers

Crow Agency has been fortunate in training and recruiting Crow-speaking staff, who made up eight of its fifteen teachers in 1986-87. Those lacking fluency in the language worked with half a dozen Crow-speaking aides from the community. Altogether there were about forty certified Crow teachers, Crawley estimates, though only about half were still teaching on the reservation, not necessarily in bilingual programs.

It was a different story that year at nearby Busby, Montana, whose Title VII program had no Cheyenne-speaking teachers and had to rely heavily on instructional aides. Because of low pay and geographical isolation, well-qualified white teachers for Indian children are also difficult to find, explains Norma Bixby, who chairs the local school board. She adds that Busby has lost some effective instructors to aggressive recruiting by other Indian schools.

At Hays/Lodge Pole, located on the Fort Belknap reservation, there were two certified Indian teachers in the Title VII program for eighty-two students in 1986-87, according to Minerva Allen.[3] Further straining local resources, the program must be *trilingual* to accommodate children from the two tribes who occupy the reservation. Some speak Assiniboine, a member of the Siouan language family; others speak Gros Ventre, an Algonquian language. The two tongues share no more grammar or vocabulary with each other than they do with English, says Allen, an Assiniboine. Initial reading is taught in each of the native languages, she says, and "all the kids seem to learn both" in addition to English, which is used for instruction about 75 percent of the time.

Knowledge of the structure of Native American languages is essential to high-quality ESL instruction, says Jon Reyhner, who administers a multicultural teacher-training program at Montana State University, Billings. For native English speakers, these languages tend to be among the most difficult to acquire. Yet, in Montana and nationwide, only a tiny proportion of those who teach Indian students are Indians themselves. "It would be a great help to the Indian children to have more," Allen says. "If we could train more teachers, we wouldn't need the federal funds."

Schools might also reduce high rates of staff turnover — a perennial problem in Bureau of Indian Affairs facilities — if more teachers had roots in the surrounding community; non-Indian teachers rarely do. On the other hand, according to Steve Chesarek, recruiting teachers locally can create "a whole new set of social and political problems that can get in the way of how people perceive bilingual education. If you're hiring a local person, it's hard to get rid of him," especially on Montana reservations, where unemployment often approaches 85 percent. He adds: "These are revolutionary programs compared to, say, Chapter 1, in the sense that they lead to dramatic shifts in who controls the schools. You see a different type of involvement from bilingual parents and from teachers who speak the language. And you may find [English-speaking Indians] who feel threatened because [bilingual teaching] is a job that can be done only by someone who knows the language." At times, he says, committed bilingual educators have been "politically pushed out" during struggles between tribal factions.

Indian educators have tackled the bilingual teacher shortage in various ways. In the early 1970s, the Navajo Nation launched an ambitious initiative to increase the number of certified Navajo teachers. It combined on-site training of instructors with summer programs on nearby college campuses. The American Indian Language Development Institute (University of Arizona) and the Summer Institute of Linguistics for Native Americans (University of New Mexico) have enabled members of several southwestern tribes to earn certification as well as college degrees. Both programs are oriented toward meeting the needs of bilingual classrooms.

Local teacher recruitment and training have been crucial to the success of bilingual education at Rock Point, Arizona, where a community school board took over the operation of elementary and secondary schools. By the late 1970s, Rock Point students, once among the lowest scoring in the BIA system, were approaching — and occasionally reaching — national norms of school achievement; they were consistently outperforming their peers in other Indian schools. Daniel McLaughlin, a former principal there, explains that in 1968,

> when the bilingual effort began at Rock Point, there were no training programs for teaching in Navajo, nor was there a pool of trained individuals to draw upon. Local people and talent were all that could be relied upon. On-site college classes were offered, and non-credentialed staff were required to make continual progress toward certification. By the late 1980s, approximately 85 percent of all instructional staff were Navajos; more than 60 individuals had gained teaching certificates while working at Rock Point; and increasingly, new teachers came from the ranks of recent bilingual-biliterate graduates of the program itself.

Using this approach the elementary school achieved a student-teacher ratio of nine to one, enabling it to teach all subjects in both English and Navajo. And self-reliance offered another advantage, McLaughlin says. Teacher training was "Rock Point-centered," focusing on the community's needs and the program's philosophy of developmental bilingualism.

By 1992, Navajos held about 1,500 of 6,000 teaching positions on the reservation in federal, public, private, and community schools, according to a tribal survey. With help from the Ford Foundation, the Navajo Division of Education continues to provide financial aid to paraprofessionals seeking certification and to match them with teacher-training institutions, many with branches in or near Navajo communities. To participate, candidates must be orally proficient — and willing to become literate — in the Navajo language.

Self-Determination and its Limits

The Indian Self-Determination Act of 1975, which authorized the Bureau of Indian Affairs to "contract out" the operation of its schools, allowed communities like Rock Point to take control of their children's education. Since then more than seventy have done so, often with excellent results. Local control has brought innovation to stagnant institutions where it was sorely needed, sometimes in the form of exemplary bilingual programs. Given significant decision-making power for the first time, Indian parents tend to feel a new responsibility for educational outcomes. And students tend to respond favorably to higher expectations for their achievement.

Community schools' potential was first tapped by an experiment involving the Navajo Nation, the BIA, and the federal Office of Economic Opportunity. The Rough Rock Demonstration School, founded in 1966, was also the first bilingual-bicultural program for Native Americans. An all-Navajo school board, largely illiterate and non-English-speaking, nevertheless set ambitious academic goals while insisting on a Navajo approach to learning. No longer was the school perceived as an alien institution run by outsiders; now it reflected community attitudes, values, and styles of interacting. Using a variety of federal grants, the school established a Navajo Curriculum Center to develop materials, a parent advisory committee, a teacher-training effort, and a transitional bilingual program.

The experiment also brought economic benefits to an isolated area, where cash incomes from farming and sheep-herding averaged $85 a year in the 1960s. The school board not only hired local residents, but it also sold hay, milk, fuel, and other commodities at a discount, constructed low-income housing, and helped set up a medical clinic. It secured BIA funding to build new classroom facilities and to pave the first road into the community, opening Rough Rock to the outside world. By 1983, per capita income averaged nearly $2,500 annually. "Though still far below the national average, this greatly enhanced the quality of life for local residents," according to Teresa McCarty, a former curriculum developer at Rough Rock who now teaches at the University of Arizona.

The demonstration school also succeeded in developing Navajo leadership, whose impact has been felt beyond the immediate community. Today many of the reservation's most respected educators trace their professional roots to Rough Rock.

So far, however, the school has produced no miraculous gains in academic achievement. McCarty acknowledges that, despite limited assessment data, by the 1980s it was clear that student progress was less than what Rough Rock's founders had anticipated. The chief explanation, she believes, is "the absence of any stable pedagogical approach over time." In the late 1970s, the bilingual program was overshadowed by a prepackaged "basic skills" curriculum that emphasized English phonics and grammar drills. Soon after, two new bilingual-bicultur-

al approaches were developed, but became controversial because of their traditional religious content. School staff divided into factions favoring each of the
three curricula, all of which had school board approval; not surprisingly, none
was well-implemented. Meanwhile, self-determination did not erase attitudes that
BIA schools had produced through years of indoctrination. Many parents continued to believe that the school's job was to "teach the white man's way," McCarty
says.

Most important, she believes, was Rough Rock's dependence on short-term
funding from federal categorical programs. Oftentimes, when the money ran out
at Rough Rock, so did the instructional approach it supported; new pedagogies
were then tailored to new funding sources. Unlike Rock Point, whose community
school board has never wavered in its financial commitment to bilingual education, Rough Rock has no guarantee that its Navajo-English program would continue without Title VII or other external assistance.

This is a pervasive problem in Indian education. Reliance on outside
financing sacrifices the stability of instructional programs, while local resources
are inadequate to sustain them. Community schools generally have a bare-bones
budget provided under contracts with the BIA, supplemented by federal grants
that are not designed as permanent entitlements. Title VII, for example, is
expected to be used for "capacity-building" — that is, to make bilingual programs self-sufficient. In high-poverty areas, such expectations are unrealistic. On
Indian reservations in particular, education is one of numerous programs competing for scarce tribal dollars. Even where public school districts exercise jurisdic-
tion, Indian lands are not subject to taxation. So schools must rely heavily on
federal assistance under the Johnson-O'Malley Act, Title IV of the 1972 Indian
Education Act, and the impact aid program, all of which suffered severe cuts during the 1980s.

Rough Rock came up with an innovative solution to this problem, enhancing pedagogical consistency even as funding for bilingual education remained
uncertain. In 1983, it entered into a collaboration with the Kamehameha Early
Education Program (KEEP), a Honolulu-based effort that made effective use of
Hawaiian culture in the classroom. KEEP wanted to see how its approach would
work in a different setting, while Rough Rock teachers were seeking an alternative to their ineffective basic-skills curriculum. The five-year partnership helped
to revive a Navajo-English bilingual curriculum and to develop a stable leadership, despite continued turnover among Rough Rock administrators. The key,
according to McCarty and bilingual director Galena Dick, was to train and

empower Navajo teachers as conscious "change agents." While modeled on KEEP, the new K-3 curriculum was developed and adapted by Rough Rock teachers themselves.[4] Hence there is a strong feeling of local "ownership," an essential factor in the success of any Indian education program.

Language Survival

When bilingual education began at Rough Rock and Rock Point, more than 90 percent of the students started school as monolingual Navajo speakers. A quarter-century later, that pattern has changed dramatically. Although these communities remain relatively isolated, virtually all children now speak some English on arrival and barely 50 percent are assessed as proficient in Navajo. Language shift has proceeded even faster in the reservation's larger towns. In 1992, a tribal survey of 3,328 entering students at 110 Navajo-majority schools found that 32 percent spoke Navajo well, while 73 percent spoke English well; only 16 percent were rated higher in Navajo than in English.[5] Within a generation the native tongue has lost enormous ground.

The number of Navajo speakers remains substantial: 148,530, or 45 percent of all indigenous language speakers in the United States, according to the 1990 census. While a majority of adult Navajos are bilingual, it is not uncommon for elders to speak little or no English. Nevertheless, the rate of language loss among youth is rapid and troubling to tribal members who had until recently taken the survival of Navajo for granted. It suggests that, as their isolated way of life disappears, so too may their tongue — a fate already experienced by many other tribes.

Native American languages began dying out almost as soon as Columbus landed in the New World. While estimates vary, somewhere between 250 and 350 indigenous tongues were spoken in North America in 1492.[6] Certainly scores, perhaps hundreds of these languages became extinct as European settlers carried out policies of Indian enslavement, extermination, removal, containment, and cultural repression. Many have blamed the BIA boarding schools, with their brutal English-only policies, as the chief cause of language loss. No doubt this experience robbed students of skills in their native language as well as pride in its use. Even when able to do so, many have declined to pass on this heritage to their children.

Yet the Navajo experience demonstrates that language shift cannot be explained by repression alone. Indeed, among several Native American groups it began to accelerate in the 1970s — a generation after the BIA abandoned its restrictionist policy and a decade after passage of the Bilingual Education Act. It has been evident even in places like Rock Point, whose schools seek to develop students' Navajo skills through the 12th grade. At Peach Springs, Arizona, where a developmental bilingual program in Hualapai has won federal recognition for academic excellence, language loss has been equally dramatic.

What is happening in these communities? Jimmy C. Begay, director of the Rock Point Community School, has several answers: "Back in the '70s, there was not a lot of electricity out in the community and there weren't a lot of televisions at the time. Now the kids are watching more television, VCRs, and so forth. So they're picking up a lot [of English] from the videos. Also, I sense that more parents are teaching their young ones more English than Navajo. From [these] parents' point of view, if you speak more English by the time you get to school, then the better you'll achieve in school. I think that's their mentality. But that isn't the truth. We tell the parents that if you teach your child the native language, then he or she [will do better] in their academics later on."

Daniel McLaughlin, now a teacher-trainer at Navajo Community College, sums up the phenomenon in simple terms: "You pave roads, you create access to a wage economy, people's values change, and you get language shift." The sociolinguist Joshua Fishman calls these "dislocations," structural changes that weaken the bonds of a language community and make it vulnerable to penetration by the dominant culture.

Why have Indian bilingual programs, despite other indications of success, failed to halt or reverse the progress of language shift? First of all, they have rarely been designed to address this problem. Most have been transitional, gradually phasing out the Native American language as a medium of instruction, while giving English top priority. The handful of developmental programs, such as Rock Point and Peach Springs, emphasize the maintenance of skills in the native tongue, not the cultivation of those skills from scratch.

Moreover, schools alone cannot counteract a community's shifting attitudes and practices regarding its vernacular. Unless a dying language is reinforced in everyday life, on the job, in religious or cultural ceremonies, in tribal functions, and especially in the home, using it in the classroom is unlikely to keep it alive for very long. Unfortunately, parents often take the attitude that "the schools can solve that problem," says Lucille Watahomigie, director of the Peach Springs bilingual program. "That's something that we're trying hard to change. We're saying it's a partnership — we all need to work together to keep Hualapai from being lost."

Since the mid-1980s, several tribes — including the Navajo, Red Lake Band of Chippewa, Northern Ute, Arapaho, Pasqua Yaqui, and Tohono O'odham (Papago) — have responded to the threat by adopting official policies to promote the use of their languages in government and education. Despite good intentions, however, the impact of these policies has remained largely on paper. Tribes enjoy no legal authority over most reservation schools; so public and private school officials feel no obligation, other than moral pressure, to honor their wishes. Even when tribes do exercise control, use of the native language remains inconsistent. For example, except in its teacher-training programs, Navajo Community College operates almost exclusively in English. As an abstract idea, language preservation remains popular on most reservations. In practice, it tends to give way to more pressing priorities like economic development. Few tribes have committed their own financial resources to the cause.

Indian educators and community activists have had to look elsewhere for funding to cope with language loss. In 1990, they successfully lobbied Congress to pass the Native American Language Act. This broad policy statement stresses the federal government's "responsibility to act together with Native Americans to ensure the survival of these unique cultures and languages." In 1992, a grant program was established to carry out that mission; two years later the federal Administration for Native Americans began to distribute the funds.[7] In 1994, Congress amended the Bilingual Education Act to make programs seeking to conserve Native American languages eligible for Title VII grants.

The availability of external support, albeit limited, combined with a growing awareness that languages are threatened, has generated new enthusiasm for preservation efforts. Naturally many Indians have pinned their hopes on education as a tool for reversing language shift. Yet questions remain about whether school programs can, in effect, replace the family in transmitting endangered languages to future generations. Three instructional approaches have recently been introduced, although it is too soon to make firm judgments about their effectiveness.

The first could be called a *foreign-language model:* teaching Native American languages to children who have little or no exposure to them outside of school. Arizona, among several states to mandate foreign-language curricula in elementary schools, allows students to meet this requirement in a few indigenous tongues. Navajo educators in particular have cited the state mandate to justify new language programs. Instruction is limited, however, typically involving 20-to-30-minute classes three to five times per week. Because of a shortage of Navajo-proficient teachers, lessons are often taught by videotape. As in non-Indian schools, where children may get a "taste" of French or Spanish at an early age,

Indian students learn numbers, colors, animal names, and other simple vocabulary in their ancestral language. Seldom do they learn to use it for communication.

Still, such programs offer other benefits. At the Lawrence Elementary School in Tucson, the Yaqui language is taught in cultural context by traditional elders, who train students to participate in deer dance ceremonies and take them to visit the tribal homeland in Sonora, Mexico. While children do not become proficient in Yaqui at Lawrence, they do acquire a deeper appreciation of their heritage. Perhaps this will motivate some to continue studying the language.

A second approach is *two-way bilingual education,* in which English-speaking children learn a second language while LEP children learn English. In 1992, the Tuba City, Arizona, school district adopted such a model for a portion of its first graders and plans to extend it to all eight elementary grades. Half the students in the dual-language program are Navajo-proficient, half English-proficient. This enables each group to learn from the other in daily "immersion activities" such as arts and crafts, games, cooking, storytelling, and drama. The program also features whole-language book-making projects that focus on a monthly theme — often related to the local culture or environment — which help to develop children's Navajo and English skills in practical contexts. Other academic subjects are taught in the students' stronger language rather than in both (unlike the practice in many two-way models; see Chapter 11). Tuba City would like to expand the program, according to bilingual director Louise Scott. But only 15 percent of its students start school speaking Navajo well enough to serve as role models for their peers. To meet Arizona's foreign-language mandate, English-speakers not enrolled in the two-way program receive instruction in Navajo as a second language.

A final alternative — perhaps the best hope of reversing language shift in its advanced stages — is *early immersion.* A preschool "language nest" approach was pioneered by Maori educators in New Zealand who believed that, to acquire an endangered language, children must be sheltered from the influence of the dominant language. Since the mid-1980s, this model has been used to teach children Native Hawaiian, a language that had declined to about 2,000 speakers, including only 30 children, mainly on the isolated island of Ni'ihau. (Most Hawaiian Natives speak Hawaiian Creole English, often called "Pidgin.") Known as Pûnana Leo, the program began in private preschools for children as young as two; later it expanded to public elementary schools. The total immersion approach postpones English instruction until the 5th grade. Yet, over the long term, students outscore their English-speaking counterparts on standardized tests, according to William Wilson of the University of Hawaii.

In 1986, Wayne Holm, a veteran educator on the Navajo reservation, adapted this model to an elementary school at Fort Defiance, Arizona. In a town where only 2 percent of five-year-olds speak Navajo fluently, parents were eager for help in preserving the language. The Fort Defiance program draws students from the one-third of kindergartners judged to have a "passive knowledge" of Navajo. English instruction is introduced slowly, from 40 minutes per day in kindergarten and 1st grade, to half a day in grades 2 and 3, to virtually 100 percent in grades 4 and 5.[8] Academic outcomes so far have been encouraging. By the 5th grade, Navajo immersion students generally score as well as, and often better than, their peers in English-only classrooms, Holm reports. As in the Hawaiian immersion program, the Navajo students are developing a command of the indigenous language "without cost" to their English or to their achievement in other subjects.

These approaches remain tentative first steps, however. Only a handful of such programs exist, and funding is limited. Meanwhile, the clock is ticking. Already it may be too late to shore up many Native American tongues, which have largely eroded away. Activists are beginning to recognize that, if languages are to be saved, indigenous communities themselves must take the lead rather than wait for outside help.

Notes

1. By 1986-87, there were 89 Title VII-supported projects serving Indian children, totaling $9.6 million, or 10.7 percent of bilingual education grants to school districts. As part of Secretary William Bennett's "bilingual education initiative," the Department of Education tightened regulations in a way that threatened to exclude many Indian students from receiving Title VII services. To be considered LEP, the department said, children would have to come from homes where there was "substantial use of [the native] language for communication." Contrary to expectations, however, the change had little or no impact on grant awards. There was no wholesale elimination of Indian Title VII programs; nor will there be under current law. In its 1988 reauthorization of the Bilingual Education Act, Congress restored the pre-Bennett definition.

2. It is important to note than neither Chesarek, Leap, nor Littlebear is espousing the view that LEP Indian children are "semi-lingual" or that they speak a "restricted code" characteristic of disadvantaged social groups. Such notions, which have supported a "verbal deficit" explanation for students' academic difficulties, have been discredited

by psycholinguistic research. Studies have shown that all normal children become competent speakers of natural languages to which they are sufficiently exposed. This does not mean, however, that they will necessarily acquire the standard language used in school. Native American children may grow up hearing their elders speak a *pidgin*, a simplified variety of English mixed with the indigenous language; along with their peers, they elaborate this code into a *creole*, a fully developed language that takes on a life of its own. Some may acquire two or more varieties of Indian English, especially in communities where more than one tribal group is present. While mastering such nonstandard dialects, at home these children receive too little comprehensible input in standard English or in their ancestral tongue to become competent speakers of these languages. Hence their need for special assistance in school.

3. Three other Indian instructors, trained under a previous Title VII grant, were teaching in nonbilingual classrooms.

4. The Rough Rock English-Navajo Language Arts Program (RRENLAP) is a transitional bilingual curriculum, however, while KEEP uses only English. In 1994, Rough Rock received a Title VII grant to provide a developmental Navajo-English program in grades 4-6.

5. Fewer than one percent of these kindergartners could understand no English whatsoever; 13 percent had no knowledge of Navajo. While 93 percent spoke at least some English, 53 percent spoke some Navajo. The study was conducted by Wayne Holm of the Navajo Nation's Office of Diné Culture, Language, and Community Services. In a Navajo Head Start survey conducted that same year, teachers rated 54 percent of preschoolers as English-only speakers, 18 percent as Navajo-only speakers, and 28 percent as bilingual.

6. These figures cover the United States and Canada, which were relatively less diverse than Central and South America. According to one conservative estimate, "In 1492, as many as 2,000 separate, mutually unintelligible languages were spoken by the many different peoples inhabiting the Western Hemisphere." These included about 250 languages in North America, 350 in Mexico and Central America, and 1,450 in South America. See Joel Sherzer, "A Richness of Voices," in Alvin M. Josephy, Jr., ed., *America in 1492: The World of the Indian Peoples Before the Arrival of Columbus* (New York: Knopf, 1992), p. 251.

7. The program's initial budget was $1 million, providing funds for eighteen language preservation projects. Even this modest amount had to be pried out of the Clinton administration with a stern letter from Senator Daniel Inouye of Hawaii to Secretary of Health and Human Services Donna Shalala.

8. In the original program design, a daily hour of Navajo activities was scheduled for the upper grades, but in practice it has not always been provided.

10 California: Coping With Diversity

$\mathcal{M}$any educators feared the worst when Governor George Deukmejian twice vetoed attempts to extend California's bilingual education law, allowing it to "sunset" in June 1987. His successor, Pete Wilson, rejected two similar bills in the 1990s. Now the state with more than 40 percent of the nation's limited-English-proficient (LEP) students had no statute to govern their schooling. The expired law had been a virtual bill of rights for language-minority children, providing guarantees unmatched in other states. Did the governors' refusal to support its extension signal a retreat from the commitment to serve English learners?

A decade later only five of California's 1,085 school districts had moved to curtail bilingual education and to substitute English-only methodologies.

Meanwhile, numerous others had expanded and improved their bilingual approaches, sunset or no sunset, beyond what the law had formerly mandated. Exemplary programs for LEP children remained exemplary. The Case Studies model and other innovative curricula continued to spread. The California Association for Bilingual Education continued to draw upward of 10,000 teachers, administrators, and researchers to its annual conference. In 1997, the state was no less a leader in the field than it was in 1987 (although soon that leadership would be severely tested by an anti-bilingual initiative; see Chapter 13.)

This is not to say that the Chacón-Moscone Bilingual Bicultural Education Act had little impact in its eleven years of existence. Especially after it was strengthened in 1981, the law served to impress upon school officials, in great detail, their obligations to LEP students:

- Bilingual classrooms had to be established where at least ten LEP children in an elementary grade came from the same language background; some exceptions were allowed for approved alternative programs.
- In elementary schools with smaller concentrations of LEP children, and in grades 7 through 12, students were to be served through "individualized learning programs" featuring at least twenty minutes a day of special language assistance.
- Schools had to identify students' native language on enrollment and to assess their oral English skills; strict procedures had to be followed when reclassifying students as English proficient.
- To avoid segregation the law required that at least one-third of the students in a bilingual classroom be fluent English speakers.
- Bilingual teacher certification meant passing examinations in three competencies: second language, culture, and methodology.
- Recognizing the shortage of qualified instructors, the law allowed districts to staff bilingual classrooms with teachers who had signed "waivers," or agreements to learn a new language and to complete other certification requirements; bilingual aides had to be assigned to such classrooms.
- Parents retained the right to insist on English-only instruction for their children.

For the most part, school districts were not inclined to retreat from these principles simply because the act had expired. Nor was Superintendent of Public Instruction Bill Honig. He announced that many of the old requirements would remain in effect, under an expansive interpretation of federal and state civil-rights laws. Native-language instruction would still have to be provided where it was feasible and necessary. Alternative approaches would be acceptable only if they reinforced children's cultural identity and used state-of-the-art methodologies like sheltered English; there would be no return to sink-or-swim. LEP programs would still have to be staffed with qualified teachers, although districts would have more flexibility in meeting this goal. Even after bilingual education advocates lost the *Teresa P. v. Berkeley* case in 1989 (see Chapter 3), Honig did not waver in enforcing these standards in triennial "compliance reviews" of school districts.

In practice, however, legal requirements meant little if a district failed to recruit adequate numbers of bilingual teachers. As the number of LEP students in California grew by more than 10 percent annually during the 1980s, so did the difficulty of staffing their classrooms. No state mandate could magically eliminate the shortage of qualified personnel.

The Los Angeles Unified School District, with the nation's largest enrollment of LEP students, illustrates the pressures created by changing demographics. In 1985-86, L.A. Unified employed 7,000 paraprofessionals to supplement its corps of 1,722 certified bilingual teachers and 1,936 teachers "on waiver." Though largely untrained, about half of these aides were providing direct instruction while waivered teachers looked on. Only 40 percent of the district's LEP children were in approved bilingual programs that year; the rest studied under vaguely defined "individual learning plans," or received no special help at all.

By 1995-96, the staffing picture had brightened. Using financial incentives to aid in recruitment, L.A. Unified nearly doubled the number of its certified bilingual teachers, to 3,077. Another 1,381 bilingual teachers were working toward certification and 9,666 bilingual paraprofessionals were assisting in the classroom. Still, the district's gains in staffing failed to keep pace with the its LEP enrollment over the decade, which doubled from 145,000 to 301,000. As a result, the percentage of English learners served in bilingual classrooms declined, to 34 percent.

New waves of immigrants have had an impact on many American communities, but nowhere more than in California. Vietnamese "boat people," rural Mexicans, prosperous Taiwanese, and Salvadoran refugees, not to mention Filipinos, Koreans, Iranians, Russians, Afghans, and Bosnians have chosen the state as their new home. Nearly 38 percent of all immigrants to the United States in the 1980s wound up in California and the trend continues. They have transformed the state's racial, cultural, and linguistic makeup. In 1970, Hispanics accounted for 12 percent of California's population and Asians 3 percent; by 1995, these proportions had mushroomed to 29 percent and 11 percent, respectively. Because of high birth rates, civil unrest, and debt crises in countries of origin, no letup in immigration, legal or illegal, is foreseen. Early in the 21st century, California is projected to become a "majority minority" state. Because immigrant groups are, on average, younger than native English speakers, their influence will be felt even sooner in the schools. In 1988-89, non-Hispanic white students became a minority in California for the first time since the Gold Rush. By the mid-1990s Latinos had become the largest group.[1]

The California Department of Education keeps careful track of demographic patterns through a statewide language census conducted each year. In the spring of 1998, schools classified more than one in four California students as limited-English-proficient. The total of 1,406,166 LEP children in grades K through 12 represented a sixfold increase over the past 20 years (see Table 10-1). More English learners were enrolled in Los Angeles County than in all of Texas, the state with the second-largest LEP population.[2] Spanish was the language most commonly spoken by California students, followed by Vietnamese, Hmong, Cantonese, Pilipino (Tagalog), Khmer (Cambodian), Korean, Armenian, Mandarin, and Russian. Among the fastest growing language groups were Ukrainian, Serbo-Croatian, Urdu, Hindi, Punjabi, and Mien/Yao.

Alhambra's Response

The Alhambra School District in the eastern suburbs of Los Angeles had no choice but to respond, if somewhat belatedly, to these demographic trends. Substantial numbers of Hispanics had begun to arrive there in the mid-1960s. They were followed a decade later by Chinese, especially in the town of Monterey Park,[3] where a real estate developer was attracting immigrants from Taiwan and Hong Kong. Despite its growing population of LEP students, however, in 1977 the district had no bilingual classes and only hit-and-miss instruction in English as a second language (ESL). At that time the federal Office for Civil Rights (OCR) determined that Alhambra was failing to meet its obligations under the Supreme Court's *Lau v. Nichols* decision.

As part of the Lau plan that resulted, school officials agreed to launch a small bilingual education program in September 1977. This amounted to fourteen classrooms for Spanish-speaking children, recalls Suanna Ponce, the district's bilingual coordinator at the time. A Chinese-language program was added the following year; in 1980, it was divided into Cantonese and Mandarin classrooms.

TABLE 10-1.

LEP Student Enrollments and Certified Bilingual Teachers in California Public Schools, 1978 through 1998

Year	LEP Students	Increase	Certified Bilingual Teachers	Estimated Teacher Shortage
1998	1,406,166	1.8%	15,783	26,751*
1997	1,381,393	4.4%	14,965	26,923*
1996	1,323,767	4.8%	13,548	20,692
1995	1,262,982	3.9%	12,105	20,692
1994	1,215,218	5.5%	10,742	20,824
1993	1,151,819	6.8%	10,014	19,906
1992	1,078,705	9.4%	9,181	18,834
1991	986,462	14.5%	8,667	16,941
1990	861,531	16.0%	8,037	14,328
1989	742,559	13.8%	7,775	11,710
1988	652,439	6.4%	7,955	8,991
1987	613,224	8.0%	8,025	7,903
1986	567,564	8.3%	8,020	6,722
1985	524,076	7.4%	7,891	5,722
1984	487,835	6.6%	7,485	N.A.
1983	457,540	6.0%	7,497	N.A.
1982	431,449	14.5%	6,497	N.A.
1981	376,794	15.7%	6,555	N.A.
1980	325,748	12.9%	5,476	N.A.
1979	288,427	23.6%	N.A.	N.A.
1978	233,444	N.A.	N.A.	N.A.

* Reflects demand for approximately 6,000 additional teachers created by the statewide class-size reduction program initiated in 1996-97.

SOURCE: Norman C. Gold, *Teachers for LEP Students: Demand, Supply, and Shortage* (Sacramento: California Department of Education, Complaints Management and Bilingual Compliance, 1997).

By 1982, there were enough Vietnamese children with limited English skills to start instruction in that language.

A decade after OCR's intervention, Alhambra's bilingual education program had grown to 120 classrooms. With 20,000 students it remained a medium-sized district, but nearly 80 language groups were represented. In 1985-86, the combined Asian population represented 49 percent of total enrollment; Hispanics, 35 percent. LEP children not accommodated in the four bilingual curricula were receiving ESL instruction and, wherever possible, individual assistance in their primary language.

Alhambra has made a substantial commitment to recruiting bilingual teachers, developing native-language materials, and hiring instructional aides for every bilingual classroom — something that was never mandated by state law. It opened two "orientation and assessment centers" to handle language testing and intensive English classes for new students. By the mid-1980s, two-thirds of Alhambra's bilingual teachers were fully certified, and all of its teachers were required to complete thirty-five hours of ESL training, freeing thirteen ESL specialists to deal with the most difficult cases.

While OCR provided the catalyst, Alhambra's turnabout was accomplished largely with the district's own resources. Although its bilingual education efforts received Title VII grants until 1986, the aid "was always very supplemental in nature," Ponce says. Using no federal funds, in 1986-87 the school system employed an administrative staff of nine to coordinate the program (as compared with just one or two in nearby districts of similar size).

Bilingual education in Alhambra also departs from the norm in a demographic sense: Hispanic children do not predominate. Ethnic diversity means that students have many "learning styles" that need to be taken into account. Training teachers in "strategies for intercultural communication" has been essential, according to Ponce:

> Sometimes an Anglo teacher who hasn't had a lot of contact with other cultural groups [doesn't understand that] children have been trained not to look up at an adult when they are being spoken to — and in this case the Asians and Hispanics are identical — because it's considered a sign of disrespect. So in the beginning, the teacher says, "Look at me," and that goes contrary to everything a child has been taught. . . . [In] the Vietnamese culture the Buddhists hold the head to be very sacrosanct. Here it's very common to touch kids on the head as they

are going by, but that's a sign of disrespect to the child. These are small nuances, but they can cause pain for the child and frustration for the teacher.

Alhambra's bilingual programs in Cantonese, Mandarin, and Vietnamese teach initial literacy in English rather than in the native tongue. Asian language skills, unlike those in Spanish, transfer less readily to English because of radical differences in alphabet, Ponce argues, while acknowledging that this remains a point of controversy among researchers. Children in the Asian programs receive prereading instruction in their first language, she explains. "What we do is a lot of oral language development. Meaning that we spend time reading stories out loud to them, discussing these stories, going down Bloom's taxonomy of higher-level thinking skills — all in Chinese. All they're *not* doing is reading Chinese characters." Continuing to develop vocabulary in the native language speeds the acquisition of English, she adds.

This approach is popular among parents, particularly Chinese Americans, who often prefer their children to learn Chinese literacy in private "Saturday schools," where old-country teachers can impart the culture in traditional ways. In public school, Ponce says, "they want to maximize the time that children hear English." Asian parents initially tend to be apprehensive about bilingual instruction. Indeed, some Chinese settle temporarily in the district to enable their children to learn English, which is becoming the *lingua franca* of Asian commerce. Gradually such parents come to understand that "using the primary language [is] a means toward that end," Ponce says.

Children are taught ESL daily, preferably by their own teacher rather than in pullout classes, she explains. "The very best kind of ESL is contextual and tied to other learning. It's only the classroom teacher who can say, 'I'm doing a unit on dinosaurs in science. For ESL I'll build dinosaur vocabulary.'"

Despite the difficulties, Alhambra's decision to offer instruction in Asian languages has paid off handsomely, according to research by Edmund Lee, formerly a member of the district's bilingual staff. In his 1986 study, 4th, 5th, and 6th graders who had completed the bilingual curriculum scored as well as, or better than, their English-speaking peers — from both Chinese and nonminority backgrounds — in reading, and significantly better in language arts. In mathematics both groups of Chinese students performed substantially higher than nonminority students.

The results, Lee says, vindicate the 36th percentile criterion typically used by California districts for reclassifying LEP students as ready for mainstream class-rooms. While some critics have argued that this standard leaves children to languish "in the LEP category forever, [the study] shows that if we use that as a target point, they really take off afterward," he concludes. Ponce seconds this assessment: "Strong primary language skills predict success in English. I can almost say that categorically about every language group there is."

At the same time, Lee's research undercuts the stereotype of Asian Americans as a "model minority." While some opponents of bilingual education assert that Asian students are succeeding academically without special language programs, Lee found that among Chinese students in Alhambra, there were significant differences in achievement. For example, Cantonese speakers — largely "ethnic Chinese" from Vietnam, who tend to come from poorer and less literate backgrounds — performed at lower levels in language and reading than Mandarin speakers from Taiwan.

The Teacher Problem

Alhambra's ability to cope with a diverse student population owes much to its ability to recruit bilingual teachers — unusual among California school districts. By 1997-98, the statewide shortage was estimated at nearly 27,000, exacerbated by an ambitious effort to reduce class size in elementary schools. This meant that only two out of ten LEP students were taught by certified bilingual teachers.

The waiver system, created by California's late bilingual education law, was a stopgap measure designed to encourage mainstream teachers to acquire new language skills. Yet it produced few certified bilingual teachers, even after the legislature extended to six years the period in which to qualify. In 1984-85, only 6 percent of waivered teachers who took the bilingual certification examination passed all three sections. For English-speaking teachers in mid-career, the prospect of being forced to learn Spanish — or worse, Cantonese, Tagalog, or Urdu — on their own time and out of their own pockets, was unpopular, to say the least. It was also an unrealistic demand, given the limitations of foreign-language classes that meet after school for a few hours each week.[4] Still, some see benefits in the experiment. Alhambra teachers who studied Vietnamese for two or more years attained nowhere near the proficiency they needed for classroom teaching, says Suanna Ponce. "But it's very important for them to have an acquaintance with the language, so that they can say a few basic phrases, put the children at ease, and also understand the structure of that language, because if you know the syntax of Vietnamese, you can remedy mistakes in English."

The Sunset Advisory Committee, a body established in 1985 to review the impact of the state bilingual education law, urged California legislators to give teachers financial incentives to acquire the extra competencies needed for bilingual certification. Thus far, however, the state has left pay decisions up to individual school districts; so practices vary widely. While the Los Angeles school board authorized yearly stipends of up to $5,000 for certified bilingual teachers, few others have been so generous. Some subsidize teachers' language courses or count academic credits toward raises; many do neither.

"There's no way my teachers are going to become proficient in Spanish," says Jean Nelson, principal of the Geddes Elementary School in Baldwin Park, California. "So if you hit them with the fact that they're going to have to learn Spanish right off the bat, you're not going to get anywhere in my district." At Nelson's school only two of fourteen bilingual teachers were certified in 1986-87. The Baldwin Park district has proven, however, that bilingual programs can work despite this handicap. Formerly LEP students are scoring at or above state norms by the 5th grade. Nelson's approach has been to give special training and support to instructional aides, for example, by relieving them from recess duty so they can meet with teachers to discuss classroom problems.

While acknowledging the success of Baldwin Park's program, Norm Gold of the California Department of Education voices reservations: "This is a solution which makes us uneasy. There are competent instructional aides who are getting instructional aides' salaries, who by all respects are credentialable teachers except for a couple of [tests] they can't pass." In 1992, there were more than 26,000 bilingual paraprofessionals working in California schools; many were interested in a teaching career. For such aides, who come largely from language-minority backgrounds, the main obstacle has been the California Basic Education Skills Test (CBEST), which all new teachers must pass. Critics say the unrealistic level of English proficiency required by the CBEST has dried up a natural source of bilingual teachers: native speakers of minority languages, including many competent educators from other countries. Among California's own teacher candidates who completed their training in 1984-85, only 46 percent of Hispanics and 56 percent of Asians passed the examination.[5]

Historically the state's institutions of higher education have paid limited attention to this problem. In 1990, they made 13,050 recommendations for teaching credentials. But only 508 — or 4 percent — involved bilingual credentials at a time when California classrooms faced a shortage of 14,000 bilingual instructors. Shelly Spiegel-Coleman, a bilingual/ESL specialist in the Los Angeles County Office of Education, says it is frustrating to see colleges turning out large numbers of teachers who are unprepared for their first assignment. "The reality is, everybody sitting in the regular teacher training program is going to find themselves in a bilingual classroom," she points out, "because those are the classrooms that are open. New teachers are not placed in the 'better schools' — quote, unquote. If you're in a system long enough, you transfer there. The openings are in the minority community, and in our county, the largest minority community is the one that doesn't speak English."

"This shortage of bilingual and English language development teachers is the greatest barrier to the improvement of instructional programs for LEP students," says Norm Gold. In 1991, the state education department launched a LEP Staffing Initiative designed to tackle the problem on several fronts: recruitment, teacher preparation, staff development, certification, and public relations. Coordinating these efforts among teacher-training institutions, professional organizations, school districts, and academic experts brought some modest gains, Gold believes, even though the legislature declined to provide any new funding. Shortages of bilingual and ESL teachers have continued to grow, but not as rapidly as before.

Some of the most encouraging gains have been achieved through the Latino Teacher Project based at the University of Southern California. While the numbers are small — 50 graduates each year — so far 85 percent have found positions as bilingual teachers and their evaluations have been glowing. Over the first three years, the student attrition rate was less than 3 percent, an enviable record for any teacher-training program. While participants receive financial help through the Ford Foundation, project director Michael Genzuk credits two other factors for sustaining their motivation. First, students get practical experience throughout, rather than waiting until their fifth year, as most teacher candidates must do. By working as aides in local schools, they also become "socialized" into the field. Second, a mentoring program helps them cope with obstacles, whether personal or professional. Genzuk adds that graduates themselves are becoming role models for other teacher aides, encouraging fellow Hispanics to follow their path.

Methodology Matters

In L.A. Unified, LEP children arrived speaking eighty-two different tongues in 1987, but the schools provided bilingual instruction in only six: Spanish,

Cantonese, Vietnamese, Korean, Pilipino, and Armenian. About 2,500 classrooms — whose enrollment is overwhelmingly Spanish-speaking — lacked fully certified teachers that year. Making the best of a difficult situation, the district has worked to upgrade the qualifications of paraprofessionals and has experimented with various ways to make better use of its bilingual teachers. Language grouping at the Eastman Avenue School, for example, was successful in concentrating the efforts of certified instructors on children who needed them most.

Another model, developed by the Roscoe School in Sun Valley, featured the use of teaming to maximize teacher resources. In 1986-87, more than 65 percent of Roscoe's students were classified as LEP, but only ten of the school's seventeen teachers had bilingual certifications. Roscoe's solution was to let Spanish-proficient teachers teach Spanish and the noncredentialed teachers teach English, grouped in bilingual, cooperative teams that made decisions on how to handle individual student needs. "Block scheduling" effectively tapped the strengths of each teacher. Students were divided each morning for a two-hour period of language arts in the native tongue, followed by a forty-five-minute lesson in the second language: ESL for Spanish speakers and SSL, or Spanish as a second language, for English speakers. Other subjects were taught in bilingual or English-language classrooms. "The teachers found that by cooperative teaching — getting together and saying, 'I can do this part, but not that part' — they were able to provide the services that were necessary," says Toni Marsnik, Roscoe's former bilingual coordinator and now an adviser in the L.A. Unified district office.

Unlike Eastman, however, Roscoe put little emphasis on instructional consistency. Some teachers used the concurrent translation method, while others alternated languages on different days. ESL was sometimes grammar-based, sometimes delivered in the form of sheltered English. "Teachers will switch and try different things — whatever seems to work," according to James Morris, the program's director. Another difference was that students' achievement test scores at the Roscoe School showed no clear improvement, while Eastman's were rising steadily.

By contrast, small and medium-sized districts in Los Angeles County are increasingly trying new methodologies and applying them with consistency. By the mid-1980s, influenced by the theories of Jim Cummins and Stephen Krashen, many had adopted approaches that stress native-language development and communication-based ESL. Meanwhile, bilingual programs in Los Angeles continued to feature concurrent translation, grammar-based ESL, and limited use of the native language. While district officials understood that these approaches were outmoded, says Shelly Spiegel-Coleman, "L.A. has a real problem with staff development." Besides the cost and logistical difficulties of inservice training — in the district's year-round schools, one-quarter of the staff is absent at any time — consultants had previously trained thousands of teachers in the old methods. Now they had to retrain them to *stop* using those techniques.

"In districts that are smaller, it's easier to get the message out," Spiegel-Coleman adds. One strategy has been the Multidistrict Trainer of Trainers Institute (MTTI), developed by Margarita Calderón. Starting with the view that staff development is crucial to effective bilingual programs, MTTI concentrates on putting the latest theory into the hands of district personnel who train bilingual and ESL teachers. Trainers are schooled in the theoretical framework developed by the Case Studies project, featuring sessions by leading researchers. Effective instructional techniques are demonstrated, and trainers learn how to coach teachers in the classroom, an essential step in initiating the new methods.

Training the trainers has had an incremental but significant impact in several districts. As graduates of MTTI rise to higher leadership positions, the new approaches are becoming firmly established, along with the whole idea of bilingual education. Student gains are converting the skeptics. From her vantage point in the county Office of Education, Spiegel-Coleman says that in the late 1970s "there were some [district administrators] who were adamant about trying to circumvent the law. Now they're asking, 'What can we do? How can we help our staffs? Can you help us recruit teachers?'"

Los Angeles 'Master Plan'

Before the bilingual education law was allowed to sunset, California's non-bilingual teachers became increasingly restive under the waiver system. In L.A. Unified, more than 300 were threatened with transfers to less desirable positions if they failed to sign an agreement to learn a second language. Assemblyman Frank Hill, a Republican who had sponsored California's successful English Only initiative in 1986, called the waiver requirement "job blackmail." Hill's opposition was instrumental in convincing Deukmejian to veto an extension of the law. Shortly thereafter, in August 1987, a dissident campaign known as Learning English Advocates Drive (LEAD) organized a referendum within the United Teachers of Los Angeles to demand an end to native-language instruction. The nonbinding measure passed by a 78-to-22 percent margin, with about 7,000 union members voting. With substantial funding from the English Only movement, LEAD has expanded into a national advocacy organization opposed to bilingual education.

The Los Angeles school board, however, was moving in the opposite direction. Buoyed by the success of the Eastman model in twenty-seven additional schools, the board voted in 1988 to adopt the curriculum, in full or in part, throughout the city. Central to this ambitious "master plan" is a major expansion of teacher recruitment and training, beginning with a $21 million increase in the district's bilingual education spending (to $114 million for 1988-89). Much of the new money went for stipends to encourage current staff to complete the bilingual credentialing process and to attract qualified newcomers.

Where schools had sufficient personnel, the Eastman-Case Studies curriculum was replicated, part of an effort called Project MORE. Where there were too few bilingual teachers, a modified version was applied, with children learning core subjects like language and mathematics in their native language, combined with sheltered English instruction in science and social studies. The district continued to experiment with various approaches "to get more mileage out of our bilingual teachers," Toni Marsnik explains, such as teaming them with teachers yet to be certified.

Staff development, with an emphasis on methodology, was seen as crucial to the master plan's success. "The goal is to provide consistent programs," she says. "Kids have often been pulled out of one program and put into another, and that doesn't help their development." An approach that proved successful in the past — sending an "instructional task force" to aid principals in teacher-training — was extended to all schools. Other features of the master plan included:

- Newcomer schools offering one-year programs for non-English-speaking students on both elementary and secondary levels.
- Model bilingual programs at the secondary level to supplement ESL, the only treatment available in the past.
- Bilingual prekindergarten instruction.
- District-financed classes in intensive Spanish for teachers.
- "Two-way" bilingual schools, in which English speakers are immersed in Spanish while LEP children learn English.

In the early 1990s, the district launched two-way experiments in diverse sections of the city, from Watts to Koreatown to West Los Angeles. School officials hoped that by expanding English speakers' opportunities to learn a second language, the public would take a fresh look at the benefits of bilingual instruction. "In the beginning, we were hesitant to get involved," says assistant superintendent Carmen Schroeder. "We have such a great need to provide bilingual teachers for LEP kids. But we realized it was a big advantage to have [a Spanish] immersion program, because living in southern California, it's almost a necessity to be bilingual. We believe it will be a wonderful way of joining hands [among] very different ethnic groups. And if the majority of the community understands that to know a second language is to your benefit, that will be a big plus." Schroeder is not alone among bilingual education advocates in believing that a greater emphasis on serving native English speakers could be the program's salvation.

Notes

1. In 1997-98, Hispanics accounted for 40.5 percent of the state's public school enrollment (K through 12), non-Hispanic whites 38.8 percent, Asians and Pacific Islanders 11.1 percent, African-Americans 8.8 percent, and Native Americans 0.9 percent.
2. In 1994-95, Texas reported 457,437 LEP students in grades K through 12. New York was third (236,356), followed by Florida (153,841), Illinois (107,084), Arizona (98,128), New Mexico (84,457), New Jersey (52,081), Washington (51,598), Michigan (47,123), Massachusetts (44,476), and Oklahoma (31,562). For further information on LEP enrollment trends, see Reynaldo F. Macías and Candace Kelly, *Summary Report of the Survey of the States' Limited English Proficient Students and Available Educational Programs and Services, 1994-1995* (Washington, D.C.: National Clearinghouse for Bilingual Education, 1996; http://www.ncbe.gwu.edu/ncbepubs/seareports/94-95/index.htm).
3. The school district serves Alhambra and Monterey Park, along with high school students in San Gabriel and parts of Rosemead.
4. According to the Educational Testing Service, minimal competence in an "easy" language for English speakers, such as Spanish or French, requires an average of 720 hours of intensive instruction for high-aptitude, motivated adult learners. In a more difficult language, such as Japanese or Arabic, it takes 2,760 hours. At this rate, assuming ideal conditions and six hours of class per week, it would take waivered teachers roughly 120 to 460 weeks of instruction to become certified in a second language. See Rebecca L. Oxford and Nancy C. Rhodes, "U.S. Foreign Language Instruction: Assessing Needs and Creating an Action Plan," *ERIC Clearinghouse on Languages and Linguistics News Bulletin* 11, No. 2 (March 1988): 1, 68.
5. In 1997-98, 77.6 percent of California's public school teachers were non-Hispanic whites, 11.6 percent Hispanics, 5.1 percent African-Americans, 4.9 percent Asians, and 0.8 percent Native Americans.

11 Two-Way Bilingual Education

*M*onolingual Americans are put to shame by the worldwide spread of our national tongue. By some estimates English is spoken today by one billion people, two-thirds of whom learned it as a second language. "Fifty million precollegiate Chinese young people are studying English," reports the American Council on the Teaching of Foreign Languages, "while less than 5,000 of their counterparts in the United States are studying Chinese, a ratio of 10,000 to one."

Disturbed by our growing trade deficit with linguistically developed countries like Japan, in 1988 the U.S. Congress created a $20 million program, on top of the $35 million it was already spending, to promote the teaching of foreign languages. That same year it appropriated nearly $90 million for Title VII programs of transitional bilingual education (TBE) designed to *replace* other languages with English. In other words, while our government subsidized instruction in 169 "critical languages" — those deemed vital to national security, economic competitiveness, and scientific inquiry — it was encouraging native speakers of those tongues to abandon them as quickly as possible. This schizophrenic approach could be summed up as *additive bilingualism for English speakers and subtractive bilingualism for language minorities.*

Senator Paul Simon, in his book *The Tongue-Tied American*, argues that we are foolhardy to discard the linguistic gifts of immigrants in our haste to Americanize their children: "Because of our rich ethnic mix, the United States is home to millions whose first language is not English. . . . We are the fourth largest Spanish-speaking country in the world. Yet almost nothing is being done to preserve the language skills we now have or to use this rich linguistic resource to train people in the use of a language other than English."

What are the costs of this wasteful policy? One way to gauge our society's loss, in part, is to consider the formidable expense of teaching monolingual Americans to speak other tongues. The Defense Language Institute in Monterey, California, each year provides instruction in more than forty languages to approximately 6,000 full-time students, who are members of the U.S. military. The school is highly regarded, and the instruction it provides does not come cheap — in time or dollars. During the mid-1980s, for example, a forty-seven-week course in Korean cost the Institute about $12,000 per student, in addition to personnel salaries and benefits. Yet its graduates achieved lower levels of oral proficiency in that language than a five-year-old native speaker of Korean typically brings to school, according to Russell Campbell and Kathryn Lindholm of the Center for Language Education and Research (CLEAR).

Though lacking literacy, the researchers say, the Korean kindergartner has "mastered completely the phonological system of adult Korean speakers [and] acquired nearly all of the morphological and syntactical rules necessary for sentence formation." Moreover, the child has attained the sociolinguistic sensitivity of native Koreans, able to choose appropriate "lexicon, honorifics, and even voice qualifiers and body-language depending upon his [or her] conversational partners."

Little is being done, however, to conserve and develop these skills. In 1993-94, there were nearly 39,000 Korean-speaking students in California public schools, but only three schools in the state offered developmental bilingual programs in Korean. The vast majority provided only English-as-a-second-language

(ESL) instruction for Korean speakers or, at best, transitional bilingual education. Lacking the opportunity and encouragement to maintain their native language, most of these children will lose it before reaching adulthood.

Opposition to bilingual education often stems from the fear that it will enhance loyalty to minority tongues and retard the process of linguistic assimilation. Ironically, the transitional philosophy that long dominated Title VII is more likely to accelerate *language loss* among minority children. As Catherine Snow and Kenji Hakuta observe:

> Bilingual education in its present form may be one of the greatest misnomers of educational programs. What it fosters is monolingualism; bilingual classrooms are efficient revolving doors between home-language monolingualism and English monolingualism. . . . The bilingual education initiatives that were taken in the 1960s have certainly made the transition easier for students. But the bottom line of all of these programs has been an almost single-minded interest in the extent and the efficiency of English proficiency development.

Impetus for Two-Way Programs

The quick-exit orientation, though still pervasive, is beginning to face a challenge from parents, educators, and even some federal policymakers. Projects like Case Studies are starting to document the benefits of extended mother-tongue instruction for LEP children, while foreign-language immersion programs are yielding superior results among English-speaking students. With parents clamoring for language enrichment programs, a growing number of educators are asking: Would it be possible to serve both groups of students with a single program? Could language-majority and language-minority children, learning side by side and assisting each other, become fluent bilinguals while making good progress in other subjects?

The answer is yes, according to Richard Tucker, a pioneer in Canadian immersion research. *Two-way bilingual immersion* — also known as *dual language instruction* — offers the benefits of additive bilingualism for both groups, he explains, despite their differing needs:

> For the language-majority youngster, there should be an opportunity to develop a far greater degree of facility in the target language

than is the case when participating in a traditional FLES (Foreign Language at the Elementary School) program. The opportunity to actually study meaningful content material via a target language and to interact socially as well as academically with native speakers of the language offers numerous benefits. In addition, for the language-minority youngster the opportunity to spend some portion of the day nurturing and sustaining mother-tongue skills and [another] portion . . . as a resource person for the language-majority youngster offers numerous social, cognitive, and academic benefits as well.

Tucker cites the successes of French immersion in Canada and developmental bilingual education in the United States. Meanwhile, there is encouraging, if preliminary, evidence from research on two-way programs.

Kathryn Lindholm and Zierlein Aclan followed the progress of 249 children enrolled in bilingual immersion programs in Northern California over a four-year period. They found a strong correlation between fluent bilingualism and academic achievement. By the 4th grade, native speakers of English and Spanish had acquired average to above-average skills in both languages. Those with the highest bilingual proficiency scored highest in English reading, Spanish reading, English mathematics, and Spanish mathematics.[1] The study ended before students had received the five to seven years of instruction that Jim Cummins and others say is needed to fully develop cognitive-academic skills in a second language (see Chapter 6). So, according to the researchers, these findings "may actually underestimate the advantages of [bilingual] proficiency on academic achievement."

Inspired by results like these, enthusiasm has grown rapidly for two-way bilingual education. A national directory compiled by Lindholm in 1987 listed thirty such programs, strictly defined. That is, all featured immersion in both English and a second language; English was used no more than 50 percent of the time; lessons were provided in a single language, without translation; and English speakers and non-English speakers were integrated for content instruction. An updated survey by the Center for Applied Linguistics found that by 1993-94, 99 districts had launched two-way programs in 176 schools. Only nine were initiated before the mid-1980s; most are at the elementary level. While 90 percent of the programs feature Spanish as the second language, others use Cantonese, Korean, Russian, Navajo, Japanese, French, Portuguese, and Haitian Creole.

Dissatisfaction with transitional approaches has been a common impetus for establishing two-way programs. Sidney Morison, principal of P.S. 84 in New York City, explains that in spite of his school's best efforts — recruitment of fluent Spanish-speaking teachers, liberal use of Hispanic culture in the classroom, and success in involving parents — its TBE curriculum was failing to produce bilingual students. Spanish-speaking children were gradually losing their language and their academic progress was unimpressive.

"Teachers taught mostly in English," Morison says, "because they felt tremendous pressure to produce good results on standardized tests. Spanish was used mainly for communication, to translate what was being taught in English." All that changed in 1983, when P.S. 84 launched a bilingual immersion approach. The new program demanded strict separation of languages — that is, no concurrent translation, and equal time for Spanish. Now the minority tongue could be "nourished, developed, and protected," and it was not long before the academic benefits became obvious, he says. "Hispanic children thought to be intellectually limited, or at least very quiet, are blossoming in Spanish-speaking classes. [They] are doing creative writing in Spanish in 1st and 2nd grade."

At the same time, many researchers believe that two-way bilingual education offers English speakers a potential advantage over "one-way" immersion education. Although the latter approach has been highly successful when compared with traditional methods of teaching foreign languages — clearly, it can produce functional bilinguals — students seldom achieve native-like skills in the second language. This finding has been consistent in immersion research in Canada and the United States, and it is usually ascribed to students' limited contact with native speakers of the second language.

The evaluator of an otherwise impressive immersion program in Culver City, California, determined that language-majority children had not fully acquired Spanish grammatical structures or phonology: "Both the tenaciousness and systematicity of [students'] errors suggest the development of a classroom dialect peculiar to Spanish Immersion Program students. The children . . . reinforce each other's incorrect usage, and fossilization at the morphological level results." Another researcher commented that if Hispanic children made errors of the same type in English, they would be candidates for remedial classes.

By contrast, in a dual immersion program with native Spanish speakers as "peer models," English-speaking children would likely acquire higher levels of proficiency in the second language, says Fred Genesee, a specialist in Canadian immersion. "Including students from both language groups creates a learning

Criteria for Effective Two-Way Bilingual Education

While evaluation research has been limited, basic research provides the following guidelines for two-way *or* bilingual immersion *programs, according to Kathryn Lindholm of the Center for Language Acquisition and Research at the University of California, Los Angeles.*

- *Long-term treatment.* A program must last four to six years for students to achieve bilingual proficiency.
- *Optimal input in two languages.* Second language input, provided through language arts and subject-matter instruction, must be comprehensible, that is, adjusted to students' level; relevant, so as to stimulate student interest; sufficient in quantity; and challenging, so that it requires students to "negotiate meaning."
- *Focus on academic subjects.* Children need more than language development. The curriculum should emphasize concept development as well, beginning in the second language for English speakers, in the native language for minority students.
- *Integration of language arts with curriculum.* Sheltered instruction alone has failed to produce native-like proficiency in the second language; students also need formal language arts. Linguistic structures are best mastered in connection with subject-matter instruction, rather than through isolated grammar exercises.
- *Separation of languages for instruction.* Sustained periods of monolingual instruction promote linguistic development better than concurrent approaches that mix languages during the same lesson.
- *Additive bilingual environment.* Enrichment approaches, in which children acquire a second language without abandoning their mother tongue, lead to higher levels of bilingual proficiency, along with improved self-esteem and more favorable attitudes toward other cultures.
- *Balance of language groups.* To ensure equity in the classroom, as well as maximum interactions among language-minority and language-majority children, the two groups should be mixed in roughly equal proportions. Never should the ratio slip below 2/3 - 1/3.
- *Sufficient use of minority language.* At least 50 percent of instruction should be conducted in the minority language, both to provide English-speaking students optimal input and to ensure that minority students develop cognitive-academic language proficiency in their native tongue.
- *Opportunities for speech production.* To become proficient in a second language, children need opportunities to practice it orally with native speakers, preferably including exercises on which language-minority and language-majority students can collaborate.
- *Administrative support.* Bilingual programs should be treated equitably within a school for many reasons; not least of these are the language-status implications that will be communicated to students.
- *Empowerment objective of instruction.* Breaking with the authoritarian "transmission model," in which teachers impart and children receive knowledge, instruction should be a dialogue in which students learn to think for themselves rather than simply to memorize information.
- *High-quality teachers.* Teachers need to be competent bilinguals, whether or not they respond only in the target language, so they can respond to children's needs and provide comprehensible input.
- *Home-school collaboration.* Especially for language-minority students, parental involvement is essential to reinforce children's native language development and to communicate high expectations about academic achievement.

environment that can be truly bilingual and bicultural. Sustained contact with members of the target language group of the same age as the learners may be necessary if students are to develop fundamentally more tolerant and positive attitudes toward each other." Successful two-way programs appear to confirm these predictions, although again research has been limited, even where such approaches have been tried for more than a decade.

The Oyster Experiment

One of the earliest experiments in two-way bilingual education was initiated at the Oyster Elementary School in Washington, D.C. At the time, 1971, there was little research evidence on second-language acquisition to guide program designers. According to Oyster's current principal, Paquita Holland, administrators were determined to avoid the segregation of Spanish-speaking children. Instead they hoped to turn the school's linguistic diversity into an enrichment experience for all students. With these goals in mind, Oyster adopted a fully bilingual curriculum for grades K through 6.

Before launching the program, the school district consulted parents on the choice of a new principal, and trained teachers for a year in bilingual methodologies. A further index of the district's commitment was its decision to hire a staff twice the regular size. With a Spanish-speaking teacher and an English-speaking teacher in each classroom, Oyster may be unique among public school bilingual programs.

In its pedagogical approach, Oyster strives for parity between the two languages of instruction, with English and Spanish used in roughly equal proportions, and with majority and minority children mixed throughout the day. The school's enrollment is 60 percent Latino, 20-to-25 percent white, 15 percent black, and 2 percent other language minority.[2] Each subject is taught in both English and Spanish — not concurrently, but on alternate days, periods, or semesters — giving students an immersion experience and also a chance to develop conceptually in their native tongue. Since children are mixed, teachers must work hard to make instruction comprehensible to one group and still interesting to the other.

An unusual feature of Oyster's curriculum is that children are taught initial literacy in English and Spanish at the same time. By the middle of the 1st grade, they are reading in both languages. The wisdom of this approach has been questioned by researchers like Merrill Swain of the Ontario Institute for Studies in Education. Citing studies in Canada, Swain warns that children who learn to read in this way may experience confusion due to "interfering and competing surface features" of the two languages. Better to let students transfer literacy skills, once mastered, from one tongue to another, she says. Paquita Holland responds that Oyster has never seen the need to change its reading program because the results have been so favorable. By the 3rd grade, children are reading two years above national norms in English. In 1987, they ranked at the 90th percentile in language and the 95th percentile in mathematics on the Comprehensive Test of Basic Skills; scores were comparable for 6th graders.[3]

One factor that may enhance the school's approach to reading is "the affirmation of the minority language," says Virginia Collier, a researcher in second-language acquisition and the parent of an Oyster graduate. "Because the whole school community is reinforcing Spanish as just as good as English," unlike the practice of many TBE programs, the Hispanic children are more likely to develop their native-language skills.

In other respects as well, Oyster is far from a typical urban school. To some extent the high test scores must reflect its double complement of teachers and its pupils' relatively high socioeconomic status. Although many of Oyster's 300 students come from the surrounding community, which is not affluent, Holland says that "we can be picky and choosy [about admissions] because we have such a long waiting list." Both Anglo and Hispanic parents have been known to camp out all night in front of school district headquarters to get their children enrolled at Oyster. Despite the demand, however, the District of Columbia has no plans to replicate the Oyster model elsewhere because of its high cost, Holland says.[4]

Moreover, the District of Columbia offers no public school programs in which English-proficient students can continue their education in Spanish after graduating from Oyster at the end of 6th grade. Affluent parents often transfer their children to private schools. By the time they graduate, Oyster students are usually sold on the advantages of bilingualism, Holland reports, "even though we're fighting all tides in society." As children grow older, the social pressure to speak English intensifies, says Collier, speaking from her own experience as an ESL teacher in the district. "Certainly, by the time they reach junior high school, many kids are putting Spanish down. Hispanic students go through a period of having mixed feelings about [their first language]."

In 1987, Collier conducted an informal survey to see what had become of Oyster's oldest graduates, those who had entered the program in the early 1970s and were now finishing college or starting careers. Had bilingual schooling strongly influenced these students? Or had its effects been transitory? Tracing eleven former students, all native English speakers who had kept in touch with

Oyster teachers, Collier found that her "biased sample" had prevailed against the odds. Over the years the graduates had continued to improve their Spanish skills. Five had studied Spanish as a part of a double major in college, and some had lived in Spanish-speaking countries. Several were involved in language teaching, social work, or other jobs in which they could use their Spanish.

Perhaps most significant, all the former students expressed positive attitudes toward bilinguals as well as toward bilingualism. Many had native Spanish speakers for friends or chose to live in Hispanic communities. By comparison, Collier notes, French immersion students in Canada, who are "schooled in a segregated setting, tend to come out with good attitudes toward French, but not toward French Canadians."

Program Variations

Though its successes are well-known, Oyster's approach — two teachers in every classroom and every subject taught in two languages — has failed to catch on elsewhere. Not only are such features expensive; they are also regarded as unnecessary, perhaps even undesirable. Other two-way program designs feature more "pure" immersion techniques, teaching subjects in one language or the other, but not in both.

A model developed by San Diego public schools in 1975 could be described as *total immersion* for English speakers, who begin their schooling almost entirely in Spanish. English is limited to twenty minutes a day in preschool, thirty minutes in kindergarten and 1st grade, and one hour in grades 2 and 3. By grades 4 through 6, half the instruction is in Spanish and half in English. In this respect the program resembles immersion in Canada or Culver City, but with an important difference: it simultaneously serves Spanish-speaking children. For the language-minority students, the program resembles developmental bilingual education.

Because students are mixed for much of the day, subject-matter teaching cannot be sheltered in the same way as in one-way immersion. When native speakers are present, there are limits to a teacher's ability to simplify oral instruction in the second language. Especially in the early years, ways must be found to compensate for the disparity in Spanish proficiency between the two groups. A 1982 report by the San Diego school district recommends two such techniques:

> First, when the K-1 class's students are receiving Spanish oral language instruction as a total class, visual aids — in the form of pic-

tures, chalkboard drawings, gestures, and pantomimes — are used to insure that the native speakers of English comprehend what is being discussed. Second, when the class is divided for individualized oral language instruction, the instructional emphasis for native-English-speaking students is on reinforcing beginning Spanish vocabulary and language patterns. (These same techniques apply to native-Spanish-speaking students during the English language period.)

On the other hand, an advantage of mixing is that children have an opportunity to acquire a second language from native speakers of their own age. Peers tend to be more influential role models than teachers when it comes to language learning. Simply throwing the two groups together, however, is not enough. The San Diego approach features a variety of structured activities that encourage children to interact, communicate, and assist each other in becoming bilingual. Such *peer tutoring* may reinforce the salutary effects of immersion, researchers predict, especially for language-majority students.

While the potential of this approach remains uncertain, the San Diego students appear to be doing well, according to periodic evaluations, although the benefits tend to manifest themselves late in the program. Children formerly limited in English make rapid gains in their oral skills from the very beginning. Generally speaking, however, it takes them until the 6th grade to score at the 50th percentile on reading and mathematics tests administered in English.[5] Native English speakers reach the 30th to 36th percentile range in Spanish reading, while exceeding national norms in their other subjects. Just as in one-way bilingual education, however, the educational payoff takes time. For the Anglo children, according to Fred Genesee, "there is generally a lag in English language literacy skills development during those grades of early total immersion programs when English language arts are not taught."

Parents' concerns on this score have inspired an alternate model, *two-way partial immersion,* in which the languages of instruction are balanced from the outset. The Key School in Arlington, Virginia, adopted this approach in 1986-87 for one 1st grade class and expanded it the following year to include kindergarten and 2nd grade. Students are taught in English in the morning (language arts and mathematics) and Spanish in the afternoon (language arts, social studies, and science). Music, art, and physical education classes are conducted in English.

An evaluation of the program by the Center for Applied Linguistics found that children were doing as well as, or better than, an all-English 1st grade class at the same school taught by the same teachers. Native Spanish speakers scored the most dramatic gains in English and conceptual development. English speakers improved their Spanish proficiency, but made relatively less progress in the second language than the Hispanic children because they had "limited opportunities . . . to acquire or practice Spanish outside of class."

All things considered, the Key School approach has been popular — "Parents do most of the selling," says evaluator Nancy Rhodes — and by 1988 the district was considering whether to make it a citywide magnet program. While English speakers value the enrichment opportunity, Spanish-speaking parents welcome the chance for their children to maintain their mother tongue.

A final two-way model might be termed *limited immersion*. This approach was tried with mixed results in Port Chester, New York, a district that had previously had little experience with bilingual education. The curriculum, which was tested from 1984 to 1987, paired two combined classes of 2nd and 3rd graders, English-proficient and limited-English-proficient, who received instruction in Spanish as a second language and English as a second language, respectively. Unlike other two-way models, Port Chester mixed the two groups only for two classes each week in social studies and joint language activities. Initially, the plan was to increase the immersion component gradually and to achieve a balance of English and Spanish by the third year, says the program's evaluator, Richard Baecher of Fordham University. "But that's a dream that was never reached. The capacity just isn't there" in terms of seasoned teachers and administrators, he explains.

After three years of the experiment, Spanish-speaking children were above grade level when tested in Spanish, although their English literacy remained very limited. On the other hand, English speakers made "remarkable progress in learning Spanish as a second language," while their skills in mathematics and English reading declined, according to Baecher's 1988 evaluation report. The disappointing results may have had less to do with the program's design than with staff problems at the school, Baecher says. He characterizes this two-way model as "a transitional form" that could be applied in similar districts outside large cities.

Uncertain Future

Port Chester's was one of seventeen pilot projects in two-way bilingual education financed by the New York State Department of Education in the mid-1980s. California and Massachusetts also began to support such programs out of state coffers. Federal funding, by contrast, was minimal during that period.

Despite Secretary William Bennett's advocacy of FLES programs as part of a "model curriculum" for elementary schools, only two bilingual immersion programs received Title VII grants in the 1980s. Ana María Farías, Bennett's deputy director of bilingual education, insisted that federal funds should be targeted to serve those most in need, LEP children. If school districts choose to provide two-way programs, "they can pay for them," she said. This attitude persisted under the Bush administration, which spent only token amounts on developmental bilingual education.

The Clinton administration has signaled a major shift in policy. Following the 1994 reauthorization of Title VII, which made fluent bilingualism an educational priority (see Chapter 12), it awarded grants to 61 two-way projects in 1994-95. But Republicans in Congress, led by English Only advocates, sought immediately to countermand this decision. In March 1995, the House voted to reduce by $38 million the appropriation already approved that year for Title VII; this "rescission" bill specifically targeted developmental and two-way programs for elimination.

Whether two-way bilingual education catches on despite ideological opposition, or whether it remains a promising but marginal experiment, depends largely on public attitudes. Thus far the multipurpose approach has shown enormous potential. From a pedagogical standpoint, English-speaking children appear to attain full bilingualism and perhaps even a cognitive advantage over their monolingual peers, although the latter outcome remains difficult to prove. At minimum, second-language acquisition is achieved at no cost to their academic achievement. For language-minority students, the benefits are well-documented: enhanced self-esteem and improved academic achievement, along with developed skills in the mother tongue. Instead of being treated as "deprived" children in need of remedial education, they are encouraged to share their valuable skills with English-speaking classmates. This can make a significant difference in their attitudes toward school and toward themselves.

In a broader context, two-way programs seem to increase cross-cultural understanding and mutual respect among ethnic groups (but again, such effects are hard to measure). The experience of acquiring a second language may sensitize English speakers to the difficulty of that process. It can also shatter unflattering stereotypes about minority cultures. Undoubtedly, successful two-way experiments have strengthened support for language learning. Writing in *Bilingual and ESL Classrooms,* Carlos Ovando and Virginia Collier report that "parents of English-speaking children in bilingual classes frequently become advocates of bilingualism when they see the unique intellectual, social, and commercial advantages it provides their children."

Finally, there is the chance that two-way approaches might reverse negative views toward bilingual education as a whole. Such attitudes tend to be highly symbolic, often reflecting racial resentments toward Hispanics and their cultures, writes David Sears, a political scientist at the University of California, Los Angeles. In a detailed analysis of opinion research, Sears determined that public support for bilingual education among non-Hispanics was strongest when respondents knew little about it. Conversely, those who were aware of its "cultural/linguistic maintenance" variant — its potential for additive bilingualism — tended to be the program's most avid opponents. Statistically speaking, Sears concludes, "opposition to cultural maintenance is linked to intolerance of minorities . . . and policies benefiting them."

Such attitudes appear, if anything, to have intensified since the data for this survey were gathered in 1983. Founded that same year, the English Only movement has grown rapidly by exploiting opposition to government-sanctioned bilingualism. Sears suggests that, as a way to avoid negative symbolism, bilingual educators might be wise to deëmphasize the language maintenance aspects of their field. Indeed, this is the strategy that most pursued in the 1980s: advertising the program's value in teaching English and shunning any mention of maintenance. ("That's a dirty word in my district," says one Title VII director.)

Yet the wisdom of this defensive response is questionable when even transitional bilingual programs inspire a "negative racial reaction," according to Sears. After TBE came under attack from U.S. English and its allies in the Reagan administration, Congress responded by trimming Title VII's preference for native-language instruction.

By contrast, two-way bilingual education may offer a way to overcome Anglo-conformist prejudice by recasting the political symbolism. A model that serves English-speaking and non-English-speaking students alike cannot be branded a "special interest" subsidy. A curriculum that turns out fluent bilinguals, unlike most foreign-language instruction, might counteract the prevailing indifference toward other tongues. A program that values minority languages as assets to be conserved and developed can only enhance their social status.

"Americans' gross inadequacy in foreign-language skills is nothing short of scandalous, and it is getting worse," concluded a Presidential commission in 1979. While bemoaning this chronic malady, the commissioners were careful to sidestep the controversies surrounding bilingual education. In so doing, they ignored what may be our best hope for a cure. With immigrants, refugees, and indigenous minorities swelling the U.S. school population, two-way programs are feasible not only in Spanish, but in Japanese, Russian, Arabic, Mandarin, and other world languages. What's more, these linguistic resources are free. All that is needed is the foresight to tap them. Perhaps some day, to become Americanized will no longer mean to become monolingual.

Notes

1. Gains in mathematics were especially striking for Spanish speakers, who were tested in English even though their instruction had been in Spanish — results that tend to confirm Cummins's interdependence hypothesis.
2. The last group of children, often coming from Washington's diplomatic community, achieves fluent trilingualism, according to Paquita Holland.
3. These are combined results for all groups; a breakdown by language background is unavailable. Also, children are not tested in Spanish. The Oyster program has never been formally evaluated.
4. While personnel costs are double those of comparable schools, Oyster does manage to save in other ways; for example, it has no need to hire outside substitute teachers.
5. These findings are consistent with Cummins's hypothesis that basic interpersonal communications skills (BICS) are acquired earlier than cognitive-academic language proficiency (CALP) in a second language.

Policy

12 Language Policy and School Reform

School Programs Assailed As Bilingual Bureaucracy
Throw Away the Crutch of Bilingual Education
In U.S. Schools, A War of Words
Bilingual Education Effort Is Flawed, Study Indicates

These headlines from the *New York Times*, appearing between 1990 and 1994, may sound harsh, but they are hardly atypical. Such messages echo the drumbeat of negativity that has dominated media coverage of bilingual education for the past twenty years. When there is bad news about programs for limited-English-proficient (LEP) children, readers of the *Times* are sure to be alerted in a prominent article.

On October 20, 1994, the newspaper reported that New York City students receiving bilingual instruction were slower to acquire English, and to be reassigned to regular classrooms, than those receiving only English-as-a-second-language (ESL) instruction.[1] These findings by the school district were cited to illustrate what the *Times* described as "a mounting debate [about] the degree to which bilingual programs may fail to help many children learn English well, and also fail to teach other subjects well." The article featured views on both sides of these issues.

The *Times* neglected to note, however, that the "study" to which it gave credence failed to meet even minimal standards for educational research. The report had made no attempt to consider students' socioeconomic backgrounds, long-term progress in other subjects, rates of school completion, or proficiency in English when they exited special programs. Did the results reflect badly on New York's bilingual programs or on bilingual education in general, as the newspaper account implied? Or did they reflect a disparity in program goals — for example, the development of bilingual skills versus a quick transition to English? Or were they due to preëxisting differences between students assigned to ESL and bilingual classrooms, or to other uncontrolled variables? School officials had no way of answering these questions. Nor could they explain the rationale for releasing a report consisting of raw and potentially misleading data about LEP student achievement.

"Bilingual Program Excels Despite Poverty, Crime, Drugs" is a headline that has never appeared in the *New York Times*. But it would have been appropriate for a story that occurred on the newspaper's doorstep and either escaped its editors' notice or failed to meet its criteria for "all the news that's fit to print." While numerous bilingual programs in New York could arguably be described by such a headline, one in particular received national recognition in 1991.

School District 19, whose bilingual program was evaluated in credible and rigorous research funded by the U.S. Department of Education, is located in one of the poorest sections of Brooklyn. Its students are 99 percent Latino and African-American, a majority from welfare families. Elementary schools in District 19 must be equipped with chains and grates, metal shields over the doors, and guards to keep muggers and crack dealers at bay. The neighborhood resembles "a bombed-out area," says researcher David Ramírez. "I've never seen a district that faced as many challenges." Nevertheless, over a four-year period its program for LEP children was rated highest among those included in the study. (Ramírez examined exemplary models of early- and late-exit bilingual education and English immersion in five states; see Chapter 7). District 19 also featured the greatest use of native-language instruction. The longer students remained in the Spanish-English developmental program, the steeper the growth curves in their achievement. By the 6th grade they showed promise of overtaking national norms in English and mathematics.

Bilingual education has recorded comparable — although rarely so well-documented — successes elsewhere. Yet seldom are these chronicled in the American media.[2] With few exceptions, journalists continue to pursue stories that highlight the political controversies surrounding the use of native languages for instruction. Thus they tend to repeat and often to reinforce stereotypes of bilingual education, as

- a self-perpetuating bureaucracy designed primarily to provide jobs for Hispanics;
- a "politicized" curriculum that puts a higher priority on ethnic pride than academic achievement;
- a pedagogy that keeps children from assimilating into the mainstream and thereby antagonizes the more "upwardly mobile" immigrant groups (i.e., Asians and Europeans); and of course,
- an obstacle to English acquisition.

No wonder public perceptions remain hostile. In a 1993 Gallup poll commissioned by Phi Delta Kappa, only 27 percent of respondents favored bilingual instruction as "the best way for the public schools to deal with non-English-speaking students." Seventy-one percent believed that schools should "require children to learn English before they receive instruction in other subjects."[3]

This difference of opinion seems intractable. Amid persistent reports of low achievement and high dropout rates among language-minority students, especially Hispanic students, many conclude that bilingual education must be to blame; others respond that it has yet to receive a fair test, with adequate resources and trained staff. Skeptics point to a failure of research to prove the effectiveness of native-language instruction; defenders say the concept should not be invalidated by poor implementation, or by programs that mainstream children prematurely. Ideological opponents argue that maintaining languages other than English will Balkanize the nation along ethnic lines; proponents cite the cognitive, social, and economic benefits of bilingualism.

If these questions are no closer to resolution than they were ten or twenty years ago, perhaps that is because when an argument becomes polarized, an honest give-and-take becomes problematic. Kenji Hakuta's 1986 book, *Mirror of Language: The Debate on Bilingualism,* contains the researcher's candid assessment: "An awkward tension blankets the lack of empirical demonstration of the success of bilingual education programs. Someone promised bacon, but it's not there." Hakuta goes on to argue that basic research makes a strong case for native-language instruction, whereas program evaluations may never do so, owing to inherent problems in this type of research (see Chapter 5). Nevertheless, his admission has been exploited by the program's political enemies. It has been quoted in numerous forums — federal courts, state legislatures, and the U.S. Congress, not to mention academic journals and the popular press — to allege that even the supporters of bilingual education have no proof that it "works." In this adversarial climate, applied linguists confront the unsavory choice of mincing their words or risking harm to the field.

Moreover, the parameters of this debate have been set largely by one side: those who stress the imperative of assimilation above all other considerations. As in the New York City study reported by the *Times*, the key issue has been: What approach will teach children enough English to allow schools to "mainstream" them as quickly as possible? Other questions, such as How can we best foster long-term academic achievement? or How can all students be guaranteed equal access to the curriculum? or How can children's bilingualism be treated as an asset rather than a liability? tend to get pushed aside. When policymakers ask, Does bilingual education really work? they usually mean, Does it remedy the "language handicap" of these students, at "reasonable" cost and without keeping them in bilingual programs "too long," so as not to offend public opinion?

Defining the criteria for academic success has given opponents of bilingual education a tactical advantage. Supporters are expected to prove that programs are teaching English within two to three years, even though basic research shows that it takes from five to seven years to acquire academic proficiency in a second language. Schools that fail to mainstream children within that arbitrary time limit are branded failures. Yet bilingual education is also blamed if students exit programs quickly and then fall behind their peers, even though there is scientific evidence that *too little* native-language development may be the problem.

No one doubts that all children need good English to succeed in American schools. Yet, as demonstrated by the failure of many language-majority students, teaching students in English is hardly sufficient to guarantee success. Neither is teaching them bilingually. Language is only one variable among many. Schooling for LEP children is afflicted by the same ills that afflict schooling for their English-speaking peers, especially those labeled "at risk" or "disadvantaged." Unequal resources and facilities, uncaring bureaucracies, insensitive treatment of parents, poorly trained staff, unchallenging curricula, low expectations — each of these factors can limit achievement, no matter what language is used for instruction.

Thus, while bilingual education is hardly to blame for failing schools, neither is it a panacea. By itself the most creative use of the native language cannot overcome a hostile environment or incompetent administration. Not that creativity is the norm. Mediocrity is no stranger to bilingual programs, as any professional in the field can confirm (even if many hesitate to do so in an adversarial climate). Although the pedagogy has advanced enormously since 1968, it has developed unevenly among states, districts, and even schools. Local attitudes toward bilingualism, relations among ethnic groups, availability of resources, and quality of educational leadership have all played a role.

Above all, this experience has shown that improving outcomes for language-minority students is a complex undertaking. It requires not merely appropriate instruction, but fundamental changes in the way schools relate to students, parents, and communities. It demands that the unique needs of LEP children be considered in every step toward school reform. And, as bilingual educators have begun to recognize, it necessitates their active participation in this movement. No longer can they remain a field apart.

School Reform Context

Following the release of *A Nation at Risk: The Imperative for Educational Reform* in 1983, the quality of American schools became a front-burner issue, achieving a prominence unseen since the panic over *Sputnik*. Educators were understandably grateful for the attention. Even if the report exaggerated the crisis with its breathless rhetoric — "We have, in effect, been committing an act of unthinking, unilateral educational disarmament" — it nevertheless inspired public concern and, in many cases, public willingness to spend more on schools to promote "excellence," however vaguely defined.

Education reform also became a site of ideological conflict, as conservatives saw an opportunity to advance their agenda. As one writer for *Commentary* explained, "Far more than any other institution in American society, the schools have become an arena for the struggle between the values of traditionalism and modernity." Politicians on the Right articulated a critique that made sense to frustrated parents. They drew connections between declining test scores, innovations like whole language and the "new math," child-centered approaches that deëmphasized rote learning, and moral relativism, as exemplified by sex education and the ban on school prayer. They had no trouble identifying the enemy: the "education establishment," portrayed as a bureaucratic leviathan dependent on big government and loyal to its liberal social agenda.

Two factors with a major impact on achievement, the growing diversity of American students and the difficulties of American schools in serving them, received relatively scant attention. So did the fact that racial, cultural, and linguistic minorities continued to receive less than their fair share of educational resources.

In his best-selling book, *Savage Inequalities,* Jonathan Kozol documented the racial segregation and despair of urban schools, with decaying buildings, overcrowded classes, and burnt-out teachers, in contrast to the ample and sometimes lavish facilities found in predominantly white suburbs. He illustrated in vivid strokes the failure of Great Society programs to abolish a two-tier educational system; if anything, inequities had increased since the 1960s. Unequal allocation of resources among school districts remained a contentious legal and political issue in numerous states.

Nevertheless, educational quality, not equality, became the rallying cry of the new reformers. Indeed, many agreed with Diane Ravitch and Chester Finn, Jr., that excessive egalitarianism was to blame for U.S. schools' low standards and limited accountability. By this way of thinking — and it appealed to many non-conservatives — "dumbing-down" the curriculum had ended up depriving poor and minority children of academic opportunities. Schools that emphasized cognitive skills over factual knowledge were turning out "cultural illiterates" unprepared for anything but menial jobs (see Chapter 3). From his bully pulpit as Secretary of Education, William Bennett denounced the "dangerous theory that content is not really important because American culture has become too fragmented and pluralistic to justify a belief in common learning." He called for a return to "the systematic study of Western civilization and its traditions."

Despite massive and often supportive coverage by the national media, however, by decade's end this ideological assault had done little to remold the schools' values, curricula, or philosophies. Although conservatives controlled the U.S. Department of Education, they failed to develop a legislative strategy for imposing their vision (other than abolishing the department itself, an idea that was never seriously pursued). As Secretary, Bennett proposed only a handful of practical initiatives, and most of these were blocked by Democrats in Congress.

One bold education proposal did emerge from Ronald Reagan's administration — "school choice" — and it was promoted heavily by his successor, George Bush. A radical idea in the strictest sense, choice is intended not to reform the existing bureaucracy, but to break its monopolistic control and allow "free market" forces to operate. Under such a plan, parents could use vouchers or tax credits to enroll their children in any school, public or private, at government expense. Thus "at-risk" students would receive the same opportunity enjoyed by wealthy students to purchase a superior education. Introducing competition would simultaneously create incentives for excellence in public schools, by rewarding innovation and penalizing inefficiency, all at no additional cost — or so the theory goes. In sum, school choice promises to empower parents, expand opportunities, and enhance quality, while keeping taxes down. It sounds almost too good to be true.

Critics believe that it is. They note that proposed subsidies to parents fall far short of expenses at most private schools; in practice, choice would mainly provide a windfall to families whose children are already enrolled there. More to the point, opponents cite the potential harm to the majority of students who would remain in public schools, including those with special needs or other traits that make them undesirable to private schools. How would these children fare when the free market diverts resources, disrupts programs, forces staff reductions, and allows facilities to deteriorate? Further concerns have been voiced about whether choice would violate the constitutional separation of church and state. Troubled by such prospects, Congress has thus far refused to consider any form of choice that might bankrupt public education or subsidize religious instruction. In any case, as the federal government's share of education spending declined to about 6 percent during the 1980s, its ability to initiate sweeping changes was limited.

It was at the state level where substantive school reforms were taking place. Political pragmatists of both parties — including Bill Clinton of Arkansas and Lamar Alexander of Tennessee — struck a deal with voters. In exchange for higher taxes for education, requirements would be stiffened in such areas as teacher certification, academic course loads, participation in extracurricular programs, promotion, and graduation. Other innovations included honors diplomas for advanced students; magnet schools dedicated to mathematics, science, and the arts; pay-for-performance and career ladders for teachers. These changes had the most impact in the South, where school systems were most starved for resources and generally had the most room for improvement. Politically the reforms proved popular, even though the overall effect on student achievement was modest.

Meanwhile, as new regulations and categorical programs proliferated, the operation of schools became increasingly complex. Educational expenditures, administrative staff, and layers of bureaucracy all expanded as a result. Changes were harder to detect in the classroom. Notwithstanding some creative and promising new programs, the success of top-down reforms had been limited, according to most observers. For the most part, teachers continued to teach and students continued to learn pretty much as before.

This recognition generated a second wave of reform efforts, more holistic than the first and less ideologically motivated. Variously described as "restructuring," "rethinking the process of schooling," and "systemic reform," the new approaches criticized the fragmentation and incoherence of education policy at all levels. They sought to overcome what Marshall Smith and Jennifer O'Day have called the "project mentality," a tendency to initiate and abandon short-lived programs "soon to be replaced by a different 'concept,' a new panacea. . . . Few leave much of a lasting trace." While some of these add-on initiatives were worthwhile in themselves, rarely were they coordinated to bring fundamental, qualitative changes in the way schools are run. Without a strategic vision, the first wave of school reform inevitably fell victim to institutional resistance. Systemic reformers, like choice advocates, saw bureaucracy as a key obstacle to change, but they worked to "reinvent" rather than wreck it. One mechanism for doing so was a movement for national standards and goals.

The first step was a 1989 "summit meeting" on education, sponsored by the National Governors Association and the Bush administration. Participants agreed on six broad goals for American education by the year 2000, involving school readiness, high school graduation, student achievement and citizenship, mathematics and science, adult literacy, and protection from drugs and violence.[4] Soon after, Congress authorized a National Education Goals Panel to measure progress in these areas and a National Council on Education Standards and Testing to study whether it would be feasible to develop national standards for "content" (what students should know), "performance," (what levels of competence they should achieve), and "delivery" (what schools must do to ensure students an adequate opportunity to learn). In 1992, the council returned an affirmative verdict. It recommended that the new standards reflect high expectations for achievement, that they be nonbinding rather than federally mandated, and that they take the form of general guidance rather than a national curriculum.

Two years later Congress adopted this approach in the Goals 2000: Educate America Act, which established a federal panel to oversee the development of voluntary standards and assessment systems. The legislation also provided funding to help state education agencies plan systemic reforms that would, among other things, raise expectations for student achievement and hold schools accountable for meeting them. In addition, it required state grant recipients to specify a minimum level of school resources and services needed to meet academic goals, although observance of such "opportunity-to-learn" standards would remain strictly voluntary.

Sprinkled throughout the new law are provisions addressing the special situation of "at-risk students, students with disabilities, students with limited-English proficiency, and students from diverse cultural backgrounds" — for example, in developing appropriate assessments and preventing biased ones from unfairly penalizing these children. The overall thrust, however, is toward comprehensive reforms that will enable all students to meet rigorous standards. For critics of the compensatory education model, which tries to overcome academic "deficits" by stressing basic skills, this has been a welcome change in philosophy. Limited goals bring limited results and limited accountability, as documented by studies of the costly but ineffective Chapter 1 program.

Yet challenging students to meet higher standards and goals is only a partial solution. What remains to be answered is whether extending the finish line will help underachievers to catch up with their peers; whether, without better coaching and without better tools to assess their progress, that strategy will cause them to fall farther behind. In the past compensatory programs have, in effect, removed such students from competition and steered them into dead-end tracks. But to include them in the race without paying attention to their needs — and without addressing their strengths as well as their weaknesses — could increase inequities and reverse gains that have been achieved through special programs. This is the dilemma facing educators of language-minority children.

'Reinventing' LEP Programs

By late 1992 it seemed clear that major policy initiatives were in the offing. In addition to Goals 2000, Congress would soon consider a five-year reauthorization of the Elementary and Secondary Education Act (ESEA), which includes Title VII and Chapter 1. Meanwhile, the transition to a new presidential administration was under way. President-Elect Bill Clinton, who had been a leader among governors in pursuing school reform, was expected to bring his activism to the federal level. Scores of Washington-based interest groups, representing virtually every aspect of education, were poised to take advantage of the favorable climate for change. But few of these had much acquaintance with the needs of language-minority students, which had been a low priority for the standards-and-goals movement.

Hoping to correct this situation, an ad hoc collection of bilingual education advocates and researchers came together under the leadership of Kenji Hakuta of Stanford University. With support from the Carnegie Corporation of New York, its first step was to convene a series of national meetings to evaluate federal policy for LEP students and to consider the opportunities and risks of comprehensive reform. While diverse views were represented, a consensus gradually emerged. The panel, known as the Stanford Working Group, compiled a series of recommendations for Title VII, Chapter 1, and Goals 2000. Released in June of 1993, its report was entitled "A Blueprint for the Second Generation."

This effort broke with the past in two significant ways. First, it sought to overcome the isolation of bilingual educators from the school reform movement. Having grown under the aegis of categorical funding and civil rights enforcement, the field was often ignored or viewed with skepticism by other sections of the education community. Insularity had served a purpose when new pedagogies were being developed to remedy the failures of mainstream schooling. But it also limited the ability of bilingual educators to influence broad changes of the kind that now seemed inevitable. Like it or not, the new standards and goals would affect language-minority education. So, rather than defending the status quo, the Working Group adopted a pragmatic strategy of working within the framework of systemic reform. Its recommendations were aimed at getting the best possible deal for LEP students under less-than-ideal circumstances.

Second, the group broadened the policy focus to include programs other than Title VII. In particular, Chapter 1 enjoyed stronger Congressional support and promised more generous funding,[5] despite its compensatory approach and poor record in addressing language barriers. In several states limited English proficiency had actually been considered a legal barrier to participation in Chapter 1 programs. Yet LEP children are three times more likely to attend high-poverty schools than their English-speaking peers; 74 percent attend schools where more than half the students are eligible for subsidized lunches, according to a 1993 study. So it became essential to open up Chapter 1 to LEP students and make it more responsive to their needs.

The Stanford report detailed its recommendations in the context of what it called "two overarching principles:

1. Language-minority students must be provided with an equal opportunity to learn the same challenging content and high-level skills that school reform movements advocate for all students.
2. Proficiency in two or more languages should be promoted for all American students. Bilingualism enhances cognitive and social growth, competitiveness in a global marketplace, national security, and understanding of diverse peoples and cultures.

The Clinton administration readily endorsed these themes. It also appointed Eugene García, a member of the Working Group and a professor at the University of California, Santa Cruz, to direct the Office of Bilingual Education and Minority Languages Affairs (OBEMLA). The administration's legislative proposals on Title VII and, to a lesser extent, on Chapter 1 were modeled on the Stanford recommendations. Highlights that became law include:

Restructuring Title VII grants. Rather than continue to categorize school programs by the amount of native language used (transitional, developmental, alternative), grants will now be defined by functional categories (program development and implementation, program enhancement projects, comprehensive school program, and systemwide improvement). The intent is to depoliticize the appropriations process, in which the language-of-instruction issue has always stirred controversy, and to encourage holistic approaches. Nevertheless, the 25 percent allowance for "special alternative instructional programs" (SAIPs) — defined as those that do "not use the student's native language for instructional purposes" — has been retained.

Increasing the state role. To strengthen systemic planning on how to serve LEP students, state education agencies will be given the responsibility to review Title VII proposals before they are submitted to OBEMLA.[6]

Encouraging bilingual skills. In awarding grants, OBEMLA is instructed to give priority to applicants seeking to develop "bilingual proficiency both in English and another language for all participating students." It is also authorized to fund programs designed to conserve endangered Native American languages (see Chapter 9).

Opening up Chapter 1. A legal provision that previously excluded LEP students has been dropped from the program, renamed Title I. Local school districts are required to take various steps to identify such students, address their language needs, assess them equitably, and involve their parents in decision-making. But the administration stopped short of mandating a key recommendation of the Working Group: language-appropriate instruction. Thus the predominance of English-only programs under Title I is unlikely to change except where districts choose to divert these funds to support bilingual instruction.

Congressional passage of a new Elementary and Secondary Education Act, completed in 1994, proved far less contentious than it had six years earlier. Democratic leaders generally supported the administration's bill, combined with a slightly modified version of Title VII proposed by the Congressional Hispanic Caucus. While some skirmishes broke out over social issues, these had nothing to do with bilingual education. (For the text of Title VII, see Appendix B.)

In committee deliberations, Republicans put up minimal resistance; most voted for the bill after exacting a concession with potentially far-reaching consequences. The "25 percent cap" on funding for "special alternative" programs could be waived if an applicant demonstrates that bilingual education is impractical owing to a lack of qualified teachers or a diverse student population. The Clinton administration has shown no interest in exploiting this loophole. Nevertheless, it would allow a future administration that is hostile to bilingual education to divert up to 100 percent of Title VII funding to English-only programs. In its practical implications, this provision is no different from the "local flexibility" proposed by Secretary William Bennett in the 1980s and opposed so vehemently by the National Association for Bilingual Education (NABE). Yet, in 1994, NABE supported the compromise rather than risk losing bipartisan support for the bill.

As it happened, a significant minority of Republicans still found the legislation unacceptable. When it reached the House floor, Representative Toby Roth of Wisconsin proposed to repeal Title VII altogether. Although the amendment lost, it attracted 58 votes, including those of several senior Republicans who would come to power a few months later.[7]

Language Policy Vacuum

Language skills received no mention in the first version of the National Education Goals. In 1994, as part of the Goals 2000 legislation, Congress added "foreign languages" to the list of subjects American students must master "so they may be prepared for responsible citizenship, further learning, and productive employment in our Nation's modern economy" (see Appendix C). Many were heartened by this decision, which may help to raise the status and quality of language education.

Still, there is no guarantee that it will cure our national schizophrenia on the subject: languages taught in school are valued, while "ethnic languages" are feared. For English speakers, proficiency in another language is seen as an educational advantage; for LEP children, an educational deficit. With few exceptions, schools still attempt to cultivate foreign languages in a barren and artificial environment, isolated from communities of native speakers. At the same time, most ignore or seek to uproot languages that have been acquired naturally in the home, insisting that English must "come first" for minority students.

Not surprisingly, this backward approach continues to yield poor results. In a multilingual world, the United States remains an underdeveloped country when it comes to language resources. Yet the linguistic gifts of new Americans are largely neglected and allowed to deteriorate, while their children lose a sense of identity that the mother tongue once conveyed. There is nothing rational about this parochial attitude. Wasting language skills is indefensible from a pedagogical standpoint. Nor does it well serve the nation's interests in trade, diplomacy, or social justice. It only begins to make sense when one considers the political context.

Representative Roth, when asked in 1993 why he opposes bilingual education, replied: "I want all Americans to be the same. That is my mission." The congressman deserves high marks for candor, if not for tolerance. Fear of diversity had a great deal to do with the emergence of English Only campaigns in the 1980s (see Chapter 3). Attacks on "bilingualism" often served as a proxy for attacks on immigrants. Proponents of official English could claim, without seeming bigoted, that they merely wanted to unite the country through a "common language."

By the early 1990s, expressions of xenophobia were more socially acceptable. Harsh approaches to restricting immigration became popular in economically troubled states like California. In 1994, voters there adopted Proposition 187, a measure designed to crack down on "illegal aliens" by excluding them from most government services, barring their children from public schools, and directing officials to report anyone suspected of being undocumented.[8] (Those who looked or sounded "foreign" would be prime candidates for deportation.) Shortly thereafter, the U.S. House of Representatives carried through on a pledge, contained in the Republicans' "Contract with America," to terminate most welfare benefits to legal immigrants, including the elderly and disabled.

English Only advocates also became bolder, offering "get tough" proposals that catered to an angry electorate. In 1995, Representative Pete King, a New York Republican, condemned bilingual education as a program that had spent "billions of dollars . . . encouraging people not to learn English." He introduced a "National Language Act" that would terminate Title VII and require schools to return unspent portions of their grants. Besides declaring English official, King would prohibit virtually all uses of other languages by the federal government, including bilingual voting, bilingual signs in public buildings, even bilingual assistance by the Internal Revenue Service. Only foreign-language instruction would be exempt from the bill's restrictions. Among other likely effects, the Government Printing Office would have to stop printing pamphlets in scores of languages; migrant health centers could no longer provide bilingual services to patients; and court interpreters would be denied to federal defendants charged with crimes.[9]

Meanwhile, the Republican majority used its power of the purse to cut Title VII appropriations by 38 percent for fiscal 1996. The most damaging reductions came in funding for teacher-training and support services, which were totally eliminated for one year.

Representative King and a growing number of his fellow lawmakers focus exclusively on the destructive potential of language diversity. Just look at how bilingualism has provoked ethnic conflicts around the world, they say. Unless we nip it in the bud, the United States could find itself in the same situation. "The strife in the Balkans has demonstrated the danger," warns Toby Roth. "Is America following Yugoslavia's path?[10] Dare we take the chance? Only by preserving our commonality — English — can we ensure that we will continue to live and work together as one Nation, one people." For English Only advocates, the policy choice is simple: *Just say no to other languages.*

Thus far the United States has never had a language policy, consciously planned and national in scope. It has had language *policies* — usually ad hoc responses to practical needs or political pressures, sometimes favoring diversity and sometimes not, but always narrow in their application. Most have been limited to states or localities; at the federal level a comprehensive approach has never been attempted. While the U.S. government spends something over $1 billion annually on various forms of language education,[11] it has never bothered to catalog these efforts, let alone coordinate them. No federal agency is responsible for doing so. The Stanford Working Group recommended that OBEMLA be charged with centralizing this information and investigating "the feasibility of a comprehensive national language policy." But during the 1994 reauthorization of ESEA, neither the Clinton administration nor Congress supported the idea.

What would such a policy look like and how would it be developed? According to English Plus advocates, a productive approach must be holistic rather than one-sided. It must encompass what Richard Ruíz has identified as the three "basic orientations" that "determine what is thinkable about language in society." *Language as problem* seeks solutions to the complications created by diversity — e.g., transitional bilingual education to overcome the "problem" of limited English proficiency. *Language as right* stresses principles of equality, self-determination, and entitlement — e.g., the *Lau* decision on civil rights for LEP students. *Language as resource* regards linguistic skills as a form of human capital to be conserved and developed in pursuit of national goals — e.g., the English Plus philosophy.[12]

While all three orientations have legitimacy, taken separately each has its limitations in formulating policy. Language as problem addresses real social contradictions, but can imply a bias in favor of monolingualism (English Only represents an extreme version of this approach). Language as right appeals to a sense of justice and equality, but can perpetuate confrontation. Language as resource is eminently rational in meeting instrumental needs, but can be naïve in confronting ethnocentric prejudices and unequal power relations. A comprehensive language policy must avail itself of all these perspectives.

Where should Americans look for enlightened policy alternatives? International comparisons are always risky — witness the strained analogies invoked to illustrate the perils of multilingualism. India, Sri Lanka, the former Soviet Union, and even Canada are very different societies from our own. But there is one country with striking parallels to the United States: a former British colony where English predominates and geographical isolation has bred a complacent monolingualism. At the same time, immigrant languages are growing rapidly, although the largest, Italian, is less dominant than Spanish in the United States (spoken by 4 percent of the population, as compared with 7.5 percent). Meanwhile, about 150 indigenous tongues still survive, all but a few of which are severely endangered. Ethnic relations are not always harmonious; conflicts have periodically flared over immigration and civil rights. Yet instead of an English Only movement, the response has been to accept, encourage, and exploit linguistic diversity.

The country is Australia. Its National Policy on Languages, adopted in 1987, incorporates four "guiding principles":

- competence in *English for all* Australians;
- *a language other than English for all,* either through the maintenance of existing skills or opportunities for Anglo-Australians to learn a second language;
- *the conservation of languages* spoken by Aborigines and Torres Strait Islanders; and
- equitable and widespread services in languages other than English, including interpreters, libraries, and media.

Australia's new policy, which has no mandatory features, has served to increase support for language education of all kinds, including ESL, adult literacy, and foreign-language instruction. It gives priority to nine "languages of wider learning" — Arabic, Mandarin, French, German, Greek, Indonesian/Malay, Italian, Japanese, and Spanish — which are considered vital to Australia's trade and international relations. It also stresses the goals of "social justice and over-coming disadvantages" through such programs as developmental bilingual education for immigrant and Aboriginal children.

In sum, Australia's approach combines respect for minority rights with the pursuit of national self-interest, primarily through educational means and without restricting anyone's freedom of choice. The United States could do worse than follow this example. Yet it is unlikely to do so unless political barriers are cleared away, notably a set of *language attitudes* hostile to diversity.

Value Judgments

Joshua Fishman has observed that linguistic minorities in this country are "given a cruel Hobson's choice — either to be 'American' and give up their languages or to maintain their languages and be 'un-American.'" This maxim, long enforced by social prejudice, originated in an earlier backlash against immigrants (see Chapter 1). Bilingualism and biculturalism are regarded not as positive ideals, not as ways to maintain community and identity, but as symptoms of divided loyalties. However unfair and shortsighted, this outlook continues to dominate popular attitudes, which in turn affect the views of politicians more powerfully than any reasoned argument.

Progress toward a just and humane language policy will necessitate a challenge to the ethnocentrism of many Anglo-Americans. While the latter tendency has flourished in the 1990s, there are also pluralist and democratic traditions to draw upon. One arena is the struggle to include LEP children in the movement for equitable school reform. Another is the movement to prevent cultural loss in minority communities, particularly Native American communities, where languages are threatened with extinction.

How a nation responds to diversity is fundamentally a question of values. Values do not change overnight. No doubt a social movement will be required to reshape them, and bilingual educators will be called upon to play a leading role.

Notes

1. The survey found that 79 percent of children assigned to ESL-only programs in kindergarten were reassigned within three years, as compared with 51 percent of those assigned to bilingual programs.
2. In fairness, it should be noted that bilingual education advocates have often missed opportunities — as in the case of School District 19 — to publicize good news about their field.

3. Of these, more than a third said children should have to learn English "at their parents' expense before they are enrolled in public schools"; 2 percent had no opinion. The national sample of 1,306 adults had a margin of error of plus or minus 3 percent.

4. In 1994, Congress added two more to the list of National Education Goals: teacher professionalism and parental participation. For a detailed list of these goals, as enumerated by the Goals 2000: Educate America Act, see Appendix C.

5. In 1993, the Chapter 1 budget of $6.8 billion was 35 times as large as the Title VII budget of $195 million.

6. Native American projects are exempted from this process.

7. Members of the House leadership in the 104th Congress who voted to abolish Title VII include Majority Leader Richard Armey, Majority Whip Tom DeLay, Ways and Means Committee Chairman Bill Archer, and Rules Committee Chairman Gerald Solomon. Speaker Newt Gingrich did not vote on the Roth amendment, but has previously cosponsored English Only legislation.

8. Most provisions were blocked by a federal court while it hears challenges to the constitutionality of Proposition 187.

9. King's proposal, HR 1005, would permit translation services for "persons over 62 years of age." Representative Bill Emerson, Republican of Missouri, sponsored a slightly less restrictive bill, HR 123, which has attracted more than 140 cosponsors in the 104th Congress. Known as the "Language of Government Act," it too would prohibit federal expenditures for bilingual education. Senator Richard Shelby, Republican of Alabama, introduced identical legislation in the Senate, S 356. President Bill Clinton, who in 1987 approved an official-English law in Arkansas, reversed his position during the 1992 campaign. He pledged to veto any English Only measure that crossed his desk in the White House.

10. This example, though timely, is a poor choice to support the view that language diversity "causes" ethnic divisions. Until its breakup the multinational state of Yugoslavia encompassed several language minority groups. As it happens, however, all parties to the recent conflicts there speak dialects of a single language, Serbo-Croatian, although Serbs use a Cyrillic alphabet, Croats use a Roman one, and Bosnians use both. It is true that Serbian and Croatian nationalists have attempted to repress each other's writing systems, seeking to use language as a tool of discrimination. Yet this merely illustrates how linguistic differences can be exploited for political advantage. As demonstrated in countless other conflicts, the roots of ethnic animosity go far deeper than mere "communication problems."

11. The estimate comes from J. David Edwards, "Foreign Languages and the State of the Union," Joint National Committee for Languages, March 1993.

12. It should be noted that English Plus has also placed a strong, if secondary, emphasis on language rights. See Mary Carol Combs, "English Plus: Responding to English Only," in James Crawford, ed., *Language Loyalties: A Source Book on the Official English Controversy* (Chicago: University of Chicago Press, 1992), pp. 216-24.

13 Disaster at the Polls

*I*t all started at Ninth Street Elementary. In early 1996, a group of Spanish-speaking parents pulled their children out of the school to protest its failure to teach English. They blamed bilingual education. The boycott lasted nearly two weeks, and it received extensive coverage in the *Los Angeles Times* — suggesting a new trend, perhaps even a sea-change, in Latino attitudes. These reports caught the eye of a Silicon Valley businessman named Ron Unz. "Parents shouldn't have to carry picket signs to get English instruction for their kids," Unz declared. Dipping into his personal fortune, he organized a statewide ballot initiative requiring that "all children ... be taught English by being taught in English." The measure, known as Proposition 227, passed overwhelmingly on June 2, 1998. It virtually outlawed bilingual education in California.

That is the official account, the story as conveyed by the victors and the news media. What actually happened — during the Ninth Street boycott and the Proposition 227 campaign — is more complicated. It is also instructive about the political adversity surrounding bilingual education. California's experience highlights a second wave of English Only activism, one with a broader appeal than the first. Avoiding the rhetoric of ethnic bigotry, it evokes the principles of equal opportunity, parental choice, and pedagogical effectiveness. Instead of warning about the menace of "bilingualism," it stresses the importance of "English for the Children." In effect, it embraces key premises of bilingual programs to undermine their public support. This strategy proved an unqualified success in California, as voters dealt the most serious setback to bilingual schooling since World War I.

Manufacturing a Myth

Located in downtown Los Angeles, on the edge of Skid Row, the Ninth Street School faces more than its share of challenges. It serves about 460 students in pre-kindergarten through the 5th grade. About half are classified as homeless, living in downtown shelters and single-room-occupancy hotels. Others are bused into the area each morning with their parents, mostly recent immigrants from Mexico who work in garment factories nearby. Nine out of ten children are limited-English-proficient (LEP); 99 percent are eligible for free or reduced-price meals. All but a few come from homes where only Spanish is spoken. These factors help to explain why Ninth Street students, like their counterparts in similar schools, score well below national norms when tested in English.

Nevertheless, prospects brightened following the appointment of Eleanor Vargas Page as principal in 1993. The school entered into partnerships with local businesses, civic groups, and social service agencies. Academic expectations increased and so did the amount of English instruction.[1] Ninth Street won a $600,000 Title VII grant to support extended learning opportunities, before and after school, and to expand the school library. Student attendance and parent participation soared. The results were impressive: children's English scores rose by 35 percent over a four-year period.

So when a reporter called on February 9, 1996, with news that a meeting of sixty-three Ninth Street parents had just voted to boycott the school, "I was in shock," Vargas Page recalls. She had always been proud of her close ties with parents and their high attendance at school functions, where complaints about bilingual education had never come up. None of the boycotting parents had asked for their children to be removed from the program; in fact, all had recently signed forms consenting to their children's enrollment. "The conflict was not here" in the school," the principal believes. "The complaints were initiated by [an outsider], not by the parents."

The outsider was Alice Callaghan, an Episcopal priest who ran a community center, Las Familias del Pueblo, that provided daycare for about one-quarter of Ninth Street students. Callaghan was also a veteran political organizer who had skirmished with city officials on numerous issues. Now she took up a new cause: abolishing bilingual education. For months she wrote to the Los Angeles Unified School District demanding English-only instruction at Ninth Street. When she received little response, Callaghan urged the parents to take direct action.

Sensational headlines followed: *"80 Students Stay Out of School in Latino Boycott ... Bilingual Schooling Is Failing, Parents Say."* For the news media, conflict means good copy. This is especially true when the conflict seems unlikely — known in the trade as a "man bites dog" story. That's what drew journalists to Ninth Street. Downtrodden immigrants, led by a colorful activist, were using civil-rights tactics to protest a "politically correct" program supported by their own ethnic leaders. Amazing! The news accounts neglected, however, to clarify a key point. This was a needless conflict, a drama that was staged precisely to generate sensational headlines.

California, like other states, has long recognized parents' right to remove their children from bilingual instruction if they so choose. At Ninth Street, all they had to do was come in, meet with their child's teacher and principal, and hear about the educational options. Then, if they chose to enroll their children in the school's alternative program taught mostly in English — as a few had done earlier that year — they merely needed to sign a consent form.[2] Vargas Page felt this procedure was essential "for a parent to make an informed decision." Callaghan called it "harassment" and "intimidation." She advised parents to refuse to attend any such conference, keep their children out of school, and send them to Las Familias (where "we will speak only English with them") until the district gave in to their demands. Several days into the boycott, she circulated a form for parents to sign — in English, although few could read the language — authorizing student transfers to the alternative program.[3]

No doubt some of Alice Callaghan's followers were convinced that bilingual education was to blame for their children's academic problems. But others told school staff they felt had no choice but to join the boycott and remove their children from the program, believing that otherwise they would lose the free daycare at Las Familias. In an interview, Callaghan denied making any explicit threats along these lines. Whatever the case, it is clear that she failed to assuage such concerns or to reassure parents that these decisions were entirely their own. Virtually none of those with children at Las Familias resisted her advice to transfer their children out of bilingual education (although a few would later change their minds).

What was the effect on LEP students? Two years later, only two out of the 74 moved into intensive English instruction had been reclassified as fluent in English. On state-mandated achievement tests, the 5th graders scored at the 11th percentile in reading, the 15th percentile in language, and the 16th percentile in math — well below peers who had remained in bilingual classrooms.[4] Questioned about these disappointing outcomes, Callaghan refused to accept responsibility. "If it's the older kids, that's not our fault," she said. "It's a result of their terrible bilingual program" provided to these children in the early grades.

Despite its dismal academic results, the boycott was a public relations bonanza for opponents of bilingual education. Soon it mushroomed into a national story. Spanish-speaking parents were quoted — often in translation — citing the importance of English to their children's future. Los Angeles Mayor Richard Riordan endorsed their protest. Ninth Street was portrayed as indicative of bilingual education's ineffectiveness and unpopularity among those it was intended to serve. Critics' views were prominently featured. Misinformation went unchallenged. The *Los Angeles Times* asserted that bilingual education "trapped" children in all-Spanish classrooms for 'six or seven years. ... That's much too long." Readers never heard an effective response.

This imbalance was not entirely the fault of the news media. Board members and district officials reacted as though the controversy concerned practices at a single school and promised to "look into it." Few bilingual education advocates came forward to assist their beleaguered colleagues at Ninth Street. Facing a hostile press, Eleanor Vargas Page and her staff were largely on their own in defending the school. Their side of the story usually came out garbled — when it came out at all. By and large, the public never heard a coherent case for bilingual education. L.A. Unified's failure to provide one conveyed an impression of arrogance and unresponsiveness to parents' legitimate demands for English.

Thus the Ninth Street myth was born. Over the next two years, it would prove more damaging than anyone had foreseen.

Calls for "Reform"

Critics had long complained that, despite the "sunset" of California's bilingual education law in 1987, the state kept most of the old requirements in place (see Chapter 10). Citing federal and state civil-rights guarantees for LEP students, the California Department of Education (CDE) continued to mandate — and enforce — the use of native-language instruction "when necessary ... [to] provide equal opportunity for academic achievement." The policy also required districts to staff its bilingual and English-as-a-second-language (ESL) programs with an adequate number of qualified teachers. In the prevailing political climate, however, Sacramento could offer them little practical help in achieving these goals.

To come from behind and win reelection in 1994, Governor Pete Wilson promoted a crack-down on undocumented immigrants known as Proposition 187. One of its provisions would have thrown their children out of public schools.[5] Not surprisingly, the Wilson administration saw little political gain in funding programs to train teachers for language-minority students. By 1997-98, the CDE estimated the shortage of bilingual teachers at nearly 27,000. This left districts unable to provide bilingual classrooms for more than a minority of their LEP students — about 30 percent, on average, statewide.[6]

Meanwhile, the California Association for Bilingual Education (CABE) resisted proposals in the legislature to allow more "local flexibility" in pedagogical matters. Since the mid-1980s, CABE had built an effective lobbying operation. It remained committed to the prescriptive philosophy, based on experience with districts that had to be prodded constantly to meet their obligations to English learners. The problem remained prevalent, for example, in the Central Valley, where language-minority communities often lacked political influence on school boards. Year after year CABE relied on the clout of Latino legislators in Sacramento to block any attempt to relax state requirements and oversight.

Yet prescriptiveness proved a double-edged sword. On the one hand, districts could be required to respond to the needs of English learners, providing additional resources, trained staff, and better designed programs. On the other hand, mandates inevitably bred resentment. The same had been true in the 1970s, when the U.S. Office for Civil Rights (OCR) imposed Lau plans forcing districts to try native-language approaches (see Chapter 2). Aggressive enforcement created a backlash that forced OCR to retreat — but not before it had established bilingual education as a viable pedagogy. The tradeoff was harder to justify in the 1990s, when that pedagogy was embraced, for the most part, by California's "education establishment." Public skepticism, English-only campaigns, and attacks by conservative politicians posed more formidable challenges than resistance at the school district level.

The CDE's encroachment on local control — and CABE's vigorous defense of the policy — presented an inviting target for anti-bilingual forces. Their charges of bureaucratic "heavy-handedness" and "one size fits all" schooling were effective, if exaggerated. No one seemed to notice that, by 1997, only five school boards — all in conservative Orange County — had petitioned the State Board of Education for "waivers" of the native-language requirement; none was denied. California's other districts also enjoyed considerable flexibility in designing programs for English learners, as testified by wide variations in program design. Nevertheless, the native-language requirement made bilingual education an easy scapegoat when schools failed these students.

Prescriptiveness also put the burden on advocates of bilingual approaches to prove their superiority in practice over English-only approaches. Given the limited quantity and quality of achievement data for LEP students in California, that was rarely possible. Nationwide, program evaluation research continued to provide relatively weak support — as compared with the findings of basic psycholinguistic research — for the effectiveness of bilingual instruction (see Chapters 5-6). It has become routine to blame bilingual educators for failing to prove the worth of their programs. Yet scientific comparisons of LEP program models are difficult to design and expensive to execute. Federal and state policymakers have seldom been generous in funding such research. Since the Ramírez report, commissioned in 1984 and completed in 1991 (see Chapter 7), the U.S. Department of Education has deemphasized large evaluation studies and concentrated instead on reviews of existing research.

National Research Council Report

The most significant of these reviews appeared in 1997. *Improving Schooling for Language-Minority Children: A Research Agenda* summarized the findings of an expert panel of the National Research Council. In addition to its chair, Kenji Hakuta of Stanford University, several other participants were prominent supporters of bilingual education. On the effectiveness question, however, their conclusions were equivocal:

> It is difficult to synthesize the program evaluations of bilingual education because of the extreme politicization of the process. Most consumers of the research are not researchers who want to know the truth, but advocates who are convinced of the absolute correctness of their positions. The beneficial effects of native-language instruction are

clearly evident in programs that are labeled "bilingual education," but they [??] also appear in some programs that are labeled "immersion." There appear to be benefits of programs that are labeled "structured immersion," although a quantitative analysis of such programs is not yet available. There is little value in conducting evaluations to determine which type of program is best. The key issue is not finding a program that works for all children and all localities, but rather finding a set of program components that works for the children in the community of interest, given the community's goals, demographics, and resources.

Complaints about politicization had been heard before. When the discussion of LEP education policy became polarized in the 1980s, focusing almost exclusively on the language of instruction, it tended to discourage open-minded efforts to analyze research evidence and improve programs. The restructuring of Title VII grant categories in 1994 was one attempt to mitigate this problem (see Chapter 12).

What was new in the NRC report was its suggestion that the debate is no longer relevant. That both bilingual and English-only program models can be beneficial. That the federal government should stop funding expensive yet futile attempts to determine which is superior. That researchers on both "sides" needed to behave more like scientists and less like advocates.[7] "We need to think in terms of program components," the panel recommended, "not politically motivated labels." It called for "theory-based interventions" that could be evaluated more scientifically and for "a developmental model ... for use in predicting the effects of program components on children in different environments."

The report also raised eyebrows with its generous, albeit ambiguous, words about "immersion." Its favorable assessment relied heavily on studies of an El Paso program whose English-only character had long been disputed; this so-called "bilingual immersion" model featured substantial amounts of Spanish instruction (see Chapter 7). Some suspected that, with its even-handed findings, the NRC panel was stretching the evidence to fit a preconceived agenda of its own.

Depoliticizing the research debate, considering the diversity of LEP students and their needs, restoring a measure of scientific detachment ... these goals sounded worthy on paper. In reality they proved problematic. Opponents of bilingual education were quick to seize on the NRC's findings as vindication of their views. Rosalie Porter's READ Institute, a project funded in part by U.S.

English, published a lengthy analysis of the report by Charles Glenn of Boston University. Its main theme was that, after a generation of experience with bilingual education, we still know virtually nothing about whether it works. Hakuta disputed this interpretation, condemning what he called "the far from impartial attempt by READ to place its own political spin on this matter." His statements, however, did little to settle what the NRC panel had meant to say. Like the research literature it criticized, the report had something for everyone, enabling partisans to pick and chose findings that served their purposes.

Meanwhile, the political divide showed no signs of narrowing. Language of instruction was becoming, if anything, more contentious. Journalists and commentators highlighted the panel's complaints about the quality of program evaluation studies — "design limitations ... poorly articulated goals ... extreme politicization" — and pronounced all research in the field useless to policymakers. If the science was inconclusive about what works, why not encourage experimentation and flexibility? they argued, reviving a familiar theme of the 1980s (see Chapter 4).

In California, State Senator Deirdre Alpert and Assemblyman Brooks Firestone sponsored a bipartisan bill along these lines. It proposed to relax the mandate for native-language instruction and allow local districts to choose their own approach, while requiring them to assess LEP students annually and show progress over time. Programs would have to be restructured if children failed to meet goals within three years. Some bilingual education advocates saw the measure as a compromise worth exploring, believing that few districts were likely to dismantle existing programs. Others objected that its accountability provisions were too weak and its sanctions too vague, thus encouraging schools to scale back their efforts for LEP children. Although the Alpert-Firestone bill easily passed the California Senate in the summer of 1997, for the third year in a row CABE managed to kill it in the Assembly. Self-described "moderates" expressed frustration and blamed bilingual educators for obstructing change. It was an opening tailor-made for Ron Unz.

English Only, Phase II

A software millionaire, aged 36 and single, with no children in school and no background in education, Unz seemed an unlikely antagonist. His first foray in politics had come three years earlier, when he challenged Pete Wilson for the Republican gubernatorial nomination. He won about a third of the vote, mainly from Far Right critics of the incumbent. Yet he also emerged as a staunch opponent of Proposition 187, earning "pro-immigrant" credentials that distinguished him from other English Only advocates. Unz believed that Republicans needed to face demographic realities and reach out to fast-growing minorities in states like California. Rather than side with nativists, he argued, the party should cater to the "natural conservatism" of Hispanic and Asian Americans on issues like welfare, crime, and abortion. Campaigning in 1994, the challenger preached the gospel of upward mobility through assimilation, while denouncing "the poisonous brew of bilingual education, multiculturalism and other ethnic separatism policies."

These views and the wherewithal to promote them gave Unz access to prominent conservatives like Linda Chávez. He helped to endow her Center for Equal Opportunity, a Washington advocacy group that opposes affirmative action and bilingual education on "civil rights" grounds. Impressed with the ideas of Peter Salins, he commissioned the sociologist to write *Assimilation, American Style*, a tendentious history that portrays earlier immigrants as eager to abandon their languages in favor of English. Meanwhile, Unz kept his distance from traditional English Only lobbies.

The influence of groups like U.S. English appeared to reach a high-water mark on August 1, 1996. By a vote of 259-167, the House of Representatives passed the so-called "English Language Empowerment Act," the first official-English bill at the federal level (see Appendix D). Mindful of a veto threat by President Clinton, the Senate declined to consider the measure. If enacted, it would have banned most federal publications in languages other than English, repealed bilingual voting rights, mandated English-only naturalization ceremonies, and shielded English speakers from "discrimination." Republicans claimed the legislation was essential to preserve the nation's "common bond" and "empower" immigrants by motivating them to learn the language. Democrats condemned it as divisive, mean-spirited, and potentially unconstitutional in its restrictions on minority access to government. In practice, the bill would have affected relatively few people. It was the precedent that stimulated interest on both sides.[8]

Likewise, in criticizing bilingual education, English Only advocates had always stressed symbolism over substance. Rhetorical attacks aside, they never dared to mount a legislative campaign to destroy the program. Fearing they would be seen as callous toward children, even the most draconian official-English proposals featured an exemption for bilingual education. Evidently they failed to grasp its vulnerability.

Ron Unz brought a different approach to English Only politics. Rather than rely on official-language declarations to oppose "bilingualism" in government, he launched a frontal assault on the most important bilingual program. Instead of gauzy rhetoric about English and "American" identity, he used specific arguments about educational effectiveness. Rather than blame immigrants for failing to learn English, he posed as their advocate against unresponsive schools.

It was a more sophisticated strategy than the visceral politics of resentment that guided Phase I of the English Only movement. Unz's arguments sounded rational and public-spirited by contrast. They also exploited ignorance about language acquisition, which extended into liberal and progressive sectors of the electorate. As a result, he effectively changed the terms of the debate. Instead of "Should bilingual education be reformed and made more flexible?" the question became: "Should bilingual education be eliminated?"

Proposition 227

Unz's first step was to disassociate himself from California's anti-immigrant fringe. In the spring of 1997, he recruited prominent Latinos to help spearhead his ballot initiative, which he dubbed English for the Children. These included his cosponsor, Gloria Matta Tuchman, a 1st grade teacher from Santa Ana and a perennial candidate for state superintendent of public instruction.[9] Jaime Escalante, the legendary calculus teacher of *Stand and Deliver* fame, agreed to serve as "honorary chairman." Several lesser luminaries also lent their support. Alice Callaghan helped to kick off the campaign with a media event at Las Familias, where scenes of brown-skinned children provided a backdrop for speeches attacking bilingual education. Unz established his headquarters nearby, just a few blocks from the Ninth Street School.

Petitions for Proposition 227 began circulating in July. Qualifying an initiative statute for the ballot required sponsors to gather 433,000 signatures from registered voters — an enormous hurdle for grassroots volunteers, but not for those able to pay. Unz simply opened his checkbook and spent $500,000 to hire canvassers.

He made a point of circulating petitions in East Los Angeles, home to a large Mexican American community. Claims of minority support became a key selling point for the initiative after a Los Angeles Times Poll, conducted in October, reported it was favored by 84 percent of Latinos. Small wonder, since the survey portrayed the measure as primarily effort to improve English instruction for children who needed to learn the language.[10] Few Californians had heard about its extreme provisions, much less read the fine print (see Appendix E).

Proposition 227 was a complex, often confusing proposal crafted to meet conflicting political and policy goals. Unz sought to outlaw a program that many parents wanted without appearing to restrict parental choice; to tie the hands of school boards that favored bilingual education without seeming to usurp their authority; and to eliminate protections for LEP students while shielding the law from civil-rights litigation. Its highlights are as follows:

- LEP students must be taught in "sheltered English immersion" classrooms "during a temporary transition period not normally intended to exceed one year." Their instruction must be delivered "overwhelmingly [in] English" by teachers who "possess a good knowledge of the English language." Students may be mixed by age and grade. They must be transferred to mainstream classrooms after they have attained "a good working knowledge of English."
- Parents may request "waivers" of the English-only rule under limited circumstances: (a) if their children already score at or above grade level in English; (b) if they are at least 10 years old and educators believe a bilingual program would foster "rapid English acquisition"; or (c) if they are under 10 and have "special physical, emotional, psychological, or educational needs" that would better be served through native-language instruction.
- Teachers, administrators, and school board members who "willfully and repeatedly" violate the law's provisions may be sued by parents and held personally liable for financial damages and plaintiffs' legal fees.
- The California legislature must appropriate $50 million each year to provide ESL instruction for adults who agree to tutor children in English.
- Proposition 227 may be repealed or amended only by a two-thirds vote of the legislature and approval of the governor, or by another ballot initiative.

When the initiative was unveiled, California's education and civil rights communities were naturally alarmed. A long list of advocates came together to plot strategy, including CABE, the California Teachers Association, the Association of California School Administrators, the Mexican American Legal Defense and Educational Fund, California Tomorrow, and the Northern California Coalition for Immigrant Rights. But an opposition campaign was slow to get under way. Finally, in mid-November, a coalition calling itself Citizens for an Educated America held its first press conference — four months after Ron Unz had launched his campaign. Meanwhile, his charges against bilingual education went largely unchallenged. Though not unreported.

News media were drawn to the high-stakes controversy and covered it in lavish detail. Unz took to the campaign trail full-time. He carefully stayed "on message," repeating the same arguments at every stop. His pitch was straightforward: "Begun with the best of theoretical intentions some twenty or thirty years ago, bilingual education has proven itself a dismal practical failure. ... Enormous numbers of California children today leave years of schooling with limited spoken English and almost no ability to read or write English." He blamed "government efforts to prevent young immigrant children from learning English," despite the wishes of parents at schools like Ninth Street. "During the past decade, the number of these non-English-speaking immigrant children has more than doubled. Yet under the current system, centered on bilingual education, only about 5 percent of these children each year are found to have gained proficiency in English. *Thus our state's current system of language instruction has an annual failure rate of 95 percent"* (his emphasis).

Unz's mantra was simplistic but powerful. It was widely disseminated by journalists, who seldom challenged his evidence or assumptions. Few prospective voters understood that, because of teacher shortages, fully 70 percent of California's LEP students were not enrolled in bilingual classrooms. If the "current system" was indeed failing, it was more logical to blame the scarcity, not the excess, of native-language instruction. Moreover, Unz's arbitrary standard of success — one year to learn English — bore no relation to the realities of second language acquisition. Educators understood that, while children quickly acquire "playground English," they typically need four to seven years to acquire the decontextualized, cognitively demanding English required to excel in school. The annual "redesignation rate" — which averaged 7 percent statewide in 1997 — fluctuated significantly from district to district. It was affected by demographic patterns, variations in assessment procedures, and other factors unrelated to achievement. Using this dubious statistic to "hold schools accountable" implied that rapid English acquisition was the best measure of student progress. Yet research showed the opposite: programs that stressed a gradual transition to English were correlated with long-term academic success.[11]

On the other hand, there was limited research supporting the "sheltered English immersion" approach that Unz sought to impose by law. There was none whatsoever showing it could successfully mainstream children within 180 school days. One of the few rigorous studies in this area, the 1991 Ramírez report, found that after one year in English immersion programs only 4 percent of students had become fluent in English. After four years 67 percent had been redesignated, as compared with 72 percent of those in transitional bilingual education.

While such rebuttals occasionally appeared in the press, they did not lend themselves to snappy sound-bites. Voters tended to remember the "95 percent failure rate." In candid moments Unz conceded the figure was misleading, but he found it too useful to abandon. Journalists never exposed the fraud. Appealing to folk wisdom about how languages are acquired — the younger the better ... through "total immersion" ... without the "crutch" of bilingual support — he dismissed research in the field as worthless, motivated by ethnic politics or ivory tower "looniness." Many reporters, after a cursory glance at the NRC report, were inclined to agree.

Unz also played to their habitual cynicism, painting bilingual educators as a vested interest — resistant to legislative reform and more interested in taxpayer subsidies than student achievement. The news media recycled these charges, while rarely questioning Unz's own motives, once it was established that he was not a nativist zealot.

Meanwhile, it seemed that every story trumpeted his lead in the polls, implying that Proposition 227 was unbeatable. This seemed to intimidate the traditional allies of bilingual education, including Latinos and liberal Democrats. Few spoke out aggressively against the measure. Those who finally did, in the late stages, conceded the program needed a complete overhaul.

How to Respond?

Bilingual education advocates were in a quandary. Anti-immigrant bias was an obvious factor in the initiative's popularity; yet Unz had immunized his campaign from the charge of racism. Voters who truly cared about LEP children were badly misinformed; yet there was little time to give them a crash course in the theory and practice of bilingual education. Media bias had become a major obstacle; yet the No on 227 campaign needed the help of journalists to get its message out. The California Teachers Association was a potential source of funds to buy TV advertising; yet the giant union was ambivalent in its support for bilingual programs. A deal remained within reach on "reform" legislation that might head off the initiative; yet the coalition was divided over whether to compromise.

Citizens for an Educated America recognized its need for professional help. It hired campaign and media consultants, along with pollsters to conduct surveys and focus groups. The professionals recommended a counter-attack against Proposition 227. This election should not be a referendum on bilingual education, but a referendum on Unz's proposal, they argued. Highlighting its extreme provisions would help to win over "swing voters" who had yet to form an opinion. Such voters were not to be found among immigrants, many of whom were noncitizens, or among Latinos and other language minorities, who usually turned out in small numbers. Given California's electoral realities, the swing voters would have to be found among white, affluent, older, English-speaking moderates. In particular, the consultants argued, the No campaign should target "Republican women over 50." A winning message — one that would appeal to the undecided — could not be built on challenging the conventional wisdom. It could not claim success for programs that were widely perceived to be failing. In short, they recommended: "Don't defend bilingual education."

This advice came as a bitter pill for many practitioners and advocates of the program. It seemed like a betrayal of everything they had worked for, a capitulation to demagogues who would risk children's futures for political gain. Lies about bilingual education were everywhere. How could Citizens fail to refute them? Still, it was hard to deny the situation was desperate. With their polling results and political savvy, the professionals were convincing. "Put aside your personal feelings," they said in effect. "This strategy is the only hope of saving bilingual education. Given a free rein and sufficient resources, we can beat Proposition 227." After much internal debate, the coalition agreed.

Others viewed the decision as not merely misguided but suicidal. In private, some said, the strategy could have hardly served Ron Unz's purposes better if he had designed it himself. Indeed, when school officials defended bilingual education, Unz warned they could be prosecuted under a California law that prohibited public employees from taking sides on pending legislation. Now bilingual educators and even immigrant advocates working in Latino communities were feeling the same pressure from the Citizens consultants. Whenever the program came up in debates or press interviews, they were advised to change the subject, saying: "I'll be happy to discuss the merits of different bilingual education programs on June 3 [after the election] — assuming the Ron Unz Initiative fails and we can still have a meaningful conversation." Unz cited the "Don't Defend" strategy as evidence that the program was indefensible.

Journalists were incredulous, not to mention frustrated, when Citizens refused to respond to his attacks. But they did not stop writing about issues of educational effectiveness. For the press and the public, Proposition 227 remained very much a referendum on bilingual education.

Some advocates chose to go their own way. Notwithstanding his long alliance with CABE, Stephen Krashen was among those who broke with its leadership. He saw the initiative as a rare opportunity to educate Californians about second-language acquisition. The more they learned about the rationale for bilingual education, he reasoned, the more likely they were to support it. Krashen joined with like-minded colleagues in a project to influence media coverage by debunking Unz's claims.[12] Numerous other researchers, teacher trainers, and school administrators came forward — as individuals — to defend bilingual education in public forums. Yet without central coordination by Citizens, these efforts were sporadic and unfocused; their impact on the press was minimal.[13] Bilingual teachers and immigrant advocates formed local committees, especially in Latino communities, to activate parents, staff phone banks, and get out the vote. They enjoyed some success. Apart from fundraising drives, however, grassroots organizing received limited support from the No on 227 campaign.

Citizens needed large sums because its strategy relied heavily on TV advertising. Based on private opinion surveys, the campaign singled out one feature of Proposition 227 for special attack: the $50 million annual appropriation for adult English instruction. Even though that was barely 1/6 of one percent of the state's K-12 education budget, Californians resented such spending to benefit immigrants, according to the Citizens polls. Ironically, Unz had inserted this provision to guard against attacks from the Left. It was intended to fortify his "pro-immigrant" defenses and draw criticism from anti-immigrant zealots, making him look moderate by comparison. Now Citizens took the bait. Advocates who had lobbied over the past decade for more immigrant ESL classes suddenly sounded like fiscal conservatives, denouncing "a new spending program — not in our schools — but to teach adults English." The hypocrisy was hard to conceal. Unz charged that his opponents were so desperate that they were willing to abandon cherished principles. For once he was right.

A lion's share of No on 227 spending — which exceeded $4.7 million for the campaign — went for media buys in the final two weeks. Unz ran little advertising; there was no need, considering the lopsided polls. Contrary to expectations, Citizens outspent him nearly five to one overall.[14] Proposition 227 still passed easily, by a margin of 61 to 39 percent.

The only surprise was the Latino vote — two to one against the initiative — exactly the opposite of pollsters' predictions.[15] In at least this one respect, bilingual educators were vindicated. The program's strongest constituency had not forsaken it, as opponents claimed. Indeed, a survey by Spanish-language media found no decline in approval rates: 68 percent of Latinos in Los Angeles favored bilingual education, including 88 percent of those with children in such classrooms.[16] Spanish-speaking parents campaigned actively to defeat Proposition 227 in some areas. In Santa Barbara and Orange County, respectively, hundreds of them staged boycotts and filed litigation against local decisions to dismantle bilingual programs. (Journalists paid little attention, however, even as they continued to publicize the two-year-old protest at Ninth Street.)

Nevertheless, parent activism against the initiative remained more the exception than the rule — an unhealthy sign. When beneficiaries of a controversial program offer mainly passive support, political trouble cannot be far away. Thus the Proposition 227 story is a cautionary one for bilingual educators across the country. Ron Unz has announced plans to finance an anti-bilingual initiative in Arizona; similar efforts are expected in other states.

Post-Mortem

Meeting at Lake Tahoe in August 1998, veterans of No on 227 shared their views about what had gone wrong. Some defended the campaign strategy and argued that defeat was inevitable, given the demographics of California voters and their appetite for racist initiatives. Others insisted the outcome might have been different if Citizens had offered a straightforward rationale for bilingual education — something most voters had never heard — instead of insulting their intelligence with diversionary gimmicks. No consensus was achieved on these matters. Still, there was no shortage of mea culpas in explaining the victory of Proposition 227:

- **Inattention to the public image of bilingual education.** Facing increasing opposition since the mid-1980s, the field has failed to respond proactively. Professional organizations have rarely used the news media to showcase success stories or to elaborate the mission of bilingual education. School districts have often neglected to communicate with parents — for example, to assuage worries about programs that stress a gradual transition to English. Researchers have seldom strived to make their findings accessible to a broad audience. Bilingual educators have tended to circle the wagons and complain to each other about unsympathetic colleagues rather than challenge their misconceptions. No wonder the field has become politically isolated.

- **Limited efforts to marshal data on outcomes.** The field has tended to ignore the importance of test scores to combat skepticism about bilingual education. Notwithstanding the difficulties in assessing LEP students, the public is not unreasonable to demand accountability for programs that have been in place for years. To their credit, a few California districts scrambled during the campaign to release data comparing the outcomes of children in bilingual and English-only classrooms. Unfortunately, the data sometimes had flaws that tended to discredit legitimate claims of success. Trained researchers are needed to assist in analyzing these results. Virginia Collier and Wayne Thomas have developed a promising model for such studies and, in the process, have greatly expanded the database on program effectiveness. Since 1994, they have reported overall patterns that confirm theories underlying bilingual education, such as a correlation between native-language development and long-term academic achievement. Their work seemed to offer powerful evidence against the claims of Ron Unz. Yet Collier and Thomas declined to release sufficient data — in the view of many colleagues — for others to assess their findings. As a result, the researchers missed an opportunity to influence the debate over Proposition 227.

- **Resistance to legislative "reform."** Over the past decade, an era of conservatism — fiscal and otherwise — bilingual educators have adopted a defensive posture, relying on backroom deal-making to block change. They have stressed mandates to maintain funding levels and force schools to meet their obligations to LEP students. In short, they have become defenders of the status quo. Refusal to compromise may be "principled," but it can also sacrifice chances to win needed improvements — for example, to remedy the chronic shortage of qualified teachers. In addition, it strengthens the stereotype of bilingual educators as a vested interest rather than a group of dedicated professionals, sometimes provoking more extreme attacks like Proposition 227.

- **Loss of ties to the grassroots.** Bilingual education was not a gift from above, but a victory of mass struggle from below. Without the efforts of determined parents and community leaders, the Bilingual Education Act and the *Lau v. Nichols* decision would never have materialized. Gradually, the program was supported by government, accepted by school boards, studied by researchers, and sustained by a corps of experts, lawyers, and bureaucrats. In short, it became institutionalized. To the extent that it became a domain of professionals, it became less of an activist cause, less of a social movement. Parents, once its strongest political base, were reduced to a passive role — as consumers of bilingual education rather than participants.

Whether any decision by No on 227 could have altered the outcome is impossible to say. There is little doubt, however, that greater attention to these problems during the campaign would have left advocates in a better position to cope with the initiative's aftermath. Because of legal challenges[17] and ambiguous language, the final interpretation of Proposition 227 could take years to sort out. Ultimately, its impact on children will depend not only on litigation but on political pressures that each side can bring to bear to influence school boards, district administrators, and state officials.

Meanwhile, the fallout from Proposition 227 is spreading beyond California's borders. In several states with the ballot initiative process, bilingual education is vulnerable to Unz-like assaults. Elsewhere, there are proposals to impose arbitrary time limits — typically three years — on children's enrollment in language assistance programs.

Rep. Frank Riggs (R-Calif.) sponsored the latter proposal in Congress during the summer of 1998, borrowing Unz's argument that students are languishing "too long" in bilingual programs. His bill, approved by the House on a party-line vote, would have also turned Title VII into a "block grant" program administered by the states, while voiding numerous Lau plans, federal court decisions, and consent decrees involving the civil rights of LEP students. With an eye on the mid-term elections and the voters' impatience to mainstream English learners, the Clinton White House was tempted to endorse a version of the three-year limit. But following an angry response from the Congressional Hispanic Caucus, it reconsidered and blocked the Riggs bill.

Nevertheless, the issue was hardly settled. It is expected to resurface during 1999 deliberations to reauthorize the Improving America's Schools Act. Similar battles loom in several states. Bilingual education will likely face jeopardy as never before. How advocates respond — whether they can regroup and formulate effective strategies to defend the program — will determine the future of language-minority schooling for years to come.

Notes

1. According to Eleanor Vargas Page, students receive a minimum of two hours of English daily in the early years, with the amount of Spanish instruction decreasing until children are reclassified as fluent English proficient (FEP), usually by the 4th or 5th grade.
2. Critics have frequently charged that children are misassigned to bilingual programs, typically on the basis of Hispanic surnames, and that parents' requests for English-only instruction are routinely denied. Such mistakes may sometimes occur. There is

no evidence, however, that such problems are pervasive. Norm Gold, the official in charge of enforcing civil rights guarantees for English learners in California, says his department receives "scores of written complaints" each year from parents unable to get bilingual instruction for their children. "But records going back over more than a decade show that there have been no complaints alleging that parents have been unable to remove their children from bilingual instruction."

3.   One parent who checked off the English-only box wrote below: "Quiero que mi hijo siga en la clase bilingüe porque quiero que es mejor para su futuro" (I want my son to continue in the bilingual classroom because I believe it is better for his future).

4.   By contrast, 5th graders in bilingual programs at Ninth Street scored at the 27th, 31st, and 38th percentiles respectively. Scores are from the Stanford 9 test administered in the spring of 1997. Direct comparisons are difficult because some students were excused from taking the test because of their limited English proficiency.

5.   This and most other features of Proposition 187 were ruled unconstitutional in 1998.

6.   Even in these classrooms, about one-third of teachers were still working toward their bilingual certification. According to the CDE's annual language census, another 21 percent of LEP students received lessons taught in English with "native-language support" from paraprofessionals. Various forms of English-only instruction were provided to 32 percent, and 16 percent received no special help whatsoever.

7.   The plague-on-both-houses theme came through even stronger in an NRC press release announcing the study on January 14, 1997: "Political debates over how children with limited English skills should be taught are hampering research and evaluation of educational programs established to meet the needs of these children. ... Much research has been used in trying to determine which type of instruction is better — English-only or bilingual. However, there is little value in using research for this purpose. ... Instead of attempting to single out one method for all students, research should focus on identifying a variety of educational approaches that work for children in their communities, based on specific local needs and available resources. ... Evaluations have proved inconclusive about which teaching approaches work best. ... Because many current studies are attempting to compare different types of programs that vary widely in such areas as funding, classroom setting, student background, and subject matter, the studies are unlikely to settle the debate over which type of instruction is best. ... Advocates on many sides of the issue have been able to use research to uphold their arguments because there are study results that support a wide range of positions. These debates confuse policymakers and muddle research agendas. ...The committee called for a model for research and development that would be grounded in knowledge about the linguistic, social, and cognitive development of children. ..."

8.   Speaker Newt Gingrich championed the English Only cause during House floor debate, hoping to give Republicans a boost in the fall campaign. But it seemed to have little impact at the polls except to drive Latinos further from the party. Gingrich would not make the same mistake again. In the 105th Congress, he refused to allow a vote on the legislation.

9.   Cosponsoring Proposition 227 gave Tuchman the name recognition to wage a seri-

ous challenge to the incumbent, Delaine Eastin, in 1998. But she lost in the November election.

10. Here's how the question was posed: "There is a new initiative trying to qualify for the June primary ballot that would require all public school instruction to be conducted in English and for students not fluent in English to be placed in a shortterm English immersion program. If the June 1998 primary election were being held today, would you vote for or against this measure?" Overall, 80 percent of likely voters said yes and 18 percent said no. Later surveys by the *Times* and the Field Poll were nearly as misleading. So was California's official ballot summary, which failed to mention the virtual ban on bilingual programs. It seems likely that many voters never got that message.

11. E.g., in a 1998 study of San Francisco students who had been redesignated as fluent in English, David Ramírez found that children had spent an average of 4.8 years in language assistance programs (bilingual and otherwise). After being mainstreamed, they usually outscored all other groups at the secondary level, including native English speakers.

12. The author was also an organizer of this effort, known as UnzWatch.

13. Spokespersons hired by Citizens, who had little background in education or knowledge of research, devoted most of their energies to debating Ron Unz and, later, to influencing editorial boards to oppose Proposition 227. But they held few press conferences and generated few news stories of any kind. Meanwhile, Unz faxed daily press releases to journalists — setting the agenda and defining terms of the debate.

14. English for the Children raised $1,289,815 but spent only $976,632, according to its reports to the California Secretary of State. Of this amount, $752,738 came from Ron Unz. Citizens for an Educated America raised and spent $4,754,157, including $2.1 million from the California Teachers Association and $1.5 million from Jerrold Perenchio, owner of the Spanish-language network Univision.

15. A week before the election, the Los Angeles Times Poll reported 62 percent Latino support for Proposition 227. By contrast, its exit interviews with voters on June 2 found that Latinos had opposed the initiative by 63 to 37 percent. African-Americans also voted No, 52-48, while Asian Americans voted Yes, 57-43, and whites voted Yes, 67-33, according to the exit poll.

16. Still, because of confusion about Proposition 227, 43 percent were inclined to support it, too. The poll was conducted in February 1998 by the newspaper *La Opinión* and KVEA-TV, the Los Angeles affiliate of Telemundo.

17. The day after the vote, bilingual education advocates sued to overturn Proposition 227 on civil-rights and constitutional grounds. A federal district judge denied their petition for a preliminary injunction in the case, *Valeria G. v. Wilson*; so the law took effect as scheduled on August 2, 1998. Litigation on the merits continues. Meanwhile, Ron Unz and Alice Callaghan have threatened to bring their own lawsuits against districts whose creative interpretations displease them. For example, some educators have cited Unz's claim of an "overwhelming" victory with 61 percent of the vote to argue that a curriculum taught 61 percent in English should satisfy the law's requirement.

Appendices

Appendix A
Glossary of Program Models

Program labels, oversimplified and misleading, often complicate discussions of bilingual education. English as a second language (ESL), English immersion, and transitional bilingual education (TBE) are often described as discrete "methods" of teaching limited-English-proficient (LEP) children. In practice, however, there is much overlap among these educational treatments. Some of the most successful programs draw techniques from all three. At the same time, there is considerable variation within each model. To follow the pedagogical and policy debates, a clear understanding of terms is essential.

* * *

Transitional bilingual education provides a portion of instruction in LEP children's native language to help them keep up in school subjects while they study English in programs designed for second-language learners. The goal is to prepare students to enter mainstream English classrooms, a transition usually completed within two to three years. In practice, TBE varies widely. Programs may stress native-language development, including initial literacy, or they may provide students with nothing more than ESL instruction and the translation services of bilingual aides. Contrary to public perceptions, studies have shown that English is the medium of instruction from 72 to 92 percent of the time in TBE programs.

Unlike TBE, *maintenance* or *developmental bilingual education* (DBE) attempts to preserve and enhance students' skills in the mother tongue while they acquire a second language. In other words, DBE programs are based on an educational *enrichment* model; transitional programs, on a *compensatory* model. "In the maintenance model, there is less emphasis on exiting students from the program as soon as possible," write Carlos Ovando and Virginia Collier. Native-language instruction generally continues through the 6th grade, although most subjects may be taught in English. DBE classrooms at the secondary level are rare in the United States.

Though it has aroused political controversy, developmental bilingual education offers sociocultural benefits for language-minority students and, according to a growing body of research, cognitive advantages over TBE as well. In two years of bilingual instruction or less, most children acquire *basic interpersonal commu-*

nication skills (BICS), also known as "playground English." But several studies have shown that *cognitive-academic language proficiency* (CALP), the linguistic foundation that children need for academic pursuits, takes five to seven years to achieve in a second language. According to the *threshold hypothesis* proposed by Jim Cummins, a LEP child must reach a minimum level of CALP in the native language before literacy skills will "transfer" to English. Failure to do so before leaving a bilingual classroom will likely inhibit the student's development of CALP in English.

DBE's goal is *additive bilingualism,* or continued development in two languages, which some researchers have linked to increased cognitive flexibility. By contrast, *subtractive bilingualism,* the attempt to replace a child's native tongue with English as quickly as possible, is associated with low levels of proficiency in both languages and underachievement in school.

Developmental programs may also function as *two-way bilingual education,* also known as *dual language* or *bilingual immersion* programs, which Ovando and Collier define as "an integrated model in which speakers of [two] languages are placed together in a bilingual classroom to learn each others' language and work academically in both languages." Most common in the United States are programs that simultaneously teach Spanish to English-background children and English to Spanish-background children, while cultivating the native-language skills of each group.

* * *

In *immersion* education children are taught a second language through subject-matter instruction in that language, with an emphasis on contextual clues and with lessons geared to students' level of competence. According to Stephen Krashen, the key is providing *comprehensible input,* or understandable messages, through which children internalize grammar and vocabulary in the target language as they learn other academic subjects. Immersion must be distinguished from *submersion,* also known as *sink-or-swim,* in which LEP children receive no special language assistance. Under the U.S. Supreme Court's *Lau v. Nichols* decision (1974), submersion is a violation of federal civil rights law.

Enrichment immersion programs have been widely successful among language-majority children, for example, French immersion in Canada and Spanish immersion in the United States, in which English speakers acquire a second language. This is a bilingual model, however, that includes opportunities for students to develop their English skills.

Secretary of Education William Bennett sought expanded funding for *special alternative instructional programs* (SAIPs) that used mostly English to instruct LEP children. Opponents of TBE have favored one such approach known as *structured immersion*, a monolingual English strategy for teaching language-minority children. Lacking evidence from the United States, proponents have cited the success of Canadian immersion programs to justify structured immersion as an alternative to bilingual education. The researchers who designed French immersion, however, have warned that this model is inappropriate and potentially harmful for minority students, whose native tongue is in danger of being replaced because of its low social status.

Alternate immersion, also known as *sheltered English* or *sheltered subject-matter instruction,* is a component of many bilingual programs. Children receive second-language instruction that is "sheltered" from input beyond their comprehension, first in subjects that are less language-intensive, such as mathematics, and later in those that are more so, such as social studies. In other bilingual program models, lessons are taught in the native language in the morning and through sheltered English in the afternoon, or the lessons may be repeated on alternate days. The *preview-review method,* frequently used in team teaching situations, features lessons taught first in one, then the other language, followed by a review session in both languages to reinforce what has been learned.

Concurrent translation, a method of bilingual instruction in which the teacher shifts between languages to communicate each idea, continues to be practiced even though it has been discredited by researchers. Studies have shown that children simply ignore the second-language portion of such lessons. Moreover, teachers tend to favor one language or the other, often unconsciously, and do little to make the English portion intelligible to LEP children. Some concurrent approaches attempt to avoid these pitfalls by training teachers to monitor their language use and to refrain from direct translation of ideas. With such modifications, the method could work, says Krashen. "But the concurrent approach is tough on the teacher, it's unnecessary, and [sheltered English] is a safer way" of providing comprehensible input.

* * *

English as a second language is a component of virtually all bilingual education programs in the United States. Owing to the shortage of bilingual teachers, for many LEP children it is the only special assistance available. In school districts where many languages are represented, students typically receive only "pullout classes" in ESL a few times each week. The rest of the time, it's sink or swim.

With ESL, as with bilingual instruction, methodologies vary considerably. Until recently the most prevalent were *grammar-based*, such as the *audiolingual method*, a behaviorist approach that emphasizes memorization, mimicry, and drills in "the structure of the week." An older method in this category is the *grammar-translation approach*, which concentrates on perfecting reading and writing skills, with less attention to listening and speaking. While grammar-based ESL may produce students who can formulate "correct" sentences, given enough time, it often fails to make them fluent communicators. The tedious content of instruction, for students and teachers alike, appears to impede learning.

Increasingly *communication-based ESL* is superseding the older methods. These approaches are grounded in Krashen's theory that language is *acquired* through exposure to comprehensible messages rather than *learned* through the conscious study of syntax and vocabulary. Representative of these *direct methods* is the Natural Approach, which stresses simplified speech and visual or physical cues to help students comprehend second-language input. It aims to create a low-anxiety environment for the ESL student and thereby to "lower" the *affective filter*, or complex of psychological factors, that prevents comprehensible input from getting through. Teachers using the Natural Approach focus on meaningful and interesting communication, while avoiding the overcorrection of student errors. They also respect children's *silent period* of up to six months, in which ability to produce speech lags comprehension.

* * *

TBE, DBE, and SAIP have also served as legal categories for purposes of grantmaking under the Bilingual Education Act of 1968 (a.k.a. Title VII of the Elementary and Secondary Education Act of 1965). As defined in the 1984 reauthorization of Title VII, TBE was

> a program of instruction, designed for children of limited English proficiency in elementary or secondary schools, which provides . . . structured English language instruction, and to the extent necessary to allow a child to achieve competence in the English language, instruction in the child's native language. Such instruction shall incorporate the cultural heritage of such children and of other children in American society. Such instruction shall, to the extent nec-

essary, be in all courses or subjects of study which will allow a child to meet grade-promotion and graduation standards.

DBE was

> a program . . . which provides . . . structured English language instruction and instruction in a second language. Such programs shall be designed to help children achieve competence in English and a second language, while mastering subject matter skills. Such instruction shall, to the extent necessary, be in all courses or subjects of study which will allow a child to meet grade-promotion and graduation standards.

As terms of legal significance, TBE and DBE were eliminated in the 1994 reauthorization of Title VII. In their place appeared a definition of bilingual education as

> an educational program for limited English proficient students that—
> (A) makes instructional use of both English and a student's native language;
> (B) enables limited English proficient students to achieve English proficiency and academic mastery of subject matter content and higher order skills, including critical thinking, so as to meet age-appropriate grade-promotion and graduation standards in concert with the National Education Goals;
> (C) may also develop the native language skills of limited English proficient students, or ancestral languages of American Indians, Alaska Natives, Native Hawaiians and native residents of the outlying areas; and
> (D) may include the participation of English-proficient students if such program is designed to enable all enrolled students to become proficient in English and a second language.

The new law retained the category SAIP, however, which it defined as:

> an educational program for limited English proficient students

that—

(A) utilizes specially designed English language curricula and services but does not use the student's native language for instructional purposes;

(B) enables limited English proficient students to achieve English proficiency and academic mastery of subject matter content and higher order skills, including critical thinking so as to meet age-appropriate grade-promotion and graduation standards in concert with the National Education Goals; and

(C) is particularly appropriate for schools where the diversity of the limited English proficient students' native languages and the small number of students speaking each respective language makes bilingual education impractical and where there is a critical shortage of bilingual education teachers.

This legal definition contradicts pedagogical practice in many alternative programs, such as structured immersion, which normally use LEP students' native language for purposes of clarification and sometimes teach it as a subject. In these respects it also departs from the California Department of Education's criteria for acceptable alternatives to bilingual instruction.

Appendix B
Title VII, Elementary and Secondary Act

Excerpts from the Improving America's Schools Act of 1994 (P.L. 103-382, Oct. 30, 1994); Title VII, Part B, Foreign Language Assistance Program, and Part C, Emergency Immigrant Education Program, are omitted.

TITLE VII: Bilingual Education, Language Enhancement, and Language Acquisition Programs

PART A—BILINGUAL EDUCATION

SEC. 7101. SHORT TITLE.
This part may be cited as the 'Bilingual Education Act.'

SEC. 7102. FINDINGS, POLICY, AND PURPOSE.
  (a) Findings.—The Congress finds that—
      (1) language-minority Americans speak virtually all world languages plus many that are indigenous to the United States;
      (2) there are large and growing numbers of children and youth of limited-English proficiency, many of whom have a cultural heritage that differs from that of their English-proficient peers;
      (3) the presence of language-minority Americans is related in part to Federal immigration policies;
      (4) many language-minority Americans are limited in their English proficiency, and many have limited education and income;
      (5) limited English proficient children and youth face a number of challenges in receiving an education that will enable such children and youth to participate fully in American society, including—
          (A) segregated education programs;
          (B) disproportionate and improper placement in special education and other special programs due to the use of inappropriate evaluation procedures;
          (C) the limited-English proficiency of their own parents, which hinders the parents' ability to fully participate in the education of their children; and
          (D) a shortage of teachers and other staff who are professionally trained and qualified to serve such children and youth;
      (6) Native Americans and Native American languages (as such terms are defined in section 103 of the Native American Languages Act), including native residents of the outlying areas, have a unique status under Federal law that requires special policies within the broad purposes of this Act to serve the education needs of language minority students in the United States;
      (7) institutions of higher education can assist in preparing teachers, administrators and other school personnel to understand and build upon the educational strengths

and needs of language-minority and culturally diverse student enrollments;

(8) it is the purpose of this title to help ensure that limited English proficient students master English and develop high levels of academic attainment in content areas;

(9) quality bilingual education programs enable children and youth to learn English and meet high academic standards including proficiency in more than one language;

(10) as the world becomes increasingly interdependent and as international communication becomes a daily occurrence in government, business, commerce, and family life, multilingual skills constitute an important national resource which deserves protection and development;

(11) educational technology has the potential for improving the education of language-minority and limited English proficient students and their families, and the Federal Government should foster this development;

(12) parent and community participation in bilingual education programs contributes to program effectiveness;

(13) research, evaluation, and data-collection capabilities in the field of bilingual education need to be strengthened so that educators and other staff can better identify and promote those programs, program implementation strategies, and instructional practices that result in effective education of limited English proficient children;

(14) the use of a child or youth's native language and culture in classroom instruction can—

(A) promote self-esteem and contribute to academic achievement and learning English by limited English proficient children and youth;

(B) benefit English-proficient children and youth who also participate in such programs; and

(C) develop our Nation's national language resources, thus promoting our Nation's competitiveness in the global economy;

(15) the Federal Government, as exemplified by title VI of the Civil Rights Act of 1964 and section 204(f) of the Equal Education Opportunities Act of 1974, has a special and continuing obligation to ensure that States and local school districts take appropriate action to provide equal educational opportunities to children and youth of limited English proficiency; and

(16) the Federal Government also, as exemplified by the Federal Government's efforts under this title, has a special and continuing obligation to assist States and local school districts in developing the capacity to provide programs of instruction that offer limited English proficient children and youth an equal educational opportunity.

(b) Policy.—The Congress declares it to be the policy of the United States, in order to ensure equal educational opportunity for all children and youth and to promote educational excellence, to assist State and local educational agencies, institutions of higher education and community-based organizations to build their capacity to establish, implement, and sustain programs of instruction for children and youth of limited English proficiency.

(c) Purpose.—The purpose of this part is to educate limited English proficient children and youth to meet the same rigorous standards for academic performance expected of all children and youth, including meeting challenging State content standards and challenging State student performance standards in academic areas by—

(1) developing systemic improvement and reform of educational programs serving limited English proficient students through the development and implementation of exemplary bilingual education programs and special alternative instruction programs;

(2) developing bilingual skills and multicultural understanding;

(3) developing the English of such children and youth and, to the extent possible, the native language skills of such children and youth;

(4) providing similar assistance to Native Americans with certain modifications relative to the unique status of Native American languages under Federal law;

(5) developing data collection and dissemination, research, materials development, and technical assistance which is focused on school improvement for limited English proficient students; and

(6) developing programs which strengthen and improve the professional training of educational personnel who work with limited English proficient students.

SEC. 7103. AUTHORIZATION OF APPROPRIATIONS.

(a) In General.—For the purpose of carrying out this part, there are authorized to be appropriated $215,000,000 for the fiscal year 1995 and such sums as may be necessary for each of the four succeeding fiscal years.

(b) Distribution.—From the sums appropriated under subsection (a) for any fiscal year, the Secretary shall reserve not less than 25 percent of such funds for such year to carry out subpart 3.

SEC. 7104. NATIVE AMERICAN AND ALASKA NATIVE CHILDREN IN SCHOOL.

(a) Eligible Entities.—For the purpose of carrying out programs under this part for individuals served by elementary, secondary, and postsecondary schools operated predominately for Native American or Alaska Native children and youth, an Indian tribe, a tribally sanctioned educational authority, a Native Hawaiian or Native American Pacific Islander native language education organization, or an elementary or secondary school that is operated or funded by the Bureau of Indian Affairs shall be considered to be a local educational agency as such term is used in this part, subject to the following qualifications:

(1) Indian tribe.—The term 'Indian tribe' means any Indian tribe, band, nation, or other organized group or community, including any Alaska Native village or regional or village corporation as defined in or establised pursuant to the Alaska Native Claims Settlement Act (43 U.S.C. 1601 et seq.), that is recognized for the special programs and services provided by the United States to Indians because of their status as Indians.

(2) Tribally sanctioned educational authority.—The term 'tribally sanctioned educational authority' means—

(A) any department or division of education operating within the administrative structure of the duly constituted governing body of an Indian tribe; and

(B) any nonprofit institution or organization that is—

(i) chartered by the governing body of an Indian tribe to operate any such school or otherwise to oversee the delivery of educational services to members of that tribe; and

(ii) approved by the Secretary for the purpose of this section.

(b) Eligible Entity Application.—Notwithstanding any other provision of this part, each eligible entity described in subsection (a) shall submit any application for assistance under this part directly to the Secretary along with timely comments on the need for the proposed program.

SEC. 7105. RESIDENTS OF THE TERRITORIES AND FREELY ASSOCIATED NATIONS.
For the purpose of carrying out programs under this part in the outlying areas, the term 'local educational agency' shall include public institutions or agencies whose mission is the preservation and maintenance of native languages.

Subpart 1—Bilingual Education Capacity and Demonstration Grants

SEC. 7111. FINANCIAL ASSISTANCE FOR BILINGUAL EDUCATION.
The purpose of this subpart is to assist local educational agencies, institutions of higher education, and community-based organizations, through the grants authorized under sections 7112, 7113, 7114, and 7115 to—
    (1) develop and enhance their capacity to provide high-quality instruction through bilingual education or special alternative instruction programs to children and youth of limited English proficiency; and
    (2) to help such children and youth—
        (A) develop proficiency in English, and to the extent possible, their native language; and
        (B) meet the same challenging State content standards and challenging State student performance standards expected for all children and youth as required by section 1111(b).

SEC. 7112. PROGRAM DEVELOPMENT AND IMPLEMENTATION GRANTS.
    (a) Purpose.—The purpose of this section is to develop and implement new comprehensive, coherent, and successful bilingual education or special alternative instructional programs for limited English proficient students, including programs of early childhood education, kindergarten through twelfth grade education, gifted and talented education, and vocational and applied technology education.
    (b) Program Authorized.—
        (1) Authority.—
            (A) The Secretary is authorized to award grants to eligible entities having applications approved under section 7116 to enable such entities to carry out activities described in paragraph (2).
            (B) Each grant under this section shall be awarded for a period of three years.
        (2) Authorized activities.—
            (A) Grants awarded under this section shall be used to improve the education of limited English proficient students and their families by—
                (i) developing and implementing comprehensive preschool, elementary, or secondary bilingual education or special alternative instructional programs that are coordinated with other relevant programs and services to meet the full range of educational needs of limited English proficient students; and
                (ii) providing inservice training to classroom teachers, administrators, and other school or community-based organizational personnel to improve the instruction and assessment of language-minority and limited English proficient students.
            (B) Grants under this section may be used to improve the education of limited English proficient students and their families by—
                (i) implementing family education programs and parent outreach and training activities designed to assist parents to become active participants in the education of their children;
                (ii) improving the instructional program for limited English proficient stu-

dents by identifying, acquiring, and upgrading curriculum, instructional materials, educational software and assessment procedures and, if appropriate, applying educational technology;

(iii) compensating personnel, including teacher aides who have been specifically trained, or are being trained, to provide services to children and youth of limited English proficiency;

(iv) providing tutorials and academic or career counseling for children and youth of limited-English proficiency; and

(v) providing such other activities, related to the purposes of this part, as the Secretary may approve.

(c) Eligible Entity.—For the purpose of this section the term 'eligible entity' means—

(1) one or more local educational agencies;

(2) one or more local educational agencies in collaboration with an institution of higher education, community-based organization or local or State educational agency; or

(3) a community-based organization or an institution of higher education which has an application approved by the local educational agency to develop and implement early childhood education or family education programs or to conduct an instructional program which supplements the educational services provided by a local educational agency.

(d) Due Consideration.—In awarding grants under this section, the Secretary shall give due consideration to the need for early childhood education, elementary education, and secondary education programs.

SEC. 7113. PROGRAM ENHANCEMENT PROJECTS.

(a) Purpose.—The purpose of this section is to carry out highly focused, innovative, locally designed projects to expand or enhance existing bilingual education or special alternative instructional programs for limited English proficient students.

(b) Program Authorized.—

(1) Authority.—

(A) The Secretary is authorized to award grants to eligible entities having applications approved under section 7116 to enable such entities to carry out activities described in paragraph (2).

(B) Each grant under this section shall be awarded for a period of two years.

(2) Authorized activities.—

(A) Grants under this section shall be used for providing inservice training to classroom teachers, administrators, and other school or community-based organization personnel to improve the instruction and assessment of language-minority and limited English proficient students.

(B) Grants under this section may be used for—

(i) implementing family education programs and parent outreach and training activities designed to assist parents to become active participants in the education of their children;

(ii) improving the instructional program for limited English proficient students by identifying, acquiring, and upgrading curriculum, instructional materials, educational software and assessment procedures and, if appropriate, applying educational technology;

(iii) compensating personnel, including teacher aides who have been specifically trained, or are being trained, to provide services to children and youth of limited-English proficiency;

(iv) providing tutorials and academic or career counseling for children and youth of limited-English proficiency;

(v) providing intensified instruction; and

(vi) providing such other activities, related to the purposes of this part, as the Secretary may approve.

(c) Eligible Entity.—For the purpose of this section the term 'eligible entity' means—

(1) one or more local educational agencies;

(2) one or more local educational agencies in collaboration with an institution of higher education, community-based organization or local or State educational agency; or

(3) a community-based organization or an institution of higher education which has an application approved by the local educational agency to enhance early childhood education or family education programs or to conduct an instructional program which supplements the educational services provided by a local educational agency.

SEC. 7114. COMPREHENSIVE SCHOOL GRANTS.

(a) Purpose.—The purpose of this section is to provide financial assistance to eligible entities to implement schoolwide bilingual education programs or special alternative instruction programs for reforming, restructuring, and upgrading all relevant programs and operations, within an individual school, that serve all (or virtually all) children and youth of limited-English proficiency in schools with significant concentrations of such children and youth.

(b) Program Authorized.—

(1) Authority.—

(A) The Secretary is authorized to award grants to eligible entities having applications approved under section 7116 to enable such entities to carry out activities described in paragraph (3).

(B) Each grant under this section shall be awarded for five years.

(2) Termination.—The Secretary shall terminate grants to eligible entities under this section if the Secretary determines that—

(A) the program evaluation required by section 7123 indicates that students in the schoolwide program are not being taught to and are not making adequate progress toward achieving challenging State content standards and challenging State student performance standards; or

(B) in the case of a program to promote dual language facility, such program is not promoting such facility.

(3) Authorized activities.—Grants under this section may be used to improve the education of limited English proficient students and their families by—

(A) implementing family education programs and parent outreach and training activities designed to assist parents to become active participants in the education of their children;

(B) improving the instructional program for limited English proficient students by identifying, acquiring and upgrading curriculum, instructional materials, educational software and assessment procedures and, if appropriate, applying educational technology;

(C) compensating personnel, including teacher aides who have been specifically trained, or are being trained, to provide services to children and youth of limited English proficiency;

(D) providing tutorials and academic or career counseling for children and youth of limited-English proficiency;

(E) providing intensified instruction; and

(F) providing such other activities, related to the purposes of this part, as the Secretary may approve.

(4) Special rule.—A grant recipient, before carrying out a program assisted under this section, shall plan, train personnel, develop curriculum, and acquire or develop materials.

(c) Eligible Entities.—For the purpose of this section the term 'eligible entity' means—

(1) one or more local educational agencies; or

(2) one or more local educational agencies in collaboration with an institution of higher education, community-based organizations or a local or State educational agency.

SEC. 7115. SYSTEMWIDE IMPROVEMENT GRANTS.

(a) Purpose.—The purpose of this section is to implement districtwide bilingual education programs or special alternative instruction programs to improve, reform, and upgrade relevant programs and operations, within an entire local educational agency, that serve a significant number of children and youth of limited English proficiency in local educational agencies with significant concentrations of such children and youth.

(b) Program Authorized.—

(1) Authority.—

(A) The Secretary is authorized to award grants to eligible entities having applications approved under section 7116 to enable such entities to carry out activities described in paragraphs (3) and (4).

(B) Each grant under this section shall be awarded for 5 years.

(2) Termination.—The Secretary shall terminate grants to eligible entities under this section if the Secretary determines that—

(A) the program evaluation required by section 7123 indicates that students in the program are not being taught to and are not making adequate progress toward achieving challenging State content standards and challenging State student performance standards; or

(B) in the case of a program to promote dual language facility, such program is not promoting such facility.

(3) Preparation.—Grants under this section may be used during the first 12 months exclusively for activities preparatory to the delivery of services.

(4) Uses.—Grants under this section may be used to improve the education of limited English proficient students and their families by reviewing, restructuring, and upgrading—

(A) educational goals, curriculum guidelines and content, standards and assessments;

(B) personnel policies and practices including recruitment, certification, staff development, and assignment;

(C) student grade-promotion and graduation requirements;

(D) student assignment policies and practices;

(E) family education programs and parent outreach and training activities designed to assist parents to become active participants in the education of their children;

(F) the instructional program for limited English proficient students by identifying, acquiring and upgrading curriculum, instructional materials, educational software and assessment procedures and, if appropriate, applying educational technology;

(G) tutorials and academic or career counseling for children and youth of limited-English proficiency; and

(H) such other activities, related to the purposes of this part, as the Secretary may approve.

(c) Eligible Entities.—For the purpose of this section the term 'eligible entity' means—

(1) one or more local educational agencies; or

(2) one or more local educational agencies in collaboration with an institution of higher education, community-based organizations or a local or State educational agency.

SEC. 7116. APPLICATIONS.

(a) In General.—

(1) Secretary.—To receive a grant under this subpart, an eligible entity shall submit an application to the Secretary at such time, in such form, and containing such information as the Secretary may require.

(2) State educational agency.—An eligible entity, with the exception of schools funded by the Bureau of Indian Affairs, shall submit a copy of its application under this section to the State educational agency.

(b) State Review and Comments.—

(1) Deadline.—The State educational agency, not later than 45 days after receipt of an application under this section, shall review the application and transmit such application to the Secretary.

(2) Comments.—

(A) Regarding any application submitted under this title, the State educational agency shall—

(i) submit to the Secretary written comments regarding all such applications; and

(ii) submit to each eligible entity the comments that pertain to such entity.

(B) For purposes of this subpart, such comments shall address how the eligible entity—

(i) will further the academic achievement of limited English proficient students served pursuant to a grant received under this subpart; and

(ii) how the grant application is consistent with the State plan submitted under section 1111.

(c) Eligible Entity Comments.—An eligible entity may submit to the Secretary comments that address the comments submitted by the State educational agency.

(d) Comment Consideration.—In making grants under this subpart the Secretary shall take into consideration comments made by a State educational agency.

(e) Waiver.—Notwithstanding subsection (b), the Secretary is authorized to waive the review requirement of subsection (b) if a State educational agency can demonstrate that such review requirement may impede such agency's ability to fulfill the requirements of participation in the State grant program, particularly such agency's data collection efforts and such agency's ability to provide technical assistance to local educational agencies not receiving funds under this Act.

(f) Required Documentation.—Such application shall include documentation that the applicant has the qualified personnel required to develop, administer, and implement the proposed program.

(g) Contents.—

(1) In general.—An application for a grant under this subpart shall contain the following:

(A) A description of the need for the proposed program, including data on the number of children and youth of limited-English proficiency in the school or school district to be served and the characteristics of such children and youth, such as language spoken, dropout rates, proficiency in English and the native language, academic standing in relation to the English-proficient peers of such children and youth, and, where applicable, the recency of immigration.

(B) A description of the program to be implemented and how such program's design—

(i) relates to the linguistic and academic needs of the children and youth of limited-English proficiency to be served;

(ii) is coordinated with other programs under this Act, the Goals 2000: Educate America Act and other Acts, as appropriate, in accordance with section 14306;

(iii) involves the parents of the children and youth of limited-English proficiency to be served;

(iv) ensures accountability in achieving high academic standards; and

(v) promotes coordination of services for the children and youth of limited-English proficiency to be served and their families.

(C) A description, if appropriate, of the applicant's collaborative activities with institutions of higher education, community-based organizations, local or State educational agencies, private schools, nonprofit organizations, or businesses in carrying out the proposed program.

(D) An assurance that the applicant will not reduce the level of State and local funds that the applicant expends for bilingual education or special alternative instruction programs if the applicant receives an award under this subpart.

(E) An assurance that the applicant will employ teachers in the proposed program that, individually or in combination, are proficient in English, including written, as well as oral, communication skills.

(F) A budget for grant funds.

(2) Additional information.—Each application for a grant under section 7114 or 7115 shall—

(A) describe—

(i) current services the applicant provides to children and youth of limited-English proficiency;

(ii) what services children and youth of limited-English proficiency will receive under the grant that such children or youth will not otherwise receive;

(iii) how funds received under this subpart will be integrated with all other Federal, State, local, and private resources that may be used to serve children and youth of limited-English proficiency;

(iv) specific achievement and school retention goals for the children and youth to be served by the proposed program and how progress toward achieving such goals will be measured; and

        (v) current family education programs if applicable; and

     (B) provide assurances that—

        (i) the program funded will be integrated with the overall educational program; and

        (ii) the application has been developed in consultation with an advisory council, the majority of whose members are parents and other representatives of the children and youth to be served in such programs.

(h) Approval of Applications.—An application for a grant under this subpart may be approved only if the Secretary determines that—

     (1) the program will use qualified personnel, including personnel who are proficient in the language or languages used for instruction;

     (2) in designing the program for which application is made, the needs of children in nonprofit private elementary and secondary schools have been taken into account through consultation with appropriate private school officials and, consistent with the number of such children enrolled in such schools in the area to be served whose educational needs are of the type and whose language and grade levels are of a similar type to those which the program is intended to address, after consultation with appropriate private school officials, provision has been made for the participation of such children on a basis comparable to that provided for public school children;

     (3) student evaluation and assessment procedures in the program are valid, reliable, and fair for limited English proficient students, and that limited English proficient students who are disabled are identified and served in accordance with the requirements of the Individuals with Disabilities Education Act;

     (4) Federal funds made available for the project or activity will be used so as to supplement the level of State and local funds that, in the absence of such Federal funds, would have been expended for special programs for children of limited English proficient individuals and in no case to supplant such State and local funds, except that nothing in this paragraph shall be construed to preclude a local educational agency from using funds under this title for activities carried out under an order of a court of the United States or of any State respecting services to be provided such children, or to carry out a plan approved by the Secretary as adequate under title VI of the Civil Rights Act of 1964 with respect to services to be provided such children;

     (5) the assistance provided under the application will contribute toward building the capacity of the applicant to provide a program on a regular basis, similar to that proposed for assistance, which will be of sufficient size, scope, and quality to promise significant improvement in the education of students of limited-English proficiency, and that the applicant will have the resources and commitment to continue the program when assistance under this subpart is reduced or no longer available; and

     (6) the applicant provides for utilization of the State and national dissemination sources for program design and in dissemination of results and products.

(i) Priorities and Special Rules.—

     (1) Priority.—The Secretary shall give priority to applications which provide for the development of bilingual proficiency both in English and another language for all participating students.

     (2) Special alternative instructional program.—Grants for special alternative instructional programs under this subpart shall not exceed 25 percent of the funds provided for any type of grant under any section, or of the total funds provided, under this subpart for any fiscal year.

     (3) Special rule.—Notwithstanding paragraph (2), the Secretary may award grants

under this subpart for special alternative instructional programs if an applicant has demonstrated that the applicant cannot develop and implement a bilingual education program for the following reasons:

(A) Where the diversity of the limited English proficient students' native languages and the small number of students speaking each respective language makes bilingual education impractical.

(B) Where, despite documented efforts, the applicant has not been able to hire qualified instructional personnel who are able to communicate in the students' native language.

(4) Consideration.—In approving applications under this subpart, the Secretary shall give consideration to the degree to which the program for which assistance is sought involves the collaborative efforts of institutions of higher education, community-based organizations, the appropriate local and State educational agency, or businesses.

(5) Due consideration.—The Secretary shall give due consideration to applications providing training for personnel participating in or preparing to participate in the program which will assist such personnel in meeting State and local certification requirements and that, to the extent possible, describe how college or university credit will be awarded for such training.

SEC. 7117. INTENSIFIED INSTRUCTION.

In carrying out this subpart, each grant recipient may intensify instruction for limited English proficient students by—

(1) expanding the educational calendar of the school in which such student is enrolled to include programs before and after school and during the summer months;

(2) expanding the use of professional and volunteer aids;

(3) applying technology to the course of instruction; and

(4) providing intensified instruction through supplementary instruction or activities, including educationally enriching extracurricular activities, during times when school is not routinely in session.

SEC. 7118. CAPACITY BUILDING.

Each recipient of a grant under this subpart shall use the grant in ways that will build such recipient's capacity to continue to offer high-quality bilingual and special alternative education programs and services to children and youth of limited-English proficiency once Federal assistance is reduced or eliminated.

SEC. 7119. SUBGRANTS.

A local educational agency that receives a grant under this subpart may, with the approval of the Secretary, make a subgrant to, or enter into a contract with, an institution of higher education, a nonprofit organization, or a consortium of such entities to carry out an approved program, including a program to serve out-of-school youth.

SEC. 7120. PRIORITY ON FUNDING.

The Secretary shall give priority to applications under this subpart that describe a program that—

(1) enrolls a large percentage or large number of limited English proficient students;

(2) takes into account significant increases in limited English proficient children and

youth, including such children and youth in areas with low concentrations of such children and youth; and

(3) ensures that activities assisted under this subpart address the needs of school systems of all sizes and geographic areas, including rural and urban schools.

SEC. 7121. COORDINATION WITH OTHER PROGRAMS.

In order to secure the most flexible and efficient use of Federal funds, any State receiving funds under this subpart shall coordinate its program with other programs under this Act, the Goals 2000: Educate America Act, and other Acts, as appropriate, in accordance with section 14306.

SEC. 7122. PROGRAMS FOR NATIVE AMERICANS AND PUERTO RICO.

Programs authorized under this part that serve Native American children, Native Pacific Island children, and children in the Commonwealth of Puerto Rico, notwithstanding any other provision of this part, may include programs of instruction, teacher training, curriculum development, evaluation, and testing designed for Native American children and youth learning and studying Native American languages and children and youth of limited-Spanish proficiency, except that one outcome of such programs serving Native American children shall be increased English proficiency among such children.

SEC. 7123. EVALUATIONS.

(a) Evaluation.—Each recipient of funds under this subpart shall provide the Secretary with an evaluation, in the form prescribed by the Secretary, of such recipient's program every two years.

(b) Use of Evaluation.—Such evaluation shall be used by a grant recipient—

(1) for program improvement;

(2) to further define the program's goals and objectives; and

(3) to determine program effectiveness.

(c) Evaluation Components.—Evaluations shall include—

(1) how students are achieving the State student performance standards, if any, including data comparing children and youth of limited-English proficiency with non-limited English proficient children and youth with regard to school retention, academic achievement, and gains in English (and, where applicable, native language) proficiency;

(2) program implementation indicators that provide information for informing and improving program management and effectiveness, including data on appropriateness of curriculum in relationship to grade and course requirements, appropriateness of program management, appropriateness of the program's staff professional development, and appropriateness of the language of instruction;

(3) program context indicators that describe the relationship of the activities funded under the grant to the overall school program and other Federal, State, or local programs serving children and youth of limited English proficiency; and

(4) such other information as the Secretary may require.

SEC. 7124. CONSTRUCTION.

Nothing in this part shall be construed to prohibit a local educational agency from serving limited English proficient children and youth simultaneously with students with similar educational needs, in the same educational settings where appropriate.

Subpart 2—Research, Evaluation, and Dissemination

SEC. 7131. AUTHORITY.

(a) In General.—The Secretary is authorized to conduct data collection, dissemination, research, and ongoing program evaluation activities in accordance with the provisions of this subpart for the purpose of improving bilingual education and special alternative instruction programs for children and youth of limited English proficiency.

(b) Competitive Awards.—Research and program evaluation activities carried out under this subpart shall be supported through competitive grants, contracts and cooperative agreements awarded institutions of higher education, nonprofit organizations, and State and local educational agencies.

(c) Administration.—The Secretary shall conduct data collection, dissemination, and ongoing program evaluation activities authorized by this subpart through the Office of Bilingual Education and Minority Languages Affairs.

(a) Administration.—The Secretary shall conduct research activities authorized by this subpart through the Office of Educational Research and Improvement in coordination and collaboration with the Office of Bilingual Education and Minority Languages Affairs.

(b) Requirements.—Such research activities—

(1) shall have a practical application to teachers, counselors, paraprofessionals, school administrators, parents, and others involved in improving the education of limited English proficient students and their families;

(2) may include research on effective instructional practices for multilingual classes, and on effective instruction strategies to be used by teachers and other staff who do not know the native language of a limited English proficient child or youth in their classrooms;

(3) may include establishing (through the National Center for Education Statistics in consultation with experts in bilingual education, second language acquisition, and English-as-a-second-language) a common definition of 'limited English proficient student' for purposes of national data collection; and

(4) shall be administered by individuals with expertise in bilingual education and the needs of limited English proficient students and their families.

(c) Field-Initiated Research.—

(1) In general.—The Secretary shall reserve not less than 5 percent of the funds made available to carry out this section for field-initiated research conducted by current or recent recipients of grants under subpart 1 or 2 who have received such grants within the previous five years. Such research may provide for longitudinal studies of students or teachers in bilingual education, monitoring the education of such students from entry in bilingual education through secondary school completion.

(2) Applications.—Applicants for assistance under this subsection may submit an application for such assistance to the Secretary at the same time as applications are submitted under subpart 1 or 2. The Secretary shall complete a review of such applications on a timely basis to allow research and program grants to be coordinated when recipients are awarded two or more such grants.

(d) Consultation.—The Secretary shall consult with agencies and organizations that are engaged in bilingual education research and practice, or related research, and bilingual education researchers and practitioners to identify areas of study and activities to be funded under this section.

(e) Data Collection.—The Secretary shall provide for the continuation of data collection on limited English proficient students as part of the data systems operated by the Department.

SEC. 7133. ACADEMIC EXCELLENCE AWARDS.

(a) Awards.—The Secretary may make grants to, and enter into contracts and cooperative agreements with, State and local educational agencies, nonprofit organizations, and institutions of higher education to promote the adoption and implementation of bilingual education, special alternative instruction programs, and professional development programs that demonstrate promise of assisting children and youth of limited English proficiency to meet challenging State standards.

(b) Applications.—

(1) In general.—Each entity desiring an award under this section shall submit an application to the Secretary in such form, at such time, and containing such information and assurances as the Secretary may reasonably require.

(2) Peer review.—The Secretary shall use a peer review process, using effectiveness criteria that the Secretary shall establish, to review applications under this section.

(c) Use of Funds.—Funds under this section shall be used to enhance the capacity of States and local education agencies to provide high quality academic programs for children and youth of limited English proficiency, which may include—

(1) completing the development of such programs;

(2) professional development of staff participating in bilingual education programs;

(3) sharing strategies and materials; and

(4) supporting professional networks.

(d) Coordination.—Recipients of funds under this section shall coordinate the activities assisted under this section with activities carried out by comprehensive regional assistance centers assisted under part A of title XIII.

SEC. 7134. STATE GRANT PROGRAM.

(a) State Grant Program.—The Secretary is authorized to make an award to a State educational agency that demonstrates, to the satisfaction of the Secretary, that such agency, through such agency's own programs and other Federal education programs, effectively provides for the education of children and youth of limited English proficiency within the State.

(b) Payments.—The amount paid to a State educational agency under subsection (a) shall not exceed 5 percent of the total amount awarded to local educational agencies within the State under subpart 1 for the previous fiscal year, except that in no case shall the amount paid by the Secretary to any State educational agency under this subsection for any fiscal year be less than $100,000.

(c) Use of Funds.—

(1) In general.—A State educational agency shall use funds awarded under this section for programs authorized by this section to—

(A) assist local educational agencies in the State with program design, capacity building, assessment of student performance, and program evaluation; and

(B) collect data on the State's limited English proficient populations and the educational programs and services available to such populations.

(2) Exception.—States which do not, as of the date of enactment of the Improving America's Schools Act of 1994, have in place a system for collecting the data described in subparagraph (B) of paragraph (1) for all students in such State, are not required to meet the requirement of such subparagraph. In the event such State develops a system for collecting data on the educational programs and services available to all students in the State, then such State shall comply with the requirement of paragraph (1)(B).

(3) Training.—The State educational agency may also use funds provided under this

section for the training of State educational agency personnel in educational issues affecting limited English proficient children and youth.

(4) Special rule.—Recipients of funds under this section shall not restrict the provision of services under this section to federally funded programs.

(d) State Consultation.—A State educational agency receiving funds under this section shall consult with recipients of grants under this title and other individuals or organizations involved in the development or operation of programs serving limited English proficient children or youth to ensure that such funds are used in a manner consistent with the requirements of this title.

(e) Applications.—A State educational agency desiring to receive funds under this section shall submit an application to the Secretary in such form, at such time, and containing such information and assurances as the Secretary may require.

(f) Supplement Not Supplant.—Funds made available under this section for any fiscal year shall be used by the State educational agency to supplement and, to the extent practical, to increase to the level of funds that would, in the absence of such funds, be made available by the State for the purposes described in this section, and in no case to supplant such funds.

(g) Report to the Secretary.—State educational agencies receiving awards under this section shall provide for the annual submission of a summary report to the Secretary describing such State's use of such funds.

SEC. 7135. NATIONAL CLEARINGHOUSE FOR BILINGUAL EDUCATION.

(a) Establishment.—The Secretary shall establish and support the operation of a National Clearinghouse for Bilingual Education, which shall collect, analyze, synthesize, and disseminate information about bilingual education and related programs.

(b) Functions.—The National Clearinghouse for Bilingual Education shall—

(1) be administered as an adjunct clearinghouse of the Educational Resources Information Center Clearinghouses system of clearinghouses supported by the Office of Educational Research and Improvement;

(2) coordinate its activities with Federal data and information clearinghouses and dissemination networks and systems;

(3) develop a data base management and monitoring system for improving the operation and effectiveness of federally funded bilingual education programs; and

(4) develop, maintain, and disseminate, through comprehensive regional assistance centers described in part A of title XIII if appropriate, a listing by geographical area of education professionals, parents, teachers, administrators, community members and others who are native speakers of languages other than English for use as a resource by local educational agencies and schools in the development and implementation of bilingual education programs.

SEC. 7136. INSTRUCTIONAL MATERIALS DEVELOPMENT.

The Secretary may provide grants for the development, publication, and dissemination of high-quality instructional materials in Native American and Native Hawaiian languages and the language of Native Pacific Islanders and natives of the outlying areas for which instructional materials are not readily available. The Secretary shall give priority to the development of instructional materials in languages indigenous to the United States or the outlying areas. The Secretary shall also accord priority to applications for assistance under this section which provide for developing and evaluating materials in collaboration with activities assisted under subparts 1 and 2 and which are consistent with voluntary national content standards and challenging State content standards.

Subpart 3—Professional Development

SEC. 7141. PURPOSE.

The purpose of this subpart is to assist in preparing educators to improve the educational services for limited English proficient children and youth by supporting professional development programs and the dissemination of information on appropriate instructional practices for such children and youth.

SEC. 7142. TRAINING FOR ALL TEACHERS PROGRAM.

(a) Purpose.—The purpose of this section is to provide for the incorporation of courses and curricula on appropriate and effective instructional and assessment methodologies, strategies and resources specific to limited English proficient students into preservice and inservice professional development programs for teachers, pupil services personnel, administrators and other education personnel in order to prepare such individuals to provide effective services to limited English proficient students.

(b) Authorization.—

(1) Authority.—The Secretary is authorized to award grants to institutions of higher education, local educational agencies, and State educational agencies or to nonprofit organizations which have entered into consortia arrangements with one of such institutions or agencies.

(2) Duration.—Each grant under this section shall be awarded for a period of not more than five years.

(c) Permissible Activities.—Activities conducted under this section may include the development of training programs in collaboration with other programs such as programs authorized under titles I and II of this Act, and under the Head Start Act.

SEC. 7143. BILINGUAL EDUCATION TEACHERS AND PERSONNEL GRANTS.

(a) Purpose.—The purpose of this section is to provide for—

(1) preservice and inservice professional development for bilingual education teachers, administrators, pupil services personnel, and other educational personnel who are either involved in, or preparing to be involved in, the provision of educational services for children and youth of limited-English proficiency; and

(2) national professional development institutes that assist schools or departments of education in institutions of higher education to improve the quality of professional development programs for personnel serving, preparing to serve, or who may serve, children and youth of limited-English proficiency.

(b) Priority.—The Secretary shall give priority in awarding grants under this section to institutions of higher education, in consortia with local or State educational agencies, that offer degree programs which prepare new bilingual education teachers in order to increase the availability of educators to provide high-quality education to limited English proficient students.

(c) Authorization.—

(1) The Secretary is authorized to award grants for not more than five years to institutions of higher education which have entered into consortia arrangements with local or State educational agencies to achieve the purposes of this section.

(2) The Secretary is authorized to make grants for not more than five years to State and local educational agencies for inservice professional development programs.

SEC. 7144. BILINGUAL EDUCATION CAREER LADDER PROGRAM.

(a) Purpose.—The purpose of this section is—

(1) to upgrade the qualifications and skills of noncertified educational personnel, especially educational paraprofessionals, to meet high professional standards, including certification and licensure as bilingual education teachers and other educational personnel who serve limited English proficient students, through collaborative training programs operated by institutions of higher education and local and State educational agencies; and

(2) to help recruit and train secondary school students as bilingual education teachers and other educational personnel to serve limited English proficient students.

(b) Authorization.—

(1) In general.—The Secretary is authorized to award grants for bilingual education career ladder programs to institutions of higher education applying in consortia with local or State educational agencies, which consortia may include community-based organizations or professional education organizations.

(2) Duration.—Each grant under this section shall be awarded for a period of not more than five years.

(c) Permissive Activities.—Grants awarded under this section may be used—

(1) for the development of bilingual education career ladder program curricula appropriate to the needs of the consortium participants;

(2) to provide assistance for stipends and costs related to tuition, fees and books for enrolling in courses required to complete the degree and certification requirements to become bilingual education teachers; and

(3) for programs to introduce secondary school students to careers in bilingual education teaching that are coordinated with other activities assisted under this section.

(d) Special Consideration.—The Secretary shall give special consideration to applications under this section which provide for—

(1) participant completion of baccalaureate and master's degree teacher education programs, and certification requirements and may include effective employment placement activities;

(2) development of teacher proficiency in English a second language, including demonstrating proficiency in the instructional use of English and, as appropriate, a second language in classroom contexts;

(3) coordination with the Federal TRIO programs under chapter 1 of part A of title IV of the Higher Education Act of 1965, the National Mini Corps under subpart 1 of part F of title V of such Act, the Teacher Corps program under subpart 3 of part C of title V of such Act, and the National Community and Service Trust Act of 1993 programs, and other programs for the recruitment and retention of bilingual students in secondary and postsecondary programs to train to become bilingual educators; and

(4) the applicant's contribution of additional student financial aid to participating students.

SEC. 7145. GRADUATE FELLOWSHIPS IN BILINGUAL EDUCATION PROGRAM.

(a) Authorization.—

(1) In general.—The Secretary may award fellowships for masters, doctoral, and postdoctoral study related to instruction of children and youth of limited-English proficiency in such areas as teacher training, program administration, research and evaluation, and curriculum development, and for the support of dissertation research related to such study.

(2) Number.—For fiscal year 1994 not less than 500 fellowships leading to a master's or doctorate degree shall be awarded under this section.

(3) Information.—The Secretary shall include information on the operation and the number of fellowships awarded under the fellowship program in the evaluation required under section 7149.

(b) Fellowship Requirements.—

(1) In general.—Any person receiving a fellowship under this section shall agree to—

(A) work in an activity related to the program or in an activity such as an activity authorized under this part, including work as a bilingual education teacher, for a period of time equivalent to the period of time during which such person receives assistance under this section; or

(B) repay such assistance.

(2) Regulations.—The Secretary shall establish in regulations such terms and conditions for such agreement as the Secretary deems reasonable and necessary and may waive the requirement of paragraph (1) in extraordinary circumstances.

(c) Priority.—In awarding fellowships under this section the Secretary may give priority to institutions of higher education that demonstrate experience in assisting fellowship recipients find employment in the field of bilingual education.

SEC. 7146. APPLICATION.

(a) In General.—

(1) Secretary.—To receive an award under this subpart, an eligible entity shall submit an application to the Secretary at such time, in such form, and containing such information as the Secretary may require.

(2) Consultation and assessment.—Each such application shall contain a description of how the applicant has consulted with, and assessed the needs of, public and private schools serving children and youth of limited-English proficiency to determine such school's need for, and the design of, the program for which funds are sought.

(3) Special rule.—

(A) An application for a grant under subsection (a) from an applicant who proposes to conduct a master's- or doctoral-level program with funds received under this section shall provide an assurance that such program will include, as a part of the program, a training practicum in a local school program serving children and youth of limited-English proficiency.

(B) A recipient of a grant under subsection (a) may waive the requirement of a training practicum for a degree candidate with significant experience in a local school program serving children and youth of limited-English proficiency.

(4) State educational agency.—An eligible entity, with the exception of schools funded by the Bureau of Indian Affairs, shall submit a copy of the application under this subsection to the State educational agency.

(b) State Review and Comments.—

(1) Deadline.—The State educational agency, not later than 45 days after receipt of such application copy, shall review the application and transmit such application to the Secretary.

(2) Comments.—

(A) Regarding any application submitted under this subpart, the State educational agency shall—

(i) submit to the Secretary written comments regarding all such applications; and

(ii) submit to each eligible entity the comments that pertain to such entity.

(B) For purposes of this subpart, comments shall address how the eligible entity—

(i) will further the academic achievement of limited English proficient students served pursuant to a grant received under this subpart; and

(ii) how the grant application is consistent with the State plan submitted under section 1111.

(3) Waiver.—Notwithstanding paragraphs (1) and (2), the Secretary is authorized to waive the review requirement if a State educational agency can demonstrate that such review requirement may impede such agency's ability to fulfill the requirements of participation in the State grant program, particularly such agency's data collection efforts and such agency's ability to provide technical assistance to local educational agencies not receiving funds under this Act.

(c) Eligible Entity Comments.—An eligible entity may submit to the Secretary comments that address the comments submitted by the State educational agency.

(d) Comment Consideration.—In making awards under this subpart the Secretary shall take into consideration comments made by a State educational agency.

(e) Special Rule.—

(1) Outreach and technical assistance.—The Secretary shall provide for outreach and technical assistance to institutions of higher education eligible for assistance under title III of the Higher Education Act of 1965 and institutions of higher education that are operated or funded by the Bureau of Indian Affairs to facilitate the participation of such institutions in activities under this part.

(2) Distribution rule.—In making awards under this subpart, the Secretary, consistent with subsection (d), shall ensure adequate representation of Hispanic-serving institutions that demonstrate competence and experience in the programs and activities authorized under this subpart and are otherwise qualified.

SEC. 7147. PROGRAM REQUIREMENTS.

Activities conducted under this subpart shall assist educational personnel in meeting State and local certification requirements for bilingual education and, wherever possible, shall lead toward the awarding of college or university credit.

SEC. 7148. STIPENDS.

The Secretary shall provide for the payment of such stipends (including allowances for subsistence and other expenses for such persons and their dependents), as the Secretary determines to be appropriate, to persons participating in training programs under this subpart.

SEC. 7149. PROGRAM EVALUATIONS.

Each recipient of funds under this subpart shall provide the Secretary with an evaluation of the program assisted under this subpart every two years. Such evaluation shall include data on—

(1) post-program placement of persons trained in a program assisted under this subpart;

(2) how the training relates to the employment of persons served by the program;

(3) program completion; and

(4) such other information as the Secretary may require.

SEC. 7150. USE OF FUNDS FOR SECOND LANGUAGE COMPETENCE.
Awards under this subpart may be used to develop a program participant's competence in a second language for use in instructional programs.

Subpart 4—Transition

SEC. 7161. SPECIAL RULE.
Notwithstanding any other provision of law, no recipient of a grant under title VII of this Act (as such title was in effect on the day preceding the date of enactment of the Improving America's Schools Act of 1994) shall be eligible for fourth- and fifth-year renewals authorized by section 7021(d)(1)(C) of such title (as such section was in effect on the day preceding the date of enactment of such Act).

. . .

PART D—ADMINISTRATION

SEC. 7401. RELEASE TIME.
The Secretary shall allow professional development programs funded under part A to use funds provided under part A for professional release time to enable individuals to participate in programs assisted under part A.

SEC. 7402. EDUCATION TECHNOLOGY.
Funds made available under part A may be used to provide for the acquisition or development of education technology or instructional materials, including authentic materials in languages other than English, access to and participation in electronic networks for materials, training and communications, and incorporation of such resources in curricula and programs such as those funded under this title.

SEC. 7403. NOTIFICATION.
The State educational agency, and when applicable, the State board for postsecondary education, shall be notified within three working days of the date an award under part A is made to an eligible entity within the State.

SEC. 7404. CONTINUED ELIGIBILITY.
Entities receiving grants under this title shall remain eligible for grants for subsequent activities which extend or expand and do not duplicate those activities supported by a previous grant under this title. In considering applications for grants under this title, the Secretary shall take into consideration the applicant's record of accomplishments under previous grants under this title.

SEC. 7405. COORDINATIONS AND REPORTING REQUIREMENTS.
(a) Coordination With Related Programs.—In order to maximize Federal efforts aimed at serving the educational needs of children and youth of limited-English proficiency, the Secretary shall coordinate and ensure close cooperation with other programs serving language-minority and limited English proficient students that are administered by the Department and other agencies. The Secretary shall consult with the Secretary of Labor, the Secretary of Health and Human Services, the Secretary of Agriculture, the Attorney General and the heads of other relevant agencies to identify and eliminate barriers to appropriate coordination of programs that affect language-minority and limited English

proficient students and their families. The Secretary shall provide for continuing consultation and collaboration, between the Office and relevant programs operated by the
Department, including programs under title I and other programs under this Act, in planning, contracts, providing joint technical assistance, providing joint field monitoring activities and in other relevant activities to ensure effective program coordination to provide
high quality education opportunities to all language-minority and limited English proficient students.

(b) Data.—The Secretary shall, to the extent feasible, ensure that all data collected by the
Department shall include the collection and reporting of data on limited English proficient students.

(c) Publication of Proposals.—The Secretary shall publish and disseminate all requests for
proposals for programs funded under part A.

(d) Report.—The Director shall prepare and, not later than February 1 of every other
year, shall submit to the Secretary and to the Committee on Labor and Human Resources
of the Senate and to the Committee on Education and Labor of the House of
Representatives a report on—

> (1) the activities carried out under this title and the effectiveness of such activities in
> improving the education provided to limited English proficient children and youth;
> (2) a critical synthesis of data reported by the States pursuant to section 7134;
> (3) an estimate of the number of certified bilingual education personnel in the field
> and an estimate of the number of bilingual education teachers which will be needed
> for the succeeding five fiscal years;
> (4) the major findings of research carried out under this title; and
> (5) recommendations for further developing the capacity of our Nation's schools to
> educate effectively limited English proficient students.

PART E—GENERAL PROVISIONS

SEC. 7501. DEFINITIONS; REGULATIONS.
Except as otherwise provided, for purposes of this title—

> (1) Bilingual education program.—The term 'bilingual education program' means an edu-
> cational program for limited English proficient students that—
>> (A) makes instructional use of both English and a student's native language;
>> (B) enables limited English proficient students to achieve English proficiency and aca-
>> demic mastery of subject matter content and higher order skills, including critical
>> thinking, so as to meet age-appropriate grade-promotion and graduation standards in
>> concert with the National Education Goals;
>> (C) may also develop the native language skills of limited English proficient students,
>> or ancestral languages of American Indians, Alaska Natives, Native Hawaiians and
>> native residents of the outlying areas; and
>> (D) may include the participation of English-proficient students if such program is
>> designed to enable all enrolled students to become proficient in English and a second
>> language.
> (2) Children and youth.—The term 'children and youth' means individuals aged 3 through
> 21.
> (3) Community-based organization.—The term 'community-based organization' means a
> private nonprofit organization of demonstrated effectiveness or Indian tribe or tribally
> sanctioned educational authority which is representative of a community or significant
> segments of a community and which provides educational or related services to individu-
> als in the community. Such term includes Native Hawaiian organizations including Native

Hawaiian Educational Organizations as such term is defined in section 4009 of the Augustus F. Hawkins-Robert T. Stafford Elementary and Secondary School Improvement Amendments of 1988 (20 U.S.C. 4901 et seq.), as such Act was in effect on the day preceding the date of enactment of the Improving America's Schools Act of 1994.

(4) Community college.—The term 'community college' means an institution of higher education as defined in section 1201(a) of the Higher Education Act of 1965 which provides not less than a two-year program which is acceptable for full credit toward a bachelor's degree, including institutions receiving assistance under the Tribally Controlled Community College Assistance Act of 1978.

(5) Director.—The term 'Director' means the Director of the Office of Bilingual Education and Minority Languages Affairs established under section 210 of the Department of Education Organization Act.

(6) Family education program.—

(A) The term 'family education program' means a bilingual education or special alternative instructional program that—

(i) is designed—

(I) to help limited English proficient adults and out-of-school youths achieve proficiency in the English language; and

(II) to provide instruction on how parents and family members can facilitate the educational achievement of their children;

(ii) when feasible, uses instructional programs such as the models developed under the Even Start Family Literacy Programs, which promote adult literacy and train parents to support the educational growth of their children and the Parents as Teachers Program and the Home Instruction Program for Preschool Youngsters; and

(iii) gives preference to participation by parents and immediate family members of children attending school.

(B) Such term may include programs that provide instruction to facilitate higher education and employment outcomes.

(7) Immigrant children and youth.—The term 'immigrant children and youth' means individuals who—

(A) are aged 3 through 21;

(B) were not born in any State; and

(C) have not been attending one or more schools in any one or more States for more than three full academic years.

(8) Limited English proficiency and limited English proficient.—The terms 'limited English proficiency' and 'limited English proficient', when used with reference to an individual, mean an individual—

(A) who—

(i) was not born in the United States or whose native language is a language other than English and comes from an environment where a language other than English is dominant; or

(ii) is a Native American or Alaska Native or who is a native resident of the outlying areas and comes from an environment where a language other than English has had a significant impact on such individual's level of English language proficiency; or

(iii) is migratory and whose native language is other than English and comes from an environment where a language other than English is dominant; and

(B) who has sufficient difficulty speaking, reading, writing, or understanding the English language and whose difficulties may deny such individual the opportunity to learn successfully in classrooms where the language of instruction is English or to participate fully in our society.

(9) Native American and Native American language.—The terms 'Native American' and 'Native American language' shall have the same meaning given such terms in section 103 of the Native American Languages Act of 1990.

(10) Native Hawaiian or Native American Pacific Islander native language educational organization.—The term 'Native Hawaiian or Native American Pacific Islander native language educational organization' means a nonprofit organization with a majority of its governing board and employees consisting of fluent speakers of the traditional Native American languages used in their educational programs and with not less than five years successful experience in providing educational services in traditional Native American languages.

(11) Native language.—The term 'native language', when used with reference to an individual of limited-English proficiency, means the language normally used by such individual, or in the case of a child or youth, the language normally used by the parents of the child or youth.

(12) Office.—The term 'Office' means the Office of Bilingual Education and Minority Languages Affairs.

(13) Other programs for persons of limited-English proficiency.—The term 'other programs for persons of limited-English proficiency' means any programs administered by the Secretary that serve persons of limited-English proficiency.

(14) Paraprofessional.—The term 'paraprofessional' means an individual who is employed in preschool, elementary or secondary school under the supervision of a certified or licensed teacher, including individuals employed in bilingual education, special education and migrant education.

(15) Special alternative instructional program.—The term 'special alternative instructional program' means an educational program for limited English proficient students that—

    (A) utilizes specially designed English language curricula and services but does not use the student's native language for instructional purposes;

    (B) enables limited English proficient students to achieve English proficiency and academic mastery of subject matter content and higher order skills, including critical thinking so as to meet age-appropriate grade-promotion and graduation standards in concert with the National Education Goals; and

    (C) is particularly appropriate for schools where the diversity of the limited English proficient students' native languages and the small number of students speaking each respective language makes bilingual education impractical and where there is a critical shortage of bilingual education teachers.

SEC. 7502. REGULATIONS AND NOTIFICATION.

(a) Regulation Rule.—In developing regulations under this title, the Secretary shall consult with State and local educational agencies, organizations representing limited English proficient individuals, and organizations representing teachers and other personnel involved in bilingual education.

(b) Parental Notification.—

    (1) In general.—Parents of children and youth participating in programs assisted under part A shall be informed of—

        (A) a student's level of English proficiency, how such level was assessed, the status of a student's academic achievement and the implications of a student's educational strengths and needs for age and grade appropriate academic attainment, promotion, and graduation;

(B) what programs are available to meet the student's educational strengths and needs and how the programs differ in content and instructional goals, and in the case of a student with a disability, how the program meets the objectives of a student's individualized education program; and

(C) the instructional goals of the bilingual education or special alternative instructional program, and how the program will specifically help the limited English proficient student acquire English and meet age-appropriate standards for grade-promotion and graduation, including—

(i) the benefits, nature, and past academic results of the bilingual educational program and of the instructional alternatives; and

(ii) the reasons for the selection of their child as being in need of bilingual education.

(2) Option to decline.—

(A) Such parents shall also be informed that such parents have the option of declining enrollment of their children and youth in such programs and shall be given an opportunity to so decline if such parents so choose.

(B) A local educational agency shall not be relieved of any of its obligations under title VI of the Civil Rights Act of 1964 because parents choose not to enroll their children in bilingual education programs.

(3) Receipt of information.—Such parents shall receive, in a manner and form understandable to such parents, including, if necessary and to the extent feasible, in the native language of such parents, the information required by this subsection. At a minimum, such parents shall receive—

(A) timely information about projects funded under part A; and

(B) if the parents of participating children so desire, notice of opportunities for regular meetings for the purpose of formulating and responding to recommendations from such parents.

(4) Special rule.—Students shall not be admitted to or excluded from any federally assisted education program merely on the basis of a surname or language-minority status.

Appendix C
National Education Goals

Excerpts from Goals 2000: Educate America Act (P.L. 103-227, March 3, 1994).

TITLE I, SEC. 102. NATIONAL EDUCATION GOALS.

The Congress declares that the National Education Goals are the following:
  (1) SCHOOL READINESS.—
    (A) By the year 2000, all children in America will start school ready to learn.
    (B) The objectives for this goal are that—
      (i) all children will have access to high-quality and developmentally appropriate preschool programs that help prepare children for school;
      (ii) every parent in the United States will be a child's first teacher and devote time each day to helping such parent's preschool child learn, and parents will have access to the training and support parents need; and
      (iii) children will receive the nutrition, physical activity experiences, and health care needed to arrive at school with healthy minds and bodies, and to maintain the mental alertness necessary to be prepared to learn, and the number of low-birthweight babies will be significantly reduced through enhanced prenatal health systems.

  (2) SCHOOL COMPLETION.—
    (A) By the year 2000, the high school graduation rate will increase to at least 90 percent.
    (B) The objectives for this goal are that—
      (i) the Nation must dramatically reduce its school dropout rate, and 75 percent of the students who do drop out will successfully complete a high school degree or its equivalent; and
      (ii) the gap in high school graduation rates between American students from minority backgrounds and their non-minority counterparts will be eliminated.

  (3) STUDENT ACHIEVEMENT AND CITIZENSHIP.—
    (A) By the year 2000, all students will leave grades 4, 8, and 12 having demonstrated competency over challenging subject matter including English, mathematics, science, foreign languages, civics and government, economics, arts, history, and geography, and every school in America will ensure that all students learn to use their minds well, so they may be prepared for responsible citizenship, further learning, and productive employment in our Nation's modern economy.
    (B) The objectives for this goal are that—
      (i) the academic performance of all students at the elementary and secondary level will increase significantly in every quartile, and the distribution of minority students in each quartile will more closely reflect the student population as a whole;

(ii) the percentage of all students who demonstrate the ability to reason, solve problems, apply knowledge, and write and communicate effectively will increase substantially;

(iii) all students will be involved in activities that promote and demonstrate good citizenship, good health, community service, and personal responsibility;

(iv) all students will have access to physical education and health education to ensure they are healthy and fit;

(v) the percentage of all students who are competent in more than one language will substantially increase; and

(vi) all students will be knowledgeable about the diverse cultural heritage of this Nation and about the world community.

(4) TEACHER EDUCATION AND PROFESSIONAL DEVELOPMENT.—

(A) By the year 2000, the Nation's teaching force will have access to programs for the continued improvement of their professional skills and the opportunity to acquire the knowledge and skills needed to instruct and prepare all American students for the next century.

(B) The objectives for this goal are that—

(i) all teachers will have access to preservice teacher education and continuing professional development activities that will provide such teachers with the knowledge and skills needed to teach to an increasingly diverse student population with a variety of educational, social, and health needs;

(ii) all teachers will have continuing opportunities to acquire additional knowledge and skills needed to teach challenging subject matter and to use emerging new methods, forms of assessment, and technologies;

(iii) States and school districts will create integrated strategies to attract, recruit, prepare, retrain, and support the continued professional development of teachers, administrators, and other educators, so that there is a highly talented work force of professional educators to teach challenging subject matter; and

(iv) partnerships will be established, whenever possible, among local educational agencies, institutions of higher education, parents, and local labor, business, and professional associations to provide and support programs for the professional development of educators.

(5) MATHEMATICS AND SCIENCE.—

(A) By the year 2000, United States students will be first in the world in mathematics and science achievement.

(B) The objectives for this goal are that—

(i) mathematics and science education, including the metric system of measurement, will be strengthened throughout the system, especially in the early grades;

(ii) the number of teachers with a substantive background in mathematics and science, including the metric system of measurement, will increase by 50 percent; and

(iii) the number of United States undergraduate and graduate students, especially women and minorities, who complete degrees in mathematics, science, and engineering will increase significantly.

(6) ADULT LITERACY AND LIFELONG LEARNING.—

(A) By the year 2000, every adult American will be literate and will possess the knowledge and skills necessary to compete in a global economy and exercise the rights and responsibilities of citizenship.

(B) The objectives for this goal are that—

(i) every major American business will be involved in strengthening the connection between education and work;

(ii) all workers will have the opportunity to acquire the knowledge and skills, from basic to highly technical, needed to adapt to emerging new technologies, work methods, and markets through public and private educational, vocational, technical, workplace, or other programs;

(iii) the number of quality programs, including those at libraries, that are designed to serve more effectively the needs of the growing number of part-time and midcareer students will increase substantially;

(iv) the proportion of the qualified students, especially minorities, who enter college, who complete at least two years, and who complete their degree programs will increase substantially;

(v) the proportion of college graduates who demonstrate an advanced ability to think critically, communicate effectively, and solve problems will increase substantially; and

(vi) schools, in implementing comprehensive parent involvement programs, will offer more adult literacy, parent training and life-long learning opportunities to improve the ties between home and school, and enhance parents' work and home lives.

(7) SAFE, DISCIPLINED, AND ALCOHOL- AND DRUG-FREE SCHOOLS.—

(A) By the year 2000, every school in the United States will be free of drugs, violence, and the unauthorized presence of firearms and alcohol and will offer a disciplined environment conducive to learning.

(B) The objectives for this goal are that—

(i) every school will implement a firm and fair policy on use, possession, and distribution of drugs and alcohol;

(ii) parents, businesses, governmental and community organizations will work together to ensure the rights of students to study in a safe and secure environment that is free of drugs and crime, and that schools provide a healthy environment and are a safe haven for all children;

(iii) every local educational agency will develop and implement a policy to ensure that all schools are free of violence and the unauthorized presence of weapons;

(iv) every local educational agency will develop a sequential, comprehensive kindergarten through twelfth grade drug and alcohol prevention education program;

(v) drug and alcohol curriculum should be taught as an integral part of sequential, comprehensive health education;

(vi) community-based teams should be organized to provide students and teachers with needed support; and

(vii) every school should work to eliminate sexual harassment.

(8) PARENTAL PARTICIPATION —

(A) By the year 2000, every school will promote partnerships that will increase parental involvement and participation in promoting the social, emotional, and academic growth of children.

(B) The objectives for this Goal are that—

(i) every State will develop policies to assist local schools and local educational agencies to establish programs for increasing partnerships that respond to the varying needs of parents and the home, including parents of children who are disadvantaged or bilingual, or parents of children with disabilities;

(ii) every school will actively engage parents and families in a partnership which supports the academic work of children at home and shared educational decisionmaking at school; and

(iii) parents and families will help to ensure that schools are adequately supported and will hold schools and teachers to high standards of accountability.

Appendix D
English Language Empowerment Act

H.R. 123, the first official-English bill to pass the House of Representatives — on August 1, 1996 — died when the Senate adjourned without acting on the measure. Reintroduced in the 105th Congress, it never came to a vote in either chamber.

SECTION 1. SHORT TITLE.
This Act may be cited as the "Bill Emerson English Language Empowerment Act of 1996".

TITLE I. ENGLISH LANGUAGE EMPOWERMENT

SEC. 101. FINDINGS.
The Congress finds and declares the following:
(1) The United States is comprised of individuals and groups from diverse ethnic, cultural, and linguistic backgrounds.
(2) The United States has benefited and continutes to benefit from this rich diversity.
(3) Throughout the history of the United States, the common thread binding individuals of differing backgrounds has been a common language.
(4) In order to preserve unity in diversity, and to prevent division along linguistic lines, the Federal Government should maintain a language common to all people.
(5) English has historically been the common language and the language of opportunity in the United States.
(6) The purpose of this title is to help immigrants better assimilate and take full advantage of economic and occupational opportunities in the United States.
(7) By learning the English language, immigrants will be empowered with the language skills and literacy necessary to become responsible citizens and productive workers in the United States.
(8) The use of a single common language in conducting official business of the Federal Government will promote efficiency and fairness to all people.
(9) English should be recognized in law as the language of official business of the Federal Government.
(10) Any monetary savings derived from the enactment of this title should be used for the teaching of the English language to non-English speaking immigrants.

SEC. 102. ENGLISH AS THE OFFICIAL LANGUAGE OF FEDERAL GOVERNMENT.
(a) In General.Title 4, United States Code, is amended by adding at the end the following new chapter:
CHAPTER 6LANGUAGE OF THE FEDERAL GOVERNMENT
Sec. 161. Declaration of official language of Federal Government
The official language of the Federal Government is English.
Sec. 162. Preserving and enhancing the role of the official language
Representatives of the Federal Government shall have an affirmative obligation to preserve and

enhance the role of English as the official language of the Federal Government. Such obligation shall include encouraging greater opportunities for individuals to learn the English language.

Sec. 163. Official Federal Government activities in English

(a) Conduct of Business.Representatives of the Federal Government shall conduct its official business in English.

(b) Denial of Services. No person shall be denied services, assistance, or facilities, directly or indirectly provided by the Federal Government solely because the person communicates in English.

(c) Entitlement.Every person in the United States is entitled

(1) to communicate with representatives of the Federal Government in English;

(2) to receive information from or contribute information to the Federal Government in English; and

(3) to be informed of or be subject to official orders in English.

Sec. 164. Standing

A person injured by a violation of this chapter may in a civil action (including an action under chapter 151 of title 28) obtain appropriate relief.

Sec. 165. Reform of naturalization requirements

(a) Fluency.It has been the longstanding national belief that full citizenship in the United States requires fluency in English. English is the language of opportunity for all immigrants to take their rightful place in society in the United States.

(b) Ceremonies.All authorized officials shall conduct all naturalization ceremonies entirely in English.

Sec. 166. Application

Except as otherwise provided in this chapter, the provisions of this chapter shall supersede any existing Federal law that contravenes such provisions (such as by requiring the use of a language other than English for official business of the Federal Government).

Sec. 167. Rule of construction

Nothing in this chapter shall be construed

(1) to prohibit a Member of Congress or an employee or official of the Federal Government, while performing official business, from communicating orally with another person in a language other than English;

(2) to limit the preservation or use of Native Alaskan or Native American languages (as defined in the Native American Languages Act);

(3) to discriminate against or restrict the rights of any individual in the country; and

(4) to discourage or prevent the use of languages other than English in any nonofficial capacity.

Sec. 168. Affirmation of constitutional protections

Nothing in this chapter shall be construed to be inconsistent with the Constitution of the United States.

Sec. 169. Definitions

For purposes of this chapter:

(1) Federal government.The term 'Federal Government' means all branches of the national Government and all employees and officials of the national Government while performing official business.

(2) Official business.The term 'official business' means governmental actions, documents, or policies which are enforceable with the full weight and authority of the Federal Government, and includes publications, income tax forms, and informational materials, but does not include

(A) teaching of languages;

(B) requirements under the Individuals with Disabilities Education Act;

(C) actions, documents, or policies necessary for

(i) national security issues; or

(ii) international relations, trade, or commerce;

(D) actions or documents that protect the public health and safety;

(E) actions or documents that facilitate the activities of the Bureau of the Census in compiling any census of population;

(F) actions, documents, or policies that are not enforceable in the United States;

(G) actions that protect the rights of victims of crimes or criminal defendants;

(H) actions in which the United States has initiated a civil lawsuit; or

(I) using terms of art or phrases from languages other than English.

(3) United states. The term 'United States' means the several States and the District of Columbia.

[(b) Conforming Amendment.]

SEC. 103. PREEMPTION.

This title (and the amendments made by this title) shall not preempt any law of any State.

SEC. 104. EFFECTIVE DATE.

The amendments made by section 102 shall take effect on the date that is 180 days after the date of enactment of this Act.

TITLE II. REPEAL OF BILINGUAL VOTING REQUIREMENTS

SEC. 201. REPEAL OF BILINGUAL VOTING REQUIREMENTS

(a) Bilingual Election Requirements. Section 203 of the Voting Rights Act of 1965 (42 U.S.C. 1973aa1a) is repealed.

(b) Voting Rights. Section 4 of the Voting Rights Act of 1965 (42 U.S.C. 1973b) is amended by striking subsection (f).

[SEC. 202. CONFORMING AMENDMENTS.]

Appendix E
California's Proposition 227

This initiative statute, entitled "English Language Education for Children in Public Schools," was adopted by California voters on June 2, 1998. Its sponsors were Ron K. Unz, a businessman from Palo Alto, and Gloria Matta Tuchman, a 1st grade teacher from Santa Ana. The measure is being challenged in federal court on civil rights and constitutional grounds.

SECTION 1. Chapter 3 (commencing with Section 300) is added to Part 1 of the Educational Code, to read:

CHAPTER 3. ENGLISH LANGUAGE EDUCATION FOR IMMIGRANT CHILDREN

ARTICLE 1. Findings and Declarations
Sec. 300. The People of California find and declare as follows:
  (a) WHEREAS the English language is the national public language of the United States of America and of the state of California, is spoken by the vast majority of California residents, and is also the leading world language for science, technology, and international business, thereby being the language of economic opportunity; and
  (b) WHEREAS immigrant parents are eager to have their children acquire a good knowledge of English, thereby allowing them to fully participate in the American Dream of economic and social advancement; and
  (c) WHEREAS the government and the public schools of California have a moral obligation and a constitutional duty to provide all of California's children, regardless of their ethnicity or national origins, with the skills necessary to become productive members of our society, and of these skills, literacy in the English language is among the most important; and
  (d) WHEREAS the public schools of California currently do a poor job of educating immigrant children, wasting financial resources on costly experimental language programs whose failure over the past two decades is demonstrated by the current high drop-out rates and low English literacy levels of many immigrant children; and
  (e) WHEREAS young immigrant children can easily acquire full fluency in a new language, such as English, if they are heavily exposed to that language in the classroom at an early age.
  (f) THEREFORE it is resolved that: all children in California public schools shall be taught English as rapidly and effectively as possible.

ARTICLE 2. English Language Education
Sec. 305. Subject to the exceptions provided in Article 3 (commencing with Section 310), all

children in California public schools shall be taught English by being taught in English. In particular, this shall require that all children be placed in English language classrooms. Children who are English learners shall be educated through sheltered English immersion during a temporary transition period not normally intended to exceed one year. Local schools shall be permitted to place in the same classroom English learners of different ages but whose degree of English proficiency is similar. Local schools shall be encouraged to mix together in the same classroom English learners from different native-language groups but with the same degree of English fluency. Once English learners have acquired a good working knowledge of English, they shall be transferred to English language mainstream classrooms. As much as possible, current supplemental funding for English learners shall be maintained, subject to possible modification under Article 8 (commencing with Section 335) below.

Sec. 306. The definitions of the terms used in this article and in Article 3 (commencing with Section 310) are as follows:

(a) "English learner" means a child who does not speak English or whose native language is not English and who is not currently able to perform ordinary classroom work in English, also known as a Limited English Proficiency or LEP child.

(b) "English language classroom" means a classroom in which the language of instruction used by the teaching personnel is overwhelmingly the English language, and in which such teaching personnel possess a good knowledge of the English language.

(c) "English language mainstream classroom" means a classroom in which the students either are native English language speakers or already have acquired reasonable fluency in English.

(d) "Sheltered English immersion" or "structured English immersion" means an English language acquisition process for young children in which nearly all classroom instruction is in English but with the curriculum and presentation designed for children who are learning the language.

(e) "Bilingual education/native language instruction" means a language acquisition process for students in which much or all instruction, textbooks, and teaching materials are in the child's native language.

ARTICLE 3. Parental Exceptions

Sec. 310. The requirements of Section 305 may be waived with the prior written informed consent, to be provided annually, of the child's parents or legal guardian under the circumstances specified below and in Section 311. Such informed consent shall require that said parents or legal guardian personally visit the school to apply for the waiver and that they there be provided a full description of the educational materials to be used in the different educational program choices and all the educational opportunities available to the child. Under such parental waiver conditions, children may be transferred to classes where they are taught English and other subjects through bilingual education techniques or other generally recognized educational methodologies permitted by law. Individual schools in which 20 students or more of a given grade level receive a waiver shall be required to offer such a class; otherwise, they must allow the students to transfer to a public school in which such a class is offered.

Sec. 311. The circumstances in which a parental exception waiver may be granted under Section 310 are as follows:

(a) Children who already know English: the child already possesses good English language skills, as measured by standardized tests of English vocabulary comprehension, reading, and writing, in which the child scores at or above the state average for his grade level or at or above the 5th grade average, whichever is lower; or

(b) Older children: the child is age 10 years or older, and it is the informed belief of the school principal and educational staff that an alternate course of educational study would be better suited to the child's rapid acquisition of basic English language skills; or

(c) Children with special needs: the child already has been placed for a period of not less than thirty days during that school year in an English language classroom and it is subsequently the informed belief of the school principal and educational staff that the child has such special physical, emotional, psychological, or educational needs that an alternate course of educational study would be better suited to the child's overall educational development. A written description of these special needs must be provided and any such decision is to be made subject to the examination and approval of the local school superintendent, under guidelines established by and subject to the review of the local Board of Education and ultimately the State Board of Education. The existence of such special needs shall not compel issuance of a waiver, and the parents shall be fully informed of their right to refuse to agree to a waiver.

ARTICLE 4. Community-Based English Tutoring

Sec. 315. In furtherance of its constitutional and legal requirement to offer special language assistance to children coming from backgrounds of limited English proficiency, the state shall encourage family members and others to provide personal English language tutoring to such children, and support these efforts by raising the general level of English language knowledge in the community. Commencing with the fiscal year in which this initiative is enacted and for each of the nine fiscal years following thereafter, a sum of fifty million dollars ($50,000,000) per year is hereby appropriated from the General Fund for the purpose of providing additional funding for free or subsidized programs of adult English language instruction to parents or other members of the community who pledge to provide personal English language tutoring to California school children with limited English proficiency.

Sec. 316. Programs funded pursuant to this section shall be provided through schools or community organizations. Funding for these programs shall be administered by the Office of the Superintendent of Public Instruction, and shall be disbursed at the discretion of the local school boards, under reasonable guidelines established by, and subject to the review of, the State Board of Education.

ARTICLE 5. Legal Standing and Parental Enforcement

Sec. 320. As detailed in Article 2 (commencing with Section 305) and Article 3 (commencing with Section 310), all California school children have the right to be provided with an English language public education. If a California school child has been denied the option of an English language instructional curriculum in public school, the child's parent or legal guardian shall have legal standing to sue for enforcement of the provisions of this statute, and if successful shall be awarded normal and customary attorney's fees and actual damages, but not punitive or consequential damages. Any school board member or other elected official or public school teacher or administrator who willfully and repeatedly refuses to implement the terms of this statute by providing such an English language educational option at an available public school to a California school child may be held personally liable for fees and actual damages by the child's parents or legal guardian.

ARTICLE 6. Severability

Sec. 325. If any part or parts of this statute are found to be in conflict with federal law or the

United States or the California State Constitution, the statute shall be implemented to the maximum extent that federal law, and the United States and the California State Constitution permit. Any provision held invalid shall be severed from the remaining portions of this statute.

ARTICLE 7. Operative Date
Sec. 330. This initiative shall become operative for all school terms which begin more than sixty days following the date at which it becomes effective.

ARTICLE 8. Amendment.
Sec. 335. The provisions of this act may be amended by a statute that becomes effective upon approval by the electorate or by a statute to further the act's purpose passed by a two-thirds vote of each house of the Legislature and signed by the Governor.

ARTICLE 9. Interpretation
Sec. 340. Under circumstances in which portions of this statute are subject to conflicting interpretations, Section 300 shall be assumed to contain the governing intent of the statute.

Appendix F
Sources and Suggested Reading

This book relies in part on journalistic sources, that is, interviews, press briefings, public records, legislative hearings, oral statements at conferences, school visits, and firsthand reporting of events. Bibliographic sources, along with recommendations for further reading, are provided below.

Introduction

Sabine R. Ulibarrí describes the experience of the Hispanic student before the bilingual education era in "The Word Made Flesh: Spanish in the Classroom," in Luís Valdez and Stan Steiner, eds., *Aztlán: An Anthology of Mexican American Literature* (New York: Alfred A. Knopf, 1972).

Einar Haugen analyzes American attitudes toward bilingualism in *The Norwegian Language in America: A Study in Bilingual Behavior* (Bloomington: Indiana University Press, 1969), and "The Curse of Babel," in Haugen and Morton Bloomfield, eds., *Language as a Human Problem* (New York: W. W. Norton & Co., 1973). See also François Grosjean, *Life With Two Languages: An Introduction to Bilingualism* (Cambridge, Mass.: Harvard University Press, 1982).

Joel Perlmann provides immigrant school attendance figures (extrapolated from the 1911 report by the federal Dillingham Commission) in "Bilingualism and Ethnicity in American Schooling before 1960: An Historical Perspective," paper presented at the Institute on Bilingual Education, Harvard Graduate School of Education, Dec. 11, 1987. Further discussion of the human costs of Americanization may be found in Stanley Feldstein and Lawrence Costello, *The Ordeal of Assimilation: A Documentary of the White Working Class* (Garden City, N.Y.: Anchor Books, 1974).

Letters responding to Secretary William Bennett's speech on bilingual education (Sept. 26, 1985) and comments on his proposed changes in Title VII regulations (Nov. 22, 1985) are on file at the U.S. Office of Bilingual Education and Minority Languages Affairs.

Demographic trends among language minorities are cited in Carlos E. Cortés, "The Education of Language Minority Students: A Contextual Interaction Model," in California State Department of Education, Bilingual Education Office,

Beyond Language: Social and Cultural Factors in Schooling Language Minority Students (Los Angeles: California State University, 1986).

In *The Undereducation of American Youth* (San Antonio: Intercultural Development Resource Association, 1988), Dorothy Waggoner uses 1980 Census data to conduct a demographic analysis of the 6 million youths, aged 16 to 24, who "were not enrolled in school and had not completed the twelfth grade." Waggoner also publishes an informative newsletter, *Numbers and Needs,* which offers extensive analyses of language data from the 1990 census. It is available from Box G1H/B, 3900 Watson Place, N.W., Washington, D.C. 20016.

Kenneth G. Wilson's misinformed tirade against bilingual education appears in his otherwise urbane and entertaining book, *Van Winkle's Return: Change in American English, 1966-1986* (Hanover, N.H.: University Press of New England, 1987).

Chapter 1. Bilingualism in America: A Forgotten Legacy

A more detailed history of language policy in the United States can be found in James Crawford, *Hold Your Tongue: Bilingualism and the Politics of "English Only"* (Reading, Mass.: Addison-Wesley, 1992). Supporting documents are reprinted in James Crawford, ed., *Language Loyalties: A Source Book on the Official English Controversy* (Chicago: University of Chicago Press, 1992).

A comprehensive and readable history of bilingual education is Diego Castellanos, *The Best of Two Worlds: Bilingual-Bicultural Education in the U.S.* (Trenton, N.J.: New Jersey State Department of Education, 1983). Useful anecdotal material may be found in Colman B. Stein, Jr., *Sink or Swim: The Politics of Bilingual Education* (New York: Praeger, 1986).

For researchers of U.S. language policy, the starting point is Heinz Kloss, *The American Bilingual Tradition* (Rowley, Mass.: Newbury House, 1977), which is unmatched for encyclopedic detail about language-minority schooling, particularly before 1968. See also his "German-American Language Maintenance Efforts," in Joshua A. Fishman, ed., *Language Loyalty in the United States: The Maintenance and Perpetuation of Non-English Mother Tongues by American Ethnic and Religious Groups* (The Hague: Mouton Publishers, 1966; rpt. New York: Arno Press, 1978), pp. 206-52.

Shirley Brice Heath has traced the neglected history of language attitudes in the colonial era in "A National Language Academy? Debate in the New Nation," *International Journal of the Sociology of Language* 11 (1976): 9-43; and "English in Our Language Heritage," in Charles A. Ferguson and Heath, eds., *Language in the USA* (Cambridge: Cambridge University Press, 1981), pp. 6-20. See also Allen

Walker Read, "American Projects for an Academy to Regulate Speech," *Publications of the Modern Language Association* 51, no. 4 (1936): 1141-79. Noah Webster's efforts to standardize American English are described in *Dissertations on the English Language* (1789) and Dennis Baron, "Federal English" (1987); both are reprinted in Crawford, *Language Loyalties*, pp. 33-40. See also Baron, *Grammar and Good Taste: Reforming the American Language* (New Haven: Yale University Press, 1982); and *The English Only Question: An Official Language For Americans?* (New Haven: Yale University Press, 1990).

For details on language use by minority groups before and after the American Revolution, see Marcus Lee Hansen, *The Atlantic Migration, 1607-1860: A History of the Continuing Settlement of the United States* (New York: Harper Torchbooks, 1961).

The Wisconsin and Illinois conflicts over English-only instruction are detailed in Louise Phelps Kellogg, "The Bennett Law in Wisconsin," *Wisconsin Magazine of History* 2 (1918): 3-25; William F. Whyte, "The Bennett Law Campaign in Wisconsin," *Wisconsin Magazine of History* 10 (1927): 363-90; and Daniel W. Kucera, *Church-State Relationships in Education in Illinois* (Washington, D.C.: Catholic University of America Press, 1955.)

Probably the most prolific writer on language restrictionism in the United States has been Arnold H. Leibowitz. Three important works are "Language as a Means of Social Control: The United States Experience," paper presented at the 8th World Congress of Sociology, Toronto, Aug. 1974; "English Literacy: Legal Sanction for Discrimination," *Notre Dame Lawyer* 45, no. 7 (Fall 1969): 7-67; and *The Bilingual Education Act: A Legislative Analysis* (Rosslyn, Va.: National Clearinghouse for Bilingual Education, 1980).

Repression of the German language during and after World War I is well documented in Carl Wittke, *German-Americans and the World War: With Special Emphasis on Ohio's German-Language Press* (Columbus: Ohio State Archaeological and Historical Society, 1936), pp. 163-79.

The seminal political and sociological analysis of the Americanization era is John Higham, *Strangers in the Land: Patterns of American Nativism, 1860-1925* (New York: Atheneum, 1963). See also Milton M. Gordon, *Assimilation in American Life: The Role of Race, Religion, and National Origins* (New York: Oxford University Press, 1964); and Edward George Hartmann, *The Movement to Americanize the Immigrant* (New York: Columbia University Press, 1948). Ellwood P. Cubberly's views on schooling immigrants are detailed in *Changing Conceptions of Education* (Boston: Houghton Mifflin, 1909). Josué M. González provides insights into ethnic politics and assimilationist pressures in "Coming of Age in Bilingual/Bicultural Education: A Historical Perspective," *Inequality in Education* 19 (Feb. 1975): 5-17.

The Language Policy Task Force examines education as an instrument of colonial rule in "Language Policy and the Puerto Rican Community," *Bilingual Review* 5, nos. 1-2 (1978): 1-39. See also Aída Negrón de Montilla, *Americanization in Puerto Rico and the Public-School System, 1900-1930* (Río Piedras, P.R.: Editorial Edil, 1971); and Pastora San Juan Cafferty and Carmen Rivera-Martínez, *The Politics of Language: The Dilemma of Bilingual Education for Puerto Ricans* (Boulder, Colo.: Westview Press, 1981).

For analyses of the linguistic repression directed at American Indians, see Senate Labor and Public Welfare Committee, Special Subcommittee on Indian Education, *Indian Education: A National Tragedy — A National Challenge*, 91st Congress, 1st Session (1969); Jon Reyhner and Jeanne Eder, *A History of Indian Education* (Billings: Eastern Montana College, 1986); and James Park, "Historical Foundations of Language Policy: The Nez Percé Case," in Robert St. Clair and William Leap, eds., *Language Renewal among American Indian Tribes: Issues, Problems, and Prospects* (Rosslyn, Va: National Clearinghouse for Bilingual Education, 1982). An excellent account of Indian education reform in the John Collier era can be found in Margaret Connell Szasz, *Education and the American Indian: The Road to Self-Determination Since 1928* (Albuquerque: University of New Mexico Press, 1977).

Leonard Pitt documents ethnic conflicts in early California in *The Decline of the Californios: A Social History of the Spanish-Speaking Californians, 1846-1890* (Berkeley: University of California Press, 1966). The modern Chicano experience is described by the U.S. Commission on Civil Rights, *The Excluded Student: Educational Practices Affecting Mexican Americans in the Southwest*, Mexican American Education Study, Report III, May 1972. See also Mario T. García, *Mexican Americans: Leadership, Ideology, and Identity, 1930-1960* (New Haven: Yale University Press, 1989); and Guadalupe San Miguel, Jr., *"Let All of Them Take Heed": Mexican Americans and the Campaign for Educational Equality in Texas, 1910-1981* (Austin: University of Texas Press, 1987). On the misclassification of language-minority children, see Alba A. Ortiz and James R. Yates, "Incidence of Exceptionality among Hispanics: Implications for Manpower Planning," *NABE Journal* 7, no. 3 (Spring 1983): 41-53.

Kenji Hakuta details the Coral Way experiment and analyzes its outcomes in *Mirror of Language: The Debate on Bilingualism* (New York: Basic Books, 1986). For additional details, see William Francis Mackey and Von Nieda Beebe,

Bilingual Schools for a Bicultural Community: Miami's Adaptation to the Cuban Refugees (Rowley, Mass.: Newbury House, 1977).

Chapter 2. The Evolution of Federal Policy

In their general histories, Castellanos, Kloss, and Stein describe the political circumstances surrounding the passage of Title VII. The educational context is sketched in *The Invisible Minority: Report of the NEA-Tucson Survey* (Washington, D.C.: National Education Association, 1966). Leibowitz summarizes the law's subsequent development in *The Bilingual Education Act*. See also Ricardo R. Fernández, "Legislation, Regulation, and Litigation: The Origins and Evolution of Public Policy on Bilingual Education in the United States," paper presented at the 6th annual Green Bay Colloquium on Ethnicity and Public Policy, University of Wisconsin at Green Bay, May 10-11, 1985.

For details of state legislation, see Tracy C. Gray, H. Suzanne Convery, and Katherine M. Fox, *The Current Status of Bilingual Education Legislation*, Bilingual Education Series, no. 9 (Washington, D.C.: Center for Applied Linguistics, 1981); with two exceptions (California and Colorado), the statutory information remains current. See also "Fourth Annual Report of the National Advisory Council on Bilingual Education," Sept. 30, 1979, pp. 113-42; and Heinz Kloss, *American Bilingual Tradition.*

Martin Gerry's recollections about drafting the Lau remedies appeared in Thomas Toch, "The Emerging Politics of Language," *Education Week*, Feb. 8, 1984, pp. 1, 12-16.

Noel Epstein's influential attack on bilingual education, *Language, Ethnicity, and the Schools: Policy Alternatives for Bilingual-Bicultural Education* (Washington, D.C.: Institute for Educational Leadership, 1977), includes thoughtful responses by José A. Cárdenas and Gary Orfield.

A helpful article in untangling the legal issues is Sau-ling Cynthia Wong, "Educational Rights of Language Minorities," in Sandra Lee McKay and Wong, eds., *Language Diversity: Problem or Resource?* (Cambridge, Mass.: Newbury House, 1988). Complete texts of several precedent-setting court decisions are reprinted in Arnold H. Leibowitz, ed., *Federal Recognition of the Rights of Minority Language Groups* (Rosslyn, Va.: National Clearinghouse for Bilingual Education, 1982).

For a detailed analysis of Office for Civil Rights activity under the Reagan administration, see James Crawford, "U.S. Enforcement of Bilingual Plans Declines Sharply," *Education Week*, June 4, 1986.

310   Bilingual Education: History, Politics, Theory and Practice

Congressional hearings on Title VII and its periodic reauthorizations are a treasure trove of information about federal policy and about the condition of bilingual education over the past three decades. The more significant sessions include:

- Senate Labor and Public Welfare Committee, Special Subcommittee on Bilingual Education, 90th Congress, 1st Session (1967), hearing on S 428; reprinted by Arno Press (New York: 1978).
- House Education and Labor Committee, General Subcommittee on Education, 90th Congress, 1st Session (1967), hearings on HR 9840 and HR 10224; reprinted by Arno Press (New York: 1978).
- Senate Labor and Public Welfare Committee, Subcommittees on Education and Human Resources, 93rd Congress, 1st Session (1973), joint hearing on bilingual education, health, and manpower programs; reprinted by Arno Press (New York: 1978).
- Senate Labor and Human Resources Committee, Subcommittee on Education, Arts, and Humanities, 97th Congress, 2nd Session (1982), hearing on S 2002.

Chapter 3. English Only or English Plus?

The debate over the English Language Amendment, and more generally, over bilingualism in the United States, has produced a voluminous literature since 1983. Analyses, editorials, legislation, court decisions, and organizational positions on both sides of the issue are reprinted in Crawford, *Language Loyalties*, along with information about the English Plus alternative. See also Harvey A. Daniels, ed., *Not Only English: Affirming America's Multilingual Heritage* (Urbana, Ill.: National Council of Teachers of English); and Karen L. Adams and Daniel T. Brink, eds., *Perspectives on Official English: The Campaign for English as the Official Language of the U.S.A.* (Berlin: Mouton de Gruyter, 1990).

The charge that Hispanics are resisting English is elaborated by Gerda Bikales and Gary Imhoff in *A Kind of Discordant Harmony: Issues in Assimilation,* Discussion Series, no. 2 (Washington, D.C.: U.S. English, 1985). Bikales outlines her views on the "price" of immigration in remarks at the Georgetown University Round Table on Languages and Linguistics, March 12, 1987. Imhoff carries these arguments further in a book he coauthored with Colorado Governor Richard D. Lamm, *The Immigration Time Bomb: The Fragmenting of America* (New York: E. P. Dutton, 1985).

The intimate ties between U.S. English and the immigration-restrictionist lobby are documented in William Trombley, "Prop. 63 Roots Traced to Small Michigan City," *Los Angeles Times*, Oct. 20, 1986, Part I, pp. 3, 20-21; and Laird Harrison, "U.S. English's Links to Anti-Immigration Groups," *Asian Week*, Aug. 15, 1986, pp. 1, 21. See also Trombley, "Norman Cousins Drops His Support of Prop. 63," *Los Angeles Times*, Oct. 16, 1986, Part I, p. 3.

Linda Chávez, as president of U.S. English, outlines her views in "English: Our Common Bond," speech to the Los Angeles World Affairs Council, Dec. 4, 1987. The "cultural conservative" educational philosophy, which underlies attacks on bilingual education by Chávez and others, is elaborated in E. D. Hirsch, Jr., *Cultural Literacy: What Every American Needs To Know* (Boston: Houghton Mifflin, 1987), pp. 92-93, 232-33.

Events leading to the resignations of Chávez, Walter Cronkite, and John Tanton as officers of U.S. English are detailed in Crawford, *Hold Your Tongue*, chap. 6.

Independent voices on behalf of official English include: George F. Will, "In Defense of the Mother Tongue," *Newsweek*, July 8, 1985; William A. Henry, "Against a Confusion of Tongues," *Time*, June 11, 1983; and Phyllis Schlafly, "Lack of English Shuts Many Doors to `Ghettoized' Hispanics," *New York Tribune*, Feb. 21, 1986.

Joshua A. Fishman looks at the movement's social psychology in "`English Only': Its Ghosts, Myths, and Dangers," paper presented at the 12th annual conference of the California Association for Bilingual Education, Anaheim, Jan. 30, 1987, excerpted in Crawford, *Language Loyalties*, pp. 165-70. Ana Celia Zentella predicts that the English Language Amendment would have a disproportionate, adverse impact on minority women in "Language Politics in the U.S.A.: The English-Only Movement," in Betty Jean Craige, ed., *Literature, Language, and Politics* (Athens: University of Georgia Press, 1988), pp. 39-53.

Linguists from several countries attack the notion of an official language for the United States in *International Journal of the Sociology of Language* 60 (1986), a special issue devoted to "The Question of an Official Language: Language Rights and the English Language Amendment." The lead article is by David F. Marshall, and there are useful responses by Tom McArthur, Eric Maldoff, Michael Clyne, Shirley Brice Heath and Lawrence Krasner, Heinz Kloss, Kathryn A. Woolard, and James E. Alatis.

Other noteworthy criticisms include: Mary Carol Combs and John Trasviña, "Legal Implications of the English Language Amendment," in *The English Only*

Movement: An Agenda for Discrimination (Washington, D.C.: League of United Latin American Citizens, 1986); Geoffrey Nunberg, "An 'Official Language' for California?" *New York Times*, Oct. 2, 1986; Roseann Duenas González, Alice A. Schott, and Victoria F. Vásquez, "The English Language Amendment: Examining Myths," *English Journal*, March 1988, pp. 24-30; Elliot L. Judd, "The English Language Amendment: A Case Study on Language and Politics," *TESOL Quarterly* 21, no. 1 (March 1987): 113-35; and Amado M. Padilla et al., "The English Only Movement: Myths, Reality, and Implications for Psychology," *Journal of the American Psychological Association*, no. 2 (Feb. 1991): 20-30.

Patterns of language loss and retention are explored by Calvin J. Veltman in *The Future of the Spanish Language in the United States* (Washington, D.C.: Hispanic Policy Development Project, 1988); and *Language Shift in the United States* (Berlin: Mouton Publishers, 1983). See also National Center for Education Statistics, *The Retention of Minority Languages in the United States: A Seminar on the Analytic Work of Calvin J. Veltman, May 13, 1980* (Washington, D.C.: U.S. Government Printing Office, 1980).

The English Only movement's attacks on bilingual education and its gains at the state level are reported by James Crawford in *Education Week*: "'Supporting' Comments Reveal Animosity Toward Ethnic Groups," Feb. 12, 1986; "Conservative Groups Take Aim at Bilingual-Education Programs," March 19, 1986; "E.D. Hires Bilingual-Education Critic for Text Study," Jan. 28, 1987; and "37 States Consider 'English Only' Bills, With Mixed Results," June 17, 1987.

Rosalie Porter's *Forked Tongue: The Politics of Bilingual Education* was published by Basic Books in 1990. Arthur Schlesinger, Jr., confounds bilingual with multicultural and Afrocentric education in *The Disuniting of America: Reflections on a Multicultural Society* (Knoxville, Tenn.: Whittle Direct Books, 1991).

Two Congressional hearings have been held on the English Language Amendment:

- Senate Judiciary Committee, Subcommittee on the Constitution, 98th Congress, 2nd Session, hearing on SJ Res 167, June 12, 1984.
- House Judiciary Committee, Subcommittee on Civil and Constitutional Rights, 100th Congress, 2nd Session, hearing on HJ Res 13, 33, 60, and 83, May 11, 1988.

For an excellent history and analysis of English Plus, see Mary Carol Combs, "English Plus: Responding to English Only," in Crawford, *Language Loyalties*, pp. 216-24.

Chapter 4. The Bennett Years

The New Right's critique of bilingual education is elaborated by Eileen Gardner, "The Growth of the Federal Role in Education," in Gardner, ed., *A New Agenda for Education* (Washington, D.C.: Heritage Foundation, 1985). Secretary William Bennett's firing of Gardner and Larry Uzell is detailed in Colman B. Stein, *Sink or Swim.*

For the views of members of the National Advisory and Coordinating Council on Bilingual Education, see Howard Hurwitz, "The Case Against Bilingual Education," *Human Events*, Jan. 4, 1986; Joan Keefe, "Bilingual Education: Costly, Unproductive," *Christian Science Monitor*, Aug. 8, 1985; and Robert Rosier, "Bilingual Education: The New Latin Hustle," *Washington Times*, June 14, 1983.

Editorials favorable to Secretary Bennett's "bilingual education initiative" include *New York Times,* "Language Is the Melting Pot," Sept. 27, 1985; *Washington Post,* "Secretary Bennett Makes Sense," Sept. 27, 1985; and *Kansas City Times,* "Citizens Speak the Language," Oct. 7, 1985.

Criticisms of Bennett's position may be found in James J. Lyons, "Education Secretary Bennett on Bilingual Education: Mixed Up or Malicious?" *NABE News* 9, no. 1 (Fall 1985): 1, 14; José A. Cárdenas, "Education Secretary Bennett and the Big Lie," *Intercultural Development Research Association Newsletter*, Oct. 1985, pp. 7-8; and "A Forked Tongue," *Miami Herald*, Sept. 29, 1985, p. 2E.

Bennett's revised estimate of the limited-English-proficient school population appears in "The Condition of Bilingual Education in the Nation, 1986: A Report from the Secretary of Education to the President and Congress." For further reading, see Dorothy Waggoner, "Estimates of the Need for Bilingual Education and the Proportion of Children in Need Being Served," *NABE News* 9, nos. 4-5 (Summer 1986): 6-9; Daniel M. Ulibarrí, "Issues in Estimates of the Number of Limited English Proficient Students," in House Education and Labor Committee, *Compendium of Papers on the Topic of Bilingual Education*, Serial no. 99-R, June 1986; Malcolm B. Young et al., *The Descriptive Phase Report of the National Longitudinal Evaluation of the Effectiveness of Services for Language-Minority Limited-English-Proficient Students* (Arlington, Va.: Development Associates, 1984); and Robert E. Barnes, "The Size of the Eligible Language-Minority Population," in Keith A. Baker and Adriana A. de Kanter, eds., *Bilingual Education: A Reappraisal of Federal Policy* (Lexington, Mass.: Lexington Books, 1983), pp. 3-32.

First-year scores from SRA's "Longitudinal Study of Immersion Programs for

Language-Minority Children" are detailed in an unpublished memorandum to the study's advisory committee from David Ramírez, Dec. 19, 1985, "Subject: Summary Results of Pre/Post Achievement Test Comparisons for Matched Groups of Target Students, FY 1984-85."

Two 1987 reports by the U.S. General Accounting Office that played a role in the legislative battles that year are *Bilingual Education: A New Look at the Research Evidence*, GAO/PEMD-87-12BR, and *Bilingual Education: Information on Limited English Proficient Students*, GAO/HRD-87-85BR.

Policy controversies during Bennett's tenure are recounted in *Education Week* articles by James Crawford: "Bilingual-Education Proposals Spark Politically Charged Debate," Feb. 12, 1986; "Bennett Proposes Bilingual Legislation," March 12, 1986; "Immersion Method Is Faring Poorly in Bilingual Study," April 23, 1986; "Lawmakers, Lobbyists Challenge E.D.'s Bilingual-Education Data," April 30, 1986; "Bennett Pushes Bilingual Bill in Congress," June 11, 1986; "Bilingual-Ed. Measure Is Vetoed in California," Oct. 8, 1986; "G.A.O. Refutes Bennett's Criticism of Bilingual Education," Nov. 19, 1986; "Finn Criticizes G.A.O.'s Handling of Bilingual Study," Jan. 14, 1987; "E.D.'s Bilingual-Education Plan Faces Second Test in Congress," Jan. 21, 1987; "Battle Lines Redrawn over Bilingual Education," April 1, 1987; "Bilingual Educators Challenge E.D.'s 'English Only' Proposal," April 15, 1987; "Accord Is Reached on Bill to Extend Bilingual-Ed. Act," April 29, 1987; "Senate Panel Would Expand Bilingual-Ed. Funding Options," May 13, 1987.

Lyons's letter on the 1988 House-Senate conference deliberations on reauthorizing Title VII is reprinted in *NABE News* 11, no. 6 (April 1988). Relevant Congressional hearings include:

- Senate Labor and Human Resources Committee, Subcommittee on Education, Arts, and Humanities, 99th Congress, 2nd Session, hearing on S 2256, June 4, 1986.
- House Education and Labor Committee, Subcommittee on Elementary, Secondary, and Vocational Education, 100th Congress, 1st Session, hearing on HR 1755, March 24, 1987.

Apparent favoritism by the Bush administration in funding English-only programs is detailed by Julie Miller, "Bias Is Charged in Awarding of Bilingual Grants," *Education Week*, March 15, 1989, pp. 1, 29.

Chapter 5. The Effectiveness Debate

Barry McLaughlin summarizes and rebuts many of the popular misconceptions surrounding bilingualism in *Second-Language Acquisition in Childhood*, 2d ed. (Hillsdale, N.J.: Lawrence Erlbaum Associates, 1984).

The American Institutes for Research study — Malcolm N. Danoff et al., *Evaluation of the Impact of ESEA Title VII Spanish/English Bilingual Education Programs* — had two significant installments: vol. 1, *Study Design and Interim Findings* (1977) and vol. 3, *Year Two Impact Data, Educational Process, and In-Depth Analysis* (1978).

For criticisms of this first major evaluation of Title VII, see Tracy C. Gray and M. Beatriz Arias, "Challenge to the AIR Report," paper for the Center for Applied Linguistics, 1978. See also Rudolph C. Troike, "Research Evidence for the Effectiveness of Bilingual Education," *NABE Journal* 3, no. 1 (1978): 13-24; and "Synthesis of Research on Bilingual Education," *Educational Leadership* 14 (March 1981): 498-504.

The Association for Supervision and Curriculum Development criticizes the pragmatist emphasis of much evaluation research in *Building an Indivisible Nation: Bilingual Education in Context* (Alexandria, Va: ASCD, 1987). Kenji Hakuta and Catherine E. Snow elaborate the lessons of basic research in "The Role of Research in Policy Decisions about Bilingual Education," *NABE News* 9, no. 3 (Spring 1986): 1, 18-21 (reprinted in House Education and Labor Committee, *Compendium of Papers*. See also Carrol E. Moran and Hakuta, "Bilingual Education: Broadening Research Perspectives," in James A. Banks and Cherry A. McGee Banks, eds., *Handbook of Research on Multicultural Education* (New York: Macmillan, 1995), pp. 445-62.

Chester E. Finn's argument about the burden of proof in bilingual education research appears in an appendix to the 1987 General Accounting Office report, *Bilingual Education: A New Look at the Research Evidence*, pp. 63-70. Christine Rossell and J. Michael Ross assert the primacy of "time on task" in "The Social Science Evidence on Bilingual Education," *Journal of Law and Education* 15, no. 4 (Fall 1986): 385-419.

There are two versions of the Baker-de Kanter report. The earlier one — Keith A. Baker and Adriana A. de Kanter, "Effectiveness of Bilingual Education: A Review of the Literature" (U.S. Department of Education, Office of Planning, Budget, and Evaluation, Sept. 1981) — received wide publicity in unpublished form, but was never officially released. "Federal Policy and the Effectiveness of Bilingual Education," in Baker and de Kanter, eds., *Bilingual Education*, is more concise and accessible; this 1983 version is relied on here.

Ann C. Willig has produced the most influential critique of Baker and de Kanter, "A Meta-Analysis of Selected Studies on the Effectiveness of Bilingual Education," *Review of Educational Research* 55, no. 3 (Fall 1985): 269-317. See also Willig, "The Effectiveness of Bilingual Education: Review of a Report," *NABE Journal* 6, nos. 2-3 (Winter/Spring 1981-82): 1-19. An exchange between Baker and Willig on their points of disagreement appears in the *Review of Educational Research* 57, no. 3 (Fall 1987): 351-76.

Chapter 6. Basic Research on Language Acquisition

The American Council on the Teaching of Foreign Languages reports statistics on our limited linguistic abilities in *ACTFL Public Awareness Network Newsletter: A Bimonthly Report on Foreign Language and International Studies* 6, no. 3 (May 1987).

Historical overviews and theories of language education may be found in Barry McLaughlin, *Second-Language Acquisition*, and Stephen D. Krashen and Tracy D. Terrell, *The Natural Approach: Language Acquisition in the Classroom* (Hayward, Calif.: Alemany Press, 1983). See also Charles A. Ferguson, "Linguistic Theory," in *Bilingual Education: Current Perspectives,* vol. 2, *Linguistics* (Arlington, Va.: Center for Applied Linguistics, 1977). Wilga M. Rivers makes a case for the audiolingual method in *Teaching Foreign Language Skills* (Chicago: University of Chicago Press, 1968).

An accessible introduction to Noam Chomsky's work, presented in the form of an extended interview, is *Language and Responsibility* (New York: Pantheon Books, 1979). For a discussion of the "language faculty," see his *Language and Problems of Knowledge: The Managua Lectures* (Cambridge, Mass.: MIT Press, 1988).

Kenji Hakuta discusses Chomsky's relationship to psycholinguistic research in *Mirror of Language*, pp. 109-11, and provides an extended analysis of research on the cognitive effects of bilingualism. See also Ellen Bialystok and Hakuta, *In Other Words: The Science and Psychology of Second-Language Acquisition* (New York: Basic Books, 1994).

Lily Wong Fillmore and Barry McLaughlin's study of variability in second-language acquisition is *Learning English through Bilingual Instruction*, Final Report to the National Institute of Education (NIE-80-0030), 1985. The findings are summarized by Wong Fillmore, "Teachability and Second Language Acquisition," in R. Schiefelbush and M. Rice, eds., *The Teachability of Language*

(Baltimore: Paul Brookes, 1989), pp. 311-32. See also Wong Fillmore, "Second-Language Learning in Children: A Model of Language Learning in Social Context," in Ellen Bialystok, ed., *Language Processing in Bilingual Children* (New York: Cambridge University Press, 1991), pp. 49-69.

A comprehensive summary of basic research on second-language acquisition, along with its implications for the bilingual classroom, can be found in a book compiled by California's state Office of Bilingual Bicultural Education: *Schooling and Language Minority Students: A Theoretical Framework* (Los Angeles: California State University, 1981). This collection includes Jim Cummins, "The Role of Primary Language Development in Promoting Educational Success for Language Minority Students"; Stephen D. Krashen, "Bilingual Education and Second Language Acquisition Theory"; Dorothy Legaretta-Marcaida, "Effective Use of the Primary Language in the Classroom"; Tracy D. Terrell, "The Natural Approach in Bilingual Education"; and Eleanor W. Thonis, "Reading Instruction for Language Minority Students."

Krashen discusses the input hypothesis and related issues in a series of absorbing essays, *Inquiries and Insights: Second Language Learning, Immersion & Bilingual Education, Literacy* (Hayward, Calif.: Alemany Press, 1985). He outlines and documents his theory more formally in *The Input Hypothesis: Issues and Implications* (London: Longman, 1985) and *Principles and Practice in Second Language Acquisition* (Oxford: Pergamon Press, 1982). See also his *Bilingual Education: A Focus on Current Research*, Occasional Papers in Bilingual Education, no. 3 (Washington, D.C.: National Clearinghouse for Bilingual Education, 1991).

Cummins develops his arguments beyond the realm of language, exploring the problem of bicultural ambivalence among low-status groups, in "Empowering Minority Students: A Framework for Intervention," *Harvard Educational Review* 56, no. 1 (Feb. 1986): 18-36. (This article was expanded into a monograph of the same title, published by the California Association for Bilingual Education in 1988.) Rudolph C. Troike summarizes arguments for the late-exit model in "Improving Conditions for Success in Bilingual Education Programs," in House Education and Labor Committee, *Compendium of Papers*.

A helpful discussion of program designs for language-minority students, along with a wealth of practical information about teaching methods, can be found in Carlos J. Ovando and Virginia P. Collier, *Bilingual and ESL Classrooms: Teaching in Multicultural Contexts* (New York: McGraw-Hill, 1985).

Barry McLaughlin elaborates his critique of Krashen's work in *Theories of Second-Language Learning* (London: Edward Arnold, 1987).

Other useful overviews of the research include: "When Children Speak Little English: How Effective is Bilingual Education?" *Harvard Education Letter* 2, no. 6 (Nov. 1986): 1-4; and Gloria R. Zamora, "Understanding Bilingual Education," Backgrounder Series (Boston: National Coalition of Advocates for Students, 1987). See also Kenji Hakuta and Laurie J. Gould, "Synthesis of Research on Bilingual Education," *Educational Leadership* 44 (Mar. 1987): 38-45.

Chapter 7. Alternatives to Bilingual Education

An introduction to immersion — its theoretical underpinnings, development of program models in Canada and the U.S., and arguments about its suitability for language-minority students — is provided in *Studies on Immersion Education: A Collection for United States Educators* (Sacramento: California State Department of Education, Office of Bilingual Bicultural Education, 1984). This anthology includes Wallace E. Lambert, "An Overview of Issues in Immersion Education"; Fred Genesee, "Historical and Theoretical Foundations of Immersion Education"; and Eduardo Hernández-Chávez, "The Inadequacy of English Immersion Education as an Educational Approach for Language Minority Students in the United States."

The genesis and development of French immersion is described in detail by Lambert and G. Richard Tucker, *Bilingual Education of Children: The St. Lambert Experiment* (Rowley, Mass.: Newbury House, 1972). Tucker argues that the Canadian immersion model is inappropriate for language-minority children in "Implications of Canadian Research for Promoting a Language Competent American Society," in Joshua A. Fishman, ed., *The Fergusonian Impact*, vol. 2, *Sociolinguistics and the Sociology of Language* (Berlin: Mouton Publishers, 1986). Another useful overview is Myriam Met, "Immersion and the Language Minority Student," paper for the Midwest National Origin Desegregation-Assistance Center, University of Wisconsin at Milwaukee, Jan. 1984.

Baker and Willig's differences over program definitions may be found in their exchange in the Fall 1987 *Review of Educational Research*. Philadelphia's ESOL Plus Immersion program and the controversy surrounding it are described in Martha Woodall, "As Refugees' Grades Sink, English Immersion Faulted," *Philadelphia Inquirer*, March 30, 1986, pp. 1B, 8B.

The El Paso pilot program is described in El Paso Independent School District, Office for Research and Evaluation, "Bilingual Education Program Evaluation: 1986-87 School Year," July 1987. Robert Rosier's erroneous characterization appears in the "Twelfth Annual Report of the National Advisory and Coordinating Council on Bilingual Education," March 31, 1988. The READ study by Russell Gersten et al. is "Bilingual Immersion: A Longitudinal Evaluation of the El Paso Program" (1993).

Gersten and John Woodward discuss the limited research evidence that exists on English-only immersion approaches in "A Case for Structured Immersion," *Educational Leadership*, Sept. 1985, pp. 75-79, 83-84. See also the response by Ramón L. Santiago in the same issue, "Understanding Bilingual Education — or The Sheep in Wolf's Clothing," pp. 79-83.

As released in 1991, the Ramírez study's full reference is: J. David Ramírez, Sandra D. Yuen, and Dena R. Ramey, *Final Report: Longitudinal Study of Structured Immersion Strategy, Early-Exit, and Late-Exit Transitional Bilingual Education Programs for Language-Minority Children* (San Mateo, Calif.: Aguirre International, 1991). For analyses of, and debate over, its findings, see the *Bilingual Research Journal* 16, nos. 1 & 2 (Winter/Spring 1992).

The review of the Ramírez study by the National Research Council is summarized in Michael M. Meyer and Stephen E. Fienberg, eds., *Assessing Evaluation Studies: The Case of Bilingual Education Strategies* (Washington, D.C.: National Academy Press, 1992).

The research on Fairfax County's ESL-only program was conducted by Virginia P. Collier and Wayne P. Thomas, who describe their findings in "Acquisition of Cognitive-Academic Language Proficiency: A Six-Year Study," paper presented at the annual meeting of the American Educational Research Association, New Orleans, April 7, 1988. See also Collier, "Age and Rate of Acquisition of Second Language for Academic Purposes," *TESOL Quarterly* 21, no. 4 (Dec. 1987): 617-41. Reactions by the school district and others are reported in James Crawford, "Study Challenges 'Model' E.S.L. Program's Effectiveness," *Education Week*, April 27, 1988.

Chapter 8. Theory into Practice: The Case Studies Project

The most comprehensive description of this program is Fred Tempes, "Case Studies in Bilingual Education: Second Year Report (1984-85)," evaluation report to the U.S. Office of Bilingual Education and Minority Languages Affairs (Federal Grant #G008303723), May 1986.

Implications of basic research for curriculum design are developed in California Office of Bilingual Bicultural Education, *Basic Principles for the Education of Language-Minority Students: An Overview* (Sacramento: California State Department of Education, 1983).

A detailed analysis of student scores in Case Studies schools and other exemplary programs is provided in Stephen Krashen and Douglas Biber, *On Course: Bilingual Education's Success in California* (Sacramento: California Association for Bilingual Education, 1988).

For a summary of early experience in replicating the Eastman/Case Studies model, see Jesús Salazar, "Eastman Curriculum Design Project, 1986-87, First Year Implementation Report," Publication no. 512, Los Angeles Unified School District, Research and Evaluation Branch, Feb. 1988.

Chapter 9. Indian Bilingual Education

Michael Krauss quantifies the threat to endangered languages, including those spoken by Native Americans, in "The World's Languages in Crisis," *Language*, no. 1 (March 1992): 6-10. In the same issue, see also Lucille J. Watahomigie and Akira Y. Yamamoto, "Local Reactions to Perceived Language Decline," pp. 10-17; and Ken Hale, "Language Endangerment and the Human Value of Linguistic Diversity," pp. 35-42. An excellent overview of the problem is Ofelia Zepeda and Jane H. Hill, "The Condition of Native American Languages in the United States," in Robert H. Robins and Eugenius M. Uhlenbeck, eds., *Endangered Languages* (Oxford: Berg, 1991). Leanne Hinton provides a unique and readable account of language preservation efforts now under way in *Flutes of Fire: Essays on California Indian Languages* (Berkeley, Calif.: Heyday Books, 1994).

William L. Leap describes the unique language situation of American Indian children in "Title VII and the Role It Plays in Indian Education: A Background Statement," paper for the National Conference of American Indians, 1982. See also Bea Medicine, "'Speaking Indian': Parameters of Language Use Among American Indians," *Focus* 6, National Clearinghouse for Bilingual Education, March 1981.

Steve Chesarek's research on the influence of native language development on later school achievement is summarized in "Cognitive Consequences of Home or School Education in a Limited Second Language: A Case Study in the Crow Indian Bilingual Community," paper presented at the Language Proficiency Assessment Symposium, Airlie, Va., March 1981.

For a detailed description of the Crow Agency bilingual program (although the district is not identified by name), see "A Well-Organized Indian Project," in *ESEA Title VII Case Studies* (Arlington, Va.: Development Associates, 1983), pp. 111-29.

A wealth of information about Navajo bilingual programs may be found in a special issue of the *Bilingual Research Journal* – 19, no. 1 (Winter 1995), including Sally Begay et al., "Change from the Inside Out: A Story of the Transformation in a Navajo Community School," pp. 121-39; Agnes and Wayne Holm, "Navajo Education: Retrospect and Prospects," pp. 141-67; and Daniel McLaughlin, "Strategies for Enabling Bilingual Program Development in American Indian Schools," pp. 169-78.

For detailed, first-person accounts of bilingual education at Rock Point, see the Holms' "Rock Point, A Navajo Way to Go to School," *Annals of the American Association of Political and Social Science* 508 (1990): 170-84; and McLaughlin's *When Literacy Empowers: Navajo Language in Print* (Albuquerque: University of New Mexico Press, 1992).

Teresa L. McCarty relates the complex and compelling story of Rough Rock in "School as Community: The Rough Rock Demonstration," *Harvard Educational Review,* no. 4 (Nov. 1989): 484-503. See also Galena Sells Dick and McCarty, "Reclaiming Navajo: Language Renewal in an American Indian Community School," in Nancy H. Hornberger, ed., *Indigenous Literacies in the Americas* (Berlin: Mouton de Gruyter, in press); and John Collier, Jr., "Survival at Rough Rock: A Historical Overview of Rough Rock Demonstration School," *Anthropology & Education Quarterly* (1988): 253-69.

For an overview of Indian bilingual education policy, see McCarty, "Federal Language Policy and American Indian Education," *Bilingual Research Journal* 17, nos. 1 & 2 (Spring 1993): 13-34. See also Jon Reyhner, ed., *Teaching American Indian Students* (Norman: University of Oklahoma Press, 1992).

Joshua Fishman provides a worldwide perspective on the problem of language loss and efforts to solve it in *Reversing Language Shift: Theoretical and Empirical Foundations of Assistance to Threatened Languages* (Philadelphia: Multilingual Matters, 1991). See also James Crawford, "Endangered Native American Languages: What Is to Be Done, and Why?" *Bilingual Research Journal* 19, no. 1 (Winter 1995): 17-38.

Details of the Pûnana Leo immersion program may be found in Larry Lindsey Kimura, "The Hawaiian Language and Its Revitalization," in Freda Ahenakew and Shirley Fredeen, eds., *Our Languages: Our Survival,* Proceedings of the 7th Annual Native American Languages Issues Institute (Saskatoon: Saskatchewan Indian Languages Institute, 1987), pp. 117-23. See also William G. Demmert, Jr., "Language, Learning, and National Goals: A Native American View," in Center for Applied Linguistics, *The National Education Goals: The Issues of Language and Culture* (Washington, D.C.: CAL, 1992), pp. 25-33.

Chapter 10. California: Coping with Diversity

California's bilingual education law and its impact are summarized in Assembly Office of Research, *Bilingual Education: Learning English in California* (Sacramento, Calif.: Joint Publications Office, 1986); and Sunset Review Advisory Committee, "A Report to the Legislature on Categorical Programs Scheduled to Sunset on June 30, 1986," Sept. 1985.

For the effects of demographic changes on education in California, see Sally Catlin, "New Kids in Class: Minorities Pace Growth in Public Schools," *California Journal,* April 1986, pp. 189-91; Assembly Office of Research, *California 2000: A People in Transition* (Sacramento, Calif.: Joint Publications Office, 1986); and Jay Mathews, "Anglos May Become Minority in California Schools," *Washington Post,* Aug. 21, 1988, p. A4.

Edmund W. Lee documents the impact of Alhambra's bilingual program in "Chinese-American Fluent English Proficient Students and School Achievement," paper presented at the 11th annual conference of the California Association for Bilingual Education, San Francisco, Jan. 15-18, 1986.

Concepción M. Valadez discusses teacher recruitment and training problems in "Effective Teachers for Language Minority Students: National Needs," in House Education and Labor Committee, *Compendium of Papers.* For a state policy expert's viewpoint, see Norman C. Gold, "Solving the Shortage of Bilingual Teachers: Policy Implications of California's Staffing Initiative for LEP Students," paper presented at the Third Research Symposium on Limited English Proficient Students' Needs, Office of Bilingual Education and Minority Languages Affairs, Washington, D.C., Aug. 12, 1992.

Chapter 11. Two-Way Bilingual Education

Paul Simon, a member of the 1979 President's Commission on Foreign Languages and International Studies, documents the sad state of our linguistic resources in *The Tongue-Tied American: Confronting the Foreign Language Crisis* (New York: Continuum, 1980). See also Catherine E. Snow and Kenji Hakuta, "The Costs of Monolingualism," in Crawford, *Language Loyalties,* pp. 394-94.

Russell N. Campbell and Kathryn J. Lindholm of the Center for Language Education and Research (CLEAR) make a case for two-way bilingual education in *Conservation of Language Resources,* Educational Report Series, no. 6 (Los Angeles: University of California, CLEAR, 1987). See also two related publications by CLEAR: Marguerite Ann Snow, *Innovative Second Language Education: Bilingual Immersion Programs,* Educational Report Series, no. 1 (1986); and

Lindholm's *Directory of Bilingual Immersion Programs: Two-Way Bilingual Education for Language Minority and Majority Students*, Educational Report Series, no. 8 (1987).

A more recent directory is Donna Christian and Cindy Mahrer, *Two-Way Bilingual Programs in the United States, 1991-1992* (Washington, D.C.: National Center for Research on Cultural Diversity and Second Language Learning, 1992), with supplements for 1992-93 and 1993-94.

G. Richard Tucker explains how two-way programs serve both language majority and language minority students in "Encouraging the Development of Bilingual Proficiency for English-Speaking Americans," paper for the Center for Applied Linguistics, June 1986. Kathryn Lindholm and Zierlein Aclan describe their research on outcomes in "Bilingual Proficiency as a Bridge to Academic Achievement: Results from Bilingual/Immersion Programs," *Journal of Education* 173, no. 2 (1991): 99-113.

Sidney Morison describes the rationale for launching a two-way program at New York City's P.S. 84 in "Two-Way Bilingual Education: The Time Has Come," paper presented at the 17th annual conference of the National Association for Bilingual Education, Houston, April 30, 1988.

Campbell, who helped design the Culver City Spanish immersion program in the early 1970s, outlines its history and effects in "The Immersion Approach to Foreign Language Teaching," in California Office of Bilingual Bicultural Education, *Studies on Immersion Education*, pp. 114-43. Also in that volume, Merrill Swain voices theoretical objections to teaching literacy simultaneously in two languages in "A Review of Immersion Education in Canada: Research and Evaluation Studies," pp. 87-112.

Virginia Collier traces the outcomes of Oyster School graduates in "Two-Way Bilingual Programs: The Longitudinal Impact of Integrated Majority-Minority Bilingual Classes on Majority Students' Attitudes and Career Goals," paper presented at the annual meeting of Advocates for Language Learning, Washington, D.C., Oct. 17, 1987.

Fred Genesee analyzes San Diego's experiment in two-way total immersion in "Considering Two-Way Bilingual Programs," *Equity and Choice* 3, no. 3 (Spring 1987): 3-7. The program's effects on student achievement are reported in Krashen and Biber, *On Course*. A partial immersion model is evaluated in Nancy Rhodes, JoAnn Crandall, and Donna Christian, "Review of the Partial Immersion Program, Key Elementary School, Arlington, VA," Center for Applied Linguistics, Washington, D.C., June 1987. The Port Chester limited immersion project is described in Richard E. Baecker and Charles D. Coletti, "Two-Way Bilingual Programs: Implementation of an Educational Innovation," *SABE Journal* 2, no. 1 (Spring 1986): 42-58; and "Two-Way Bilingual Programs: Language-Learning-as-Resource," paper presented at the annual meeting of the American Educational Research Association, New Orleans, April 9, 1988.

Deborah L. Gold provides a comprehensive overview of two-way programs and policymakers' responses in "2 Languages, One Aim: 'Two-Way' Learning," *Education Week,* Jan. 20, 1988, pp. 7, 24-25.

Public attitudes toward bilingual education are analyzed in David O. Sears and Leonie Huddy, "Bilingual Education: Symbolic Meaning and Support among Non-Hispanics," paper presented at the annual meetings of the American Psychological Association, New York, Sept. 1, 1987, and the American Political Science Association, Chicago, Sept. 4, 1987.

Chapter 12. Language Policy and School Reform.

The unfavorable report on New York City's bilingual programs is Sam Dillon, "Bilingual Education Effort Is Flawed, Study Indicates," *New York Times*, Oct. 30, 1994. See also Edna Negrón, "Bilingual Critique Flawed, Backers Say," *Newsday,* Oct. 21, 1994, p. A37.

Adverse attitudes toward bilingual education are documented in "The 25th Annual Phi Delta Kappa/Gallup Poll of the Public's Attitudes Toward Public Schools," *Phi Delta Kappan*, October 1993, pp. 137-52.

Thomas Toch provides a useful account of 1980s school reform efforts in his book *In the Name of Excellence: The Struggle to Reform the Nation's Schools, Why It's Failing, and What Should Be Done* (New York: Oxford University Press, 1991). A discussion of the movement's limitations can be found in Marshall S. Smith and Jennifer O'Day, "Systemic School Reform," *Politics of Education Association Yearbook, 1990,* pp. 233-67.

Jonathan Kozol's *Savage Inequalities* was published in 1991 by Crown Publishers, New York.

For a history of the standards-and-goals movement, see Cynthia D. Prince and Pascal D. Forgione, Jr., "Raising Standards and Measuring Performance Equitably: Challenges for the National Education Goals Panel and State Assessment Systems," in Center for Applied Linguistics, *National Education Goals*, pp. 11-22.

The Stanford Working Group's report, released in June 1993, is "Federal Education Programs for Limited-English-Proficient Students: A Blueprint for the Second Generation."

Richard Ruíz offers a broad perspective on U.S. language policy in his influential article, "Orientations in Language Planning," *NABE Journal*, no. 2 (1984): 15-34; rpt. in McKay and Wong, *Language Diversity*, pp. 3-25.

Australia's approach to managing diversity is described in Joseph LoBianco, *National Policy on Languages* (Canberra: Australian Government Publishing Service, 1987). Further information on this policy is available through the Australian Advisory Council on Languages and Multicultural Education (AACLAME), Department of Employment, Education, and Training, GPO Box 9880, Canberra ACT 2601, Australia. The council publishes a newsletter and a quarterly journal, *VOX*.

Joshua Fishman makes recommendations for U.S. language policy in an interview with *BEOutreach* (Fall 1994, pp. 26-29), the newsletter of California's Bilingual Education Office. For a detailed discussion of policy alternatives, see Crawford, *Hold Your Tongue*.

Chapter 13. Disaster at the Polls.

Initial coverage of the Ninth Street School boycott appeared in the *Los Angeles Times* between February 13 and 26, 1996. Another side of the story was provided by James Crawford, "The Ninth Street Myth: Who Speaks for Latino Parents?" in an article syndicated by the Hispanic Link News Service, May 25, 1998.

The National Research Council Study, *Improving Schooling for Language-Minority Children: A Research Agenda,* was published by the National Academy Press (Washington, D.C.: 1997). Charles Glenn's "political spin" on the report is posted at http://www.ceousa. org/nrc.html.

Ron Unz outlines his strategic ideas for Republicans in "Immigration or the Welfare State: Which Is Our Real Enemy?" published in the Heritage Foundation journal *Policy Review*, Fall 1994. Peter Salins's *Assimilation, American Style* was published by Basic Books (New York: 1977). Unz makes his case against bilingual education on a campaign Web site: http://www.onenation.org/. Commentaries, analysis, debates, poetry, opinion polls, research briefs, resource links, and an archive of news articles on Proposition 227 can be found at http://ourworld.compuserve.com/homepages/jwcrawford/unz.htm. Official materials of the No on 227 campaign are posted at http://www.noonunz.org/.

Wayne Thomas and Virginia Collier's most extensive summary of their research is *School Effectiveness for Language Minority Students* (Washington, D.C.: National Clearinghouse for Bilingual Education, 1997), an online publication available at http://www.ncbe.gwu.edu/ncbepubs/resource/effectiveness/index.htm.

Internet Resources

James Crawford's Language Policy Web Site & Emporium: http://ourworld.compuserve.com/homepages/jwcrawford/ – A compendium of news and commentary on bilingual education, English Only legislation, language rights, endangered languages, and other issues of U.S. language policy.

National Clearinghouse for Bilingual Education: http://www.ncbe.gwu.edu/ – An unparalleled reference source, featuring a searchable database of research on language-minority education, email discussion groups for practitioners, and "occasional papers" of interest to the field. NCBE can also be reached at 2011 I Street, N.W., Suite 200, Washington, D.C. 20009; (800) 321-NCBE or (202) 467-0867; or askncbe@ncbe.gwu.edu.

Center for Multilingual, Multicultural Research: http://www.bcf.usc.edu/~cmmr/ – Based at the University of Southern California, this site tracks current developments in bilingual education and ESL, professional development, educational technology, and education of ethnic minorities.

Professional, Research, Governmental, and Advocacy Organizations

Center for Applied Linguistics, 4646 40th Street, N.W., Washington, D.C. 20016. (202) 362-0700; info@cal.org; http;//www.cal.org/.

Joint National Committee for Languages, 4646 40th Street N.W. Suite 310, Washington, D.C. 20016. (202) 966-8477; info@languagepolicy.org; http://www.languagepolicy.org/.

Linguistic Minority Research Institute, Building 528, Room 4722, University of California, Santa Barbara, Santa Barbara, Calif. 93106. (805) 893-2250; infodesk@LMRINet.ucsb.edu; http://lmrinet.gse.ucsb.edu/.

Mexican American Legal Defense and Educational Fund, 634 South Spring Street, 11th Floor, Los Angeles, Calif. 90014. (213) 629-2512; info@maldef.org; http://www.maldef.org/.

National Association for Bilingual Education, 1220 L Street, N.W., Suite 605, Washington, D.C. 20005. (202) 898-1829; http://www.nabe.org/.

National Council of La Raza, 1111 19th Street, N.W., Suite 1000, Washington, D.C. 20036. (202) 785-1670.

Office of Bilingual Education and Minority Languages Affairs, U.S. Department of Education, 600 Independence Avenue, S.W., Washington, DC 20202-6510; obemla@ed.gov; http://www.ed.gov/offices/OBEMLA/.

Puerto Rico Legal Defense and Education Fund, 99 Hudson Street, New York, N.Y. 10013. (212) 219-3360.

Teachers of English to Speakers of Others Languages, 1600 Cameron Street, Suite 300, Alexandria, Va. 22314. (703) 836-0774; tesol@tesol.edu; http://www.tesol.edu/.

Index

controversy over extent of, 88-90
demographic trends and, 15, 99, 197-98
shortcomings of term, 17-18n
Lindholm, Kathryn, 210, 212, 214
Linguistic Society of America, 77
Literacy transfer between languages,
        106, 128-29, 130-31, 170, 200-1,
        215-16
Littlebear, Dick, 179-80, 181, 184, 193n
Little Big Horn Community College, 182
Locke, John, 119, 123, 136n
Lodge, Henry Cabot, 26
López, Simón, 168
Los Angeles Times Poll, 251, 261n
Los Angeles Unified School District, 197,
        204-5, 206-7, 244-45. *See also*
        Eastman Curriculum Design Project
Louisiana, 23
Lyons, James J., 55, 86, 87, 97, 98

Magallanes, Ramón, 145
Mahon, George, 60n
Maori, 131
Marsnik, Toni, 205, 206-7
Martínez, Matthew, 84, 95-96
Martínez, Ricardo, 87
Massachusetts, 42, 219
Massachusetts Institute of Technology, 182
Mathew, Alfredo, 50
Matta Tuchman, Gloria, 251, 260n
Matthews, G. H., 182
May, Cordelia Scaife, 78n, 80n
McCain, John, 55
McCarthy, Eugene, 66
McCarty, Teresa, 187-88
McCormick, Washington J., 79-80n
McLaughlin, Barry, 118, 122, 132, 134, 135
McLaughlin, Daniel, 186, 190
Meléndez, Sara, 90
Melikoff, Olga, 140
Melting pot myth, 14, 20-21, 49. *See also*
        Cultural assimilation
Mexican American Legal Defense and Educa-
        tional Fund (MALDEF), 84, 252
Mexican-American War, 32
Mexican Americans, 11, 42, 58, 131
    educational neglect of, 34-35, 41
    English-only school policies for, 32-33
Mexico, 166

Secretaria de Educación Pública, 174n
Meyer v. Nebraska (1923), 29
*Mirror of Language: The Debate on
        Bilingualism* (Hakuta), 227
Mississippi, 78n
Missouri, 78n
Modern Language Association, 77, 119
Moll, Luis, 156n
Monitor hypothesis. *See* Krashen, Stephen,
        theories of
Montana, 78n, 178
Monterey Park, Calif., 70, 79n, 198
Morison, Sidney, 213
Morris, James, 205
Muhlenberg, F. A., 37n
Mulder, Dick, 73
Multicultural Education Training and
        Advocacy project (META), 57, 59
Multidistrict Trainer of Trainers Institute
        (MTTI), 205
Murphy, George, 41
Myers, John, 168-69

National Advisory and Coordinating Council
        on Bilingual Education (NACCBE),
        82-83, 97, 146, 155n
National Americanization Committee, 26
National Association for Bilingual Education
        (NABE), 52, 55, 77, 84, 87-88, 93-94,
        96-97, 98, 158, 236
National Clearinghouse for Bilingual
        Education, 89, 130
National Council of La Raza, 84, 90, 94, 96
National Council of Teachers of English, 77
National Defense Education Act of 1958,
        136n
National Education Association, 41, 52, 84
National Education Goals, 232, 236, 294-97
National Governors Association, 232
National Research Council (NRC), 152, 156n,
        247-49, 254, 260n
Nation at Risk, A, 229
Native American Language Act, 191, 194n
Native Americans. *See* American Indians
Nativism:
    against Hispanics, 67-69, 250
    anti-Catholic, 24-25
    bilingual education and, 13, 85
    displaced anxieties and, 72-73

ALSO AVAILABLE FROM

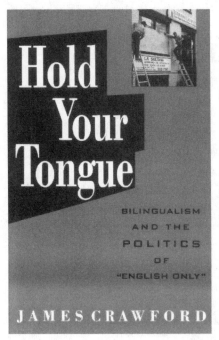

Hold Your Tongue:

Bilingualism and the Politics of "English Only"

by

James Crawford

Now in paperback, this award-winning exposé of the English Only campaign traces the hidden agenda and social consequences of today's backlash against bilingualism.

"A very timely book that is more timely than ever."

Los Angeles Times

"Crawford is at once a scholar, advocate, and journalist – all those voices are heard in this book and masterfully woven into a gripping indictment of seemingly innocent attempts to legislate English."

Kenji Hakuta, *Stanford University*

"Readers looking for insight into the tangled politics of language are well served by Crawford['s] . . . extensive and illuminating discussions."

The Nation

"Jim Crawford's news-gathering prowess and insider's knowledge shine through *Hold Your Tongue*. Rich in anecdotes, majestic in its sweep and scope . . . a ground-breaking study of the English Only movement."

Henry Cisneros, *U.S. Secretary of Housing & Urban Development*

"Richly informative . . . a valuable discussion of the US' past and present difficulties with intolerance and discrimination against immigrants."

Harvard Educational Review

"Convincingly argues that multilingualism is a significant economic resource and that English Only sends a xenophobic message to the rest of the world."

The Washington Post

Hold Your Tongue:
Bilingualism and the Politics of "English Only"

by **James Crawford**

Author of

*Bilingual Education: History,
Politics, Theory, and Practice*

As a journalist who closely monitors developments in legislation, research, and the classroom. James Crawford examines bilingual education from all sides:

CONTENTS

324 pages • Paperback

BILINGUAL EDUCATION SERVICES, INC.
2514 South Grand Avenue
Los Angeles, CA 90007-9979
(213) 749-6213 • (800) 448-6032
Fax: (213) 749-1820

urchase Order # _____

❑ Check enclosed
❑ Bill the following credit card number:

lame on the Card _____

ccount # _____

xpiration Date _____

ignature _____

# of Copies	Unit Price	Total
	$14.95	
Total Amount of Order		
California Sales Tax*		
Shipping and Handling (9%)		
Total Amount Paid		

*All California customers must add 8% of the merchandise total for state sales tax. All Los Angeles County customers must add 8.25% of the merchandise total for state and county sales taxes.

Ship to _____
Address _____
City _____ County _____
State ____ Zip _____ Phone _____
Name _____ Title _____

FREE  BILINGUAL EDUCATIONAL SERVICES INC

CATALOG

BES, publishers of *Bilingual Education: History, Politics, Theory and Practice* and *Hold Your Tongue: Bilingualism and the Politics of "English Only"* by James Crawford, also carries thousands of other titles of interest to bilingual and multicultural educators.

- Award Winning and Highest-Rated Books in Spanish for K-12 in Library Prebound Binding
- Bilingual Books
- Crane Publishing Reading Program in Spanish and English
- Textbooks
- English as a Second Language (ESL) Books, Tapes, and Programs
- Interactive CD's in Spanish and English
- Audio/Visual Programs (CD-ROMs, Cassettes, and Videos)
- Dictionaries & Encyclopedias
- Teacher's Resources